AT
ARM'S
LENGTH

For
Elizabeth
and
Mathew, Rhodri and Edward

AT ARM'S LENGTH

Recollections and reflections
on the arts, media
and a young democracy

Geraint Talfan Davies

seren

Seren is the book imprint of
Poetry Wales Press Ltd
57 Nolton Street, Bridgend, CF31 3AE, Wales
www.seren-books.com

© Geraint Talfan Davies, 2008

ISBN 978-1-85411-436-5

The publisher works with the financial assistance
of the Welsh Books Council.

Cover photograph: Betina Skovbro
Cover design: Mathew Talfan
Index by Penny Brown

Printed in Plantin by CPD Ltd, Blaenau Gwent

Contents

Foreword   7

RECOLLECTIONS
1: Roots   13
2: In the beginning was the word   27
3: Up and down the Taff   44
4: Wales on the agenda   52
5: ITV Swansong   63
6: Going North   85
7: Coming home   92
8: Nations and regions   113
9: Thinking about Wales   137
10: Who killed Hadid?   149
11: To opera sideways   161
12: A not so poisoned chalice   180
13: The bonfire lit   201
14: Grappling with Government   207
15: Suspended animation   224

REFLECTIONS
16: The arts in a young democracy   247
17: Appetite and access   255
18: What are culture ministers for?   265
19: Anywhere but Cardiff   275
20: The cities we deserve   287
21: Voices on the edge   294
22: If you can't be big, be smart   316
23: Politics one can touch   325

Index   342
About the Author   358

Foreword

There was always a strong chance that this book would never be written. One of the drawbacks of being a generalist rather than a specialist is that life presents too many interesting distractions. When I returned to Cardiff in 1990 to head BBC Wales I went to see my uncle, Alun Talfan, then in his late seventies but still exhibiting a keen appetite for public life. He advised me that in such a position I would be asked to do many things. 'You must learn to say no,' he said firmly, and then paused. 'Mind you, don't say no too often. Got to stay in the swim.'

Primed by my parents' involvements, as a journalist I sensed quite early the satisfaction of getting close to events and the people who shaped them or were battered by them, as well as the deeper satisfaction of discovering subterranean realities or motives – the thrill of the scoop. I have been fortunate since to have spent forty years in organisations that have examined our society in different ways: newspapers and broadcasting, even a small think tank. At the BBC it was a privilege to be positioned at a point where so many of the overlapping circles of society meet – politics, business, academia, the arts, sport. When I left my main fear was how I would react to being thrown onto the dry banks beside the river of information in which I had swum all my working life.

That said, one of the frustrations of journalism is that you inevitably remain at arm's length from many things. You are, after all, paid to be a spectator not a player. But in a small society the temptation to be a participant is ever present. The extra-curricular has always had an extra appeal, and I have seldom been able to resist. The community outside the workplace beckons in quite a different way.

In work you have a contract that imposes obligations. At a minimum it will require you to turn up – at a workplace or perhaps only at a laptop somewhere in the world. At home you have other obligations, those of love and marriage and parenthood. Outside work and the home is a wider community that doesn't impose or tie you to a contract. It is content to leave you alone. Occasionally, it will rattle a tin in your face or sell you a flag or ask you to vote. But you can always say no and, more often than not, there are no immediate consequences.

But to say no to that community is to forego an endless source of stimulus and satisfaction as well as to limit the capacity for change. We are not just colleagues at work, or just members of the same family behind our front door, we are citizens of a community – many communities, like a Russian doll, one inside the other – the neighbourhood, the town or city, the region or nation or even the globe. All of them affect us; and if we want to, we can affect them, not necessarily by becoming politicians – though somebody has to do the job, and I think we should respect them for that – but through the million ways in which people volunteer, at every level, their time, effort, care, ideas or knowledge.

Most of my working life has been spent in Wales. That is not to deny the intoxicating appeal of metropolises, but Wales has been the place where I could be fully myself. Some may see that as parochial, but in the United Kingdom of all places, I think there is value in asserting the centrality of the peripheral and, when needed, in pinpointing the parochialism of the metropolis. At the same time, I believe Wales's recent past has a relevance for the rest of the United Kingdom that is seldom acknowledged. Devolution has broken the mould of the unitary state. What is happening in the least assertive of the three 'devolved nations' is a benchmark to note.

The first part of this book is more memoir than autobiography, perhaps because I was resistant to the latter or because the only time in my life that I kept a diary, and even then intermittently, was during my period with the Arts Council of Wales. But some element of recollection was necessary to give context to the reflections in the second part.

For that reason I am hugely grateful to all those friends who have jogged my memory recently and shaped my opinions over the years through both gloomy and jolly conversations. They are too numerous to list here in full, but I must make special mention of Rhys David, Trevor Fishlock, Patrick Hannan, Keith James, John Osmond, Menna Richards, Dai Smith, William Wilkins and my sister, Elinor Delaney. I must also thank Genista McIntosh, Brian McMaster, Kevin Morgan and John Punter who read substantial parts of the manuscript, and Gwyneth Lewis and John Osmond who read it all. Penny Fishlock edited the manuscript with a sharp pencil and even sharper eye, in the process saving me from many grievous errors. Caroline Morris provided similar rigour. My son, Mathew Talfan, and his wife, Betina Skovbro, contributed the design and photography for the cover. The advice of all these people was invaluable, although any faults in the pages that follow remain attributable only to me.

One of the privileges of my life has been working with so many teams of energetic and stimulating people – at the *Western Mail*, HTV, Tyne Tees, the BBC, the Institute of Welsh Affairs, Glas Cymru, Cardiff Bay Arts Trust, Wales Millennium Centre, Welsh National Opera and, by no means least, the Arts Council of Wales. All these organisations are full of committed people from whose talent, knowledge and friendship I have benefited beyond measure. I thank them for it.

Behind all this have been my wife, Elizabeth, and sons, Mathew, Rhodri and Edward. For me, Elizabeth has been a massively sustaining force for the last forty years and more, and not only during the obsessive travail of writing this book. It would not have been finished without her, something that could be said of everything I have ever done. Beyond endless encouragement, she and my sons have kept me grounded and have kept smiling, even at times when it was thought that my BBC identity badge was for showing at my own front door. No words of mine can adequately express what I owe them or thank them enough.

Cardiff, December 2007

RECOLLECTIONS

1 Roots

Recollections of childhood are like a swim in a deep and cloudy sea. You cannot be certain of the bottom. The passage of time is deceptive and clarity fleeting, its arrival and disappearance sudden and unpredictable. Some patches of water are colder than others. On the dry land of the present you cannot be certain where you have been, or what you may have only narrowly missed. The boldest shapes are clear, the detail sometimes gauzy, and even the brightest colours are washed out. Recollection is not a precise chart of what was there.

At one level I was extremely fortunate. I did not lack for love or affection or company. My parents were both of a gentle disposition, intelligent, engaged and active. I had an elder brother and a younger sister, the one to look up to and live up to, the other to treasure or tease. There were uncles, aunts and cousins aplenty. The house was full of books, music, visitors and conversation in two languages. My parents were deeply rooted in their community and anxious that we should be too. Life was not dull. I do not remember my childhood as idyllic, but neither do I remember it being unhappy. That says much for my parents stoicism, for over the course of the years they had much to be unhappy about – the effects of war, illness and the death of a child.

Both mother and father came from West Wales stock. My mother, Mari, would proudly claim to be from a seafaring family that straddled the border between Cardiganshire and Pembrokeshire either side of the salmon-rich Teifi. They had been part of the great migration from west Wales to the docks at Cardiff and Barry at the height of the coal trade. Since no-one in Wales is allowed to be imprecise about these things she would say they came from St. Dogmaels, which is on the Pembrokeshire side of the river, although her care with money was attributed to Cardiganshire blood.

The fact that this ignored her father's Glamorgan background was the result of her mother's death in childbirth in 1912 and that she was brought up by her mother's sister and her husband. Her real father was a restless and not very successful entrepreneur from Pencoed who ended up running a dairy business in Barry. Her adoptive father, who I knew as my grandfather, started as a coal trimmer at Barry docks in

1901 after twenty years as a merchant seaman. Other relatives were
ships' pilots who guided larger boats into the docks through the tricky
waters of the Bristol Channel and their massive tides. They were all
stalwarts of the town's multiplicity of Welsh chapels, that naturally had
a habit of feuding. Years later my mother played the organ regularly to
a dwindling congregation at Calfaria Baptist chapel in Cadoxton.

My father, Aneirin, also professed to come from two counties. His
grandfather was a weaver from Ysbyty Ystwyth in north Cardiganshire,
although my father was born in rural Drefach in Carmarthenshire in
1906. He grew up in industrial Gorseinon, where his father, the
Reverend William Talfan Davies, was the Calvinist minister of Libanus
chapel. Close by was Loughor where the religious revival of 1904
began its short ecstatic course, during which newspapers ranked
chapels in league tables of conversions. William had been christened
simply William Davies, but since there were several of the same name
in the village school, they were encouraged to take a nickname. William
chose Talfan (literally, the high place) the name of an outcrop of rock
above his parents' cottage, and it stuck for the rest of his life and
succeeding generations.

Father's education was somewhat less conventional than my
mother's. He had left Gowerton Grammar School at the age of
fourteen, and sought an apprenticeship at a chemist's shop in Swansea,
under the misapprehension that this would allow him to pursue an
interest in photography. One can only imagine his disappointment at
finding that all the films deposited there were sent elsewhere for
processing. Illness intervened and he found himself bedbound for
almost a year with suspected TB.

It was a crucial turning point since, in that year, with the windows
half open and the curtains constantly drawn, he began the habit of
reading that was to change the course of his life and interests. He also
began to write, encouraged by a visit from Saunders Lewis, the son of
another minister. Lewis, sixteen years his senior and setting about the
launch of the Welsh National Party, was a literary hero to father for the
rest of his life, although he later became estranged from his politics. But
if literature was to be father's world, it was still not a living. Recovered
from the illness, he went to Cardiff Technical College to qualify as a
pharmacist.

Mother meanwhile had done her teacher training at Barry Training
College just as the export trade in Welsh teachers was in getting into
full swing. In the mid-1930s they both, separately, headed for London

and away from the unemployment of south Wales – mother to teach infant children in the impoverished East End at Hoxton and father to work in chemists' shops in King's Cross and later in the rather more plush neighbourhoods in Kenton and Harrow. The London Welsh chapel community brought them together and they married in 1936, beginning a strong and close partnership bonded by common ideals and severe challenges.

In the same year, at the age of 27, father began his first literary venture. From a bedroom at the unlikely address of Swiss Avenue, Watford, he began to edit and print a Welsh language literary magazine *Heddiw* (Today) to publish the early works of several young poets and some of the Welsh greats, to support language campaigns and to rail against Franco's warring regime in Spain. His co-editor was Dafydd Jenkins, a pacifist lawyer and historian who later relinquished the editorial role to organise a petition for official status for the language in courts of law – *Deiseb yr Iaith*. This bore fruit in the Welsh Courts Act of 1942, removing an exclusion that had persisted since 1536.

A year later father and another poet, W.H. Reese, collaborated in the first published volume of *vers libres* in the Welsh language, better known for its strict metrics. They each provided a separate introduction. Father's began with Eric Gill's dictum, 'All art is propaganda', and expressed dissatisfaction that the recent Welsh literary renaissance had not, he thought, addressed the pain of the world. He bemoaned the fact that young Welsh poets had, at that time, to look to English writers and critics for a discussion of the problems of their art in such uncertain times. It was a volume designed to unsettle. Like many an autodidact, he would forever stay outside the academic mainstream and even take a pride in that position.

As the war curtailed publishing he thought it important to sustain his magazine, even in a slimmed down form, and reduced its price from a shilling to sixpence. One of the articles that appeared in a tiny wartime typeface was on 'felling trees' by T.J. Morgan, father of Wales's current First Minister, Rhodri Morgan, in which he argued that the axe always took precedence over the plough.

Father was the second of four brothers. The eldest, Elfyn, worked in a bank, though in his spare time was ever active in fostering the Welsh language through all kinds of performance including amateur drama. In the 1980s several television reporters and presenters would admit how his training influenced them. Behind father came Goronwy, who became an Anglican priest after a rather short stay at a teetotal nonconformist college that ended in a row over a crate of stout. Alun was the youngest, the only one to attend university, and became an eminent and somewhat theatrical silk of the old school. It was while studying law at Gonville and Gaius at Cambridge that he would travel to Watford at weekends to help father print his new magazine on a small Adana press. It was the start of a collaboration that saw the launch, even before *Heddiw* ceased publication in 1942, of a new Welsh publishing house, Llyfrau'r Dryw (Wren Books), that lasted for sixty years.

My parents returned to Wales in 1938 to open a pharmacy in Heathfield Street, Swansea, now known as Kingsway. It was just around the corner from the Kardomah café, where Dylan Thomas, and his friends, Vernon Watkins, Daniel Jones and Alfred Janes, would meet. The shops of pre-war Swansea had a certain Victorian swagger about them, that spoke of better times as the world capital of copper production. This shop was hardly in that category, but that it was a Welsh pharmacy was unmistakable: the sign above the window said Aneirin Davies and beneath, in brackets, was the more traditional Welsh version Aneirin ap Talfan, under which name most of his earlier literary work appeared. More discreetly in the window display was the word *fferyllydd* (chemist).

It is unclear to me how the business survived, since the back room was given over to my father's growing library and was becoming a meeting place for writers and poets and any one else interested in Welsh cultural issues. Out front mother held the mahogany fort, though she would have had to call on father to dispense. It was not a good business for him to be in, since it also fed a hypochondria that stayed with him for the rest of his life. Long after he had left the pharmacy behind, he would keep a pharmacopoeia in the house and would buy pills as if they were some interesting new confectionery.

The business lasted only three years. The first bombing raids over Swansea had damaged the shop in September 1940, but those of the following January and February were of a different order. The Luftwaffe obliterated the centre of Swansea. Not only was the shop completely destroyed – it was said by a last, late bomb – but another bomb landed twenty yards in front of my parents' rented home, a tall terraced house just off the impossibly steep Constitution Hill that faced the targeted docks.

Father's own account was published as *Dyddiau'r Ceiliog Rhedyn* (Grasshoppper Days), a reference to the Book of Job: 'Canst thou make him afraid as a grasshopper?' He told how a friend pulled him back behind the stairs just as the explosion blasted the front door and a large bay window into the centre of the house. Mother and my brother, Owen, then just short of his third birthday, escaped unhurt from a neighbour's cellar. The upright piano in the front room took the full force of the window. It was eventually pieced together by a local craftsman, but for thirty years thereafter whenever a piano tuner called he would finish by brushing up small shards of glass shaken loose from the wood casing by mother's accomplished playing.

The bombing must have been devastating for the young family – mother was not yet thirty – yet I can never recall it being talked about in that way nor even relished for its drama. Others had suffered worse fates. Besides, although the financial impact was felt for some years, even after the war, in other ways it was a surprising piece of good fortune. Father took a job as a part-time newsreader and translator with the BBC and remained with the organisation for thirty years. Hitler had released him to pursue his real interests and talent.

From May 1941 until the middle of 1944 he travelled to London for one week each month to read the news in Welsh from the basement of Broadcasting House, in company with another son of the manse, Hywel Davies. The careers of both men shadowed each other until father succeeded him as head of programmes at BBC Wales after his premature death in 1965.

While father was getting into broadcasting mother and Owen decamped to a rented farmhouse twelve miles away in Tycroes, a village near Ammanford, poised between rural Carmarthenshire and the western edge of the south Wales coalfield. They were not to know at that time that the blitz on Swansea would not recur. It was through this accident of war, rather than because I was rooted in the county, that I was born in a maternity hospital in Carmarthen on 30 December 1943.

Until the end of the war mother sold what cosmetics she could from the front room of the farmhouse, and took in a lodger, Marged Jenkins, a teacher who became a surrogate aunt and would send me a birthday postal order until I was past forty. She became an inspector of schools and proofread all father's books. I gained the impression from my parents that even during the war it was a lively and enterprising community, though I could never be sure whether tales of black market food hidden in the local undertaker's finest ebony coffin were fact or fiction.

At this time father wrote some short plays, one entitled pleadingly, *Heddwch* (Peace). He also wrote a nativity play in Welsh for the church, with a section for a recitation party whose names were listed in the printed programme. Among them was A. Watkins, Alan Watkins, now the doyen of British political columnists. Years later, during a chance and bibulous meeting on the train to Paddington, Alan, returning from a visit to his mother, remarked on the transformation his homeland had undergone. 'Who would have thought, thirty years ago, that one day you would be able to walk into the Co-op in Ammanford and buy a perfectly drinkable bottle of claret.'

★ ★ ★ ★

The lush fields of Carmarthenshire were not to be my home. Until the age of nine my landscape was instead the stone-walled back lane of Maes-y-Cwm Street in Barry. I knew every foot and hand-hold in those walls and cursed the spoilsports who planted broken glass in cement on their ridges. My marbles and Dinky cars rattled down every gully at their foot. My wild west was Barry's Central Park, two streets away, still a green amphitheatre. The two dominant edifices were the rather dumpy Barry Town Hall on the park edge that housed the public library and whose clock chimed every quarter, day and night. Further away, the mock rock face of the big dipper at Barry Island looked as if it were made of papier mâché.

As a family we had moved into my grandfather's terraced house two streets behind the town hall. The house still had gaslights with their hissing mantles – the sound remembered in Dylan Thomas's line, 'I labour by singing light'. Children were sent into the street to collect horse manure left by the ponies that pulled the carts of the milkman and the rag-and-bone man. I have only a faint memory of my grandfather, a moustachioed disciplinarian who kept a bamboo cane, thankfully never used, that he would slide into the polished brass rod over the fireplace. It was hardly surprising that he should be grumpy, since a family of five had suddenly filled the place where he had been living alone for some years. He would squat for hours in the garden shed, chopping up the oily offcuts of railway sleepers into the most flammable firewood. Outside the shed was an earth-filled Belfast sink in which my sister and I buried, with druidic ceremony, a dead goldfish named Cynan, after the then archdruid who, my parents thought, had papal pretensions. Our elder brother, Owen, would lead us into mischief but protect us from its consequences.

We had gone back to my mother's home because by the war's end father had graduated from a talks assistant to a talks producer. He moved from the BBC's wartime base in Carmarthen to Cardiff, and worked alongside Philip Burton, famous for turning Richard Jenkins into Richard Burton. Father looked after talks in Welsh, Burton the talks in English. When Burton transferred to London father's plea to have his own post redesignated as 'bilingual' was turned down, after which he made it clear that if the talks posts were to be advertised again as Welsh or English, he would, apply for the English post – a fact that is as significant as it will be surprising to some.

As a young turk committed to opening out the Welsh literary scene, he had run WEA classes during the war in modern Welsh and English literature at Glanamman, which he was told were some of the best attended in the valley. He had commissioned the first of Dylan Thomas's radio talks, *Reminiscences of Childhood*, back in February 1943 and a second, *Quite Early One Morning*, in 1945. Both were broadcast on the BBC Welsh Home Service, the latter having been rejected by London on account of the 'breathless poetic voice'. Some years later he drove Dylan, his wife, Caitlin, and daughter Aeronwy to Llangollen for the International Eisteddfod. It was a long journey. There are many pubs between Swansea and Llangollen and not a few in Llangollen itself. Dylan, father recorded, wrote notes on the back of ripped-up fag packets but turned up at the studio with a handwritten script that required no amendment.

He, along with some others in the BBC, championed Dylan and father produced all his radio talks and many of his readings from the work of other poets, later editing and publishing the former under the title *Quite Early One Morning*. The latter came together in *The Colour of Saying*, an anthology he co-edited with an American academic, Ralph Maud. Just as important was his championing of Dylan within Welsh literary circles at a time when writers in Welsh and English in Wales tended to look at each other over mental barricades. His insistence on a religious dimension in Dylan's poems, that years later he thought were confirmed by entries in the poet's notebooks, was novel although not unchallenged. After Dylan's death in 1953 he was left with a limp cheque made out to A.T. Davies and signed Dylan Thomas in a tight boyish hand. It was for one pound only. At the top left in red were the words, 'Refer to Drawer'.

Soon after the war my father published studies of T.S. Eliot, Pushkin, Poe and James Joyce, and commissioned a series of 'radio odes', that included a poem entitled *The Minister* by R.S. Thomas, later published in Thomas's collection *Song at a Year's Turning*. Vernon Watkins, Glyn Jones, Brenda Chamberlain and Dannie Abse, and in Welsh Kitchener Davies, were other poets who wrote for him.

Domestically, we lived our lives in what today would be called a Welsh-speaking community of interest – the nursery and infant schools, mother's chapel and its drama society, father's church, the Cymmrodorion, the Eisteddfod, even holidays at Pantyfedwen, an outsized Victorian hotel, beached on the Cardigan coast at Borth, that had been given to the Urdd, the Welsh language youth organisation, by a London Welsh philanthropist after the war. These were the years of the slow post-war emergence of the language from decades of social ostracism encouraged even by Welsh-speaking parents. The census continued to record the language's decline, without the comforting accompaniment of a kaleidoscope of official support that was shaken into place from the 1960s onwards.

The years also saw the beginnings of the Welsh language school movement. The first school had been established in Aberystwyth. Its headmistress, Norah Isaac, was a close family friend. Mother taught in Welsh nursery schools that were crucial in generating the demand, and my sister Elinor and I were volunteered for service. I was first in, travelling by bus to Cardiff each day to the two rooms, in a Grangetown primary school near the Ninian Park football ground, that constituted the city's first Welsh language school. Within a year a group of parents had started the Barry Welsh school, predictably in the vestry of a chapel. I stopped travelling to Cardiff and my sister and I became founder pupils. A move to Swansea meant two years at a third such school, Ysgol Lonlas, in the sight and frequent smell of BP's oil refinery at Llandarcy.

Parental involvement in these schools at that time was intense, since it was they rather than local authorities that truly created them. However, in one case my father was able to give added support as he had been elected the sole independent councillor in Barry in 1951. This caused much banter in the extended family where one of mother's cousins and her husband were both Labour councillors and later mayors of the town.

Attending a Welsh language school when there was only one in a town, tended to put you apart from other children in the street who went to the neighbourhood school – less of an issue in Cardiff today where there are no fewer than fifteen Welsh language primary schools. But there were other markers. Whereas my friends' autograph books were full of the scribbled names of footballers and cricketers – Allchurch, Parkhouse, Watkins, Wooller – in mine they could find literary and broadcasting luminaries whose significance was only slowly dawning on me: Cynan, Dyfnallt, Douglas Cleverdon, who produced *Under Milk Wood*, John Arlott, Peter Dimmock, Huw Wheldon. P.H. Burton's name was cherished, not because of the association with Richard, but because he bought me my first pair of football boots.

At home there was a privilege above all others: conversation. As children we had realised that hanging in on our parents' conversations with visiting friends required some artifice and the application of the craft of total silence. Participation came later. A stool behind father's winged armchair was a good place not be noticed, and infinitely preferable to being outside on the stairs, even if you could slip the living room door ajar. On the stairs a punchline could be missed, muffled by laughter or the clatter of crockery as my mother served tea and cakes. The clink of glasses was less frequent, though not unknown.

It seemed normal, but the range of it was wonderfully wide. Hilarious evenings when my father and Hywel Davies would run through the repertoire of pulpit perorations they had known, were a feast of mimcry; better than actors swapping stage stories. As two sons of the manse, whose childhood homes had been like theatrical boarding houses for touring and reverend Wolfits, their standing joke was that one or other would write a book on 'preachers I have slept with' – a joke whose innocence has usually to be explained more fully today.

Conversation, be it with broadcasters or bishops, politicians, actors or editors, could be serious or could be fun. It was never without purpose. There was always an end product: a programme, a sermon, a column for the *Western Mail*, an editorial for the current affairs magazine *Barn* (Opinion), that he edited even while holding down a senior post at the BBC. There was Welsh music to be promoted through a new guild, which he chaired; a libretto for a Festival of Britain oratorio; a programme to be devised for the annual Welsh jamboree at the Royal Albert Hall; a pamphlet to be written on the need for bilingual bishops; a bishop or archbishop to be elected by the Governing Body of the Church in Wales of which he was a member; the prayer book to be revised with other members of a liturgical commission; another scheme from his brother Alun's fertile mind to be explored and, perhaps, implemented.

He worked behind a closed study door that deadened the noise of the clacking typewriter. A small brass knocker, in the shape of a cross, was more of a jest than a deterrent. It was mother who stopped my sister and me, and every other aspect of domestic life, from intruding on father's work. She was as central to our family as any fictional Welsh Mam, her practicality sharpened by a frugal upbringing, wartime hardships and post-war austerity. Behind the softness lay an astonishing inner strength and seriousness of purpose, albeit accompanied by an earthy sense of humour. A Baptist by upbringing, she was confirmed in the Anglican church for the sake of family solidarity, although not until her foster-father had died. Her one extravagance was household gadgets – bargains, usually of dubious value. I remember her as beautiful and photographs attest that that was more than a son's exaggeration. She was also endlessly conscientious about keeping in touch with the extended family, necessitating frequent and, to a child's mind, overlong visits to elderly uncles and aunts.

She taught only fitfully, since the successive illnesses that afflicted her provided a dark counterpoint to her life. Within months of Elinor's birth in 1946 she contracted meningitis, complicated by a haemorrhage that put her into a coma from which no-one expected her to emerge. She was 34. Father sat with her in the hospital for days on end. Two weeks had passed when, one night, he squeezed her hand and felt the lightest pressure from her own hand in return. She recovered. Nine years later, in her mid-forties, cancer was diagnosed and she underwent radical surgery and intense but crude radiotherapy. My father was warned that she might not live for more than nine months.

She lived for another sixteen years – until 59 – with iron determination but suffering side effects that constrained her natural gentleness in ways that we children failed to comprehend, not least because, according to the fashion of the time, the word cancer was not mentioned. Eight years later, as she coped with the disease and the drugs as well as further surgery, she also had to face the death of her firstborn, in a car accident, at the age of 25.

★ ★ ★ ★

Owen was my elder by almost six years, and one of life's brilliant cavaliers. He was intelligent, independent, witty and ambitious and, in tune with his generation, always likely to rebel against the staidness of British, let alone Welsh life in the fifties. He did not disappoint. For nearly six years he had been the only child, cherished by my parents and the apple of father's eye, a fact which made the decision to send him away to school, after only a year at Barry Grammar School, all the more inexplicable. Father had let himself be persuaded by a friend in the church, the Reverend Gwilym O. Williams, then headmaster of Llandovery College and later Archbishop of Wales. The fact that Llandovery was in Wales and that its headmaster was putting a new stress on its Welshness, made it no less of a disaster for my brother's relationship with my parents than if he had gone to an English public school. I declined the invitation to follow him.

Although I never got the impression that he was unhappy there – he may even have wanted to go – during school holidays there was much fierce quarrelling as he and my parents adjusted again to each other's presence. Even today I dislike raised voices. Owen sought what little glamour Swansea could muster in the fifties, cutting a dash at tennis clubs, and even finding the cash for a private flight in an aircraft. It had its effect, since he entered the Royal Air Force to do two years of national service and be challenged by new responsibilities given to a young officer at an improbably young age. After the RAF he never settled at Trinity Hall, Cambridge, where he went to read law, and dropped out after one year of high living, even borrowing a Chipmunk trainer from the university air squadron to fly to St. Athan so that he could attend, unannounced, my sister's confirmation.

It was while working as a freelance reporter for the BBC that he met a vivacious, red-headed actress, Rita Street, then familiar as an announcer with TWW. It was a passionate relationship and they were married by a chaplain friend in Paris, without either set of parents knowing. It was painful for my parents and sharpened the feeling at home that their son's life was being lived urgently and impatiently on the brink. Insistent on not taking a staff job in Cardiff, where father was by now the assistant head of programmes, Owen went to London – with Rita and their two-year-old son, Simon.

It was a pioneering time, society and television were both being prised open. The BBC's director general, Hugh Carleton Greene, was pushing the shutters wide. Huw Wheldon was running the arts programme *Monitor*, Grace Wyndham Goldie was a legendary presence in current affairs, and Donald Baverstock and Alastair Milne were running *Tonight*. David Frost was leading the satire charge. Owen joined presentation, producing the first *Points of View* programme with Robert Robinson, and writing occasional scripts for the new show, *That Was The Week That Was*. He directed film reports for the *Tonight* programme, presented by the avuncular Cliff Michelmore, that was becoming compulsive viewing for the nation. Its reporters included Alan Whicker, Fyfe Robertson and Julian Pettifer. It was a heady time but it was difficult for the young family – their son, Simon was born in June 1961 – to make ends meet in London or to establish a stable home.

A six-year gap in the teenage years is almost unbridgeable, so it was not until I was nineteen and looking forward to Oxford in the autumn of 1963 that I felt myself getting closer to Owen. I spent some days with him in London during which he relished showing off his new friends to his younger brother. We talked about how easy it would be for me to travel up from Oxford regularly.

I had been at Jesus College for only two weeks, when I returned to college from a lecture at the Examinations Schools at the end of the morning to find Idris Foster, the Professor of Celtic, waiting for me with news that Owen had been involved in a car accident in Scotland and that things were pretty bad. Friends were on their way to pick me up. I should go home. They arrived some hours later with the news that Owen had died the previous night in a hospital at Elgin. He had been in the car with Julian Pettifer and a production assistant, Vivien Duret, who both escaped. I felt angry that frantic prayerful hours had been in vain even before they began, and constantly replayed in my mind the moment when a black baton of truth was passed to me in the middle of the college's serene quadrangle.

Owen had been difficult, outrageous, and at times impossible, but confident and imaginative enough to chase wild dreams, and charismatic enough to take others with him. He was life-enhancing company. His death was a shattering blow, and father took it hardest of all, worryingly silent for days after. The pain was such that he was never able to talk to me about Owen throughout the remaining seventeen years of his life, although, after my mother's death, he published a volume of poetry, *Diannerch Erchwyn*, that centred on his memories of her and my brother.

Despite her illness mother coped better with the tragedy. She did so perhaps because, unlike father, her faith was unquestioning, something felt in the gut rather than in the mind. Her practicality was now a means to blot out darker thoughts, a device that the cancer had already honed. Her first words to me, after the unspoken ones, when I returned home after Owen's death were, 'Have you eaten?' Welsh and Jewish mothers have much in common. The combination of the trauma and the practicalities of dealing with mother's illness meant that Elinor, who had always idolised Owen, and I had to cope as best we could.

Alasdair Milne wrote a warm tribute in the BBC staff magazine, *Ariel*. A month later as we watched Millicent Martin sing her elegy to the assassinated John Kennedy on *That Was The Week That Was*, we cried for more than one reason.

For Rita and Simon the rollercoaster of the last few years had come to a disastrous end, as it often threatened to do. A long period of disorientation, and some strain between my parents and her, ended when, in 1965, she married Herbert Davies, a radio drama producer who had been a regular visitor at home. Peter O'Toole was best man at the ceremony. Soon after, Herbert, Rita and Simon emigrated to Australia, where Herbert pursued a career in broadcasting and Rita came to be lauded in her community as an inspirational drama teacher. There was one final tragedy left. On 18 June, 1981, less than a fortnight after his twentieth birthday and on the eve of a round the world trip that was meant to end with his first return to Wales, Simon committed suicide.

* * * *

The novelty of university and the delights of Oxford were not a wholly effective distraction from the loss of Owen, although fellow students were supportive, jolly and determined that I should play. Elizabeth, whom I had then known for less than a year, carried me. She had never met Owen, but he had made her laugh and blush when he spoke to her once on the phone and mischievously pretended for some minutes to be me. She was an acute and caring listener even in her teens – a gift that has never left her – and the emotional turmoil of that period deepened our already intense relationship. She visited Oxford regularly, so that despite the dark backdrop, it also became a period of happiness, even in the cold, grey Februaries of the Hilary term.

I plunged into sport, captaining the college at rugby and coxing a college eight. There were also the dubious pleasures of the Elizabethan Society in a college then unconstrained by the civilising influence of women undergraduates. It was said that the university turned boys into young men. The Elizabethan Society usually did the reverse. Although I never got involved in university journalism, I was not averse to committing opinions to paper. A friend, David Bartlett, and I had the temerity after only three terms, to write a memorandum to the Franks Commission, then investigating the workings of a university that measured itself in centuries, telling them how it should be run, how students should get a better deal and how dons should be better trained. This was all very well as a piece of private cockiness, but when the contents got ten inches in the *Oxford Mail* on the alleged shortcomings of dons, it made us both blush almost as much as when I recall it now.

I enjoyed the study of history, but was not a diligent student. My headmaster had once written in a school report, 'He may yet have time to confound the critics.' Yet the history school made a mark, for I have read more history since leaving Oxford than I did while I was there. Some disciplines are absorbed unconsciously. Constitutional history was of continuing use, and the history of slavery transformed a later visit to the southern states of America. At Jesus I was guided by Dr. John Walsh, then a kindly, young tutor with the lean frame of a climber, and a specialist on English Methodism. My one small triumph was to introduce him to the diaries of Welsh Methodist leader, Howell Harris. As my final year approached, Dr. Walsh was honest in his appraisal: 'Davies, you will get a second with ease and, I'm afraid to say, a third with even greater ease.' My problem was that I regarded this assessment as ambiguous, more comforting than worrying.

It did not help that I already had offers of two jobs: a traineeship in journalism or in personnel management with a steel company. It was not difficult to choose. When I got my degree father sat on the stairs and wept.

2 In the beginning was the word

The first newspaper feature to imprint itself on my mind was the *Western Mail*'s Birth Marriages and Deaths column. Mother was always impressed by the orderliness of Wales, people dying in alphabetical order. She would announce arrivals and departures across the kitchen table over breakfast: mainly unknown relations from the distant west whose three lines in the *Western Mail* might presage a full three paragraphs in the *Tivyside Advertiser* that would arrive by post.

I cannot remember a time without newspapers. One of the joys of urban living is having a newsagent that will deliver the papers early to your door – the day's essential beginning – their absence a signal for grumpy frustration. No matter that turning the pages of the 'national newspaper of Wales' has normally been a preliminary to curmudgeonly chuntering about insufficient substance, or the unnecessary daily bulletin on the imagined doings of Catherine Zeta Jones, or the inability of some near-teenage journalist to recall an historical precedent more than three months distant from the day. What counts is the feel of the newsprint, and the hope and belief that the next page just might enliven the day, through some new journalistic insight, folly or outrage.

The family habit was confirmed by twelve years in the newspaper business, twelve years that instilled a fogeyish belief – long ago discarded by the public and even by many print journalists – that the printed word is more important and valuable than the broadcast or online image. Even the subsequent twenty-five years in broadcasting could not scour that belief from the soul. It was a defining period.

I began as one of twelve university graduates that Thomson Regional Newspapers thought it should recruit but without any idea why. Six were allotted to the morning newspaper, the *Western Mail*, and six to the evening paper, the *South Wales Echo*. Another of the twelve was Alun Michael, later to become, albeit for a very short period, the first First Minister of the National Assembly. We were greeted with suspicion by more seasoned hacks whose minds had not been narrowed by fancy education. Our main value was to spare them the more mundane tasks of rewriting press releases, or sitting through the minor committees of Cardiff City Council or any committee at all of

Cardiff Rural District Council.

The influx caught the organisation and the staff almost literally on the hop. Thomson had a religious dedication to parsimony, and the Thomson House newsroom contained fewer chairs than reporters. It explained why, after lunch, many would walk back from the pub unnaturally quickly. Slower reporters were left loitering around the newsdesk or, if anxious to avoid an assignment, in the library. Management gurus have since sought to make this shameful economy respectable under the fashionable label, hot-desking.

The *Western Mail* newsdesk was run by John Humphries, a man of manic energy and an inexhaustible supply of ideas that we would be obliged to pursue, however madcap we thought them to be. Many newspapers have characters that become legendary among those that pass through their eccentric hands. Humphries is such. No two members of staff who ever worked for him can meet for more than five minutes without his name being taken in vain. (I use the past tense only because he is now retired.) I worked for and learnt from him as news editor, and later worked with him when he was deputy editor and I assistant editor. He lived for the paper and the night before my wedding took me aside to tell me to remind my wife-to-be that she would be 'marrying the *Western Mail*'.

He exuded tension. He worked with shirt sleeves rolled up rather too tightly, well above his sharp elbows. His intense ballpoint doodles would cut clean through several sheets of the admittedly thin newsprint offcuts that Thomson gave us as notepaper. He spiked weak stories with a vehemence that, in the days of a real spike, made you surprised at the lack of stigmata. He saw himself as a scourge of lazy journalists and lazy journalism, though more successful in the former role than the latter.

Reporters dreaded his return from leave. He would always take his annual holiday in Wales, a notebook on the company Cortina's dashboard to jot down ideas to be explored by the staff on his return. He was more than willing to generalise from the particular. A half-page spread on oil pollution on Welsh beaches contained a long quote from an unnamed 'irate holidaymaker'. No prizes for guessing who that holidaymaker was. In one post-holiday fit of enthusiasm he summoned the agricultural correspondent: 'I want you to break this racket. There are potatoes on sale in Pembrokeshire for a shilling. In Cardiff they're five times that price. What's going on?' The operation of the market was too simplistic a notion to be accepted and, besides, would not have entailed the obligatory two days of phone calls to the obviously bemused and the potentially irate.

When I finished my two and a half years of indentured training, he called me to one side, said some complimentary things and informed me that it had been decided I should become a specialist correspondent. 'What do you want me to specialise in?' said I expectantly. 'Everything,' said Humphries. Elsewhere in the Thomson empire this was the era of the *Sunday Times* Insight team. Away from London this was a way of doing it on the cheap. Thus was the *Western Mail*'s first Welsh Affairs Correspondent created. In similar fashion Patrick Hannan became the 'News Focus team'.

The tautology of creating the post of Welsh Affairs Correspondent at the 'national newspaper of Wales' was not lost on anyone and was, in part, the result of a wish to walk around the word 'politics' and so avoid offending David Rosser, the paper's rotundly conservative political editor who resided at Westminster and saw little need for a new and uncontrollable presence on the politics beat in distant Cardiff. He may have foreseen that thirty years hence, in reporting Welsh politics, the boot would be firmly – and not entirely healthily – on the other foot.

In 1969 the paper felt it had to respond to the growth in the powers and size of the Welsh Office, the rising fortunes of Welsh nationalism, the burgeoning of the Welsh language movement and the imminent appointment of a Royal Commission on the Constitution. Nevertheless, it made for occasionally tense relations and some schizophrenic reporting: myself digging out material from civil servants in Cardiff (a source to which current Welsh journalists should give more attention), and David often providing the rebuttal from their own Ministers at Westminster. Through the seventies, too, the fact that groups within the Labour Party in Wales tended to take a more radical approach to devolution than their own MPs at Westminster echoed our different journalistic inclinations. It was often John Humphries' job to reconcile the two.

Humphries' excesses, not to mention his occasional scorn for graduates, made him an easy target for condescension, and yet that would have been unfair. He was of that generation that slipped through the inadequate university net. He was an inspired news editor, intuitive and tireless. You could forgive every wild idea just to have the ones that worked, to have the added value that his quivering nose and terrier-like persistence could bring. If there was one mantra that stayed in the mind it was 'Ring 'em, again'. And we did. It was a discipline that I later found to be much less rigorously employed in the corresponding morning newspaper in Newcastle-upon-Tyne or even on *The Times*. It is rare in broadcast newsrooms that are now dominated by the demand for swift and regular reports around the clock.

Humphries was particularly hard on the team that covered the National Eisteddfod every year. He wanted controversy – not necessarily cultural – and in the late sixties it was what he got. My first working Eisteddfod was at Bala in 1967. The paper had booked the team of five reporters into this inland town's Ship Hotel, but had neglected to tell us that we were to share one room. The personal hygiene deficit was made worse by the fact that this was, by common consent, the booziest Eisteddfod in history, with what seemed like ten thousand drinkers converging each night on the central High Street, turning the town into one huge pub. This may well have fuelled the escalation of the first day's news into the realms of the surreal.

The Eisteddfod, although marketed as a cultural festival is, more importantly, the annual general meeting of the Welsh-speaking community, and had convened as usual in the first week of August. On Monday afternoon the choirs were competing in the main pavilion, then made of flimsy wood panels topped with a tin roof. A choral competition was in full flow when a low flying jet buzzed the field, severely rattling the roof and obliterating one choir's collective climax. Result: fury all round. Aggrieved choir, aggrieved officials, nationalists complaining about this insult to Wales, pacifists aghast at this military intrusion, reporters absolutely delighted to have a 'real' story, rather than all that dreary human interest stuff about winners.

Day two saw the local MP, the jolly, rather raffish Wil Edwards, delivering his speech as President of the Day. He was keen to show that he had been active in his protests to the Ministry of Defence, who had claimed one of their pilots had strayed from his prescribed course. 'I have their categorical assurance that this will not happ....' The end of the sentence was lost as a second jet screamed across the field. This time reporters swore it had dipped a wing in salute, pulling the rug from under the excuse of cartographic ineptitude. Result: embarrassed, incandescent MP goes off to ring the MOD again.

By day three the MOD had discovered – as if pulling a Welsh rabbit out of a hat – that it had an Air Chief Marshal by the name of Sir Hugh Pugh Lloyd. He was dispatched to Bala – by car not jet – to calm the waters. The RAF, while talking to the natives, was clearly not talking to its pilots, one of whom had clearly purchased a ticket for the week and continued to come like a bee to the honey, though for a rather shorter time than most bees. At the newsdesk Humphries was now both delirious and untiringly imaginative as he goaded his team on.

In the *Western Mail*, by day five, the handful of jets had grown in number to something resembling the Berlin airlift. Air Chief Marshal Pugh Lloyd had been robust in his denials, so the jets had now become American, while a quick glance at a map of north Wales was enough to convince any right thinking sleuth that the not-too-distant Mawddach estuary must be a training ground for American pilots bound for Vietnam's Mekong delta. It was duly reported as such. Humphries reckoned we had had 'a good Eisteddfod'. I believe poets also won a chair and crown.

Accounts of his doings, like this one, inevitably concentrate on the more bizarre episodes, but he was perhaps the most powerful influence on the paper for more than two decades, as news editor, deputy editor and editor, before moving on in 1989 to launch and edit the new stablemate, *Wales on Sunday*. Significantly, that paper in its early days was considerably more ambitious and thoughtful than it has now become. John Humphries believed in his paper, believed in Wales and in reporting it thoroughly, and he was more fortunate than his successors in having the journalistic resource to carry out that task.

The staff, augmented by a now defunct network of freelancers across Wales, filled more than half a dozen localised editions, as well as the new 'main Welsh' page, another reflection of an intensifying national dimension. Although always rightfully sceptical of his more politically engaged specialists, and more inclined to black and white argument than shuffling shades of grey, he eventually moved, with characteristic decisiveness, to a passionate pro-devolution stance. This included, after he had left newspapers, the formation of a short-lived fringe independence party for Wales. Gwent shook hands with Gwynedd.

His greatest triumph lay elsewhere. He devoted the same intense focus and energy, not to say ruthlessness, to battering down the doors of medical bureaucracy to create the British Bone Marrow Donor Appeal – the largest bone marrow database of its kind – in a long and blessedly successful attempt to save his son from leukaemia. It was the biggest pay-off of all for refusing to take no for an answer.

*   *   *   *

Print journalism was an education that came in a number of very different forms. The darkest came quickly, within six weeks of starting my training: 21 October 1966 and the Aberfan disaster. I hadn't been due in the office that morning, and it was Elizabeth – then working as a physiotherapist at Cardiff Royal Infirmary – who alerted me, ringing to say her department had no patients because all ambulances had been diverted to an accident in the valleys. As a raw trainee I was despatched not to Aberfan, but up the Rhymney Valley to check on water supplies that had been disrupted, but with instructions to get round to Aberfan later if I could. By mid-afternoon I had parked my car some miles north of the village, and walked in. Turning a corner into a row of terraced houses, one faced a wall of slurry, rooftop to rooftop. Emergency services and volunteer rescuers swarmed over the school site where 116 children and 28 adults died.

In truth I did not stay there long, but was recalled to the office, feeling much like a willing soldier posted to a desk job. There was an enormous amount of copy to be reworked under John Humphries's staccato instructions. Calls were made regularly to the Met Office to check whether the rain that caused the disaster would persist. With darkness, the newsroom in Cardiff began to fill with foreign correspondents eager to find a desk and a reliable phone. Wales was used to disasters. My own brother, Owen, had covered one at Six Bells Colliery in June 1960. This was different.

Local reporters and cameramen hesitated before the unbearable poignancy of the tragedy. It was said an over-eager *Paris Match* photographer had been thrown over a wall by enraged rescuers. The *Western Mail*'s seasoned industrial correspondent, no stranger to mining disasters, was sick beneath the same wall. It was unforgettable not only because of what it was but because its aftermath knew no end: the funerals and memorials, the clearance of the threatening tips that still covered that and other hillsides, the argument with government and the Charity Commissioners over who should pay, the bickering over the disaster fund, the appeals for privacy between the inevitable anniversaries. Unforgettable, too, because of its wider effects, not just the creation of a political edge, but the opening of eyes to the general despoliation of the valleys and its continuing threat, and ultimately, the beginning of a re-creation of a landscape that could be special again.

The memory of Aberfan comes back every time the malign slope above the village comes into view on a dualled curve of the A470, a piece of history that nature struggles to sweep under its carpet. Rather too much of Merthyr's history has been swept away, and not always by nature.

* * * *

The passions generated by Aberfan, and by a host of other issues, would be the stuff of debate in the back bar of Cardiff's Old Arcade pub, where it was possible to do a beery post-graduate degree in politics, although only of a reddish hue. Rhodri Morgan, who thirty years later would be Wales's First Minister, exercised his formidable powers of total recall on economic development. Ted Rowlands, now Lord Rowlands, then in the gap between serving as MP for Cardiff North and later Merthyr, was his passionate self about planning matters in Cardiff, having just vanquished the Hook Road project – Colin Buchanan's egregious scheme for cleaving Cardiff in two with a motorway of breathtaking insensitivity. An activist's intensity, particularly on housing, emanated from Bob Dumbleton, from the Cardiff Housing Action Group. Another academic, Barry Jones, was deep into Labour's working groups on devolution. Jack Brooks, (now Lord Brooks of Tremorfa) who was Jim Callaghan's agent, brought a roguish cunning to the table, not to mention an encyclopaedic knowledge of Frank Sinatra's repertoire. He was looking forward to leading the new South Glamorgan County Council, an authority that was to last only 20 years, although the 1979 referendum dashed his hopes of playing a part in a Welsh Assembly.

The most consistent denizen, consistent enough to have his own reserved oak seat, was the least known – Ellis Goldstone, the loquacious owner of a chain of dress shops in the city, who was far more interested in politics than in the rag trade, and given to handing out volumes by Ralph Miliband to enlighten the wage slaves of Thomson House. Ellis was also the source of sage advice. I once told him that my wife and mother-in-law were thinking of starting a dress shop. 'Have they got good taste,' he asked. 'Yes,' said I. 'It'll be a disaster,' he said crushingly.

Political conferences and rallies punctuated the calendar at regular intervals. Each party's event had its own character. The Welsh Labour conference was the biggest and the most male – the party had yet to embrace the equality agenda fully. Etiolated miners, florid steelmen, rumpled teachers and academics composited away in Swansea or Llandudno, on threats to coal and steel plants, plans to make local authorities larger or smaller, or to go into or get out of Europe, depend-

ing on where in the cycle we were. To devolve or not to devolve was the
thread that ran through every gathering, the delegates often unaware of
the subtle manipulations of their secretary, Emrys Jones, who did more
than anyone to circumvent opposition to devolution in the party: long,
soporific filibusters stating the Executive's position drove even the
most rabid opponents to the bar, while votes taken early after a short-
ened lunch break seemed always to go the Executive's way.

Party conferences generate passion, almost as if speakers plug into
a high voltage socket under the lectern. But passion is often trumped
by humour. In the seventies Michael Foot, in a rattling Patti Pavilion in
Swansea, argued with unpunctuated eloquence for his Government's
'measure of home rule'. Neil Kinnock, regretfully attacking his mentor,
scoffed, 'A measure of home rule? You can no more have a measure of
home rule, than a measure of pregnancy.' Emrys Jones, a skilled casting
director, called the Llanelli trade unionist, Dai Davies, to the rostrum.

In his high and hoarse voice Dai extolled at length the sacrifices that
generations of working men and women had made to give their
children an education to escape the pit. 'I'm very disappointed to know
this morning that even after all that education, Neil still can't tell the
difference between home rule and pregnancy.' Even Neil applauded.
Dai Davies must have been a frustrating opponent in a negotiation.
Some years later at HTV I dispatched a reporter to interview him
about the proposed closure of one of three south Wales tinplate works.
'It's true, we may not need three works, but we need more than two,' he
said without blinking.

Some conferences are smaller than others, a fact that is less obvious
in newspaper coverage than on television where camera angles
contrive, unsuccessfully, to avoid the rows of empty seats. Questions of
identity that were to the fore the world over, also afflicted the political
parties and in the Wales of today their titles seem drawn from another
age. A body called the Wales and Monmouthshire Area Council of the
Conservative Party did not exactly chime with the times, even then,
though its annual meeting that took all of a Saturday afternoon, was
rightly named since it would have been an exaggeration to say that the
party conferred.

It did at least meet at Llandrindod, which was an advance on the
fifties when it met outside Wales at Chester, Ludlow or Shrewsbury. Its
'debates' usually amounted to one speech by a frontbencher or MP,
supporting an anodyne motion that would then be formally seconded
by a somnambulant colonel or major. The real focus was usually a

middle-ranking cabinet minister. It was not, therefore, a surprise when the party failed to win a single Welsh seat in the 1966 General Election.

The Liberal Party of Wales, though occasionally frequenting Llandrindod, was more at home deeper in the Cambrian Mountains in a hotel that had seen better days at Llanwrtyd. Largely untroubled by power, it preferred to hold 'Liberal weekends' that required rather less organisation and money, both of which the party lacked. They resembled a large house party, with guests including junior academics, an assortment of London Welsh, an overseas speaker to add breadth, and a relative of Lloyd George. The two MPs, Geraint Howells and Emlyn Hooson, a farmer and lawyer respectively, were as different as the constituencies they represented, canny Ceredigion and lush Montgomery. The party seemed blessed with pianists, leading to much singing of the first verses of various Welsh hymns and, rather surprisingly, choruses from Gilbert and Sullivan. Policy discussion was earnest but diffuse.

All parties drew, if in varying degrees, on the output of Welsh academics who were starting to show much more interest in Wales, both in terms of a flowering of Welsh historiography and a real, though less widespread, study of the Welsh economy – an entity whose existence many found to be questionable. The search for numbers was a particular fascination, since the freshly formed Welsh Office was now churning out a new annual for the anorak class, the *Digest of Welsh Statistics*.

Professor Edward Nevin at Aberystwyth and later Swansea had done pioneering work on the structure of the Welsh economy, demonstrating, not for the last time, that optimistic political rhetoric was unlikely to be borne out on the ground. In 1966 he resigned from the Welsh Economic Council, an advisory body to the Secretary of State for Wales, after Eirene White, the Minister of State, allegedly tampered with the Welsh Office's first stab at a strategy for Wales – the 1967 White Paper, *Wales, The Way Ahead*. Nevin insisted to me that she had deleted the number 59,000 – solely on the grounds of political expediency – and inserted 15,000 as an estimate of the 'jobs gap' likely to accumulate over the next five years. The original estimate had been based on Nevin's own researches. Five years later the actual shortfall was 56,000.

Those looking for something more meaty than the White Paper included the young turks of Plaid Cymru, not least Dafydd Wigley, an economist with Mars, and Phil Williams, an astro-physicist at home with the whole universe. Over a weekend at Aberystwyth in January 1969 they unveiled a 'budget for an independent Wales', to an audience that ranged from the credulous to the sceptical, and to those, like economist Roger Opie, who were surprised that it should be done at all.

A more unpredictable presence at the seminar came with a thick Germanic accent and a mischievous twinkle in the eye. He was Leopold Kohr, who was to Plaid what Kaldor and Balogh were to Harold Wilson. Kohr was a pioneer of the 'small is beautiful' school, and many claimed that E.F. Schumacher, the public hero of the movement, had been too grudging in confessing his debt to him. Born in the Austrian village of Oberndorf, where the carol 'Silent Night' was written, Kohr tended to turn up in small nations, even writing an economic plan for Anguilla that was subverted by gangsters and finally sunk by the invasion of the Metropolitan Police, ordered there by Wilson. Aberystwyth was quieter.

After the Plaid research team had finished their presentation Kohr rose, adjusted his outsize hearing aid and started to rip a piece of paper slowly. 'I take your feeegures,' he told the conference, 'and I rip them apart. Let me tell you, the only feeegures that are completely unassailable are feeegures that you invent!! I will invent a budget for you!' He never did, but he did publish one volume, entitled *Is Wales Viable?* reminding people that the real question was at what standard of living it became viable.

His penchant for deploying metaphors rather than data was hugely entertaining, though the despair of more conventional economists. In a television interview Joan Bakewell attempted to counter him by saying: 'We cannot turn the clock back.' 'My dearrr....' he replied, hovering between refutation and flirtation, 'your analogy is as weak as your argument.' Whereupon he took a large pocket watch from his top pocket. 'There, I have turned the clock back,' he beamed, leaving Joan Bakewell's face a cross between a smile and a gape.

All this was a far cry from Plaid rallies where the rhetoric could often telescope centuries into days. Hacks at tables beneath the platform would occasionally bet on the earliest date to be mentioned by Gwynfor Evans – 1536 (the Act of Union), 1282 (the death of Llewelyn, last of the Welsh princes) or the fifth century, and Britain's first poem, *Y Gododdin*. Gwynfor, whose habit of kindly encouragement was ecumenical, sent me a copy of his somewhat romantic history of Wales, with a note thanking me for my work for Wales, *trwy gyfrwng amheus* (through a doubtful medium).

★ ★ ★ ★

The daily leader column is a feature that many papers still take to be intrinsic to their self-importance. This is why such columns have survived in many newspapers, even if by now they are – London broadsheets apart – little more than succinct expressions of a populist knee-jerk. Today, in a 'regional' newspaper, it would be regarded as irresponsibly luxurious to allow a member of staff to spend the whole day perusing every imaginable newspaper and magazine, along with *The Observer*'s foreign news service that arrived daily on green paper, and the black, weighty files of Keesing's Contemporary Archive that ate up shelf space at an alarming rate; all this to produce 750 words of considered thought that would be ignored by a large majority of the readership.

There was also the added benefit of a nightly visit from Henry Reynolds, the head reader, who, in a hierarchical pre-Wapping print industry, claimed the right to read the proof of the leader column and to convey to me his commanding knowledge of Fowlers' *Modern English Usage* and his sharp eye for any 'infelicities'. Sadly, this post no longer exists in newspapers, providing grist to the mill of Lynne Truss and other guardians of the language.

It is easy to dismiss leader columns as an outdated indulgence, a corporate vanity. More sceptical journalists will tell you of the futility of the exercise, usually reminding you of that famous pre-1914 Irish newspaper headline: '*The Skibereen Eagle* warns the Tsar.' Yet, tackled in the way it was, I would defend it as an assertion of a paper's continuity and an investment in its consistency, even if it made this young journalist impossibly opinionated in the process. Apart from any impression it might or might not have made on the reader, the leader and the process of arriving at its message had an internal value for the paper. A subject would be researched and argued about, and in the process the question would always be asked, 'What have we said in the past?' Sometimes we would defend a long standing position, at other times we would change tack, but if we did it was done consciously and with a sense that the change needed to be justified. Often it would lead to hours of argument between John Humphries and myself, with the editor, Duncan Gardiner, as umpire.

In the wake of the Birmingham pub bombings in 1974 John and I rowed about the return of capital punishment, though the fact that I won that one had as much to do with the fact that that the editor's wife was a Catholic Irishwoman as with the paper's respectable abolitionist track record. A few years later we argued for days about whether to support a referendum on devolution, myself with a foolishly long memorandum that referred us back to the paper's opposition to a referendum on European membership in 1975. John took a more succinct and populist line that had more reason behind it than I allowed at the time. The editor, fresh from being metaphorically beaten up by anti-devolution MPs at a Westminster dinner, and sensibly choosing not read beyond the first page of anything, came down on Humphries's side. Duncan's crisp memo, dictated by telephone, simply said, 'I have decided there should be a referendum. I will explain my reasons when I return.'

Even this does, of course, exaggerate the purity of the process. During the 1970 election readers would have been bemused by a series of leaders, organised by the then deputy editor, John Rowley, a cerebral individual, who would interrupt a discussion to swivel his chair and gaze wistfully out of the window. We would write leaders, not only about Wales but also about world events – the Prague Spring and the Biafran War – and trends including, rather frequently, population control. He left to edit the journal of the International Planned Parenthood Federation. Assisted by willing graduate trainees, Rowley was heading towards an endorsement of the Labour Government, if only by studied circumlocution, only to find that on the day before polling – and without much argument – the then editor, John Giddings, stepped in and insisted on the paper's traditional default conservatism.

The *Western Mail*, founded by the Marquis of Bute in 1869 to counter the dominant Liberal interest in south Wales, had a long right-wing pedigree. Although it had had some sporadic attacks of social conscience during nineteenth-century industrial disputes, its instinct was to champion the employers' cause. Its Toryism became less liberal in the twentieth century and it railed against Aneurin Bevan in what Michael Foot called a campaign of 'unexampled virulence'. In the late sixties its conservatism moved from upper case to lower case, though the touchstone of its politics was still found somewhere between the bars of the Cardiff and County Club and the Cardiff Athletic Club.

Its gradual switch to a largely non-party championing of Welsh issues, although a nod to the liberalisation of the sixties, was not always benign. In the six months before the Investiture of the Prince of Wales in July 1969, every story on opposition to the event and the campaigns of the Welsh Language Society had to be referred to the editor, with the

blue pencil much in evidence as a result. The morning after the conference where Plaid revealed its economic blueprint, I left Aberystwyth
early only to see every road sign for miles painted out – the first action
in a major new campaign of civil disobedience by the Welsh Language
Society. It got a few paragraphs.

This anxious compliance was partly a reaction to law-breaking,
partly an acute discomfort with cultural issues but also the result of an
unfortunate coincidence between the Investiture and the paper's centenary on 1 May that year. It meant that it was especially keen not to blot
its copybook. I had been given six months to write the paper's history
which appeared in a 24-page supplement which, as the security guard
told me as I left with a first edition under my arm, would 'make the chip
shops happy tonight'.

The centenary celebration took a form difficult to imagine today,
and not just on the grounds of its cost. At the suggestion of the managing director, David Thomas, a man rather over-fond of style who also
rode with the Glamorgan hunt, a lavish dinner was held at the Savoy in
London attended by the Prime Minister and the Leader of the
Opposition. At a civic dinner at Cardiff Castle, the paper's owner, Lord
Thomson, presented the city with a large solid silver rose bowl that
must have cost far in excess of a junior journalist's salary.

★ ★ ★ ★

Thomson's newspaper empire was widespread, and in 1971 it was
decided that I should leave the *Western Mail* and set off on an educational peregrination. First stop was Newcastle and its morning
newspaper, *The Journal*, with the intention that I should learn about the
technical end of newspaper production. However, since this was a
company that allowed nothing to go to waste, it was decided that, first
of all, my four months of daily attendance at the public inquiry into the
redevelopment of Cardiff should be put to good use in writing a series
of investigations into the redevelopment of almost every town in the
north east of England – Newcastle, Gateshead, Sunderland, Durham,
Middlesbrough, North and South Shields, and, for the sake of the
readers *trans montem*, Carlisle.

It did not lift the spirit of this journalist any more than it lifted those
of the shoppers of the region. Charting the redevelopment of decent
towns, some of which had endured more than their share of the
century's hardships, was to face a repetitive catalogue of misconceived

ambitions, uneven battles between the public and commercial interests, rough-hewn compromises and cut-price architecture. Some, such as Durham, with the breathtaking glories of its cathedral and castle, cried out not just for something better but for the very best. It did not get it. In most of these towns, local authorities have, in more recent decades, been struggling to ameliorate the effects of this period.

It was a relief to reach the cosy security of the sub-editor's bench, though that could prove equally repetitive. I had been warned about the potential boredom of the work by the poet and film-maker, John Ormond. As a young sub on the *South Wales Evening Post* – before his days at the BBC – he had, in order to test that the night editor who checked his work was awake, constructed a stultifying three-line headline: 'Swansea Man / Weds Swansea Woman / In Swansea'. The night editor cast a beady eye at Ormond. 'We'll have none of your smart London tricks down 'ere,' he said deleting the third line.

Ormond was right. It was dull, quiet work. 'Cut and paste' was a physical reality, not a couple of icons on a computer; the biro, the scissors, the conical pot of Gloy, were the simple toolkit. The real interest came several floors below, amidst the clank of Linotype machines and the clatter of the printers' stone – the metal bench that stood between an impecunious sub and the aristocrats of the union movement. A place of banter, but which was never allowed to blunt the sharp edge of incomprehensible demarcations; also a place where you could relish the disciplined sculpting of a page in metal, learn to savour the beauty of a serif, to spot an errant font, and to develop that skill, much treasured by journalists and spies, the ability to read type upside down and back to front.

If you were lucky you could finish by 2.30 a.m., in the winter to get back to a candle-lit home struggling against power cuts caused by the latest battle between Edward Heath and the miners but, on clear summer nights, heading due north from Newcastle on the A1, to catch the most southerly shimmering trace of the *aurora borealis*.

The Times, the next stop on my journey, was a different matter. These were pre-Murdoch days, Fleet Street's last decade. Harold Evans was at *The Sunday Times*, setting new standards in investigative journalism. William Rees-Mogg was editing *The Times*, then in Printing House Square, from a Kennedy-style rocking chair, and giving the place the air of a senior common room. Peter Jay was writing abstruse articles on monetary policy designed, he confessed himself, to be read by only three people in the UK. Louis Heren presided with heavy authority over foreign coverage, and Ion Trewin over the books pages, in a department where one could drink jasmine tea from porcelain cups. Bernard Levin was the star columnist of his day, regularly reminding us of how he had been swept away by the voice of the young Kiri Te Kanawa, but who, from time to time, swept Wales and its language under a carpet of condescension, woven with the threads of his interminable subsidiary clauses.

It operated at a different level but also at a different pace from regional newspapers. On my first day in the newsroom I was given a press release about the conserving of a rare fritillary somewhere in Dorset, and told to turn it to a story. Hardly big news, but presumed to be of interest to its country readership. It was the sort of story that in Cardiff or Newcastle you would turn out at the rate of three or four a day. A few hours later I delivered it to the news desk. While pleased with the outcome, there was a degree of surprise and it became clear that they would have been happy if I had taken a day or two over it. It was an early lesson in the resource differential between operating in the regions and in London.

Given my interest in politics, I was despatched for a period to join the political team at Westminster. The political editor, David Wood, managed a welcome that was somehow both warm and gruff. He was of the old school, grey-suited with a sprinkling of ash from an ever-present cigarette. He was so much part of the place that it was difficult to imagine him going home. Not long before I arrived he had written a column attacking the notion of devolution, on the basis that 'the tribal Welsh and Scots would, thereby, cut themselves off from the voices of moderation and reason at Westminster'. I rose to the bait, but with no visible effect. It was an issue that was the cause of bemusement rather than real intellectual curiosity; good for a column, but Royal Commissions not withstanding, not something that was ever going to happen.

He could also play the aloof uncle. The Palace of Westminster is a sweaty place in high summer. One hot day, I turned up in a light coloured suit, looking rather like Martin Bell in his heyday. 'Good God, Davies. You look like a Hoover salesman from a Graham Greene novel,' he said with a look of alarm on his face. I didn't wear it again.

The letters page of *The Times* carried a prestige in the seventies that it has now almost completely lost in its modern tabloid form. It was a very English institution, with much emphasis on 'doing the right thing'. Its editor, Geoffrey Woolley, tended his formal garden with meticulous care, shaping it for impact and balance. The views of peers, principals, professors, bishops and others who had a propensity to live in houses with no numbers – if not in central London, then in Wiltshire – were carefully sifted for their interest, significance, topicality and style. All letters were acknowledged, the favoured being told of the degree of the editor's interest. More letters were set in type and proofed than could be accommodated on the page. If they were lucky, those who fell by the wayside at this last stage might be sent a copy of the proof as evidence of quite how close they had come to a prize in one of life's great contests.

This was a paper where tradition and nuance counted, as became evident when the death of the Nazi, Martin Bormann was confirmed. the *Daily Express* had, rashly, claimed to have proof that he was alive and well and living in South America, billing it as a 'world exclusive'. Unfortunately for the paper, a few weeks later a body was dug up in Germany, and dental records proved conclusively that it was the said Herr Bormann. Rees-Mogg suggested that, now that the death was confirmed, *The Times* should carry an obituary. I'm afraid not, said those older than him. At the end of the war *The Times* had not run obituaries of any of the Nazi leaders, only biographical details. What was the difference? It was this: an obituary in those days always began with the phrase, 'We announce with regret the death of'. Since the paper did not regret the death of any Nazi leaders, it carried only biographical details without risking the hypocrisy of the introductory phrase.

It was said, though I have been unable to confirm it, that in times past the newspaper even had degrees of regret, like an in-house honours system, depending of the departed's station in life. 'We announce with regret the death of. We announce with much regret the death of. We announce with deep regret the death of. We announce with the deepest regret the death of' and last, reserved for only the most distinguished, was the accolade of having the whole sentence turned around. 'It is with the deepest regret we announce.' Ronnie Barker and Ronnie Corbett could not have scripted it better.

The letters page of the *Western Mail* was rather different – more an inchoate platform for the public than a sharpened tool for the political community. The addresses were more down to earth. Alongside those who felt they had been traduced by the paper's reporters and columnists were the party supporters obliged to keep up their partisan letter count. On a bad day the rabid and the nutty would turn up as if the page were a drop-in centre for the deranged. There was sometimes more than a suspicion of the Welsh penchant for noms de plume. It appears saner and duller, though no less partisan today, younger and livelier souls having taken to blogging.

I have often pondered why I returned to the *Western Mail* from *The Times* when there was an opportunity to stay there. It was certainly not the money or the title, more a conspiracy of aspiration and circumstance. The attraction of that more intimate connection with the reader was always something to savour, but that has the hint of a later rationalisation. There was certainly the pull of unfinished business – an urgent desire not to miss an historic period, and a naive wish to change the paper I left. But as a family we were not keen to repeat the trials of bringing up children through a steamy summer in a cramped flat in Raynes Park. It was also a period of personal turmoil – my mother's death in 1971 and, on the very first anniversary of that event, my father suffering a stroke while addressing the assembled pharmacists of Newport. It was to be the first of several strokes during the remaining eight years of his life. For whatever reason, the family returned home.

3 Up and down the Taff

Frank Lloyd Wright's mother, an educational progressive, gave her precocious child a set of wooden blocks. Later in life he would recall running those smooth blocks through his fingers every time he set about designing a building. I was given a second-hand Meccano set. Had it not been for the missing long bits and the bent screws I am sure I could have designed the Eiffel Tower or the Pompidou Centre, but it was not to be. I have had to content myself with being a spectator rather than designer of the world around me, a world that has been irredeemably urban.

The inadequacies of the British planning system turned up on my parents' doorstep in suburban Llandaff one Sunday afternoon in the late sixties when my father was informed by our neighbour, a medical consultant, that a bulldozer would arrive the very next morning to clear his own garden to make way for consulting rooms two-storeys high. Urgent calls to the planning department revealed only that all protest would be in vain, permission had been given some time ago and there was no requirement to inform anyone. Councillors offered no comfort, and my parents lived in the shadow of the building and the hurt for their remaining years in the house. The fashionable cause of 'public participation in planning', a response to the excesses of sixties development, became for me a keen matter of personal and journalistic interest.

These were the years of the escape from the drab fifties, the years of comprehensive development, and increasing local government ambition, based on assumptions of rapid population growth. The consultant, Colin Buchanan, was telling everyone to cater for the car. Reports told us we had to plan for a whole new Severnside region, and for new towns everywhere across the UK. The Welsh Office came up with a bizarre idea for a 'linear new town' running along the Severn from Newtown to Llanidloes, presumably on the flood plain. Though it would clearly have been an environmental nightmare – and not only in retrospect – it was taken seriously. Plans for a new town at Llantrisant, where the old settlement saddles the mountain at the foot of the valleys, resulted in a characteristic Welsh fudge: the idea of a new town corporation being rejected, but the building going ahead anyway without the burden of a plan. From the ridge to the north the garish retail sheds now look as if some white-tented army of barbarians has squatted across the whole plain.

These were also the black years of growing corruption scandals, worryingly prevalent in poorer regions like south Wales and the north east of England. T. Dan Smith, John Poulson and George Pottinger in the north, Ernest Westwood and Gerald Murphy in south Wales, were not the only people to be entertained for a while by Her Majesty. Cardiff missed out, although narrowly. The arrest of four Cardiff councillors, one of them in his dressing gown, in the early hours of a Saturday morning, prompted the *News of the World* headline, 'Pyjama Swoop Rocks City'. The ensuing case was abandoned, the judge having found himself in 'uncharted waters'.

By the late sixties Cardiff City Council was at war with its citizenry. Armed with the Buchanan study the Council had proposed an urban motorway that would have carved its way through relatively prosperous suburbs in north Cardiff and poorer areas alike, before hooking around a redeveloped city centre. Los Angeles was coming to Cardiff, and the citizenry didn't like it any more than the City Planning Officer, Ewart Parkinson, who was placed in the uncomfortable position of having to defend his council's position at an inquiry, despite disliking the scheme himself. The size of the citizens' revolt, and the political and planning expertise that they mustered saw it off. That left the issue of the redevelopment of the shopping centre, to be undertaken by a property company called Ravenseft, that had redeveloped Swansea's blitzed centre too hurriedly and cheaply after the war. While living in Swansea my mother had taken my sister and me regularly to watch them excavate the site where my father's chemist shop had stood until the blitz of February 1941, in the hope of seeing and perhaps rescuing some relic. Nothing.

The battle over Cardiff's centre was fought with great ferocity, not only dividing the council but also its planning department, which began to leak like a colander. Two schemes – one large scale, the other more modest – had been assessed by the council, and it had opted for a grandiose version and, with expensive help from a public relations company, a lavish exhibition. Predictably, it also sought to suppress all public knowledge of the more sensible alternative. Happily, one morning I came into the office to find a large brown parcel waiting for me, containing every conceivable document relating to the secret Plan

B. Within days the newspaper had taken over an empty shoe shop in Cardiff's High street to stage our own exhibition of the other plan. On the morning we announced our intention to publish, the council leader, Alderman Ferguson Jones, came through the newsroom's swing doors like John Wayne into a cowboy saloon, accusing me of larceny of documents belonging to the city council. I suggested that 'receiving' might be a more appropriate charge. This promised to be good sport.

The eventual public inquiry was held in the City Hall's circular council chamber, festooned with the symbols of the city's earlier prosperity. It was a practical course, that I attended every day for four months, in the way our cities are shaped. It was also a place of theatre where preening lawyers contended, representing developers and agents, councils, department stores, campaigners of all kinds. Leading for the city council was a tall English peacock, Mr Peter Boydell, QC – sharp pinstripe, gold chain, plenty of double cuff, with a silk handkerchief ostentatiously available in one sleeve. He was assisted by his junior, Hywel ap Robert, who made a more jolly, rather agricultural impression. Daily, they padded up against fast bowlers and spin bowlers, not to mention a few stiff-arm tackles from the counsel for the David Morgan department store, Tasker Watkins, later to become a deputy chief justice and president of the WRU.

In the sixties lawyers tended to gather in the Royal Hotel, where Captain Scott dined before his fatal journey to the Antarctic. Here they would polish their barbs nightly. One silk – an apt appellation – had clearly been burning the midnight oil in this task and began his final plea with an affected mystification at the modern world, delivered in cut-glass tones: 'There are places of refreshment that I do not frequent wherein are contained devices known as juke boxes. The rationale behind these devices is that if you place a coin in the slot and press the appropriate button, you may hear the song and the singer of your choice. At this inquiry, whichever button you press, you hear precisely the same song, the only choice is whether you hear it andante cantabile in English from Mr Boydell, or allegro vivace in Welsh from Mr ap Robert.'

Tasker Watkins, more used to the criminal bar, and a VC to boot, took on the head of the letting agents, a man who – so claimed the more emotional protesters – had *actually* sold his grandmother. The first knife went in between the second and third rib.

'I believe you were associated with a similar development at Newport that, I'm told, was not attended by a marked degree of success – The Kingsway Centre.'

'Er, yes.'

'Perhaps you would explain to the Inspector what the problem was,' said Tasker, looking around the chamber with a half smile.

'It was difficult because the Kingsway Centre was... well...off-centre.' This was going to be too easy. Tasker adjusted his gold half-glasses the better to see the next target spot.

'And about how far off centre, would you say?'

'About a hundred yards,' said the agent, his eyes cast downwards.

'A hundred yards. A... hundred... yards.' Tasker repeated the words with an old-fashioned Welsh rallentando and, looking the inspector in the eye, despatched his victim.

'Not too far in the age of the motor car, you may think.'

The dynamics of urban development were crystallised in that chamber: private versus public interest, the pressures for public acquiescence, the possibility and the impossibility of resistance, the value and the vulnerability of professional expertise, the siren call of 'inevitablity'. The dogmas of the day are often the flaky, even comical opinions of tomorrow. The late Henry Mansfield, then the Cardiff city treasurer, told the inquiry with aquiline authority that 'land values are such that building homes in the city centre of Cardiff will never again be possible'. A tall block of flats now sits on the very site he was talking about, and the David Morgan department store has closed, its upper floors, too, turned into apartments.

Opponents of the scheme lost the battle but won the war. They had argued throughout that what was proposed for the city was overblown, and would have created far too much shopping space too quickly. The inspector disagreed, but he could not have foreseen the Yom Kippur war in the Middle East in 1973 and the quadrupling of the price of oil. The war blasted the developer's calculations to smithereens, and Ravenseft paid the city £3m. to get out of the deal – probably worth at least £30m in today's prices. The money was put aside, and became the down payment on our national concert hall, St David's Hall, built as part of the much smaller St David's centre shopping development less than a decade later. Art had the last laugh.

Not everybody was laughing, however. It was the first of the serial disappointments that anybody interested in the shape and quality of our towns and cities has had to endure over recent decades; the deep seam of mediocrity, and worse, alleviated by rare nuggets of quality. Another disappointment soon turned up a short distance to the north.

★ ★ ★ ★

Travelling on motorways is like travelling by air, you get on at one end
and get off at the other. You see scenery but get no sense of place. It
used not to be like that. The long street from Cardiff to Merthyr was
familiar territory – Tongwynlais, Treforest, Cilfynydd, Fiddler's Elbow,
Hoover's, Cyfarthfa, Cefn Coed – a narrow defile to be passed through
behind bus or lorry before breaking out into the glories of the Brecon
Beacons.

Less than a decade after the cataclysmic event at Aberfan, I found
myself nervously chairing the Newydd Housing Association that had
almost 500 homes across the valleys in its care. It still exists and its
portfolio has expanded to 2,500. The 1974 Housing Act had rightly
insisted on dislodging all the construction professionals from the
boards of the associations because of conflicts of interest that were as
plain as a pikestaff. I and assorted other lay men and women were
charged with imposing some semblance of independent corporate
governance on associations across the land. It was also an opportunity
to look at the south Wales valleys anew, and I managed to persuade the
Western Mail to give me a month's sabbatical to write a report on Welsh
housing conditions, with Gareth Hughes, a Labour activist who ran the
Welsh Federation of Housing Associations. It was a not a pretty
picture, with housing in the same clutch of south Wales valley authorities appearing at the wrong end of almost every league table of
disadvantage.

At one point the Newydd attempted to overturn the decision to
demolish The Triangle, a uniquely shaped group of industrial houses
and a familiar landmark opposite the town's Hoover factory at
Pentrebach. It was the kind of story that had been repeated in Merthyr
time and again, as a combination of local authority philistinism and
public apathy eroded the town's astonishing industrial heritage at an
alarming rate. Only a determined effort by the Merthyr Heritage Trust,
aided by another housing association, had stopped the local authority
from demolishing the Dowlais stables.

History was written into every stone, brick and slate of The
Triangle. The houses were double fronted and whitewashed, and their
long low form seemed to be a reminder of a more rural Merthyr that
passed swiftly away as the ironmasters, Crawshay, Hill and Guest,
competed to expand their empires. Much of the forestation in the area
had been cleared for fuel. Work on The Triangle, designed to accom-

pany Anthony Hill's Pentrebach rolling mill, was begun in 1839, the year of the Chartist march on Newport, but not finished for another five years. Jeremy Lowe, an authority on the history of housing in Wales, reckoned that they were built to 'above average standards of space, durability and finish', which was all the more remarkable since during the same five years the price of bar iron had slumped to an historic low. More than 130 years later we thought that they could now be restored, creating modern family homes as attractive individually as in their group setting. We wanted The Triangle to be more than just a monument.

Despite the protection of listing, Merthyr's application for compulsory powers and consent to demolish were granted by the Welsh Office even before the Newydd Housing Association came into existence, so there was little doubt that we were on the back foot. Dewi Prys Thomas, the already legendary head of the Welsh School of Architecture, weighed in on our behalf pointing out that The Triangle had been sufficiently important not only to adorn the cover of the National Museum's booklet, *Welsh Industrial Villages*, but also to feature with Yorkshire's Saltaire – now made famous by David Hockney – as one of only two industrial villages featured in an exhibition touring the UK at the time under the title *Villages of Vision*.

A dispute over costs – that we felt was a mere pretext – gave the Welsh Office sufficient reason to turn us down, unless the local authority was itself willing to come up with the money. As so often, Merthyr was broke. So yet one more part of its history was buried. The only consolation was a fine mixed metaphor. After I had delivered the bad news to a meeting of the full council, one councillor rose to voice his disappointment: 'I came here tonight expecting a carrot, and we haven't had a sausage.'

It was a painful failure, not only because of bureaucratic obduracy but also because what stands there now is so depressing: an architecturally shoddy retail park that houses some commercial offices and shops – Halfords, Bikehut, Poundstretcher and, irony of ironies, a kitchen and bathroom centre for home improvers. At the time of writing, the biggest unit is empty, and I would guess that the majority of people who use these buildings now have little idea why it is called The Triangle Business Park. Such lowest common denominator development has not and never was going to make a difference.

Most painful of all was that so many of the people I spoke to in the local authority at the time had no appetite for saving those houses. One councillor told me that all they represented to him were poverty, disease and an awful past and they should come down. It is not for people who have had the benefit of a more comfortable suburban upbringing to scorn such sentiments – Merthyr had, at that time, already experienced nearly half a century of painful economic depression – but understanding such reactions makes them no less a failure of the imagination. It is perhaps unfair to single out Merthyr which has no monopoly on municipal short-sightedness or communal neglect. Some of the sins of the capital city are as grievous and fall into the same category. But Merthyr could less afford to lose any part of its heritage.

★ ★ ★ ★

The Triangle and Aberfan apart, Merthyr is a place I have not been allowed to ignore. History placed it on a pedestal, chipped and tarnished though that pedestal may now be. Before decamping for Paris, King Edward VIII went there and, famously, demanded that 'something must be done'. That something, in the view of Whitehall civil servants in the thirties, involved closing Merthyr down and moving the population lock stock and barrel to the coast. This startlingly Stalinist plan has been recorded in a book by Ted Rowlands, a convivial contributor to political argument in The Old Arcade pub, who in 1972 succeeded S.O. Davies as MP for the town, and became the youngest minister in the Wilson Government.

My uncle, Alun Talfan Davies – who early in his legal career had championed the bids of miners for compensation – was Recorder of Merthyr and chaired the Aberfan Disaster Fund Committee. But no-one could possibly sharpen your appreciation of the place more than the historian Gwyn Alf Williams, not just in reading his book on *The Merthyr Rising*, but in talking to him over a long period during the making of the HTV series, *The Dragon Has Two Tongues*. You could not leave his company without knowing that Merthyr is completely central and pivotal to our history, or that that history could and should even now be central and pivotal to the future of Merthyr. It is easy but sometimes necessary to bemoan the great heritage losses of the last decades. What is much more important now is the issue of our care for what remains and the quality of new elements of the public realm that we are creating for future generations.

Despite the losses of the past, Merthyr's built assets are substantial but underexploited: Cyfarthfa Castle, its contents and its magnificent setting, Crawshay's furnaces, the Town Hall, John Guest's Memorial Library, the Dowlais and Ynysfach Engine Houses, the YMCA, and the old Synagogue. In some cases the fabric has been saved, but people have been slow to find imaginative uses. Valuable though sports facilities are, converting every piece of heritage into a sports hall cannot, surely, be the limit of our imagination.

Cyfarthfa Castle, built by Crawshay, the demonised ironmaster, in only one year, needs and deserves significant investment. Its museum, in recent years without even a curator and beginning to resemble someone's attic, needs new spaces and resources to display its collection more expansively, to put itself in the forefront of museum practice, and to tell the story of Merthyr not just to its own people, but to its nation and to the world. West of the castle and its park, Pandy Farm, once Crawshay's stables, the Taff and the great curving wall of his furnaces have yet to be brought together into an imaginative whole.

There was an opportunity to have joined hands with Blaenafon's ironworks site in the latter's successful bid for World Heritage status, but Merthyr let it slip. As so often, there is a consultant's master plan with the usual array of pretty impressions, but some of its most important proposals for the Cyfarthfa Heritage Area are grouped in the medium and long term categories where they could easily be jostled into oblivion by competing pressures. The proposals are modest, some would say realistic, but its language does not fully convey the area's potential as a wonderful public space of European or world significance, not to mention a profound educational experience, nor its capacity to provide both a physical and psychological breakthrough for a wider area. Money and quality development will be the key issues, and tough ones for Wales's smallest local authority whose very viability, with a population of only 55,000, has been called into question.

But Merthyr's story is not just a local story. Its history is of national and international, political and industrial importance. Its historic assets should be at the heart of an international project, perhaps drawing support from the steel industries of the world. For Wales, it is a national issue.

4 Wales on the agenda

The 1960s was an extraordinary time to be in the news business, even if you joined late. Wherever you looked there was tension, turmoil and transition. Kennedy, Johnson and Nixon traced an arc from light to dark in America. In the Soviet Union the change from Khruschev to Brezhnev represented a slide back from a hopeful, though volatile, pragmatism to a familiar, implacable absence of imagination. In Britain Macmillan, Home, and Wilson traced both a social and generational mental shift. Cuba and Vietnam were pivotal crises, the one sharp, the other lingering. In Prague another cold war tragedy was played out, but with greater poignancy. The war between Israel and its Arab neighbours was anything but cold. China turned on itself under the banner of Mao's Cultural Revolution.

In the west, race, feminism, homosexuality and censorship were more productive battlegrounds. Popular music and drugs both made and reflected the new mood. Across the world the Kalashnikov, the Molotov cocktail and the placard were weapons of choice, though in Paris the cobblestone also proved popular. In the same way that 1848 was a phenomenon in the nineteenth century, 1968 seemed set, if only for a moment, to be so for the twentieth. Protesters and public authorities everywhere were unable to see eye to eye through the tear gas. In these islands, as if tuning in to the decade, the Celtic countries also changed key, Wales seeking some recognition for itself and its language, the Scots doing likewise but also pondering the political significance of the discovery of North Sea oil and, in Ulster, Republicans and Unionists resuming their war.

The decade had opened with Harold Macmillan's Pretoria speech about the 'wind of change' sweeping through Africa. Wind knows no boundaries. Two years later, in 1962, the year Algeria, Uganda, Rwanda and Burundi, Jamaica and Trinidad and Tobago celebrated their independence, an ascetic Catholic writer from Wales delivered a BBC Wales radio lecture that launched the Welsh Language Society, arguably the most successful British civil disobedience campaign of the twentieth century. Only the suffragette movement could have claimed to match it in effectiveness.

If its author Saunders Lewis were alive to deliver that speech today, with its demand for the use of 'revolutionary means', the boys from the anti-terrorist squad would undoubtedly have been knocking on his door in Penarth waving the latest derogation from Magna Carta. They would have needed their wits about them to read between the lines. According to Rhys Evans, biographer of the Plaid Cymru leader, Gwynfor Evans, Lewis's aim was not to establish a language movement, but rather to undermine the nationalist party's more conventional political strategy, and more specifically its pacifist leader, putting 'hate and persecution' in the place of 'peace and love'. The law of unintended consequences saw a Welsh Language Society formed by August 1962 and Gwynfor Evans, redoubling his constitutional efforts, elected as the first Plaid Cymru MP in July 1966.

Gwynfor Evans was right to be cautious. The bombings of the mid and late sixties in Wales – unconnected with the language society – at reservoir sites, at the Welsh Office, at the Temple of Peace in Cardiff, and on the eve of the Investiture in Caernarfon, pointed in a bleak and bloody direction. Too many enjoyed the frisson of the higher stakes, even while abhorring the consequences. Saunders Lewis, always an enemy of Gwynfor Evans's pacificism, was among them. After the explosion at the military base at Pembrey, in which a warrant officer was seriously injured, I rang Lewis for his reaction. He professed himself to be appalled at the injury, although he said his 'heart leapt' at news of every explosion. It was a doublethink that did not impress.

Since 1964, and the formation of the Welsh Office, Labour, the party of power, had been establishing the basis of Welsh governmental administration. (By happy coincidence in the same year BBC Wales was given its own television frequency, freeing it from its Siamese twin, BBC West, and allowing the new government department to be reported more fully across Wales.) The enthusiasm of the first Welsh secretary of state, James Griffiths, and the second, Cledwyn Hughes, for these developments was not shared by the third incumbent, George Thomas. Behind the born-again bonhomie lay a waspish lack of charity that often extended to his own party colleagues as well as his opponents. In private one would be hard pressed to know whether Cledwyn Hughes or Gwynfor Evans was the enemy. There was something visceral about his politics that went beyond political ideas or rational conviction.

There was calculation even in his humour. At a Labour rally in the now demolished King's Hall in Aberystwyth he introduced Roy

Jenkins, then Chancellor, and whose accent owed more to Winchester than Abersychan. 'Roy,' said George, rolling the R with scarcely hidden glee, 'is a Welshman, like you and like me.' Jenkins rose. 'Yes, I am a Welshman, fwoo and fwoo.' This small vignette of the politics of identity, was completed by the local MP, Elystan Morgan – who had made the jump from Plaid hopeful to Labour Minister – and who, in thanking the Gwent-born Chancellor, described the people of Gwent as the 'Sudeten Welsh'. This put Morgan into the too clever by half category, and for the historian Jenkins it seemed an unwelcome balm. His obvious discomfort may be a clue to why Lloyd George is the only major British statesman of the nineteenth and twentieth century on whom Jenkins did not expend his great gift for biography.

A non-smoker myself, I spent much time passively smoking George Thomas's cigars that seemed to grow in size as the years wore on. He would sometimes come into a press conference, cigar in hand, only to put it ostentatiously into a drawer if a camera entered the room, 'lest Mam should see'. The largest was reserved for a morning in February 1971 when, after attending the birth of our second son, Rhodri, I rushed to the top floor of the Hodge building in Cardiff to find Julian Hodge and George Thomas celebrating in a cloud of blue smoke the registration of the Commercial Bank of Wales, for which Hodge had been campaigning for years, and on which subject I had written some supportive columns. In the 1970s it appeared a more important victory than it turned out to be. By the end of the century it had been taken over by the Bank of Scotland (with scarcely a murmur of protest in Wales), and the name and brand of the only Bank of Wales lies hidden in an HBOS drawer on the outskirts of Edinburgh – a symbol of the attrition of Welsh business.

The cigars had not shrunk significantly even when I sat with George in the kitchen of his bungalow the weekend after the Labour defeat in 1970. He looked physically broken. Defeat had not entered his head, and, hand over mouth like a naughty schoolboy, he admitted neglecting to clear his ministerial office as tradition dictated. Even in this domestic setting there was no let up in the partisanship. I pointed out that his Conservative successor, Peter Thomas, spoke Welsh. 'He'll go down alright in druid-land,' he said, with only the most wan smile.

In 1968 Thomas had been instrumental in scotching Cledwyn Hughes's plan to sneak in an elected Council for Wales as part of a reorganisation of local government, hoping that the use of the word 'council' might make it seem more innocuous than Assembly or

Parliament. Thomas was sharp enough to spot the subterfuge. He would have been on his guard since, in his book, Hughes came from the wrong end of Wales. Many Welsh people joke about the differences between north and south, for Thomas they were a balloon to be inflated with all the huff and puff at his disposal.

In 1973 the editor of a book of essays, to which I also contributed, had the unconscious wit to ask a future Archdruid, Robyn Lewis, and the future Speaker of the House of Commons – two people who enjoyed their roles and their costumes overmuch – to put the social and political case for and against Welsh nationalism. For Thomas these were two different countries: 'The mountains of mid-Wales create a massive barrier between the north and south ... deep differences, both in habits and customs have distinguished the people.' Listing the imbalances of Wales he carefully counted the number of Welsh-speaking MPs, point-ing out that five of them represented 'anglicised constituencies'. It was a starting point very much of its time.

The fashionable kick to touch of governments at the time was the Royal Commission, and devolution seemed just the right subject for this kind of heavyweight pondering. The Commission on the Constitution – first chaired by Lord Crowther, and, after his sudden death, by a Scottish lawyer and peer, Lord Kilbrandon – bridged two decades. It had been established by Harold Wilson but, after 1970, it laboured away throughout the Heath administration, publishing its report in October 1973. By the time that the 1974 election had returned Wilson – after Heath's disastrous double brush with the miners – Britain was part of the European Economic Community, changing fundamentally the context in which the constitution commis-sion worked. As a journalist I was fortunate that one of the two Welsh representatives was my father's brother, Alun. He was an increasingly well informed sounding board, although frustratingly for this tyro journalist, he never leaked anything.

Geoffrey Crowther was a journalist himself, having edited *The Economist* for 18 years from 1938 to 1956, and always staunchly defending the hallowed anonymity of everything written in his magazine as 'a form of ancestor worship and a source of momentum in thought and principle'. He died in 1972, midway through the commission's work. I interviewed him after its first open session in Cardiff's City Hall, when the Welsh Office's permanent secretary, Sir Goronwy Daniel, had delivered his idiosyncratic mix of mandarin wisdom, mischievous thought and lugubrious utterance.

Crowther, who had already been to Scotland to take evidence, had spotted a difference between Wales and Scotland. 'The Scots want to do,' he told me, 'the Welsh want to be.' It was a succinct and perceptive observation that reflected differences in national psyche as much as the different stages that each country had arrived at in the evolution of their respective civil societies. It is interesting to ponder whether an English editor would have held the commission together more effectively than the Scottish lawyer who succeeded him.

As it was, only eight members – a bare majority – supported the most radical recommendation for full legislative devolution for both Scotland and Wales, although that did include the two Welsh members. They echoed, remarkably closely, the finding of the Richard Commission, thirty years later, that there was no satisfactory halfway house. In this, even the two who accepted legislative devolution for Scotland but not for Wales, seemed to agree, for they opted for an elected Welsh advisory council with absolutely no power at all.

Two further academic dissenters were Norman Crowther-Hunt and Alan Peacock (the latter more famous for his 1986 incursion into the funding of broadcasting), who peeled off and wrote their own report. It had its own theoretical attractions, constructing a scheme of devolution to be applied symmetrically to Scotland, Wales and every English region, but its neatness was insufficient to persuade most English politicians that the pair were not inhabiting another planet.

As proof of the dangers of academics venturing into politics, in 1979 Crowther-Hunt (by now a Minister), delivered a *coup de grâce* to his own side – the failing Yes campaign – at its final rally in Cardiff's Sophia Gardens Pavilion. Supposedly speaking in favour of devolution, and pressed to respond to the allegation that the proposed Welsh Assembly would be powerless, he anticipated Ron Davies's famous adage – 'a process not an event' – by twenty years, by saying that it would be a dynamic situation. He predicted that very soon 'the Assembly would have the power to raise income tax'. As the hacks scribbled, on the platform Michael Foot and James Callaghan put their heads in their hands. A few years later the pavilion's roof caved in under heavy snow, which seemed appropriate.

After the 1974 election, Wilson's sidelining of George Thomas in favour of John Morris put the devolution issue, but not Kilbrandon's more radical recipe, back on the agenda. While Thomas was packed off to the Speaker's Chair and radio fame, John Morris, a contender for the title of the most constructive of Welsh secretaries of state, started planning a scheme that might stand some chance of withstanding the scorn of the anti-devolutionists within his own party. He was advised by Gwilym Prys Davies, a cerebral solicitor, whose gentleness hid intellectual steel, and who kept effective communication with the pro-devolution elements in the Labour Party's Cardiff offices and with myself and John Osmond at the *Western Mail*.

The paper, meanwhile, continued to churn out polls that seemed to suggest Wales would look with favour on an Assembly or Parliament of its own, even if this required making dodgy assumptions about the large number of Don't Knows. John Osmond, who had taken on the 'Welsh Affairs' mantle in 1972, traced every twist and turn. I had the task of commissioning weightier pieces than would be likely to surface in the paper today, by such as John Mackintosh, the charismatic Scottish proponent of the cause, the historian Kenneth O. Morgan and Crowther-Hunt, and opponents such as Neil Kinnock, Leo Abse and Enoch Powell. My visit to Enoch Powell's Belgravia home to commission an article was the toughest viva examination I have endured. He had allotted 30 minutes in his narrow study and reminded me when 29 were up.

The paper had to share its thoughts not only with our readers but with a whoosh of flying correspondents. Local journalists were a first port of call for London feature writers who trod a steady path to the restaurants of Cardiff and an unsteady path away from them. The more intrepid got as far as Carmarthen and the teetotal welcome of Gwynfor Evans, the first Welsh nationalist MP. A little Welsh Language Society seasoning of civil disobedience completed the dish. Though this was hardly the stuff of bus stop conversations in Pontypridd let alone Pimlico or Preston, in the 1970s the story at least had the advantage of novelty. It was a change from coal and steel and strikes, and it was a story in which Wales mattered.

Americans, Germans, French, even Russians turned up. *Newsweek*, *Pravda*, *Le Monde* and the *Los Angeles Times* came to take a peek at us. The Russian arrived with his wife, in winter, both in fur coats, great bears who so filled my cubby-hole of an office in the *Western Mail* that I had to stand outside the door as they attempted to call Moscow. Embassies sent scouts, often proferring invitations to visit their countries to study their arrangements. A Breton *préfet* arrived to convince us that French centralisation was a thing of the past. All things are relative.

A press counsellor from the West German Embassy, Rolf

Breitenstein, came more often than most. He had taken a liking to Wales when picking potatoes in Pembrokeshire during the Queen's coronation year in 1953. This and, no doubt, a brush with a Welsh Mam had inspired him to invent the 'the potato principle' that, contrary to popular wisdom, states that demand is determined by supply not the other way round. *'Die kartoffeln sind da; nun werden sie auch gegessen'* (The potatoes are there and are meant to be eaten). It's strange to think that Pembrokeshire's early spuds spelt out a theory on which the extremes of western consumerism could be based.

One result of this cultural exchange was that in April 1976 a group composed of mainly Welsh, Scottish and English journalists headed for Germany to study the constitution of its free and federal half. One of the party was Neal Ascherson who, fired with devolutionary hope, had left *The Observer* to return to *The Scotsman* in Edinburgh as its deputy editor. His fluent German and immense knowledge of Eastern Europe meant that we learnt as much from him as from any official. Trevor Fishlock of *The Times* and myself represented the Welsh interest.

The two English journalists, from the *Daily Mail* and the *Manchester Evening News*, had clearly won the newsroom raffle for the next trip, and didn't feel obliged to put pen to paper. They were baffled that anyone could take time out to listen to a presentation on the 'political implications of revenue equalisation in Germany'. The Mancunian, a man with a keen eye for the bizarre, was rather more intent on knowing why a German dog licence was three times more expensive in an urban area than in a rural area, and his final question about what would happen in the event of the arrival of six urban puppies stopped the minister of finance of Nordrhein-Westfalia in his tracks.

The Americans, on the other hand, while only politely interested in happenings in this part of the Celtic fringe, saw a chance to generate some interest in their coming bicentennial in 1976 and, through a US State Department scheme, packed me off to look at state government as well as to research links between Wales and America. My employers were doubly content since the visit was made to coincide with a jamboree dreamt up as a last fling by the Development Corporation for Wales, the impecunious predecessor of the Welsh Development Agency that was soon to replace it.

A Boeing 707 took off from Cardiff airport, complete with the secretary of state for Wales, the Bishop of Llandaff, assorted industrialists, three journalists – Patrick Hannan, Trevor Fishlock and myself – and the Morriston Orpheus Choir. It touched down in Shannon to refuel – drink as well as gasoline. Several hours later, approaching a cheap slot at Newark because a plane had overshot the runway at JFK, the none too steady secretary of the choir, well-trained on rugby coaches and keen on a safe landing, stalked the aisles intent on a 'whip-round for the driver' and managed to collect forty quid.

Meanwhile the development corporation's PR man was starting to wonder how they would pay for a variety of receptions at the posh hotel where we were due to stay. Undaunted, despite the lateness of the hour, he bribed half the choir to buy one bottle of duty-free gin and scotch each on the strict understanding that they would deliver it to the rooms of the three journalists who would store it for emergencies. Such was the hand to mouth existence of Welsh business evangelism before the WDA. The fact that we arrived in New York on Labour Day weekend when most of New York was out was quite incidental.

I left Patrick and Trevor and pursued the rest of my six-week American grand tour and experienced the energising shot that knocks most first visitors to the USA sideways. In the place of that enervating southern English reserve that seems to regard enthusiasm as a weakness, here were people who were endlessly curious, who asked questions, who were keen to tell you their own tale, who had no compunction in wearing their hearts on their sleeves. Here was an open society that, at one level, spurned the privet castellations of Britain's suburbia in favour of expansive unfenced gardens, in their minds a people of the prairie not the paddock, and a place where freedom of expression rather than official secrets had the protection of the law. I had to answer as many questions as I asked.

Occasionally the enthusiasm was overplayed. A state department telex – these were days before e-mail – informed all my hosts that I had an MA (Oxon.) in history. My hosts right across this more rational country were unaware that the Oxford MA is a quaint medieval fraud whereby a seven-year wait for a presumed accretion in wisdom and a small cheque converts your modest – in my case, very modest – BA into something grander. I was, for the first and last time in my life, feted as a scholar. I particularly treasure the newspaper cutting that appeared in the local paper at Wilksbarre, Pennsylvania after I had visited the bank's senior vice president, a man of Welsh stock. It read, 'Noted Welsh Historian Visits Bank.'

Whether in New York or Chicago or in the small town of Ruston in Louisiana's Bible belt – a town dominated by the James family, descendants of a Carmarthenshire poacher – one could not help being struck

by the civic vitality of America, the geographic and institutional dispersal of power, and the defence of the local, by state, city and
municipality, even in the face of the still swelling might of federal
power. Inter-governmental relations (IGR), an academic discipline,
described relationships between tiers of American government rather
than international relationships. In lighter moments, some said that the
growth of federal power dated from the invention of air-conditioning
that enabled legislators, for the first time, to endure Washington's
steamy summers. In the sixties and seventies such summers did
nothing to cool the passions occasioned by racial conflict and the still
vivid memories of the Vietnam war.

The new British interest in the devolution question had for some
years overlapped with the excitement caused by the other constitutional issue: Britain's entry to the EEC in 1973 and the subsequent
confirmatory referendum in 1975. For journalists the run up to the
European referendum meant briefings on every conceivable subject.
There were special events for business correspondents, agricultural
correspondents, legal correspondents and almost any other kind of
specialist you could imagine. Since much of the appeal was the quality
of the hospitality, if your journalistic beat was ill-defined it was possible to justify going several times. It was a privilege to share some of
these briefings with Hugo Young, whose later work *This Blessed Plot*
charted the insular timorousness of Britain's European relationship.

Welsh journalists took full advantage, encouraged by Gwyn
Morgan, who ran the first EEC office in Cardiff after a period as *chef
de cabinet* for the first Commissioner for regional policy, George
Thomson. Gwyn's name is at the centre of one of the great 'what ifs'
of British political history. In 1972, as deputy general secretary of the
Labour Party, he narrowly missed being appointed general secretary,
losing to Ron Hayward only on the casting vote of the NEC's chairman
at the time, Tony Benn. The destructive history of the party over the
next decade might have been very different had Gwyn's outward
looking vision had more support.

As sociable as he is bright, for a period Gwyn brought a certain élan
to political life in Cardiff that cemented in many minds a natural affinity
between two causes – Europe and devolution. Years earlier he had
presented the Labour Party's evidence to the Commission on the
Constitution. Gwyn and two other senior European Commission
staffers – Hywel Ceri Jones and Aneurin Rhys Hughes – were immensely
influential at the time in opening new avenues of understanding. They

also began to affect greater contact with the Irish, who showed, as ever, an intelligent interest in events in Wales and Scotland. Visits were arranged.

In the splendour of Iveagh House in Dublin, Garret FitzGerald, then the Irish Minister for Foreign Affairs, painted for us a sophisticated picture that interwove British membership of the EEC, Ireland's aspirations for its own economy and for European regional policy, devolution in the UK and a distant resolution of the troubles in the north. His cultured intelligence left a deep imprint, making him an ambitious template in any aspirations for a mature Welsh political class.

One of the joys of the newspaper business is the freedom to get involved, which is much more circumscribed in public service broadcasting, where statutory impartiality creates constraints. Therefore, when the first Scotland and Wales Bill came before the Commons late in 1976, it proved too much of a temptation both for myself and John Osmond. In December we co-authored a briefing paper that looked forward to the referendum with misplaced optimism, putting as positive a gloss as possible on polls (mostly commissioned by our own newspaper) that were, on the face of it, extremely discouraging. It was more realistic in predicting that Labour would divide in the campaign and that Liberals would be far from unanimous, given the varying stances of their two MPs. Any Plaid doubters would probably suppress their misgivings about the Government's proposals. Tories would be against, despite some teasing hints of sympathy for devolution from Geraint Morgan, the MP for Denbigh and, more surprisingly, Raymond Gower, Barry's MP. But what was needed was an all-party Yes campaign organisation.

The action committee first met in Gwyn Morgan's Cardiff office – Gwyn, George Wright, the no-nonsense secretary of the Wales TUC and Les Paul, his treasurer, Jack Brooks, who lived for politics and saw on the horizon something more glamorous to lead than South Glamorgan County Council, Sir Alun Talfan Davies, Kilbrandon's flag carrier in Wales, John Osmond and myself. In his absence a professor of banking and finance, Glyn Davies, well known as an adviser to Julian Hodge and for a forbiddingly bushy black moustache, was appointed chairman. But the referendum that most of us expected would happen late in 1977, was not the main talking point.

The more pressing concern was the possibility of a Tory amendment to delete Wales from the Bill. The Bill itself was a jumble and attracted more than 700 amendments – some seeking to improve it, but a fair proportion seeking to wreck it. There was a lot to be said for separating everything out into two bills, as eventually happened, but we thought that if the Commons voted simply to delete Wales, a Welsh Bill might never surface. Blocking any such amendment was the first priority.

Elizabeth, in daily contact with the 2,000-strong workforce at BP Chemicals in Barry, where she was then working, already sensed the game was up. There was no detectable public appetite. So it was to the consternation of our families that John and I took two weeks annual leave in January 1977 and, holed up in an attic above the EEC office, proceeded to collect 700 signatures for a grand declaration that would be carried in the *Western Mail* and *Daily Post* and register the certain affront that we believed the proposed deletion would occasion across the nation. Other members of the action committee agreed to twist arms for the necessary costs. Copies of both newspapers and a letter to every MP were driven to Westminster on the eve of the vote. Wales survived by 24 votes. However, in crafting the declaration John and I had placed it under the rash heading – 'Parliament must let Wales decide.' That's just what Parliament did, and two years later Wales rejected an Assembly by four to one. This was not how it was meant to be.

5 ITV Swansong

1980. It was a cold Sunday morning in December, dangling between Christmas and the New Year, an icy breeze blowing down an almost empty Brompton Road. Turning their backs on it were huddles of anxious television executives, PR men and journalists. Ronald W. Wordley, late of the British Army, and now Managing Director of HTV, had arrived from some European ski slope and was still sporting woolly ankle-warmers. His boss, Lord Harlech, chairman of the company, was outwardly all languid elegance, despite wearing the jacket of one suit, the trousers of another and a deeply stained silk tie to give a whiff of sixties bohemia. The casual attire clothed two confident yet unrelaxed people. They were there to find out from the Independent Broadcasting Authority whether their company would continue to run a commercial television licence for Wales and the West for another decade. They need not have worried.

The only opposition had come from a company called Hafren Television, led by Emlyn Hooson QC, the MP for Montgomery, Alf Gooding, a genial and serial entrepreneur from south Wales and, hovering in the background, though not on the Board, the managing director of the *Western Mail and Echo*, David Thomas. It was not a well-researched bid and, at the IBA's public meeting in Cardiff, a badly briefed Gooding promised that, if they won, 'half their programmes would be in Welsh, half in English and the rest bilingual' – a promise that amused the audience as much as it perplexed Lady Plowden, the IBA's chair. He was not alone in discomfiture.

The meeting had been packed by people campaigning loudly for a Welsh language television channel. Repeated pleas from the chair to stick to the subject of the meeting – the merits of the two candidates for the ITV franchise – fell on deaf ears more than once. Exasperated, her ladyship rashly asked whether she or they were 'being stupid about this'. 'Let's vote on it,' came the richly accented reply from the back of the hall. Discomfited or not, Lady Plowden awarded the contract to HTV.

It was, in fact, two companies in one, linked by two bridges across the Severn, a single bridging television licence, and the charismatic authority of Lord Harlech, a former British Ambassador to Washington, over both local boards when they sat together. Both sides liked to affect an incomprehension of the other. The HTV West board, dotted with 'merchant venturers' and often caricatured by colleagues across the water as 'the slavers', focused on commerce, while the HTV board was unmistakably Welsh in the profusion of cultural credentials: an opera singer, a rugby international, a journalist, a poet, a county librarian, an expert on childrens' books, and a lawyer for whom publishing was a hobby. There were sensitivities. The pages allocated respectively to Wales and the West in glossy brochures were carefully counted, and capital investment in Cardiff and Bristol had to be carefully apportioned, like lollipops to siblings.

This fusion of culture and cash, under the name of the Harlech Consortium, had wrested the licence for the area from TWW in 1967. Any one of four people would claim the credit for the idea, by far the most convincing being the journalist, John Morgan, for whom constructive mischief was not only a pleasure but a democratic obligation. Like many, he had come to feel that TWW was run from London and "invented a campaign to seize it by compatriots". If the late sixties were to be historic in any way, he wanted to be part of it. He roped in Wynford Vaughan Thomas, and Alun Talfan Davies, before spreading the net to the starry diaspora of Richard Burton, Elizabeth Taylor and Stanley Baker. Harlech himself, renowned for his connections with the Kennedys and his role in the Cuban missile crisis when he was British ambassador in Washington, also brought a kind of glamour to the table, along with establishment bottom. It was a considerable coup for Welsh romanticism.

A decade later the company still retained an informality characterised and shaped by its Cardiff headquarters, Pontcanna, a Victorian farmhouse on the edges of Cardiff's castle grounds. It had been converted and extended beyond recognition, and its endlessly varying levels and sharp stylistic switches demanded agility of both body and mind. Its very modesty, especially compared with the swank modernism of the BBC's new HQ at Llandaff, only confirmed the underdog spirit of the staff, a spirit that managed to survive, even after the company built its own new campus at Culverhouse Cross. Chippiness was a common ITV phenomenon since, unlike the BBC, it was a channel that informed society professed not to watch. It did not matter that audience research told a different story. At a party, a medical consultant, addressing our director of programmes, Huw

Davies, said he was a heart specialist and only watched the BBC. 'That's alright,' said Huw, 'I only see foot specialists.'

Ron Wordley was a big man with a big voice. His bark may have been worse than his bite, but the bark could be very loud, in person and on paper. His voice went ahead of him, rising then fading like a passing aircraft as he went by your door. The army marked his style. You always felt that he was carrying an imaginary swagger stick, though it was difficult to swagger when short corridors were wont to drop you unexpectedly into a half landing every few paces. Momentum was not easily attained. As befitted a Royal Artillery officer memos arrived like artillery shells, either in sharp, numbered paragraphs or handwritten in appropriate red ink, their contents repeated *forte* at meetings larded with the choicest parade-ground profanities. Harlech is said to have described him as 'a good guard dog, but not house-trained'.

Although undoubtedly a leader, it was a sensitive time in Wales for which he was not, in all respects, suited. Language issues and campaigns had been dividing society for more than a decade. The campaign for a Welsh television channel was reaching its apogee at the very time that the company was fighting for the renewal of its franchise – inter-connecting issues in which the company's direct interests were at stake. On language matters, the Welsh board would teach him the words, but he could never quite pick up the tune. While the company was investing heavily in Welsh-language programmes, as well as blazoning its support for the language and culture on the back pages of brochures for every cultural event in the land, he preferred to portray it only as an unfortunate necessity, lest it encourage anyone to ask for more. He didn't have to like it. For instance, conceding contracts in Welsh for Equity members had to be accompanied, in a long, five-page memo, by adamant and totally unnecessary protestations that the administrative language of the company was English. It had the touch of a retreating Raj.

With my newspaper background, it was easy to get cast as the office wordsmith. Wordley would send down drafts of his next blast, and I would rush to his office to try to avert a PR disaster. 'You just can't say that, Ron.' Eventually, after a decent interval, he would give in, 'Alright...but you're chicken.' The battle over, he could relax and laugh at himself, but not for long. He relished his image as the hard outsider, able to juggle with grenades. To the extent that it was a front that had to be kept up, I learnt to deal with it, and even to like him. We got on well, but there were limits. Suspicious that most Welsh-speaking members of the news staff were sympathetic to the language channel campaigners, I was once asked to remind the staff that 'they are paid in English pounds'. On the whole, I thought it best not to.

HTV was far from a philistine place. Beneath the hard crust a softer tone had been set, first by Wynford Vaughan Thomas, better known for his brilliant wartime radio reporting. He became HTV's first programme director, but having soon shaken off the cares of office, was the resident television storyteller to the nation, not to mention boardroom wine critic. His successor, Aled Vaughan, had joined the company from the BBC. Although he had appointed me, I was not sure that he was hugely interested in journalism, believing it to be a diversion of resources from the world of the spirit. He was a writer as well as a documentary producer and steered HTV, with gentle enthusiasm, not only towards spectacularly photogenic documentaries depicting unlikely and dangerous activities around the world, but also into the arts and music and, with an extra push from Sir Geraint Evans and John Morgan, into opera – the least likely genre for an ITV company. Across the water in the West Country, Patrick Dromgoole, a perpetual performer, played the great white shark.

Huw Davies, who succeeded Aled Vaughan, was fond of Latin tags, as befits an Oxford classicist, and a pragmatic pivot between the board and the cats he was obliged to herd. He hankered after the role of drama director that he had now set aside. Peter Elias Jones harnessed and developed a prodigious number of talents in light entertainment and children's programming that, in various guises, served S4C for two decades, although the channel's commissioning decisions eventually dispersed the critical mass of his department without adequate replacement.

Also working in the Welsh language was Gwyn Erfyl, the like of whom can rarely have been found in an ITV company – a nonconformist minister, a philosopher, a conscientious objector, a man of immense wisdom, curious and insightful about the world, holding a commendably high opinion of his audience and worryingly perceptive about his close colleagues. He took confession from many of us, mainly in fine restaurants. His death in 2007 was the closing of a book.

For a journalist whose only tools had been a notebook, a biro and a typewriter, television had been at first bewildering, not to say irritating, in its complexity. Cameras, sound, lights, film processing, editing, dubbing, studio schedules and union rules stood between you and the communication of the simplest idea. So what seemed on paper a large department, was a desperately thin resource in practice. The title of Head of News and Current Affairs was also a misnomer, since there was no current affairs department of any kind, simply a reporter pinched from the newsroom for a day or two. It meant that the new head of the department had to get his hands dirty, not least because 1979 would see the devolution referendum, a general election and the first direct elections to the European Parliament packed into less than four months.

Devolution, an issue that had been a total preoccupation for a decade, now faced its critical test, as did I. I had taken television's shilling in September 1978, six months before the referendum, and my appointment at HTV had won the doubtful distinction of being one of the few junior appointments in broadcasting to have been criticised on the floor of the House of Commons. During the debate on the referendum orders, Michael Roberts for the Tories, a jolly and gregarious ex-headmaster, and Leo Abse for Labour, the most destructive of the anti-devolutionists, had both questioned HTV's wisdom in appointing a known devolutionist to head their news department, and demanded safeguards. Waiting in Palace Yard for a taxi after the debate, Abse said it was meant in the friendliest way. While I was pondering this surprising gloss, Michael Roberts, rather more practical, pulled me out of the queue and back to the Strangers' Bar for an unhealthily long and friendly session.

Still a television novice, I would have to prove them wrong. The armies of Don't Knows evident from the opinion polls showed that there was a need for more explanation of the issue. It proved an opportunity to work with John Morgan for the first time, and to learn something of the chemistry of words and pictures that he had mastered while working for the BBC's *Tonight* and *Panorama* programmes. Elis Owen, now Managing Director of ITV Wales, was the project's researcher, and set about finding an impoverished family so that we could illustrate the hoped-for effect of devolution on real lives.

Some history was unavoidable. On a freezing January morning beneath the old Severn Bridge, John stepped forward to the water's edge, chin up in cheeky hauteur, the unmistakable Swansea voice all fruit and fags: 'It was here at Aust 1400 years ago that St. Augustine came to meet the Welsh bishops. The meeting was not a success and ended in much snarling and rumours of fisticuffs. The tone of Welsh politics was set.' It was a witty telescoping of history, and made a change from 1282 and 1536. But despite John's pithy script, in truth we struggled to make our case intelligible to a wider audience more concerned with the queuing corpses and rubbish filled streets of Callaghan's winter of discontent.

Heated studio debate was easier although, as ever, the devil had the best tunes. Since I had been steeped in the subject for so long, and despite the political criticisms of my appointment, I decided to risk presenting these debates myself and got away with it. At the end of the campaign Neil Kinnock wrote to thank me for the balance of our coverage and added that he would have said the same even if the result had gone the other way, 'if then I could have recovered my powers of speech.'

For the defeated minority the scale of the referendum disaster was a shattering event. Even those who dared think recovery possible felt it was over for their lifetime, a task now for other generations. By then, what would Wales be? And what kind of nation was it now, that it could reject so decisively any increase in its autonomy, however cabined and confined? After all, the No campaign had hardly been a call to rally round a bold, competing vision for its future, rather a call to confirm a depressive's dependence, and a fear that the doctor would be Welsh-speaking. The gloom was not just about a campaign lost, but about what it said about ourselves. The elements of the debate were uncannily similar to those of the debate in the 1990s between pro and anti-European forces. In 2007 UKIP is the one party calling for the abolition of the Welsh Assembly.

There were many reasons for the failure, but at a more fundamental level it was inexplicable. That was captured for me in a comment from a surprising source. Some months later Elizabeth and I were invited to lunch by Sir Cennydd and Lady Rowena Traherne. They were a remarkable couple. Sir Cennydd became the longest-serving Lord Lieutenant in the country and, unique amongst the landed gentry of the Vale of Glamorgan, both had been supporters of the devolution project. Lady Rowena, given to using words like 'spiffing' and 'topping', confessed she was depressed by the result. 'It was the most dreadful rout, you know.' I agreed. 'Yes,' she said breezily, 'all our friends in Bavaria were totally perplexed.'

The 1979 referendum did not define the 1980s in Wales, but the decade was played out in its shadow: Thatcher's victories, the Falklands war, the shakeout of jobs in steel, the absolute decline of coal, the miners' strike and, on the cultural front, the formation of S4C and the resultant transformation of Welsh broadcasting in both its languages.

Ironically, given what had happened in the referendum, the last of these also transformed the broadcasters' capacity to report Wales to itself.

* * * *

It is hard now to imagine Welsh television before the advent of S4C. ITV viewers in Wales would see a Welsh language news programme – *Y Dydd* – from six o'clock to 6.15 followed by English language news – *Report Wales* – for the next fifteen minutes. On Mondays, each language would get half an hour – Welsh at six, and English at 6.30. Later that evening, at 8.30, *World in Action* would be displaced by a Welsh language current affairs programme – *Yr Wythnos* – serious, not to say earnest, though more for the lack of money than of wit. Viewers wanting to see such things as *World in Action*'s famous clash between Mick Jagger and the William Rees-Mogg would have to wait until 10.30.

Similar displacements of networked programmes happened most nights on BBC1. Paul Fox had once written to my father – then head of programmes at BBC Wales – to complain that he had played ducks and drakes with the network schedule and received a reply to the effect that he was paid a decent salary to do just that. At HTV the ducks and drakes job was the preserve of Chris Grace, the head of programme planning, who also monitored the company with catlike antennae, retreating to his portakabin in the car park to ponder the latest intelligence and to welcome both the temporarily and the permanently disgruntled.

Although Welsh-speaking broadcasters had fought for such a dispensation for the language over several generations, they were not unconscious of the discomfort it caused to the majority, or the inadequacy of the services in each language. Neither had room to grow. Complaints from monoglot viewers, and even from Welsh speakers not immune to the delights of *Z Cars*, *Dallas* or *Opportunity Knocks*, were legion. The issue was a staple ingredient for the letters columns of Welsh newspapers.

That the arrangement was tenable for almost two decades was due only to the existence of an escape route for monoglots to English transmitters to the east of the country, as well as a wider pool of support for the language than people often give credit for. A key fact that is often forgotten in language debates in Wales is that the Welsh-speaking minority, a fifth of the population, is spread across a much higher proportion of households, extending the language's reach. It ensured that a quiet, subterranean respect for the language breathed beneath the vehemence of public debate and protest.

In judging the best alternative arrangement HTV found itself out of step with prevailing opinion. The notion of confining all Welsh language programmes to one channel where they could have primacy had wide public appeal, even amongst those who fulminated against the Welsh Language Society's civil disobedience campaign. The one side wanted a channel to succour the language, the other simply to be shot of it. The society's arguments and sharp methods made their mark on the official mind. The IBA's Welsh Advisory Committee and the BBC's Broadcasting Council for Wales backed the concept, the former even contradicting the view of its parent body.

In 1974, a Government committee – the Crawford Committee – concurred. Its recommendations for an 'investment in social harmony' were accepted by successive Labour Home Secretaries, Roy Jenkins and Merlyn Rees, two differently accented Welshmen, though it has to be said that neither moved with any expedition. Their department's scepticism would eventually contribute to Willie Whitelaw's abandonment of the plan, despite his own party's manifesto commitments in the 1979 election. It was a misjudgement that provoked Gwynfor Evans to declare, in the early summer of 1980, that he would fast unto death for the cause.

HTV had been firmly wedded to the general ITV line that the ITV companies should be given the fourth channel so that they could play on an equal footing with the BBC's two channels. Its stance was also affected by the fact that a third of HTV's licence area was outside Wales. In this the company was no more and no less self-interested than any of the other ITV companies, but in arguing its case it had to take a firm view that the interests of the language would be better served by being broadcast across a combination of two of four channels. one controlled by the BBC and the other by itself, rather than on one channel. In this the company was not entirely alone, nor was it necessarily disingenuous, as I had reason to know, since it was influenced by the relationship between my father and his brother, Alun, who chaired the company's Welsh board.

The two brothers had been close collaborators in Welsh-language publishing for nearly forty years. In matters cultural Alun tended to defer to my father, his elder brother, who, on this matter, had taken an early line against what he saw as a possible 'ghettoisation' of the language. Father had retired from the BBC in 1971, before the debate on the fourth channel was truly joined, but was invited back to give the BBC Wales annual lecture in 1972. The need for dialogue between Welsh speakers and English speakers in Wales had been a constant theme throughout his career, both within and beyond the broadcasting field. In 1966, in a speech as 'day president' at the National Eisteddfod at Aberafan, he had called for greater understanding between both communities and had been excoriated by the leading nationalist philosopher, J.R. Jones, for his pains.

The lecture, *Darlledu a'r Genedl* (Broadcasting and the Nation), was, in part, a considered response, but it went on to argue against any system that would 'push the language under the counter like the Post Office's [Welsh language] forms' or that would 'push Welsh into a Patagonian wilderness of a network'. He also warned against 'creating, in our rush for a treatment for the problems that ail us, networks that can solve those problems for a period, but which will, in the long run guarantee the extinction of the language'. Whatever the rights and wrongs of the argument, there is no doubt that my father's view weighed heavily with Alun, persuading him to listen to others who took a similar view, in particular, the educationist, Professor Jac L. Williams, who argued forcibly for a two-channel solution until his death in 1977.

In retrospect, it is easy to see this as a blindness to the possibilities of the single channel solution, as well as a shade apocalyptic, but at the very beginning of the 1970s, and particularly in the bitter climate that prevailed, no-one foresaw the scale of investment that governments would eventually make in S4C, or the more benign attitudes towards the language that followed S4C's creation. Neither did they foresee the digital age, multi-channel television or video on demand – a new technological environment where the arguments for corralling the language in only one place seem, once again, less certain.

HTV's pursuit of its increasingly lonely line had predictable conse-quences in the fevered atmosphere created by the ratchet of a referendum defeat, a Conservative victory, an unforeseen reversal of policy and Gwynfor Evans's pitch for martyrdom. In the summer of 1980 at the Lliw Valley Eisteddfod, having already laid siege to the secretary of state's car, the protesters descended on the HTV stand and studio and trashed it thoroughly. Ron Wordley, military reflexes twitch-ing, had to be restrained from setting about them with a golf umbrella.

The matter was settled by Gwynfor Evans's threat, the intervention of a deputation of 'wise men' – Gwilym Williams, the archbishop of Wales, Cledwyn Hughes, a former secretary of state and Sir Goronwy

Daniel, a former Welsh permanent secretary – Whitelaw's capitulation, and the 1980 Broadcasting Act. Some years later, at a dinner in Tyne Tees Television's London flat, I asked Whitelaw why he had acted as he did. He confessed that he had no idea whether it would be better to have the language on one channel or two, but thought it was hardly worth anyone dying for a difference he couldn't truly assess. A deceptively simple but honourable answer.

Within a period of 18 months a referendum might have been lost, but HTV also found itself with a new government, a new franchise, and a substantial new customer. If the loss of the referendum was a matter for personal gloom, work would be an intense therapy, for the creation of S4C was not just an addition to the Welsh broadcasting infrastructure, but a transformation for us all. Both BBC Wales and HTV Wales would have to increase their Welsh language output and, henceforth avoid duplication, and both would eventually double their English language output. An independent production industry would also spring to life, changing the ecology of television programme making for ever.

Above all, Welsh language broadcasters and producers could begin to think through what it meant to provide an independent national service on S4C, rather than opt-outs from UK networks. Nowhere was the difference more evident than in news and current affairs. But who was to do what? Both HTV and the BBC had nightly news programmes in Welsh – though they were very different in character – and had aspirations to deliver the news service for the new channel. We at HTV believed our programme to be sharper and harder than the opposition, so despite the fact that the strategic logic favoured the choice of the BBC, we were determined to make it a contest.

On a June weekend in 1982, our team of Welsh-speaking journalists, some outright rookies, descended on the St. George's Hotel, in London, cheekily close to the BBC, and within a stone's throw of ITN's old offices at Wells Street. With the help of ITN we recovered all the material for a single day's news and proceeded to edit it into a programme that sought to blend world, UK and Welsh news seamlessly and to give some sense that a Welsh perspective on the world had validity. At the end of the day we shipped everything across from the hotel to ITN, re-edited the pictures and recorded two programmes under the title *Y Byd ar Bedwar* (The World on Four).

ITN colleagues, including David Nicholas, ITN's chief executive, marvelling that it was done at all, thought it was done well. The authority of Elinor Jones and Alun Ffred Jones, the two presenters for a proposed ten o'clock programme, and Tweli Griffiths for a shorter early evening version, seemed to grow instantly simply because they were delivering a wider world agenda. It was a revelatory moment and a concept that, fifteen years later, was to create panic amongst the most senior BBC managers in the wake of the referenda in Scotland and Wales.

The BBC produced its own pilot programmes, but in the end it was never a beauty contest. The BBC's unity was a decisive advantage, for despite ITN's collaboration in the experiment, it was not ready to relinquish daily editorial control of its UK and world material to a 'regional' broadcaster – quite an irony given its present day business model. Moreover, giving HTV the news brief would have tied up too much of S4C's cash in the news field, leaving it with less editorial and financial flexibility in other programme areas. The BBC could supply news within its obligatory 'free' ten hours a week. News and current affairs was thus split cleanly between the two organisations. BBC would supply news, HTV current affairs. *Y Byd ar Bedwar* survived as the title of HTV's current affairs flagship for S4C and, a quarter of a century later, is still on air.

The challenge, defined by a mixture of programme ambition, commercial considerations, and the need to fill a whole channel, was to create three current affairs programmes a week. However, it was the commercial dictates that demanded that these three should each run for 48 weeks of the year, a length of run unheard of in television current affairs anywhere else in the UK. That it was achieved spoke volumes not only for the commitment of the team but also for the tenacity of my deputy, Cenwyn Edwards, an unsung hero of television journalism in Wales, whose knowledge, cool judgement and total unflappability gave confidence to old hands and novices alike.

By far the most novel challenge for any non-metropolitan team of journalists, let alone one working in a language other than English, was our brief to cover the world. It was a brief that defined the difference between opt-out services and an independent channel, and it meant developing quite a different perspective on the weekly agenda. Suddenly, elections in American or Germany or South Africa were as much within our purview as Welsh politics. It would be fair to say that our international output was more exposition than investigation, but we determined to stamp this international brief into the audience's mind from the outset. Our very first foreign report came from Emyr Daniel, who explored 'Reaganomics' in the context of US mid-term elections.Unburdened by a BBC coat of arms we also found our way into unlikely places, particularly in Latin America. In Honduras Russell Isaac interviewed John Negroponte, the US Ambassador, then turning a blind eye to human rights abuses in order to gain Honduran support against the Sandinista government next door in Nicaragua. Tweli Griffiths succeeded in getting us into Cuba, perhaps the first British current affairs crew to paint a considered portrait of that country. Early the following year Emyr Daniel also fronted an hour-long programme on the German federal elections, with a timely interview with Petra Kelly, the leader of the Green Party that went on to win 27 seats, their first in the German Parliament. We also had strokes of luck. Russell Isaac, covering Israel's withdrawal from Lebanon, found himself being searched by an Israeli soldier speaking Welsh with a distinct north Wales accent. The soldier, from Holywell, had gone to work in a kibbutz, married a Jewish girl and had been conscripted into the Israeli army.

Our very first venture abroad had taken place even before the S4C service came on air in November 1982. Tweli Griffiths put together a graphic account of protests in Plogoff, a small, coastal village in Brittany, against the building of a nuclear power station. This had been a sustained and sometimes violent campaign, reminiscent of 1968, but which had been completely ignored by the British press, despite presaging the construction of a chain of nuclear stations directly opposite the English coast. French policy stood in stark contrast to the British approach to nuclear power, comforted as we were by the early days of North Sea oil.

An even more revelatory report had come from Russell Isaac, who became the last journalist to take a film crew into Argentina as the Falklands crisis developed through 1982. In Welsh minds Argentina meant Patagonia, a centre of Welsh migration in the nineteenth century, where remnants of the Welsh language still existed, encouraged by all kinds of links and, today, even by the Welsh Assembly Government. There were more people of Welsh extraction in Patagonia than there were British on the Falklands islands themselves, which lent an entirely different slant to the concept of 'kith and kin' that was playing so strongly in the press.

Russell, who knew Patagonia well and spoke fluent Spanish, had found a family where the wife spoke Welsh and the husband was a colonel in the Argentine army. To hear the Argentine case being argued in Welsh by people who naturally used the term Las Malvinas rather than the Falklands was a jolt to us and to our audience at home. It also led to a dispute about whether, in order to avoid confusion if not for any reason of principle, we should use the name Las Malvinas rather than Falklands in the remainder of our reports. We decided that to do so would be misinterpreted by many, not least the families of Welsh soldiers. As the war began Russell was arrested, not far from the naval base of Comodoro Rivadavia, along with his crew and Simon Winchester of *The Times* and Ian Mather of *The Observer*. It was a phone call to the Argentine colonel that got him and his crew out and, eventually across the River Plate to Uruguay.

When it was over we sent Russell to the Falkland Islands themselves, where he discovered a young soldier, Milton Rhys, who was secretary and official translator for Menendez, the post-invasion Argentine governor. Rhys was from a Welsh-Patagonian family from the Gaiman and spoke fluent English, though no Welsh. He spoke emotionally about the fact that the first native Welsh people he had met were the Welsh Guards who had entered Port Stanley. Russell's reports were journalistically rigorous and in no way sentimental, but they were also fascinating for the cultural disorientation they engendered, challenging any easy assumptions about the bonds created by a common language.

In some ways the journalists producing the English language news output and the new current affairs programme, *Wales This Week*, faced a more difficult task in establishing a new agenda. Unlike their counterparts serving S4C, their brief was limited to Wales. Whereas their colleagues enjoyed a wide canvas, they had no option but to drill deep in their own backyard. It was at times an uncomfortable asymmetry, not helped by the very different budgets to which both teams worked – although both were generous by today's ITV standards – but the team's competitiveness was sharpened not only by an unspoken contest with their colleagues but also by knowledge of the BBC's vastly greater resources.

BBC Wales's current affairs output at that time was heavily dependent – some said over-dependent – on the considerable presence of Vincent Kane, who specialised in studio interrogations in *Week In Week Out*. The HTV Wales team took the alternative course of investigating stories on film, and did so effectively enough to persuade the BBC in time to change tack. The competition was truly healthy. *Wales This Week* kept lawyers busy with programmes on some WDA investments, training scams in west Wales, and the debated attribution of a number of

Rubens cartoons in the National Museum of Wales's collections. In year-long filming projects it tracked the cultural tensions in R.S. Thomas's parish of Aberdaron and the social stresses in the community around Cwm Colliery during the miner's strike. Whether in English on HTV or in Welsh for S4C, journalists, given the right space, freedom and money, stretched themselves and moved Welsh journalism on.

It was no surprise to me that they should take to their new agendas so eagerly, and they did so with élan, but if we were to produce three current affairs programmes a week in Welsh for the new channel – in truth, an over-provision that sometimes strained the quality – as well as establish a properly resourced current affairs unit for the HTV Wales service, the team had also to be reshaped and augmented. Early 1982 was a period of unending interviewing for new staff, and for many it was their first job, but we also needed anchors of experience and authority.

Emyr Daniel and Menna Richards, two key talents, were enticed across from the BBC amidst much secrecy and rumour to front the S4C output. The former, faced with a sceptical BBC lifer asserting that 'I wouldn't go to HTV for £30,000,' calmly replied, 'Neither would I'. Both brought not only the highest presenting skills but real breadth and political acuity to the task.

In English David Williams brought a similar sharpness to *Wales This Week*. Elis Owen, steeped in print journalism, had already come aboard to research the devolution output, and stepped up to edit the programme. Bruce Kennedy and John Osmond were two other recruits from newspapers, though after the 1979 referendum the latter had left the *Western Mail* to try to give Welsh civic society the kiss of life through an incisive but short-lived current affairs magazine, *Arcade*. It was a nicely balanced team – Elis Owen, the terrier, David Williams, the Alsatian, Bruce Kennedy, the bloodhound, and John Osmond, an intellectual Welsh sheepdog.

It was to prove an influential stable of talent. At one point in the late nineties virtually every senior position in news and current affairs across BBC, HTV and S4C was held by ex-HTV Wales people who had been instrumental in recasting the output in 1982: Aled Eirug and David Williams at the BBC, Elis Owen and Bruce Kennedy still at HTV and Cenwyn Ewards as the senior commissioning editor at S4C. Emyr Daniel, Menna Richards and Elis Owen all became, successively, Managing Directors of HTV Wales, Menna later succeeding me as Controller of BBC Wales. By that time John Osmond had left broadcast journalism but, as director of the Institute of Welsh Affairs, was editing

Wales's only regular journal dealing with public policy, as well as a
steady stream of weightier volumes.

★ ★ ★ ★

Although greatly enlarged, the scale of the company made it possible
for an executive to set aside management tasks from time to time in
order to make programmes. The documentary form was hugely attractive, offering the space to develop an issue or a story, and to make
wider connections not always possible within the tighter confines of
news and current affairs. Although the burden of union crewing levels
was often irksome, the other side of that costly coin was the widespread
pride in specialist craft. Working with lighting cameramen who, on
another day, might be filming a network drama, was a privilege that is
now virtually extinct in regional television. Rare too, are directors and
editors with the time and resource to agonise over shape and structure.
In those terms it was a luxurious time.

In this way the spate of arson attacks on holiday homes in Wales
could become a means of exploring a nexus of problems – steel
closures, recession, poverty, poor and scarce housing, language – that
together might have generated an aggressive and combustible despair.
The film's title, *A Real Fire*, played on the words of a then current
British Gas advertisement, 'Come home to a real fire', that today seems
so environmentally extravagant. Amusingly, although the film delved
into planning policies in the Lake District and the Channel Islands, a
London reviewer thought it had 'a heavy bias to the Welsh point of
view'. Quite. It may have had something to do with the inclusion of
R.S. Thomas reading one of his poems on the beach at Aberdaron.

Nearby, in the bar of the Bwlchtocyn Hotel at the furthermost
extremity of the Lleyn Peninsula, the crew met a holiday homeowner
from Stoke-on-Trent, talking in irresistibly provocative terms. He
agreed to be interviewed the following day. It required no great inter-
rogation. He could see no link between attitudes to immigration in his
own home town and any native nervousness about a culture clash in
Lleyn. I asked him whether he and his wife travelled. Yes, indeed, they
holidayed regularly in the Caribbean. With a completely straight face
he said that on a visit to Barbados, while taxi-bound from the airport
to the hotel, he had tapped the black driver on the shoulder and said
'By Jove, you've got a colour problem out here.' To recollect it is to feel
like Sam Tyler in *Life on Mars*, propelled back two decades into a place

of different values. It is also a corrective to the usual view that life has become coarser in the last few decades.

We went with Lucy Rees, the zoologist daughter of Goronwy Rees, to tame horses in Arizona, contrasting her 'horse whisperer' methods with the rougher ones of traditional cowboys with names out of fiction, like Wes Lance and Joe Scaggs, and guns to match. For a month we stayed in a tiny settlement, topically enough in 1983, named Thatcher. It could have come from a *Guardian* cartoon. It had one police car, with the words Thatcher Police written on its side. On a semi-derelict wooden building, the paint peeling in the dusty sun, were hung crookedly the words 'Thatcher Municipal Building'. In the township's sole bar we had our first encounter with redneck America, passportless people who were only too ready to recommend, during breaks in the line dancing, that we 'nuke the Russians'. Some miles out of town and into the stunning Arizona wilderness, was a missile silo.

A different America offered itself in New York on the thirtieth anniversary of the death of Dylan Thomas. Television has an excessive but utilitarian regard for anniversaries, and this one was not to be missed. Dylan is pre-eminent in the short roll-call of Welsh artistic heroes, a dead cert for our imagined Mount Rushmore. My father's association with him had provided an added push, as had the writer Rob Gittins's research into the last weeks of Dylan's life. It proved a warm and emotional experience, although we also lowered our bucket into a deep well of hurt. The fact that the poet had died in New York rather than Laugharne had clearly exacerbated the anguish felt by his friends in this country – helplessness multiplies grief. But there were also implications of a lack of care and understanding, even that America had killed Dylan. Thirty years later his circle of American friends still felt wronged – perplexed and hurt that their experience was being written down as something superficial.

Somehow we had managed to pull together a group that had been key to Dylan's last visits to the States. They were three of the actors who had taken part in the very first concert reading of *Under Milk Wood* – Roy Poole, Allen Collins, and Sada Thompson. They were joined by the two central figures who could not have been more different: John Malcolm Brinnin, who had arranged Dylan's last tours and who, in 1953, ran the New York Poetry Centre where *Under Milk Wood* was first performed, and his assistant there, Liz Reitell, who had produced that performance and with whom Dylan had had an affair. He had collapsed into his final coma in her bed.

It was not difficult to see why Dylan should have fallen in love with
Liz Reitell. Even thirty years later she was tall, slim and ramrod
straight. Her black hair framed an aquiline face that had the look and
poise of a Sioux chief, except when animated by her exuberant enthusiasms. She confessed to being a 'rather large, conspicuous person',
noticed when she came into a room, but was also proud that Dylan had
called her simply, 'very long and very gentle'.

This last may have been a lover's perspective, for Liz Reitell was a
force. She had needed no persuasion to get on a plane and fly from
Montana to New York. She had a story to tell, and saw this as an opportunity set the record straight. She was part of the legend and would not
have disagreed with the verdict of Dylan's biographer, Paul Ferris, that
she had 'joined the throng of those who were never the same again'.
She told the tale in a strong but quiet voice, and though not above
theatricality – after all, we did film the interview in a room in the
Chelsea Hotel – we were all convinced that this was no mere performance.

Brinnin, on the other hand, was much more reluctant. He had told
his story in *Dylan Thomas in America*, a book that had provoked a
ferocious and sometimes abusive response on this side of the Atlantic.
Only a year earlier he had been at the unveiling of the plaque to
Thomas in Westminster Abbey, attending only 'for the symmetry of the
occasion'. One felt the wounds were not entirely healed. After a long
phone call, he agreed to come to New York. Some books were harder
to close than others. Even then you felt him stand back one pace,
sympathetic to Reitell's story, understanding of her motivations, nevertheless more detached and more private about his own deep feelings
for the poet.

There were two very different postscripts to that film – *A Far Ago
Land*. Some years later I received a letter from the sculptor, Dave
Slivka, whose ex-wife, Rose, had been one of the three women partic-
ipating in the bedlam at St. Vincent's Hospital in 1953 – the others
being Liz Reitell and Dylan's wife Caitlin. He had made a head of
Dylan, based on a death mask he had taken at the hospital. He offered
a final cast to the BBC and it stands in the entrance hall at Llandaff.
Liz Reitell, after a period as assistant to Arthur Miller and Marilyn
Monroe during the filming of *The Misfits*, took up causes with a drive
and conviction that won awards from the environmental movement,
and ended up working for the Columbia River Inter-Tribal Fish
Commission. She visited our family in Newcastle and railed tirelessly

against the environmental policies of the Reagan regime, pausing only once in deference to the architecture and organ of Durham Cathedral. She died in 2001.

Although the 1979 referendum verdict had cast many of us into gloom, and the fate of coal and steel gave the impression of the bailiffs coming in to take away the furniture, the new broadcasting arrangements gave us an opportunity to claw back some territory. The need to convey the history of Wales to our audience now had an added urgency. If nothing else 1979 had demonstrated the gulf that existed between an assumed intelligentsia and the bulk of the population. But there were other reasons, too.

Welsh historiography had been transformed in recent decades, there was talk of a golden age. Glanmor Williams, Kenneth Morgan, Gwyn Alf Williams, Dai Smith, Rhys Davies and John Davies contributed to a treasurehouse of new scholarship about Wales's past that deserved wider recognition. At the new Channel Four Jeremy Isaacs was also keen. He was a distinguished producer of historical documentaries, and two years earlier was in the middle of producing Robert Kee's television history of Ireland when he travelled to Edinburgh to deliver the lecture that wags described as the James McTaggart memorial job application. It got him the job as Channel Four's first Chief Executive, and amongst his first commissions was a 24-part history of Scotland.

Wynford Vaughan Thomas had had a draft of a series on Wales in a drawer for some time, and claimed to have a gentleman's agreement with Isaacs. It was important to him personally, since below the bubbly surface was a serious man trying to get out. Yes, he was an entertainer. Yes, he revelled in mountains and pathways, castles and narrow gauge trains, myth, legend and quirkiness, but he was much more than a frothy presenter, hinterland came in by the hodful. Anyone who had visited his home in Fishguard knew that it housed one of the finest private libraries on all things Welsh.

He knew every inch of his country. I once saw the amazement on the face of one of the world's leading experts on Turner's work as Wynford explained to him that a particular depiction of Snowdonia could only have been painted from the south, naming, as he toured the canvas, every rock, ridge and summit. But he had also created, perhaps as a result of the trauma of reporting Belsen, a better known mask of frivolity, and we worried about his capacity to put that aside when faced with the camera. We were also conscious that such a series would only be done once in a lifetime, and would have to measure up to the critical scrutiny of an uncomfortably large number of distinguished historians.

Colin Thomas, the producer, brought the solution. Colin had gained some notoriety, following his resignation from the BBC as a protest against the cutting of references to British atrocities from a documentary on Northern Ireland. Following a spell at RTE in Dublin, he had come to HTV to produce *And did corruptly receive*, a documentary on local government corruption. This film had ended in a confrontation, umpired by John Morgan, between the two protagonists, Gerald Murphy, an errant local government leader from Swansea, and Paddy French, the editor of *Rebecca*, a magazine that, it has to be said, had done much more than any mainstream medium to unearth corruption. This confrontation of cavalier and roundhead was a pre-echo of what was to come.

From the outset Colin had been keen to have a two-headed series for a mix of reasons, to explore differences and create dramatic impact, to have a variation in style – 'the poetic and the prosaic' as he said in a note. The series should examine social history as well as the actions and decisions of great men, appeal to all age groups and include women. There was also a competitive reason – 'an opportunity to outflank the BBC's choice of David [Dai] Smith for its own series' that became *Wales! Wales?* Wynford was resistant and, as a former director of the company, carried a lot of clout, forcing me to weigh in on Colin's side.

On the eve of the Brixton riots, and with a copy of Colin McArthur's British Film Institute treatise, *Television and History*, in his pocket, Colin went to Fishguard to persuade Wynford to co-present the series with a woman historian, Angela John. Wynford jumped the co-presenter fence, albeit reluctantly, but sharing the task with a female proved a fence too far for someone shaped in a different age. Seeing that the chemistry was not going to work, Angela John tactfully withdrew. Then fortune smiled. Although we were far from ready to start filming the series, Colin, with a deal of prescience, decided to film the 150th anniversary celebrations of the 1831 Merthyr Rising. There, on the steps of Merthyr's Town Hall, in the pouring rain and with his fist in the air, was Gwyn A. Williams in full declamatory flow. Colin had found his man.

Gwyn Alf, as he was known, was claimed by socialists and nationalists. On the left he was applauded for destroying many nationalist myths, but saved nationalist blushes by demonstrating that the importance of myths did not lie in their factual basis or lack of it. In the seventies he had given me an fascinating foretaste of his later books – In *Search of Beulah Land* and *Madoc: the making of a myth* – before I ventured on my first visit to the United States, a year before the American bicentennial. It proved particularly useful, if a shade embarrassing, when I addressed the Chamber of Commerce in Mobile, Alabama, who were particularly proud of their monument to Prince Madoc, 'discoverer of America', on the Mobile foreshore. It was a community committed to not letting the facts spoil a good story.

It was the pairing of Wynford and Gwyn that allowed the series to become a debate rather than a single narrative, to be about the nature of history as well as about Wales's continuities and discontinuities and, as Jeremy Isaacs observed, 'to move history on television on a step'. It also allowed the series to have a focus on the future, as well as being steeped in the past and, in relation to what seemed at the time a very precarious future for Wales, to engage both pessimists and optimists. Gwyn Alf had himself captured the more pessimistic mood in the BBC Wales annual lecture delivered less than nine months after the referendum: 'We are living through what may be our end. The end of Wales and the Welsh as distinct entities.' But being a champion of 'that Aneurin Bevan of Italian communism, Antonio Gramsci…who worked to the motto 'pessimism of the intellect, optimism of the will', he had also offered a chink of light:

> There is no historical necessity for Wales; there is no historical necessity for a Welsh people or a Welsh nation. Wales will not exist unless the Welsh want it. It is not compulsory to want it. Plenty of people who are biologically Welsh choose not to be Welsh. That act of choice is beyond reason. One thing, however, is clear from our history. If we want Wales, we will have to make Wales.

At their first meeting Gwyn had charmed Wynford by recounting that he had listened to his radio despatches on the liberation of Rome in June 1944 while himself crouching in a landing craft heading for the Normandy beaches. That created a bond that made later disagreements short-lived. Initial wariness was mixed with surprise. Gwyn, the professional historian, in his mid-fifties and at the height of his powers, was surprised at the depths of Wynford's historical knowledge. Wynford, in his mid-seventies and undertaking his last big project, was also surprised, alarmed even, at how good a performer Gwyn could be, notwithstanding his stammer. Over the next two years I put on weight lunching Wynford regularly, usually at his request. Towards the end of every meal, he would lean across the table and, exhibiting the insecurity of all performers, even in his seventies, whisper hesitantly, 'Am I winning?'

It was Colin's abiding integrity and seriousness of purpose that steered these two volatile entities to a harmonious conclusion over two years of filming and editing, but not without its scares along the way. The most serious happened in Aberystwyth, a place that Wynford had likened to an onion: 'It has many layers, and each one can reduce you to tears.' Colin reported that Wynford and Gwyn had rowed furiously about the significance of William Abraham, usually known by his bardic name of Mabon, a miners' agent who represented the Liberal-Nonconformist world that was about to be eclipsed by Labour early in the last century. Both presenters were capable of passionate excess, and the backdrop of the cataclysmic miners' strike of 1984-5 made ignition easier. Gwyn, in full firebrand mode, was scornful and, frustrated by Wynford's dismissive obduracy, stormed out. Colin fretted that he would not return. The following morning over breakfast Gwyn appeared, knelt ostentatiously at Wynford's side, kissed his hand and confessed that he had ended up in a pub from which he fled, alarmed at being mistaken for the singer-comedian, Freddie Starr.

When the series began its thirteen-week journey in January 1985, the air was heavy with significance. The miners' strike was entering its eleventh month and heading for almost certain defeat. Construction of the final episode was delayed until the strike's end in March so that both Wynford and Gwyn could deliver a contemporary verdict. The last image of the final programme was of the return to work at the Maerdy pit. The ground was fertile in other ways too. There had been a burgeoning of curiosity in history and genealogy. Industrial archaeology was also beginning to excite interest and, only a year before, the government had established CADW to conserve and to exploit the Welsh abundance of historic monuments, something that had prompted Gwyn Alf's fear of Wales becoming 'a nation of wine waiters and museum attendants'.

We were determined to make the fullest use of the series, assisted by Channel Four's innovative commitment to education and by an enterprising team at Gwynedd Archives. Wynford and Gwyn did, of course, produce their own very different books on the series, Gwyn's *When was Wales?* becoming a classic text. Wynford gave Gwyn a copy of his own book, inscribed 'to my beloved enemy'.

We also produced document packs and wallcharts and information on each episode specifically designed to allow people to carry on their own debate. They did so with gusto. We logged 136 viewing and discussion groups, involving more than 2,000 people. The groups would meet to watch that week's episode and continue the argument. More than 1,500 document packs were sold and, at the end of the series 200 people paid to attend a weekend conference in Cardiff to discuss television and history and take part in rambunctious workshops, one of which carried the label, Wales: Dead or Alive? Wales had taken a lot of punches over the previous decade and sustained a lot of damage, but it was far from comatose.

6 Going North

ITV's Tyne Tees Television in 1987 was far from being an identical twin. The north east of England is different. In many ways more isolated and more self-contained than Wales, in the mind it is an island region, bounded by the North Sea to the east, the Pennines to the West, the Scottish borders to the north and the North Yorkshire moors to the south. For this reason it seems more self-sufficient. It does not have a Bristol or a Liverpool on its doorstep. Leeds is as far from Newcastle as London is from Cardiff. In the late 1980s, London was four hours away by train, against Cardiff's two. The business class flew to Heathrow instead. Scandinavian suffixes abounded in the telephone directory, and it was no accident that Newcastle's Town Hall was opened in 1968 by the King of Norway not the Queen of England.

Vying with Wales for bottom place in most regional league tables – it still does – but also sharing a border with Scotland, it was suspicious of devolutionary schemes because it worried about losing out to its northern neighbour. Its councillors and MPs played a large part in scuppering devolution in 1979. At the same time it fretted about its own impotence, especially after the abolition in 1986 of the Tyne and Wear County Council, a metropolitan authority of 1.2m people that had brought cohesion and clout, and the Nissan car factory, to the region over two decades.

It may have shared with Wales a deep male chauvinism, but it exceeded Wales in its dismissal of London as the habitat of effete southerners. In 1987, the weekend after a hurricane devastated large parts of southern England, I heard this exchange on a Sunderland street: 'Helluva wind down south.' 'Aye, serve the buggers right.' Although, in its own referendum in 2005, it voted against the idea of a regional assembly as heavily as did Wales in 1979, it would be best not to leap to premature conclusions.

When I left HTV for Newcastle and the chance to steer a complete programme operation, I expected that, some cultural differences apart, life would be rather like home. Like Wales, the region's economy had been devastated by the decline in coal and steel, and its shipbuilding industry was going the same way. Both places put up with similar stereotyping, even if the accents were different. 'Blaydon Races' and 'When the boat comes in' took the place of 'Calon Lan' and 'Men of Harlech'. For Cardiff's Ely estate read Newcastle's Scotswood Road; for Ebbw Vale, Consett; for St. David's Cathedral, Durham. But there were important differences, not least the extent of private schooling. Unlike Wales, behind a superficially familiar industrial and political culture one could find the vestiges of a feudal past distinctly different from our own. Behind this bastion of old Labour, there stood the region's old money, a handful of landed families who seemed ubiquitous in the institutions of the north east.

Among the many things that they dominated was Tyne Tees Television. Its chairman, Sir Ralph Carr-Ellison, and another director, the fourth Viscount Ridley, between them owned a substantial chunk of the region. They simply reversed roles on the board of Northern Rock. The Queen Mother would sometimes holiday at Sir Ralph's home. Another director, Paul Nicholson, occasionally monocled, brewed the region's beer. A solicitor, Robert Dickinson, connected to the old coal-owning Joicey family, seemed to be *consigliere* to them all. It was as if in Wales the Crawshays and Powell Duffryn had survived to own and run HTV, the Principality, Cardiff University and, for good measure, the WDA. Sir Ralph, being also the Lord Lieutenant of the county, would often appear in the office in military uniform, allowing me to observe that it is easier to walk upstairs than downstairs while wearing spurs – something I would never have learnt at the national eisteddfod.

These were assured, shrewd and genial people, infinitely polite even when menacingly decisive, although it was reassuring that Viscount Ridley, a Lord Steward of the Household who had chaired Northumberland County Council for 12 years, thought his brother, Nicholas, a Tory minister, 'quite mad' to have proposed the privatisation of the water industry. There was something of a social gulf between half the board and its senior directors, let alone the staff. Ward Thomas, whose roots were in Wales, and who had presided over the previous merger of Tyne Tees and Yorkshire under Trident Television – a merger that the IBA had forced apart – was the only broadcasting professional amongst its non-executives. He was a tiger who slept with one eye open.

It was an unlikely board to preside over a company that had its roots in light entertainment, and had gained some notoriety through the 1980s with its weekly live music offering to Channel 4, *The Tube*, presented by Jools Holland and Paula Yates. This had been a brilliant departure initiated by my predecessor Andrea Wonfor, but the risks of live broadcasting, especially in the anarchic, devil-may-care world of pop music, had produced a crisis just before I arrived.

Jools Holland, doing the regular, unscripted live promotion for the show in the middle of ITV's childrens' programmes, had finished by inviting children everywhere to switch to Channel 4 'where all the groovy fuckers are'. ITV switchboards had lit up across the nation, and the IBA issued Tyne Tees with a formal reprimand. It was something of a disappointment to arrive in Newcastle to read, on my first day, a letter from Jeremy Isaacs saying that Channel 4 was not going to recommission the show. It was nothing to do with the reprimand – Jeremy's shoulders were quite broad enough to deal with that – but more his wish to end it, as with many shows, before it risked going stale.

Andrea Wonfor, an inspired programme maker, and her managing director Andy Allan, had built a sizeable reputation for the smallest of the middle ranking ITV companies, also creating and handling Harry Secombe's Sunday evening religious programme *Highway* for the ITV network. Unfortunately, when Allan handed over to David Reay in 1984, he left him with a staff of nearly 850 only shortly before ITV revenues took a sharp downward turn. This had led to an acrimonious dispute over programming ambitions that led to Andrea Wonfor's departure. It was not a promising climate in which to take over in the spring of 1987, and it didn't get any easier after Black Monday – the stock market crash the following October – that reduced the company's share price dramatically. The prospect of auctioning ITV franchises, raised by the Peacock report the previous year, and confirmed in the 1988 White Paper, only deepened the gloom.

I had worked with David Reay at HTV, where, as Director of Engineering, he had been responsible for the design and commissioning of its Culverhouse Cross centre. Now he was running the ITV company that covered his home patch. Born in Sunderland, he had started as a transmission engineer, but though a card-carrying member of the union in his day, was now determined to be in the van of ending the restrictive practices that drained the souls of programme makers as much as the coffers of the company, and brought ITV into such disrepute in the eyes of the Prime Minister. The irrationality of Britain's adversarial post-war industrial relations still had a last spark of life in it, despite what had happened to the miners in 1985. In retrospect it seems like two sides walking either side of a high wall, each with a different view of the world, vaguely conscious of those on the other side, but neither heeding the common pit ahead into which they would both fall. The strike by the company's electricians was short-lived, but its collapse after three weeks forged a new realism that soon took hold across the ITV system, although too late to avert the catastrophe of the 1990 Broadcasting Act.

If anything the company seemed even more immersed in the community than HTV, although this may have been an illusion created by the fact that the region itself is more compact geographically. It is less than half the size of Wales, although having a population only some 15 per cent smaller. Newcastle was then much more dominant as an expression of the region than Cardiff was of Wales. The Tyne eclipsed the Wear and Tees, and the building of the The Baltic gallery and The Sage concert hall confirmed this despite both being, strictly, in Gateshead. There being relatively few regional institutions, the city was the region's most important available champion, and Tyne Tees was closer to local television than HTV could ever be.

Its nightly news programme, *Northern Life*, vied with the BBC for domination, but since the latter had no regional output beyond news and current affairs, the north east had no option but to look to Tyne Tees for anything like a full reflection of its life. There was scarcely an initiative in the city in which the company's staff were not involved. I was drawn into several organisations, including the new public-private partnership, The Newcastle Initiative, the Northern Sinfonia and the Northern Stage Company.

It was also another opportunity to strengthen current affairs, in order to build some deeper examination on the back of daily news. It was put to a long and strenuous test during the child abuse scandal in Cleveland, in which 121 children were identified as victims of child abuse by a single doctor, Dr Marietta Higgs, at a hospital in Middlesbrough, mainly on the basis of a single and controversial diagnostic method. Our programme had been the first to break the story and its initial impact was strong enough, but it seemed to enter another dimension when the local MP, Stuart Bell, uttered the words, at the top of our programme, 'Salem has come to Teesside.'

The story led the programme almost every night for a year, earning a special Royal Television Society commendation in 1988 for the local reporter, Luke Casey, and the RTS's main current affairs award for the documentary *Crying in the Dark* that included sensational tapes of a Cleveland social worker interrogating a child. Even the mammoth inquiry under Dame Elizabeth Butler-Sloss failed fully to resolve the issues. The Medical Officer of Health in the region thought the diagnosis of abuse was correct in 70 per cent of the cases, although court cases involving 96 of the 121 children were dismissed.

A rather different controversy arose from our religious programme, *Inner Space*, when the Bishop of Durham, the Rt. Rev. David Jenkins, ventured the thought that the resurrection might have been a spiritual rather than physical event. Despite the thundering of the press, who suddenly discovered an interest in theology, he was not struck by lightning, although shortly afterwards I did receive a proposal to do a televised version of Eliot's *Murder in the Cathedral* at Durham.

As was to be the case later in the BBC, access to the ITV network was a constant issue around the regional controllers' table. The system of network financing in ITV's asymmetric federation was reaching new heights of complexity as the middle five companies sought a better deal from the big five. We would joke that in the event of being hijacked in a plane, we would talk the terrorists through the issues, a process we thought would, with absolute certainty, produce a collapse of any terrorist's will. It said much for the system that a deal in which Tyne Tees was given a ration of four hours a year was regarded as a major step forward.

We had tried to maintain the popular music output that had been built in the eighties, although I am not sure I myself was ever comfortable in the world of pop music. ITV tendered for a competitor show to BBC's *Top of the Pops*, which we won, but network controllers were never fully behind the concept. As a result the programme, *The Roxy*, was scheduled at different times in different parts of the country which, ultimately, killed it. In a joint venture with Harvey Goldsmith we televised the gothic exuberance of the Monserrat Caballe and Freddie Mercury concert at the beginning of Barcelona's cultural Olympiad, which set new records for going over the top. A music education series with Jim Henson, *The Ghost of Fafner Hall*, tried to do for music education what *Sesame Street* did for literacy. I introduced Henson to our chairman. He had not met a knight of the shire before and after the encounter asked me whether he could copyright him.

In drama the North East had rich potential. Live Theatre, a small stage in a crumbling warehouse on the quayside, was a crucible of good writing. It was established by two actors, Val McLane and Tim Healy, in 1973, and made much use of work by C.P. Taylor, Tom Haddaway, Alan Plater and Sid Chaplin, the father of Michael Chaplin, who joined me at Tyne Tees from London Weekend and worked with me later at BBC Wales. Plater and Sid Chaplin's *Close the Coalhouse Door* had been a national success as had C.P. Taylor's *A Nightingale Sang*. It was with the latter that we decided to begin, in co-production with Portman Productions and Victor Glynn, who some years later produced Mike Leigh's film *High Hopes*. The television script was crisp, as was only to be expected from Jack Rosenthal. Performances by John Woodvine, Joan Plowright and Stephen Tomkinson helped it to an audience of 10 million, rather more attainable then than in today's fragmented world.

A more sustained contribution was based not on a playwright but a novelist from the region, Catherine Cookson. She was the area's pre-eminent storyteller, and the most borrowed author from British libraries until well after the millennium. Strong plots and strong characters, even if it could be said that they were sometimes stereotypical, were a true treasure chest.

Ray Marshall, a business partner of the writer Ted Willis in Worldwide Television, had opened discussions with her agent and Ray and I went to see Catherine in her home in the Tyne Valley. She was not in the best of health, suffering from a rare vascular disease, and was being carefully nursed, as ever, by her husband Tom. She told us she dictated many of her books into a recorder, acting out the dialogue in front of a mirror. Although seeming to marvel at our interest and enthusiastic for the venture, she was also canny, but in time we made an arrangement that gave us exclusive access to the books.

To get its place in the network schedules it needed the support of one of the network controllers, and it was to the credit of Greg Dyke, then at London Weekend, that he spotted immediately that this would be strong British drama that would appeal to the home audience rather more than deracinated transatlantic co-productions that were essentially deal driven. This was what regional companies were for. The first that we made was *The Fifteen Streets*, in which the Welsh actor Owen Teale had his first major television role alongside Sean Bean, Ian Bannen, Bille Whitelaw and Jane Horrocks. Greg's support guaranteed a Sunday slot and another 10 million audience and, as a consequence, an immediate start on the next, *The Black Velvet Gown*. Sadly, I had left Tyne Tees before it was screened, but in the following years eighteen Cookson novels were adapted for television under Ray Marshall's guidance.

Nevertheless, the region's fragility in television terms was never far from the mind. It had been evident in other ways too. In 1989 the Wilding Report for the Arts Council of Great Britain had recommended merging Northern Arts with Yorkshire Arts. The protest it produced was loud from both the arts and the business community. It was as if someone had suggested merging the Arts Council of Wales with the South West of England. At the recording of the Northern Arts Awards that we had just initiated, the presenter Melvyn Bragg used the platform to powerful effect, and the plan was withdrawn.

There was some irony, therefore, in the fact that the non-executives on the board of Tyne Tees were increasingly convinced that the company should and would merge again with Yorkshire, even if there was some doubt about when. Some of them had been part of the previous Trident arrangement and had been reluctant to acquiesce in the separation that the IBA had insisted upon. I argued a case against, more in order that the board should understand the precise consequences for programming and the region, than in any hope that such a prospect would be averted. It was demoralising for the executive directors, and although not in the public domain, the effect trickled down. Newcastle had been a stimulating city in which to work. I loved its people, its dramatic river and elegant streets, and the mystic allure of the Northumberland coast but, in the circumstances, it was a relief to receive more than one invitation to go back to Wales, and, for the first time, to the BBC.

Wales and the north east of England exhibited great similarities, and great differences. Both ITV companies had an intense relationship with their own areas – the one perceived as a nation, the other a region. Although Wales benefited from a more robust production ecology, the division of local output for Wales between the two languages meant that it was not until after 1982, and the launch of S4C, that the English language service for Wales caught up with the scale of service in Tyne Tees and other English regions. Even when it did, it is arguable that the underdeveloped institutional apparatus of English regions placed a greater burden on English ITV companies, especially given the BBC's very limited regional services at the time.

It was evident in both that the sense of mission of programme makers was more serious, and the texture of their services far richer than implied by the common English metropolitan perception of regional programming as merely 'cider and Cornish pastie' culture. But it was the last decade in which the ITV regions felt secure.

Tyne Tees was absorbed once again by Yorkshire Television in 1993 and is now part of the single ITV company. In 2007 I visited Newcastle. For Sale signs festooned the company's unlovely premises near the river. A shrunken staff of little more than 100 were encamped instead not far from the giant Metrocentre shopping mall some miles away. Studio 5, the grey, metallic cube that that once rocked to bands for *The Tube*, is the temporary home of a Pentecostal church.

7 Coming home

Let's start at the post room, I said to the 'Major' who liked nothing better than arranging an event with military precision, and not a little flair. It was day one at BBC Wales and the 'Major' – the public relations manager, Iwan Thomas – had promised a tour to every nook and cranny in the building. In the post room two uniformed men turned from their sorting to be introduced to the new controller. Then, from a door behind me came another, and then another and another until I was faced with half a dozen postmen who delivered mail to and collected mail from offices four times a day. They did it five times day for the management floor, since the BBC is an organisation that believes in hierarchy, despite its staff being blessed with an abnormal number of congenital dissenters. To express a preference for having my mail only once a day was, apparently, to send a frisson of fear through the building.

To join the BBC was to undergo an involuntary change of image. From having been, at Tyne Tees, the programme softie, slightly uncomfortable with the company's confrontational attitude to the unions, I was now cast in the unlikely role of ITV hatchet man come to sort out BBC Wales. It was not an image I cared for. 'Need more of you chaps,' the BBC's chairman, Duke Hussey, had barked down at me when we first met, compressing several questionable assumptions into a short phrase that, in his customary style, combined a kind of warmth with the peremptory.

The BBC was preparing its defences, conscious of the damage that was about to be done to ITV by the franchise auction, and convinced that the BBC was now firmly in Margaret Thatcher's sights. Michael Checkland, a shrewd and affable Director General, and respected as a critical friend of programme makers, made it clear that my first task was to take a big slice out of the cost base of BBC Wales, even while extolling the delights that lay ahead of me. I went to see his deputy, John Birt, the most famous recruit from ITV and asked about the risks of going native in an organisation with such a strong culture. He thought he had been too long in ITV for that to be an issue for him, but, as an insurance, it was 'best to have your own cadres around you'.

There was a chill about the word cadre.

It was a rather different problem for me. Although I was to work for the BBC for less than a quarter of my working life, I had first entered the corporation's records in January 1944 – at two weeks old – when my father had written to 'Admin' in London to claim the BBC's 'post-natal allowance'. My elder brother had been a tyro director on the groundbreaking *Tonight* programme and had died in the BBC's service. When I joined in 1990 I first worked in an office my father had occupied as head of progammes in Wales in the sixties. It was truly a case of *Cadw ty mewn cwmwl tystion* (Keeping house midst a cloud of witnesses). I may not have worked for the BBC but I had lived with it for most of my life. I expect still to be a BBC pensioner when my file is closed. And yet I have not been nor ever felt a BBC lifer, which is just as well because a few years rather than weeks after joining I was introduced at a BBC function with the words, 'Of course, he is not a BBC man.' What else did you have to do to be admitted fully to the Opus Dei of public service broadcasting?

The BBC is an extraordinary British invention that the novelist Penelope Fitzgerald described as 'a cross between a civil service, a powerful moral force and an amateur theatrical society that wasn't too sure where next week's money was coming from'. She could never have envisaged that its annual income would one day be three billion pounds. It is an organisation that is at once creative and bureaucratic, inspiring and infuriating. It manages to embrace the popular, the populist and the esoteric without any sense of discomfort, and is both wonderfully unworldly and cunningly political. It contemplates the world and its own navel with equal enthusiasm, its core skills being programme-making and lobbying. While managing to seek out the new, it remains a vital agent of continuity in an age when novelty arrogantly aspires to be the highest virtue. But in 1990 the negatives provided too much ammunition to the BBC's enemies with which they could threaten all that was good and noble.

The BBC had been subject to regular bouts of cost-cutting, a necessary scraping of barnacles from the bottom of the boat. Geraint Stanley Jones, the BBC's first managing director of regional broad-casting, and Michael Checkland and others had only just completed an exercise known as 'black spot'. Now the BBC was into another round under the title Funding the Future. It would be followed by the television and radio resources reviews, the overheads review, the production efficiency study, ad infinitum. None of this would have been unfamiliar to managers in any large corporation, but in the BBC – then and now with a staff the size of a small town – it produced a loud collective groan, relayed with extraordinary speed and regularity to unsympathetic newspapers.

On his retirement Colin Morris, who had been a missionary in Africa long before becoming controller of BBC Northern Ireland and was much respected by colleagues, made light of his disillusion and likened the job of a BBC regional controller to that of a district commissioner in the colonies: 'You have only two jobs – to maintain law and order and to count things … and having counted them, to count 'em again.'

While all its staff could portray these battles as ones between 'creatives' and 'bean counters', outside London the clash between centre and periphery provided added seasoning. Scotland, Wales and Northern Ireland have always been lumped together in BBC jargon as the 'national regions', or, more recently, the 'nations'. This is to ignore the differing impulses driving each country, impulses that sometimes strained Celtic alliances though never Celtic friendship. The Scots, as in most spheres, were always confident of their political muscle, and as the Tory era drew to a close were increasingly certain that a Scottish Parliament would soon follow. They could also rely on Scottish newspapers to whip up a storm. Ron Neil, the warm and ebullient, and Scottish, managing director of regional broadcasting, despairing of his compatriots resistance to cost-cutting protested that 'you can't take a copy of the *Glasgow Herald* out of Scotland without a furore'.

In contrast, in the poker game of politics Wales had, in the 1979 referendum, disclosed the weakness of its hand to the rest of the country. It had only the Welsh language card up its sleeve, and that had already been played to maximum effect. Talking up the prospects for a Welsh Assembly in 1990 could sound like whistling in the dark, particularly when the storms generated by Welsh newspapers could be contained within teacups. Meanwhile the Northern Irish marched to a different drum, at least until the Good Friday agreement introduced the concept of the peace dividend. It was the first Roman Catholic controller of BBC Northern Ireland, Pat Loughrey, who stunned a meeting of the regional broadcasting directorate by ending a defence of the local with the last lines of Patrick Kavanagh's poem, *Epic* –

> Till Homer's ghost came whispering to my mind.
> He said: I made the Iliad from such
> A local row. Gods make their own importance.

The 1990s were unprecedented years in the history of the corporation, the first in which its income failed to rise like a cake. One of my predecessors, Alun Oldfield-Davies, who presided over BBC Wales for an unheard of 22 years, from 1945 to 1967, had seen the BBC's income grow inexorably as the population increased, and as television spread. In the year that he retired, colour television came to BBC2, prompting another increase in the licence. That growth had stuttered in the 1980s, but now the fee was to be cut by 3 per cent for one year before being pegged to the retail price index. In addition the BBC had to accommodate a new 25 per cent quota for independent production. Funding the Future was but one stab at handling the consequences, but it became a relentless decade's work driven first by the cannily pragmatic Michael Checkland and then by John Birt, in a very different style as he sought a more fundamental and controversial systemic change.

Wherever you sat in the corporation it was not difficult to see that change was necessary. On a very hot day in my first weeks, working in a room overlooking the Taff that faced the early morning sun, and in which I could have grown tomatoes even in winter, I asked whether someone could find a fan. Within minutes a suspiciously clean box arrived containing a pristine fan in a polythene bag. This is when I discovered the stores, an Aladdin's cave that suggested that Aladdin was stocking up for a nuclear winter and, judging by the number of fans, a nuclear summer too. Like a boy scout the BBC was prepared for every eventuality, but with considerably more kit at its disposal. At the cheap end were the fans, at the expensive end were outside broadcast units with seven figure price tags. It was possible to marvel at this commitment to quality, but it was a commitment beyond price that could not now be sustained.

I had tried to resist making comparisons with ITV, but when it was put to me by one manager that we could not afford to lose a single job in costume, design and make-up, the temptation proved irresistible. Costume and design – BBC Wales 22, Tyne Tees 2; make-up – BBC Wales 17, Tyne Tees 1. Making all necessary allowances for the differences in output – BBC Wales did have a daily soap opera, *Pobl y Cwm* – there was, at the very least, room for compromise.

In February 1991, after a thorough review of the operation I had the painful task of announcing 300 redundancies, from within a staff that had risen to nearly 1400. Half of the redundancies involved employees who transferred to contractors delivering out-sourced services, which is commonplace today but was unprecedented then in the BBC. As elsewhere in the BBC there were many warnings about throwing the baby out with the bath water, but the fact that staff protests were so muted, even in the face of the changes being proposed suggested a new realism. Trades unions wrote to Welsh MPs but later, at a meeting of the Welsh Labour group at Westminster, after sincere but ritualistic concerns had been expressed, the reception was friendly.

The BBC's capacity to deliver Kafkaesque surprises surfaced on the day of the announcement. After an arduous morning of separate briefings for unions, managers and the press and, in the orchestral studio, a crowded open meeting that fluctuated between deep silence and emotional protest, I collapsed back into my office at two o'clock. On the top of the in-tray was Personnel Circular 443, emanating from London, informing me that the BBC had decided to increase the size of its wedding presents to staff from £50 to £75, after the application of RPI since the last uplift, and describing a new and centralised administrative procedure by which I could trigger this bureaucratised act of good will. You did not have to be Scrooge or against the institution of marriage to think this was madness. A template letter setting out how I and other controllers should convey the corporation's bounteousness to each happy couple seemed, on that day, to take the ultimate prize for incongruity.

It is not a comfortable feeling to be the dispenser of so many P45s, though even to say so seems to imply, quite wrongly, that you put your own discomfort above that of people whose livelihood you have ended or put at risk. First you have to be persuaded that it is the right thing to do, and then conquer the thought that however convincing the case, you may be wrong, or that the changes you are introducing are merely an expression of managerial fashion. Inevitably in large companies people scan the internal horizons to spot inequity between departments. In an organisation with some level of humanity the process of implementation takes some months, during which time you look at people in the lift and try to remember whether they were amongst the unlucky ones. People leave, staff see gaps at nearby desks or around canteen tables, a process of corporate bereavement begins. The incoming tide of fresh preoccupations seems to cover only a part of the beach.

Despite the torrid start, the first two and a half years at the BBC were the most exhilarating of all. Although on the organisational charts the controllers in the nations might be classified as middle managers, the territorial responsibility and distance from London gave the job a more elevated feel. Some reckoned that the four best jobs in the BBC were DG and the three national controllers. National controllers had a distinct territory, a visible headquarters, a direct link to a governor, and a symphony orchestra to boot. Despite the common assumption of successive controllers that they enjoyed greater freedom than their successors, the degree of financial discretion was large and liberating, and one that regional directors of clearing banks, if any remain, would have envied.

The touch from London was, at first, light. Michael Checkland, who had developed a close relationship with Geraint Stanley Jones, understood the psychology of the BBC's 'nations'. It was said he scarcely ever attended a Broadcasting Council meeting without springing some new money from his back pocket. When we delivered 40 per cent more savings than asked for from the review of the BBC Wales operation, he understood the value of incentives and the needs of a new controller, and contrived to allow us to keep the excess for investment. This lightness transmitted itself to Ron Neil, who brought passion and humanity to the task, and created an easy collegiality around the regional directorate table, even when some of us were at our tetchiest. There was soon to be a distinct change of tone.

Succession at the top of the BBC is never easy. The selection of popes seems more open, and it is no doubt easier to get permission for a small chimney to poke out of the Sistine Chapel than out of Broadcasting House's listed bulk. A funnel would suit the latter better. The sacking of Alasdair Milne in 1987 was still fresh in people's memory, as was the part played in that event by the National Governor for Wales, John Parry, whose vote switch was thought to have done for the Scot. This time round the closed, pre-Nolan nature of the process, if such it could be called, rankled with some of the would-be *papabile*, notably John Tusa, and drew a final riposte from Michael Checkland at his own nervously jolly farewell dinner. He made a pointed reference to being interviewed for the top job when he himself became DG in 1987, adding, 'a fact that I mention only for those historians amongst you'. The toss-up between a full extension of Checkland's contract and the appointment of his deputy was decided in favour of Birt, with a limited extension for Checkland, obliging both men to endure a cruelly long, 20-month handover period.

The fact that a whole decade in the BBC's history was subsequently demonised around the name of John Birt seemed excessive then and absurd in retrospect. It resulted in both an undervaluing of what

Michael Checkland had put in train and a quite irrational level of criticism of his successor that had the same rabid quality as the neocon assault on Clinton, though the latter gave rather more spectacular cause. There were big issues at stake, but it didn't help John Birt that his name was so short and began with B. The irresistible lure of alliteration to subeditors meant that it became Birt's BBC, the identification was total. It's possible that his seven years in office might have played differently in the press had his name been more like Carleton-Greene.

The conventional analysis is that Checkland wanted to work with the grain of the institution, whereas Birt did not. There is little doubt that the BBC's civil service organisational model, put in place by Lord Reith, needed changing. But if there is some validity in the portrayal of Checkland as the Gorbachev of the BBC, it is a nonsense to try to portray Birt as either Lenin or Stalin. Whereas Checkland and Birt may have differed on the degree of necessary organisational change, they were indistinguishable in their regard for the BBC's core purpose.

There was also the chairman factor. Neither Checkland nor Birt were helped by having as chairman someone who, despite his qualities, could not but seem anachronistic. Whereas Checkland-Hussey might have made for a soft cop-hard cop duo in that order, the Hussey-Birt pairing meant only old cop and young cop, both hard. When the playwright Dennis Potter launched a wildly abusive attack at the Edinburgh Festival in 1993, although attacking John Birt's reforms, it was the Hussey-Birt pairing and Hussey's tones that, cruelly, enabled him to use 'croak voiced Daleks' as the headline grabbing metaphor. Even before Birt and Hussey fell-out over the Martin Bashir interview with Princess Diana (Hussey's wife was a lady in waiting to the Queen), Hussey may have given Birt full support, but he did not have the skills or image to give him cover. For that reason Christopher Bland's arrival as Chairman in 1996 was greeted with immense relief, and not only by the besieged DG.

The choice of John Birt set a course for a pivotal decade in which the BBC was faced with its own version of climate change: an all encompassing ecological shift evidenced in fundamental changes in technology, and in the competitive, political and cultural environments. It moved us from income growth to real term decline, from duopoly to multi-channel, from analogue to digital, from studio to desktop, from the centrality of the producer to the centrality of the audience, from cheap sports contracts to cripplingly expensive ones, from a monopoly on its own production to statutory quotas for independent producers, and from public good to private subscription in the wider market. In short, from the comfort of universal belief in the corporation to the reality of agnosticism and the first poisonous shoots of atheism amongst competitors, politicians and, more worryingly, a measurable fraction of the public.

That the BBC managed to respond to this complex, ever-changing external environment, and to emerge as a stronger beast at the end of the decade, spoke volumes for the resilience of the staff, but spoke most loudly of all for the remarkable strategic insight of John Birt, that secured for public broadcasting in the UK not only a space but a dominance in the new environment that its biggest rival, Rupert Murdoch, would have given his right arm to prevent. The same unusual degree of focus that was needed to prevent a large organisation with a deeply ingrained culture from falling back on older default positions and habits, also meant inevitable disagreements and an unavoidable unpopularity. That might have been mitigated somewhat if John Birt had had the skills of Olivier and Shakespeare for a speech writer, but I doubt that any director general pushing that amount of change for that long would ever have been loved.

As each wave of change broke onto the beach the rising swell of the next could be seen rolling in. Flotillas of consultants surfed in on each, before paddling out to catch another. To adopt a more inland metaphor, it was said that the BBC had consultants like some people had mice. For the most part the mice that scurried along our skirting boards were fearsomely bright, though often alarmingly young. Ron Neil once joked that it was not difficult to arrange a meeting with them, 'as long as you avoid their bath time'.

The best were intellectually challenging, awesomely well-informed, and a privilege to work with, even if it soon became apparent that for any problem there were always four possible solutions, and the right one, in all circumstances, was number three. For those interested in such things, Option 1 was the status quo, Option 2 mere tinkering, Option 3 the option for real change while Option 4 was going too far. The jokes themselves, especially among the upper echelons, seemed more an expression of nervous discomfort about the effects of reform than of hostility to its substance. Even senior people convinced of the necessity of radical measures fretted lest the surgery should produce a permanent personality change, rather than just a cure, in a cherished old aunt. The jokes were also sometimes a handy bridge to some of the more sceptical troops.

* * * *

The unavoidably painful start in Wales had to have a creative purpose beyond mere survival. It was all very well to tell the staff that we were cutting in order to grow, on the sound gardener's principle that a well-pruned tree bears more fruit, but they wanted and deserved proof. Within two years we were producing more than ever before, both for Wales and for network radio and television, though the latter was, in my view, far from sufficient.

The main opportunity for development was transparently clear. Since 1982 and the launch of S4C, the Welsh-speaking community, as both audience and producers, had enjoyed a hard won but generous dispensation, in terms of hours of output, pounds spent, and programme range. Total output in Welsh far exceeded the English language programming made in, by and for Wales, notwithstanding the expansion of English hours after all Welsh language programmes moved from BBC1 and ITV to S4C.

The disparity held, even if you added together the services of BBC Wales and HTV Wales, and seemed even greater when you took into account that the majority of the output for Wales consisted of the BBC Wales and HTV news services, whose two main early evening programmes at that time ran head to head. S4C's non-news output in Welsh ran to 26 hours a week in 1990-1, against a total of twelve hours a week in English from the combined forces of BBC Wales and HTV Wales. There was also a disparity in funding, with the cost of the S4C/BBC output in Welsh greatly exceeding the combined BBC/HTV spend on English language programmes for Wales – £65m against £25m.

While it was possible to argue that these comparisons did not take account of the vast range of English output available from UK networks – a belief that regional programmes are a local vitamin supplement and not the main meal – it was obvious that the monoglot English-speaking majority did not enjoy as full a reflection of Welsh life and talent as the Welsh-speaking minority, and the demand for more was evident from research, phone-ins and letters to newspapers as well as my own gut.

Similarly, the creative community felt that there were fewer opportunities available to work in English. Writers griped about having to get their scripts translated into Welsh if they were to stand a reasonable chance of being commissioned. They were right. The funding for BBC

Wales services was not ungenerous compared with ITV's regions or even compared with the BBC's own English regions, but it had to be split across both languages in radio and television. It was best illustrated in radio, where BBC Radio Scotland's annual budget was not far short of the combined budget of Radio Cymru and Radio Wales.

In television, the service was also necessarily predicated on being an opt-out from a UK service rather than a free-standing national service as on S4C. In this situation it was only by winning a bigger share of UK network output, particularly in more expensive genres, that those working in English could enjoy the range of opportunity afforded by S4C, and at the turn of the decade that output was minimal.

There were also complaints that career paths in the BBC were considerably shorter for non-Welsh-speakers. One back room worker, convinced until the day of his retirement that he was the victim of linguistic discrimination had a badge made for his last day carrying the words 'Faith, Hope and Parity'. While this was a handy grievance, especially for the untalented, it was not always without substance. There was plenty of anecdotal evidence that much good talent had been lost to Welsh broadcasting as a result. It was not even in the interests of the Welsh language to allow such grievances to fester.

Not only was new investment needed, but the new priority had to be made clearly manifest. For that reason the posts of head of radio and head of television, both of which required bilingual appointments, were replaced with two posts that joined radio and television under a head of Welsh language programmes and a head of English language programmes, thus clearing one avenue of advancement for non-Welsh-speakers. It is perhaps significant that through all the organisational changes that have naturally ensued in the subsequent sixteen years, it is one change that has endured.

The first occupants of the two posts came from outside the BBC. Michael Chaplin, followed me from Newcastle to Cardiff. A man of confident style and a witty, Geordie directness, he also enjoyed taking risks, the first being to turn up for the interview with the Welsh National Governor in a loud tartan jacket that looked unmistakably Scottish. Michael became the first head of English language programmes, and brought to it an unusual mixture of easy urbanity and a robust non-metropolitan sensibility. Always at heart a writer – very much his father's son – he later left us in order to write full time and gave the BBC the long running series, *Monarch of the Glen*.

Gwyn Pritchard, who had been a colleague in current affairs at

HTV, took on the equivalent Welsh language job, joining from Channel 4 where he had been the senior commissioning editor for education. His Channel 4 experience had given him an empathy with independent producers to add to the seriousness of the documentary maker. He soon plugged a long-standing gap in that genre for S4C.

The scale of change also demanded an urgent refocusing of all the technical areas. Stephen Reid, a music-loving resources manager, joined us from Granada to drive the process with both flair and punctilious care. Wyn Mears, who had been the UK marketing director at the Wales Tourist Board, came aboard to tread the difficult ground between the executive, its governors and the Broadcasting Council for Wales, as the latter's secretary and our head of corporate affairs. Keith Rawlings, a personnel professional from the steel industry, joined to face the unenviable task of dealing with the consequences of a decade of painful organisational change, which he carried out with calm and warmth. Helen Manson, who had been my PA at HTV, came to keep a firm rein on my office. Phil Davies, the head of finance, provided crucial continuity and rock-like assurance. Quiet, not to say, lugubrious, he understood even the most arcane idiosyncrasies of the BBC's systems and, unfazed by crisis or by change, adjusted us all, quietly and with Stakhanovite application, to each successive wave.

Despite the endless demands for further economies, that persisted from my first day in the BBC to my last, it was a team that did manage to produce a deal of creative change and a significant increase in the total output for Wales. Michael Chaplin and Gwyn Pritchard were both keen to extend the range of the services in their care. Michael had found that 80 per cent of his output was tied up in news and sport, while Gwyn found that the service to S4C was dominated by long running strands, notably the daily soap opera, *Pobl y Cwm*, but also a weekly programme of hymn-singing. Both needed to get outside their respective straitjackets. Michael had the advantage of being able, quite quickly, to increase and broaden the weekly output in English.

Gwyn, constrained by the statutory ten hours the BBC had to deliver to S4C, decided to hand over the hymn-singing programme to S4C so that they could commission it from independents. With the money that was freed up he launched S4C's first substantial single issue documentary series, *O Flaen dy Lygaid* (Before your Eyes), as well as commissioning some dramas. We came to an ageement with S4C that they would buy additional weeks of *Pobl y Cwm* to extend its run and renegotiated the deal that had given HTV a monopoly of current affairs programming on S4C from 1982. There was no sense in refusing to exploit fully, through an extended format, the journalistic talent that had been nurtured in BBC Wales news on radio and television. The resulting current affairs programme, *Taro Naw* (On the stroke of nine) proved to be competitive and long lasting and became the first Welsh language programme to lift the Royal Television Society's regional current affairs award.

In radio new schedules were launched, although we had to wait a little longer for investment to extend the transmission hours of both Radio Wales and Radio Cymru through the evening, something that was standard practice for any other station. Radio Wales was particularly disadvantaged by being able to transmit only on the Medium Wave, a frequency band that, as audiences well knew, gave an inferior sound quality to VHF. It took an eight-year battle to put that right. While Radio Cymru needed to be revamped to appeal, without loss of substance, to a younger audience – in this case we meant anyone under 50 – the priority for Radio Wales was to give the output much greater substance and bite. The work of Dai Smith and Nick Evans, the station editor, paid off in 1997, when Radio Wales was not only named Sony radio station of the year but also won a total of seven Sony awards, then the record number by a single station in one year.

News was more than well represented in the BBC's senior management. John Birt, when deputy director general, had recast the whole news and current affairs directorate, choosing Ron Neil to lead the process. The latter had by now become managing director of regional broadcasting, with Mark Byford, another network news graduate as his deputy. A decade later it was Mark who took the hospital pass as Acting DG, after the Hutton inquiry and Greg Dyke's precipitate departure. Together, Ron and Mark, led a crusade to get regional news to report 'that which is significant in people's lives' rather than to peddle a clichéd diet of frothy human interest stories laced with a catalogue of criminal acts and convictions. This was one issue on which I needed no persuading.

The need to scrutinise, assess and present Welsh affairs with at least the same rigour, seriousness and intelligence as is given by the main networks to British and world issues has always seemed to me to be the one worthwhile mission for Welsh journalism: to create a purposeful journalism that is both local and national but has none of the pejorative overtones of the provincial. But it is not an easy mission to accomplish, partly because the culture of journalism outside London is underdeveloped and usually under-resourced, and, it has to be said, the conduct

of public affairs is not always pursued at a level that encourages such
an approach. However, presenters and correspondents such as
Vaughan Roderick, Glyn Mathias, Guto Harri, Dewi Llwyd and David
Williams showed that our aspirations could be realised.

Wales Today, the bedrock of the BBC Wales television service was
revamped, more specialist correspondents were recruited to bring
greater expertise to bear on health, education, business and the
environment. Bethan Kilfoil became our European correspondent in
Brussels, the first full-time BBC foreign correspondent from any
region, and it was revealing to find that the more open habits of the
European Commission sometimes allowed her to find out more about
Welsh policy intentions than her colleagues were able to do in Cardiff.

We also had a gap to fill in the arts. On the back of a report I had
commissioned on the relationship between BBC Wales and the arts, we
established an arts and music department under Hilary Boulding. She
came to us from BBC Scotland and quickly pulled together a young
and talented team that built a high reputation for music programmes
and for a regular arts programme, *The Slate*. Within the next five years
it became one of the few programme titles that, in surveys, the public
could recall unprompted. It also became noted, not to say notorious for
Eddie Ladd's actorly presentation.

The aim was to create a regular presence for the arts for 40 weeks
of the year, in a conscious rededication to the purposes that had been
pursued by BBC staff in Wales through seven decades, even if shifting
the emphasis way from constant evaluation of the past to reflecting
contemporary Welsh culture. It produced documentary treatments of
subjects as varied as the painter Shani Rys James, Welsh rock music,
men's magazines, and collaborations with companies such as Moving
Being and Cyrff Ystwyth, a dance company for the physically and
mentally disadvantaged, the last effectively the commissioning of a new
work. *The Slate* was complemented by long running arts programmes
on Radio Wales and Radio Cymru as well as S4C.

The department, this time in harness with a new department for
factual programmes, also began a chain of programming on architecture that I was keen to encourage. It started in spectacular fashion with
a series on the decommissioning of the Trawsfynydd nuclear power
station – two great cubes designed in the early 1960s by Basil Spence,
the architect of Coventry cathedral, a fact that most people had forgotten. I have always believed that the series was a model of imaginative
public service broadcasting, in that it bridged current affairs, education

and art and tackled the connections between supposedly different problems and very different disciplines. Here were two small communities in Blaenau Ffestiniog and Trawsfynydd confronted by a scientific and environmental problem of world significance as well as by a local economic crisis. To confront those issues we assembled the nuclear industry, engineers, architects, artists and employment agencies, as well as the local people.

The architectural line-up was impressive. James Wines, a pioneer of 'green architecture' came from New York, the Ushida-Findlay partnership, a husband and wife team, from Tokyo and Arup Associates and Wil Alsop from Britain. They each gathered teams from across the arts and sciences. In addition, the landscape photographer, John Davies, produced highly atmospheric photographs of the surrounding area, and a charity assembled an education programme for local primary and secondary schools. The teams were given a month to talk to local people and organisations.

In the final debate recorded in the turbine hall Wil Alsop's scheme seemed to be a favourite until, under questioning, he became rather contemptuous of his audience, confirming prejudices about arrogant architects. Nevertheless, in the final vote Arup's scheme pipped his own by only one vote. Arup envisaged entombing Basil Spence's cubes in sculpted hills of waste slate that had disfigured Blaenau Ffestiniog for a century and a half, thus killing two birds with one stone. Although *Power to Change* became the only 'regional' programme I know to have warranted a half page in the *New York Times*, the decommissioning debate, sadly, resumed a more sterile course.

We had better luck a few years later when we ran an architectural competition to find, a 'house of the future' that ended, thanks to the National Museum's support, in the building of the winning proposal at the Museum of Welsh Life at St. Fagans. The house still stands, even as the future slowly overtakes it.

Although many of these developments were already underway we had been obliged in 1993, as part of a BBC-wide exercise, to embark on a further review of our programme strategies. The overall project was led by Alan Yentob and by Liz Forgan, who had not long arrived from the *Guardian* to take control of BBC Radio. She told a staff meeting in Cardiff that she had found the BBC to be a remarkable place: 'Open any cupboard and strategies fall out on top of you.' Dai Smith, who had by this time forsaken his history chair at Cardiff University to become, first, editor of Radio Wales and then a successor to Michael Chaplin as head of English language programmes, was a powerful influence on the work in Wales. We shared a liking for the big picture, and the project allowed us to project a coherence for our plans across all our services, in a way that fitted the organisation and its output to an emerging Welsh *zeitgeist*.

It was the sort of exercise that the BBC's critics at the time could easily have lampooned – BBC Wales's own report ran to more than 200 pages – but it was an extraordinarily informative exercise that gave us a much more nuanced view of the audience and community that we were serving. The research that underpinned it challenged some hunches and gave real substance to others. It also counselled us against easy generalisations. It certainly went beyond rhetoric.

The work reminded us of the vanishing monoliths of Welsh life in industry, religion, language and attitudes, and forced us to ask whether our responses had kept pace. We became acutely conscious of a more varied and plural Wales than the common stereotypes allowed for. For instance, it showed us that whereas in England, Scotland and Northern Ireland the percentage of their populations born within their borders was still well above 90 per cent, in Wales it was below 80 per cent, significantly different despite the concentrations of immigration elsewhere. The assumption that those who identified themselves as primarily Welsh were more likely to be Welsh-speaking – an assumption challenged by Denis Balsom's survey in the 1980s – was further confirmed in this work, 62 per cent of 'Welsh identifiers' did not speak the language.

When we came to look at the interest in money and business we concluded that if the average Welshman was 'no longer a hymn-singing miner reading Engels, [he or she] was never a yuppie'. Although share-holding amongst Welsh people had risen over the decade from 1983 to 1993 from 7 per cent to 21 per cent, close to the UK average, they were far less likely to use credit cards. The proportion with medical insurance was half the UK average.

The observed appetite for history programmes was underlined by a higher propensity to read history books and visit historic buildings, as well as the profusion of historical societies in every county. We concluded that nostalgia was a valid response to the scale and rapidity of economic and social change. It more than justified the effort that went into *All Our Lives*, an 18-part series that created an oral history archive of the twentieth century that is now lodged at the National History Museum at St. Fagans. The success of history on television persists, as the continuing diet of such programmes shows. Given the investment that we had started to make, as well as the continued journalistic push within the BBC, it was reassuring to find that Welsh people also displayed a greater appetite for news and current affairs and documentaries than elsewhere.

Such work was often disparaged as research driven programming, a mechanistic process that devalued the producer's creative impulse and judgement. But critics seldom stopped to consider how it was used. The project gave our commissioners and producers a clearer picture of Wales and the ways in which it differed from other parts of the UK. Knowing our terrain better, that knowledge sparked creative responses. It told us where we were in touch with our audiences and where we were ahead of or behind them. It also equipped us to fight the battle for resources more intelligently in tight times, taking account of changes that required one to justify developments with a robust case rather than rely, as of old, on annual increases in baseline funding. Such work also informed those in London who allocated money to nations and regions that they often knew only at a distance. Comfortingly, it found that satisfaction with the BBC in general and with regional news in particular was higher in Wales than in any other part of Britain. We were not getting it wrong.

There were two areas where our services for Wales ran into trouble, the one problem rather exotic and the other more serious. The former had to do with the revamping of Radio Cymru that brought about the strangest strike in the history of British industrial relations. The new editor of the station, Aled Glynne Davies, who had done some pioneer-ing work in establishing a style and vocabulary for the Welsh language suitable for a popular radio service, had been appointed its editor on the strength of an amusing job application. It purported to be a letter from Mrs Jones, Llanrug, the mythical average listener to the station. The wrong side of 70 and living in a village on the edge of Snowdonia 'she' reminded us that her son had married Mandy, a girl from the fleshpots of south Wales, who did not speak Welsh, although her children, Jonathan and Adrian, attended Welsh language schools. She lamented the fact that the station had little appeal for her own children and grandchildren, although plenty for Mrs Griffiths, her lemon-sucking neighbour.

On the back of a witty and perceptive bid Aled set to, repositioning Radio Cymru in order to draw younger families and Welsh learners into the folds of its listeners and dispelling the impression that, polished service though it had been, the station was the 'Welsh tannoy in God's waiting room'. Change in radio is never easy, as I had found out in my first months at the BBC when trying to defend the moving of Radio 4's Woman's Hour from the afternoon to the morning to a frighteningly hostile audience at the British conference of the Women's Institute at Aberystwyth – they wanted blood rather than jam and Jerusalem.

But the sound of a more demotic Welsh at key points on Radio Cymru and, during the evening hours, a willingness to play some English records, albeit requested and presented in Welsh, proved too much for some traditionalists. It also aroused an existential reflex that had developed in the Welsh language community in recent decades, 'I campaign, therefore I am.'

The opposition to the changes was at times vitriolic and some of the attacks on Aled Glynne Davies savagely and inexcusably personal. Our stand at the National Eisteddfod was liberally fly-posted with protest leaflets, a familiar hazard of Welsh institutional life. But we were dumbstruck when, without warning, we were faced with a strike by the poets who took part in our weekly contest of poetic skills, *Ymryson y Beirdd*, between teams drawn from villages across Wales.

We issued a statement to the effect that this was an historic moment in industrial relations and that we were prepared to commission a *pryddest radio* (a radio ode) to commemorate it. Given that the strikers were experts in the traditional strict metres, we acknowledged their astonishing ability to work to rule but in any negotiations could not guarantee that our representatives would have the same skills. Although the bardic strike was short-lived, the issues became a matter of more serious debate within the Broadcasting Council for Wales. To anyone outside and to a fair few within, it all seemed esoteric, but it rumbled on for more than a year, before petering out, though some protesters threatened not to pay their licence fee. Aled's changes were fully vindicated by the growing audience and a 50 per cent increase in listeners in the middle age ranges.

A year into these changes, during the annual performance review ritual, Aled explained his approach to a team from London that included an accountant with a loud voice, who had come from the consumer goods industry and would have looked at home in the bar of a Surrey golf club. Aled described his diverse audience. 'Ah. I see,' said the accountant, 'Two groups, children and peasants in the hills.' There was a heavy thud as our jaws hit the table.

A more serious problem arose over rights to Welsh rugby, a dispute that threatened to disrupt the whole relationship with S4C. The BBC had made a massive investment in rugby over decades, in airtime and in skill. In the 1970s and 1980s a BBC Wales director, Dewi Griffiths, had written the early rule book on rugby coverage, and on screen it was easy to spot an English or Scottish director, more used to soccer, struggling to master the very different flow of the rugby game. In the 1990s the cash investment increased exponentially as competition from Sky drove up the price of sports rights. Corporate strategists had warned us that in the new climate it was inevitable that the BBC would, from time to time, lose sports contracts. That did not make it any easier when it happened.

Early in 1997, the newly appointed national governor for Wales, Roger Jones and I had just emerged from a function in Gwydyr House in Whitehall when I took a call from Arthur Emyr to say that we had lost the rights to Welsh rugby to S4C. It was a massive blow, far and away the lowest point in my ten years at the BBC. Rugby was at the heart of our television service, both its content and its economics, and a key to our identification with the Welsh audience. Much of our rugby coverage had been available back to back on both BBC Wales and S4C, serving both languages alike. Now it was to be available primarily in Welsh only, with a junior ration delivered, as part of the deal, to our main competitor, HTV. Audiences to rugby would be smaller, while the non-Welsh-speaking majority would be significantly disadvantaged in a central portion of popular viewing.

We had no complaint about HTV's involvement. ITV was an acknowledged competitor and they were, understandably, taking advantage of the situation. But S4C's action raised serious policy issues. Whereas our bid was backed by additional money for Wales from London, the S4C bid was, inevitably and substantially, a diversion of its existing and already tight resources. It also raised the question of whether two publicly-funded organisations should compete against each other to create a false market, what economists would call nugatory competition. Interestingly, I discovered later that in Ireland, RTE and TG4, the Irish language channel, have a protocol that prevents such competition.

More worryingly, the row fundamentally altered attitudes towards S4C at the centre of the BBC overnight. The BBC's contribution of 10 hours a week of programmes to S4C had, at its inception, been the first ever example of the use of the licence fee for the benefit of another public service broadcaster. The annual value of those programmes was, by 1997, more than £17m. Now the cushion of that free resource was being used against us. Suddenly, this was a competitive relationship, rather than the collaborative one that had been envisaged in 1982 when Willie Whitelaw, reminded of the complexity of the new arrangements, had said that 'good chaps could make anything work'.

Welsh-speaking programme makers in the BBC, all of whom believed deeply in S4C's mission and in their own contribution to it, felt disoriented. Roger Jones indulged his liking for military metaphors with abandon. The degree of anger at the centre was such that I had to remind many London colleagues that the BBC had to remain committed to Welsh language broadcasting and that we should do everything to avoid a meltdown. That was not easy in the face of such clear signals that there was no reciprocity in the relationship.

A helicopter view of this fracas would paint a slightly different picture. In 1982 S4C had naturally felt at some disadvantage to the two big suppliers. HTV had secured a programme supply contract whose generous terms left a bitter taste in S4C mouths. The BBC, unlike HTV, had been supportive of the creation of the channel and even supplied its first two chief executives, Owen Edwards and Geraint Stanley Jones. But at the outset it had adopted a somewhat paternal tone towards the newcomer that rankled with S4C and did not fit the 1990s. As someone who had come from ITV, I hoped that I was more sensitive to their feelings, but some negativity towards the BBC seemed to be almost hard-wired into S4C's thinking.

The 1990 Broadcasting Act had cut S4C loose from its ties to ITV's Independent Broadcasting Authority, making it an authority in its own right and switched its funding from a levy on the ITV companies to a straight subvention from government. It had also allowed S4C to sell its own advertising. The subsequent 1996 Act gave it further freedom to operate commercially, especially in the digital field. S4C had also lobbied to end the system whereby the BBC's national governor was, ex-officio, a member of the S4C Authority. Despite the regular routines of collaboration that still saw BBC programmes providing most of S4C's top ten and top twenty most popular programmes year in year out, and despite the continuing deep commitment of our programme staff, these changes to the institutional framework began to change the underlying psychology of the relationship.

During the 1990s, too, both BBC and S4C were operating with less buoyant revenues than in the 1980s. Huw Jones, S4C's first chief executive without a BBC background, was starting a long struggle to fund the move into digital broadcasting and to shore up the Welsh-speaking audience in a multi-channel world. At the BBC I was struggling to end the under-provision in English, again within a tightening financial corset, inevitably restraining any growth in our spend on S4C. It was nevertheless a disappointment to find that many at S4C thought the BBC's involvement was a problem for the channel rather than an asset. The relationship did not break down after the rugby row, but had a different edge to it thereafter.

The decade ended with a double coda – devolution and digital television – that both spoke of the place of Wales within the broadcasting system. The prospect of digital had occasioned much excitement in the BBC, encouraged by John Birt whose enthusiasm had been fired by a visit to Microsoft's founder, Bill Gates. At the time it felt as if the mist was slow to clear on these issues although, with hindsight, things moved with extraordinary rapidity. Websites had started to develop all over the BBC in a completely ad hoc fashion, depending on whether a programme team had within it someone who was early into exploring the web. More often than not their design was amateurish. Individuals were often ahead of the institution. Similarly in radio, the pace at which we moved to desktop technologies for editing sound was accelerated, in part because some staff started taking work home where they could edit material on computers in their bedrooms, rather than on outdated technology at work.

There was much gnashing of teeth when the order came to shut down every BBC website, but it was the essential precursor to creating the BBC online site that, within a short space of time proved to be one of the most visited sites in the world. Keith Jones, the only graduate in the Wales management team from a non-arts background – in a previous career he had taught my children mathematics – pulled our own plans together. They included *Cymru'r Byd*, the Welsh language news site that became, in effect, the first daily Welsh language newspaper.

Digital broadcasting was a trickier proposition to grasp as the gap between its theoretical potential and its practical capacity in the earliest stages was substantial, and seemed to change by the month. At one minute we were enthused by the prospect of unlimited spectrum to develop our services, only to be discouraged the next by some newly discovered limitation. There were the usual alarums about engineering-led propositions that had a poor fit with the geography of community. Conscious of the battles over radio and television transmission in Wales that had studded the last eighty years and still persisted, we were anxious that the mistakes of the past should not be repeated.

Our worst fears were confirmed in radio, when the government allocated space for the new digital services. Whereas it gave the BBC's UK services their own digital multiplex, BBC radio services in the 'nations' and local radio in England were simply guaranteed space on a multiplex that would be controlled by commercial radio. In a speech at the Celtic Film and Television Festival I protested that this was mixing oil and water, and would put Radio Wales and Radio Cymru at a huge disadvantage on their very own patch. If anything it was an understatement. BBC Radios 1 to 5 in digital form reached parts of Wales a whole decade before the two Welsh services. Under the still current dispensation some parts will be denied them for the foreseeable future.

There was more at stake in television. At least our radio services were free-standing stations with their own frequencies on VHF or Medium wave. That was not the case in television, where our services were opt-outs from BBC1 and BBC2, the equivalent of leasehold plots in a wider estate. We did not want to be rid of these opt-outs, after all they were in a prime position on the first channels at the top of the new electronic programme guides. But we did want to secure for Wales a chunk of freehold digital real estate, a place where the service for Wales could exist and develop less bound by the constraints of a highly competitive schedule designed elsewhere for another purpose.

The first digital service went on air in 1998, under the title BBC Choice, but it was obviously experimental, little more than radio on television produced from a shoebox of a studio at Llandaff. The BBC's ultimate decision to make space for four national versions of BBC2 available in digital was an important milestone. By simultaneously transmitting English, Scottish, Welsh and Northern Irish versions of BBC2 it took away the argument that every opt-out deprived someone else of the service from London, and took us out of a cul de sac into an open-ended avenue of possibilities.

In the wake of the devolution referendum of 1997, it seemed a fitting development.

8 Nations and regions

The BBC is a reasonable analogue for the pre-Assembly British state. It is centrally driven by two legislative chambers, the executive board and now the BBC Trust. Its chief executive, the director general, is granted presidential status and has a remarkably direct influence on the tone of every part of an institution employing more than 20,000 people. In Scotland, Wales and Northern Ireland it has territorial administrations, with substantial freedom of action but no formal autonomy, and in receipt of funding that, in England, is regarded as generous.

These administrations are headed by national Controllers who are obliged to face in two directions – in my case, representing the BBC in Wales and Wales in the BBC, like the pre-1999 Welsh secretaries of state. From time to time this can produce a degree of mistrust at both ends of the M4, staff in Cardiff sometimes suspicious that you are simply doing London's bidding, senior managers in London suspicious that they are spending hard cash in response to cultural and political forces that they dimly understand or, perhaps, believe overstated.

Outside the institution titles such as Controller Wales or Controller Scotland are often regarded as either hilarious or bombastic depending on your inclination. When linked to a country rather than a task, they have a communistic ring. One academic commentator would write articles that always referred to me by the title rather than by name, which implied, purposely I assume, some impersonal Orwellian Big Brother. Ironically, it was just at this time that the BBC stopped using job titles or their initials internally and started using names instead.

In Cardiff the staff happily followed suit, with the exception of union officials who, presumably, liked the implied distance and, rather more surprisingly, our foremost television presenter at the time, Vincent Kane, a Welsh Paxman whose fearless interrogations on radio and screen masked a more conservative bent.

At the centre of the BBC you would normally encounter three very different reactions to the nations in general and Wales in particular: first, the instinctive understanding and empathy of some, usually because of a direct connection or some non-metropolitan past; second, the jocular reaction of a larger group who, with a broad grin and a wink, would consider the 'national regions' a bit of a ramp; third, and uncomfortably common, an incomprehension that saw the BBC's regional role as a tiresome irrelevance, to be put up with like a distant and nerdy cousin at a wedding.

I gently suggested to the BBC's Governors on their visit to Cardiff in 1991 that where such negative attitudes existed they were 'at least as worthy of the BBC's imaginative attention as the perils of sexism, racism or sexual harassment', and offered them lines from the geography lesson from G.K.Chesterton's *Songs of Education*:

> Gibraltar's a rock that you see very plain
> And attached to its base is the district of Spain.

The following summer the chairs of fifteen task forces, created to reformulate the BBC's purposes in preparation for the renewal of our Royal Charter, met in a swank hotel on the edge of Salisbury Plain to consider our draft reports. I was there as chair of the task force on entertainment. Unfortunately, the report on regional broadcasting was one of the weaker documents and it allowed sceptics to pounce. On a sunny day, with the conference room's French windows open to the lush garden, John McCormick, controller Scotland, Mark Byford, then number two in regional broadcasting, and I had to argue long and hard against some who thought that the BBC should get out of regional broadcasting altogether. We could not conceive that the BBC would ever do such a thing, and comforted ourselves that thinking the unthinkable was in the spirit of the exercise. Nevertheless, the rumble of army artillery in the distance increased the sense of foreboding.

Of the handful of policy issues that dominated the 1990s – money, efficiencies, charter renewal, digitalisation, and devolution – access to the BBC's UK networks was the most constant concern.

By now there is a general appreciation within Wales of the importance of contributing to the UK networks, but in 1990 that feeling was not universal. There were a number on the staff who thought that our job was solely to deliver a service in Wales for Wales, all else was a distraction designed to solicit empty approbation from without. That was not a view shared by successive BBC Wales controllers or by their heads of programmes, even if most of us thought that primacy should be accorded to giving Welsh people 'a sense of themselves'. But the task had been sufficiently uphill over decades both to arm sceptics and discourage the optimistic. It was clear that the primary virtue for broadcasters outside London was not genius but stamina, an ability to return to the upright position like a weighted doll after every punch.

While attitudes towards Wales on the sixth floor of Television Centre have rarely paid much attention to political correctness, it is true that network production was not a priority for Welsh broadcasters during a long period, particularly following the launch of S4C in 1982, when the development of the services within Wales, in both languages, became a major task. This was not the case in Scotland where both BBC Scotland and Scottish Television, undistracted by local expansion, made more concerted attempts to build their network output far earlier than Wales, in a decade when the BBC's income was still growing, so that gains did not necessarily come at the expense of London departments.

In contrast, HTV's network output, primarily drama, came mainly from HTV West in Bristol. HTV Wales, charged with developing and delivering nine profitable hours of programmes a week to S4C and increasing its hours in English for Wales, provided only an occasional network programme for ITV or Channel Four. As part of a more unified organisation than ITV's often dysfunctional federation, BBC Wales was better placed and it had a notable success in the late 1980s with *District Nurse*, produced by Tony Holland and Julia Smith, brought in fresh from their success in launching *Eastenders*, but also involving a number of Welsh writers. In an era when BBC2 ran regular live orchestral concerts, St. David's Hall was also much visited, not least for the biennial Cardiff Singer of the World competition. When the channel's enthusiasm for live concerts cooled, only Cardiff Singer survived and by the beginning of the 1990s BBC Wales's total network contribution was worryingly low.

This was not altogether unwelcome in Television Centre, and not only because relationships between Cardiff and London had been tense. When I paid my first courtesy call on Paul Fox, one of the giants of the industry, then in his last year as Managing Director Television, I told him I hoped to increase Wales's contributions to the network. 'Why would you want to do that?' he replied, releasing a discouragingly long sigh. That said, he was as solid as a tank when it came to negotiating the rugby contracts.

Drama was an area of painful frustration, interspersed with sporadic achievement. Michael Checkland had kept the flame of network drama alive in Wales in the late 1980s with a direct subvention,

needed to counter resistance from the Controller of BBC1, Jonathan
Powell. As part of the agreement on my first round of savings, this was
made permanent, giving Ruth Caleb room to build on her first projects
after her secondment to Cardiff in 1989. Ruth is one of the BBC's star
drama producers, though her predilection for weighty single dramas
dealing with social issues, is now less in vogue with commissioners
pressured by a more competitive climate.

She had already produced, in the aftermath of the 1985 miners'
strike, Karl Francis's *Ms Rhymney Valley*, and her personal reputation
was a key factor in securing the commissioning of two further Karl
Francis projects, one that dealt with alcoholism and abuse, *Morphine
and Dolly Mixtures*, and *Civvies*, a raw series depicting the impact of
Northern Ireland on a group of paras who had left the army. *Trip Trap*
with Kevin Whateley dealt with wife battering, and Dawn French, in
Tender Loving Care, played a nurse given to murdering old people.

Not that it was all dark. *Sticky Wickets*, depicting an embarrassing
hotel double-booking between a German business delegation and a
local cricket team decked out in Nazi uniforms for a fancy dress party,
mocked civic boosterism at the height of Wales's inward investment
boom. Karl Francis finally turned Dylan Thomas's film scenario,
Rebecca's Daughters, into a romp of a film with Peter O'Toole, Paul
Rhys and Joely Richardson. *Filipina Dreamgirls*, both poignant and
funny, followed a group of Welshmen in search of wives. The script was
by Andrew Davies who also delivered a masterly adaptation of
Kingsley Amis's *The Old Devils*, that many found more roundly satis-
fying than the novel.

Two things changed that had a significant impact. First, BBC 1 and
BBC 2 began to cut back on single dramas and to concentrate on
longer running series, where the search was always for a returning
series. Charles Denton, who had arrived as the BBC's Head of Drama
in 1993, came to Cardiff. He said he was quite keen on costume drama,
'but, please, nothing in sandals'. Second, the advent of Producer
Choice – the BBC's internal market system – in April 1993 had a
profound effect in that it removed from Wales and from the other
nations and regions a potential incentive for network commissioning.

Before Producer Choice, commissioning had always involved an
element of financial bargaining, where London would offer a price that
would (or would not) cover the marginal costs, while the nations threw
in, below the line, the technical resources that they managed independ-
ently, or even some cash. If one of the regions chose to commit its

resources to a particular network project, a network commissioner might achieve his commission at relatively little cost to his own budget. In the last year of the old system, BBC Wales network income was a mere £5m, to which we added £3m worth of technical resources. We forfeited more than £2m of that latter contribution as budgets were adjusted for the new system.

The separation of BBC Resources from the programme side undoubtedly taught us a huge amount about our costs and about financial discipline, but it also removed a lever that we ourselves controlled. Perhaps the degree of opacity attached to such bargaining was always unlikely to survive a consultant's eye, particularly if the centre wished to take a firmer grip. There were times, too, when network controllers tried to use it to burrow too deeply into Welsh resources, but the ultimate effect of the change was to reinforce the narrowness of the commissioning funnel and to reduce the likelihood of a more culturally diverse outcome.

Much has been made in the rhetoric of regional broadcasting about the importance of a 'sense of place'. But it meant different things to BBC colleagues working at either end of the M4. Commissioning controllers would worry lest a drama be 'too Welsh' and yet be equally perplexed if one offered a play that wasn't obviously from the patch.

A sense of place can be many things: an incidental location that simply suits the director's visual requirements – for example, Snowdonia for China in *The Inn of the Sixth Happiness*; a place, any place, needed to anchor an idea – say Manchester in *Life of Mars*; work that consciously sets out to represent a community – *Coronation Street* or, as we attempted in the 1990s, *Tiger Bay* and *Belonging*; a story or passion or issue that is precisely located – *Boys from the Blackstuff* or Karl Francis's *Streetlife*. Commissioning controllers are, by and large, content with the first of these, which is why the decentralisation of production has not led to any great increase in cultural diversity. Drama departments in Wales have tended to struggle to get commissions for anything culturally more distinctive and substantial.

The operation of the system, before and after the Producer Choice change, was exemplified in two very different dramas: *Selected Exits*, an adaptation by Alan Plater of Gwyn Thomas's autobiographical novel, *A Few Selected Exits*, and Karl Francis's *Streetlife*.

Strangely, the story of *Selected Exits* began in Newcastle, in what was a tatty but cherished theatre space, Live Theatre. Alan Plater and my colleague at Tyne Tees, Michael Chaplin, had collaborated on a theatrical adaptation of *In Blackberry Time*, a collection of stories by Michael's late father, Sid Chaplin. During a conversation at the end of the first night, Alan Plater mentioned to me that Gwyn Thomas was one his heroes, and *A Few Selected Exits* a particular favourite, so when both Michael Chaplin and I ended up back at BBC Wales it was one of the ideas that was high on our list.

Despite an excellent script from Alan Plater – that fully reflected Gwyn Thomas's acerbic wit – the experienced Geraint Morris as producer, a well-regarded director in Tristram Powell and, to cap it all, Anthony Hopkins in the lead role, network resisted the project and particularly the notion of paying for it. Perhaps we paid the price of our commitment, but in the end BBC Wales, able to deploy technical resources that were already paid for, financed the whole project.

A few years later Karl Francis was pushing *Streetlife*, a drama based on the story of a single mother on a council estate. He saw it as a riposte to John Redwood's strictures on single mothers during his brief tenure as secretary of state for Wales. This time, with the internal market in place, technical resources had to be fully paid for out of the programme budget. Since this was also a project to which the network – always somewhat wary of Karl – was willing to make only a small contribution, the only way in which it could be made by BBC Wales was on a budget that was a third of that which we had been able to muster under the old system for *Selected Exits*. That it was such a success was not only down to the anguished brilliance of Helen McCrory, in her first leading television role – and matched by Rhys Ifans – but also to Karl's fierce commitment to the project that had been sharpened into bloody-mindedness by the process.

The pattern was to be repeated, in part, in 1997 over Trevor Griffith's play to mark the centenary of Aneurin Bevan's birth, *Food for Ravens*. The project had been pressed by our head of English programmes, Dai Smith, himself an historian of the left who had written much on Bevan. Brian Cox was to play Bevan and Sinead Cusack, his wife, Jennie Lee. The network's reluctance to take the show ended in a messy and, in this instance, public compromise in which it was shown at nine o'clock in Wales but at a very late hour on BBC2 in the rest of the country. In fairness, this was one occasion when the centre, in the person of Will Wyatt, then chief executive of BBC Broadcast, admitted that it had perhaps misjudged matters. Given the centrality of Bevan's NHS to our post-war history as well as to current political debate, it was a case of the BBC not so much refusing to respond to Welsh sensitivities as failing to be British enough.

Such difficulties were not confined to Wales and could easily generate one of the less attractive facets of regional broadcasting, a culture of grievance. Survival in the BBC requires you to bury it quickly. There is a fine line between persistence and nuisance – and I cannot swear that I never crossed it – but there were always other battles to be fought. The relentlessness of programme schedules in radio and television and, in particular, television's need for long term planning, meant that one always had to judge whether to risk tomorrow's business for the therapeutic attractions of today's scrap.

Besides, there were real reasons for optimism. John Birt's television resources study, that recommended the introduction of the internal market, had identified the startling fact that four-fifths of all television output was produced in London, with a mere 19 per cent being produced outside the south East of England. It was the kind of factual nugget that produces change. In a situation where the licence fee was collected from every home in the land, he deemed the current imbalance unacceptable and set an objective to raise the output from outside the south east first to 25 per cent and then to 'broadly a third'. This was a seminal moment, for which he has received less credit than he deserves, and fundamentally altered the terms of the debate even if it did not provide a total or swift solution.

David Hatch, who had run radio for the BBC with wit and tenacity and was now assistant to the director general, was deputed to put flesh on the policy of 'proportionality'. He came to Cardiff where Michael Chaplin and I argued our case with some vehemence. At the end David looked at me and said, 'Let's get this clear, Mr Davies, are you a Welshman or a member of the BBC?' At least with David you could be sure he was pulling your leg, but he was also satirising some of his London colleagues. In the end Scotland, Wales and Northern Ireland were given some assurances on drama, and Wales was designated as a centre of excellence for music and earmarked for a larger education output for the networks.

But it was not plain sailing. Had John Birt's policy and David Hatch's targets been put in place in the 1970s when the BBC's income was still growing fast it might have been implemented with good cheer and speedy effect. Coming, as it did, in a decade when its income was in real term decline, it caused a near revolt amongst London departments who were already having to slim down in response to the mandatory 25 per cent production quota for independent producers.

Whereas we worried about assembling critical mass, London departments worried about losing it. As a result, further down the hierarchical chain, the policy was implemented with sullen reluctance or sometimes even circumvented by sleight of hand.

Moreover, an overall target for output from the 'nations' was never set, so that the predominant benefit in the early years accrued to the regional outposts in England – Bristol, Birmingham and Manchester – that had always been, primarily, centres of network production. But we had our own weaknesses, too. We did not have sufficient producers and writers in Wales who had already been blooded for this competitive challenge and it would take longer to hone those skills than we thought. The net result, despite the policy breakthrough, was that network production from the three Celtic countries languished way below 10 per cent for most of the rest of the decade. It was not until 2004 that Mark Thompson, by then director general, decided that Scotland, Wales and Northern Ireland and Wales would deliver 17 per cent of network output – their population share – by 2012, a full 21 years after John Birt identified the issue. Even then, the calculation of the 17 per cent has deliberately excluded news, sport, daytime programmes and *Eastenders*.

There was one disappointment that particularly saddened me. Wales had made a pitch for a presence in the field of history programmes, for which we thought ourselves well-equipped. Dai Smith's background was tailor-made for such a brief, and he and I had both been involved in major history series for television. Gwyn Pritchard had made documentaries on history for the Open University and HTV. Our factual programmes department was also headed by Roy Davies, who had joined us from the BBC's history department in London where he had been editor of the *Timewatch* series. But, oddly for a policy that purported to be about cultural diversity as much as redistributing spend, factual programmes were left out of the equation.

We also had to contend with the law of unintended consequences. For example, Wales had regularly contributed films for the religious series, *Everyman*, but when, as part of the decentralisation, the religious programmes department was moved to Manchester – where, as one wag suggested, they would be closer to the Archbishop of Wales, then at St. Asaph, than the Archbishop of Canterbury – our contributions were no longer required.

We all felt it was a lost opportunity, especially as one of our senior producers, Phil George, had had a notable success with *Blood and*

Belonging, a compelling series exploring the light and dark side of modern nationalism, that had grown out of conversations I had had with a Canadian producer, Pat Ferns, while in ITV. It was presented by Michael Ignatieff, himself a Canadian, and took in Germany, the Ukraine, Kurdistan, Northern Ireland and naturally, Quebec. It was memorable for many things, not least chilling scenes from the Balkans of erstwhile next-door neighbours in cellars, now streets apart, threatening, via a radio telephone, to bomb each other into oblivion. It was a warning about how thin is the veneer of civilisation. The series demonstrated our capacity to handle large subjects and we were keen to do more.

A few years later John Geraint, then my chief assistant but later our head of production, wrote a dissertation on factual programmes in the BBC that played a part in persuading Mark Thompson that this was an area that would have to addressed. By the end of the decade we were gaining a toehold in programmes that dealt with the landscape, including *The Fruitful Earth*, a beautiful series on the history of Britain's land and agriculture, and *Visions of Snowdonia*, narrated by Anthony Hopkins, that brought a young bird lover, Iolo Williams, to the fore.

The most significant advance was on the music front, where Hilary Boulding's success in arts and music was rewarded with a brief to become the main source of music output outside London. It needed her terrier-like qualities, not only because her equivalent in Television Centre saw this as a considerable threat but also because the ink was hardly dry on the policy before network controllers reduced their total spend on arts and music quite sharply. At one meeting my only slightly mischievous suggestion that Radio 3 should be moved, lock stock and barrel, to Cardiff where it could be produced more economically, was greeted by its controller, Nick Kenyon, with speechless horror.

Nevertheless, contributions to Radio 3 and to BBC 2 grew and included memorable programmes such as a day's live radio broadcasting from Moscow to celebrate the eightieth anniversary of the October revolution, and a sublime television production of Brahms's German Requiem from the Musickverein in Vienna, with Claudio Abbado, the Berlin Philharmonic, Bryn Terfel, Barbara Bonney and the Swedish Radio Choir. After Hilary left to go to a senior post in Radio 3, her successor, David Jackson, took the reins and, after the turn of the decade, took responsibility for network music output from Wales, Scotland and Northern Ireland.

In the field of drama we struggled to make the shift from single plays and films to popular long-running series that commissioners required and which demanded a different sensibility. Pedr James, who had a distinguished pedigree in theatre and television, put much effort into developing writers while he was head of the department, including, with Dai Smith's backing, the launching of two soaps – *Station Road*, a daily effort for Radio Wales, and *Belonging* for BBC Wales television – both designed to paint a less stereotyped picture of Welsh society than British media normally manage. We tried to do the same for the network with *Tiger Bay*. That it did not succeed was a crueller disappointment than most, as we and critics felt it broke new ground by presenting a true and unforced picture of an multi-racial community. As such, we thought there was something bigger at stake.

A substantial commitment, but one that was not related to the new policy, was to major animation projects being produced in conjunction with S4C. It had an unusual origin. In the late 1980s while representing Tyne Tees at one of the international television markets in Cannes I met two American educationists. We talked about educating children in the classics of literature and one of them expressed a view that it was high time Charles Lamb's *Tales from Shakespeare* was updated for this generation. Animation seemed the obvious medium.

Having little knowledge of animation production myself, the following Christmas I talked to Chris Grace, an old HTV friend who had moved to S4C and single-handedly established a prolific animation output, created an embryonic industry in Cardiff, and had started to raise S4C's international profile into the bargain. I asked him whether he would be interested in animating Shakespeare. Chris never does anything half-heartedly and he reacted with enthusiasm. Soon he and I and Michael Chaplin were holding meetings with Leon Garfield, who had written so well for children, and it looked set to be an S4C-Tyne Tees collaboration. However, not long after I left to join the BBC, Tyne Tees themselves pulled out and soon Chris was knocking on my door at BBC Wales to see whether we would be interested in coming on board. There was no question, and in truth the concept sat more comfortably with the BBC and S4C than with ITV.

With Chris's single-minded drive and irresistible salesmanship behind it, S4C and the BBC were soon joined by HBO from the United States, Fujisankei from Japan and a large Moscow animation house, Christmas Films, led by Eliza Babachina, a shrewd, creative and very determined businesswoman. Foreseeing the direction of perestroika, she had spun the company out of the old state animation house,

Soyuzmultfilm, surviving both the coup against Gorbachev – when they had to stop filming every time the tanks passed by – and the anarchic days of Boris Yeltsin.

We produced two series encompassing twelve of Shakespeare's plays, scripted by Leon Garfield in English and with translations into Welsh of exceptional quality by the poet Gwyn Thomas – the Welsh versions for S4C and the English for BBC2, although its success saw it move quickly to BBC1. There was some grumbling from Welsh animators that, although overseen by Welsh producers, the bulk of the production was located in Moscow, but the truth was that there was no other animation house in the world that had the capacity to handle a project of this scale within the time frames of television commissioning.

In 1991 the whole production team, including Leon Garfield, Gwyn Thomas and the series consultant, Stanley Wells, travelled to Moscow to see progress. The work, done in a wide range of techniques each chosen to suit a particular play, was inspiring, but Moscow was in a truly tragic state. People lined the pavements trying to sell a canned drink or a jar of sugar, anything to keep body and soul together. The economy was at its worst point in the transition from communism. We took with us sacks of basic necessities to sustain the team. They were emotional in their gratitude, but we also sensed the humiliation that they felt about the desperate state of their country.

The group stayed in a hotel of brash and clumsy architecture that had previously been reserved for members of the central committee of the communist party. A deep red carpet swept down a wide staircase between walls and pillars of white marble, like the blood of a seal on an iceflow. The young Russian director, Natalya Orlova, who was tackling Hamlet, came to meet us there for dinner. She had not been in the building before. She stopped, looked around and smiled a sad smile. 'Ah,' she said, 'the taste of tyrants.'

In time Chris and I managed to persuade the BBC to make a longer term investment so that S4C and BBC Wales could plan almost a decade of work in this vein. Shakespeare was followed by biblical tales in *Testament*, the story of Jesus in *The Miracle Maker, Beowulf, Moby Dick*, and Chaucer's *The Canterbury Tales*. *The Canterbury Tales* won four Emmys, a BAFTA and an Oscar nomination, while *The Miracle Maker* was shown in America in peak time coast to coast on the ABC network on Easter Sunday for two successive years.

It was a major enterprise that demonstrated the S4C-BBC partnership at its best, not to mention the joint commitment from Cardiff and

London, that tied in the main channels, BBC Wales, BBC Children's Department and BBC Education. It involved a substantial and consistent investment from both sides that attracted international partners, both financial and creative: the extraordinary vision and technical skills of Russian animators, and talented Welsh producers – Dave Edwards, Naomi Jones, Penelope Middleboe and Martin Lamb from the independent sector, and Alison Hindell, Jane Dauncey and Lyn Jones from BBC Wales. Alison, by good fortune a fluent Russian speaker, produced many of the English soundtracks, Lyn the Welsh.

Although by the end of the decade we had more than doubled our total network output in radio and television to £17m. it was still a fragile advance. It required yet more effort in Wales and a further advance in policy to move things forward again. Unlike his two predecessors in charge of regional broadcasting, Mark Thompson, who would soon depart to Channel 4, had been a Channel Controller. He was well aware not only that there were remaining talent issues to be dealt with, but also that the commitment to Scotland, Wales and Northern Ireland would have to become more substantial and specific. The commitment in 2003 to the production of *Dr. Who* in Cardiff, a project brilliantly secured, managed and executed by Menna Richards and Julie Gardner, was a remarkable breakthrough and a sign that the new targets for the 'nations' were beginning to be seriously meaningful.

★ ★ ★ ★

All this was watched through the 1990s by a feisty BBC Broadcasting Council for Wales, since replaced in the 2006 Royal Charter by the awkward sounding Audience Council under the new BBC Trust. It had always been easy for sceptics to dismiss the BCW and its equivalents in Scotland and Northern Ireland. The councils took no decisions, and disbursed no money. Their members enjoyed neither the legitimacy of election nor the comfort of payment. Their chairman or chairwoman had a prior loyalty to the BBC Board of Governors on which they represented Wales. An American consultant I worked with had seen such forums before and was wont to dismiss them as 'the once a month for lunch bunch'. He was wrong.

The 1952 Royal Charter that created the councils gave them, arguably unrealistically, 'the function of controlling the policy and content of the programme in the Home Services which the corporation provides primarily for general reception in that country'. It was hard to see how this function could be discharged since they had no power over finance or resources. Nevertheless the prescribed function sat there like a nuclear device, designed not be used, but ensuring that people listened. The BCW's role had been particularly constructive in the 1970s in the decision to create the two radio services for Wales, Radio Wales and Radio Cymru, and in securing the BBC's support for the creation of a Welsh language channel. The changing moods of councils acted as warning signals both to London and to local managements.

Council members had questioned me sharply about the proposed job losses in BBC Wales and I came to the conclusion that, whatever their formal power, if you could not persuade a dozen intelligent, well-informed and independent minded people that your plans made sense, you had better think again. The first sign of a capacity for revolt came unexpectedly on Friday, December 13, 1991, the last meeting of the BCW to be chaired by John Parry, a large and genial vet and President of the Royal College of Veterinary Surgeons, who had been involved in recruiting me and had given me unstinted support. During his term he lived for the BBC and became an enthusiastic groupie for its Welsh orchestra.

The government had treated him discourteously by not announcing in timely fashion who his successor would be. At his final meeting he was asked by Jim Morris, a canny trade unionist from north Wales, whether there was any truth in the rumour that it would be Dr. Gwyn Jones, the chairman of the Welsh Development Agency, whose successful but racy tenure at the WDA had been under a cloud, not to mention under the hammer of the Public Accounts Committee. John Parry obviously knew the answer but was sworn to secrecy. He did not utter a word but his naturally florid face said it for him. Uproar ensued.

Management were asked to leave the room. Four council members peeled off into another office across the corridor to draft a letter to the Home Secretary, Kenneth Baker, protesting at a conflict of interest that could 'not only embarrass the National Governor but might inhibit the proper activities of the news and current affairs department' and would be 'detrimental to the integrity, independence and reputation of the BBC'. Eventually, I was called back in and, out of courtesy, the letter was read to me. It was despatched under the name of Lady Hooson. I thought it was a sad and unseemly end to a governor's term, and it did not bode well for his successor, but I had underestimated the resilience of the council. The protest made, we all descended to the hospitality suite, put on paper hats and ate a jolly Christmas lunch.

Gwyn Jones was a very different animal from John Parry and, in truth, better suited to contribute to the debate on the tougher agenda that John Birt was laying out. He was more interested in the BBC's overall strategy than in the service in Wales. He had made a deal of money in the burgeoning IT business, though not without controversy, before being plucked by Peter Walker, then secretary of state for Wales, to run the Welsh Development Agency. Although from the private sector, he was from the world of the owner-managed business rather than the large corporation and, with a low boredom threshold, tended to see a good deal of the BBC's admittedly heavy corporate governance as tedious.

He also relished playing it tough. Acquaintances at the WDA warned me to start looking for another job, as they thought he preferred playing executive rather than non-executive chairman. This misread the BBC situation where my lines of accountability ran to London and not through the National Governor. Gwyn, in very straightforward fashion, did make it quite explicit that he did not want a cosy relationship, but he was more adversarial in theory than in practice. We would irritate each other from time to time, and had one serious fall-out over a programme that involved the WDA, yet the relationship never broke down. He could be good company, and out of the blue could show a warm side. But he was not the man for the coming period of Labour Government and returned to the private sector.

When Gwyn joined, the BBC was deep into its preparations for charter renewal, Michael Checkland was still in place and John Birt had not yet elaborated his detailed plan for the future that would include the separation of programmes and resources. At that point the controller's job in Scotland, Wales and Northern Ireland embraced every facet of the business and was more akin to the managing direc-tor of an ITV company, a situation that all three of us cherished. Although John Birt was right about his central reform, he mistakenly assumed that we would be happy to be shot of responsibility for the 'bogs and boilers', not spotting that some of us actually enjoyed the holistic sense of responsibility not only for the fabric of the building but for everyone who worked in it. Even long after the split it was argued that everyone in Wales still played in the red shirt, no matter on which side of the fence they ended up.

The BCW started turning its mind to what charter renewal might mean for itself and for the shape of things in Wales and was keen to join in the spirit of 'thinking the unthinkable'. The council encouraged me to sketch out an exhaustive list of constitutional options for Wales's place in the BBC with the relative pros and cons. While this was an interesting academic exercise that ran from the status quo to the federalisation of the BBC, it caused alarm bells to ring in London. Ron Neil, who would exhibit genuine pain at the thought of any dissension in his regional broadcasting family, took me to Odin's in London for a very expensive meal that I took to be a 'disciplinary dinner'. It was a mark of the gentle nature of the man and the corporation, a languid reminder to keep things under control and a warning against too much free thinking. Controllers in the nations are often accused of 'winding up' their councils but in this instance it was more a matter of holding them back.

On one of their triennial visits to London to dine with the BBC governors, the BCW met in the afternoon to hear from John Birt himself. John did not beat about the bush, and gave short shrift to some of the council's arguments for a better deal for English language television, advising members in no uncertain terms that the status quo was the best they could hope for. The directness of his language left some raw feelings and at the dinner that night Gwyn Jones, who had an occasional taste for mischief, made a shrewd choice when picking a member of the council to say a few words of thanks.

Ossie Wheatley is not a five-foot-six Celt but a tall Englishman with a mane of blond hair rather like Michael Heseltine, not a fiery Welsh preacher but an urbane England cricket selector. Ossie reminded the governors that he was chair of the Sports Council for Wales that had a royal charter of its own, like all the other countries in the UK. Although Ossie was only tweaking the lion's tail, it challenged a core belief in 'the one BBC' and the dinner ended with nervous huddles and whispers.

Eventually the future of the Broadcasting Councils was settled. There was no radical change. The controlling function was dropped with no noticeable effect and a raft of other measures to improve accountability adopted, one of which involved a delegation from each of the Broadcasting Councils meeting annually with the governors for an hour or so to discuss the previous year's performance.

Efforts to improve mutual understanding were clearly necessary. On one such occasion the BCW delegation was led by the retired vice chancellor of Bangor university, Eric Sunderland, an internationally respected anthropologist and a past president of the Royal Anthropological Institute. He is also Welsh-speaking. At the buffet lunch following the meeting, one governor, an English businessman, opened a conversation with Eric with the breathtaking observation,

'You speak English rather well,' to which Eric replied with his usual dry wit, 'Oh, one tries.'

Everyone by now was getting accustomed to living with paradox. Producer Choice was giving producers the freedom to spend their money in ways that best suited their programmes, even if there was often less of it. At the same time there was a clear centralising trend that was more than simply a sharpened accountability. The regional directorate was becoming as much a control mechanism as a champion. Professional heads of finance, marketing and personnel wanted direct control of their fellow professionals in the nations, with only 'dotted lines' to the controllers, rather than vice versa. At one stage I had to fend off pressure to centralise the production of all programme promotions in London, despite the fact that our own had been winning awards around the world and had built the highest levels of satisfaction with BBC1 of any nation or region. It was depressing to be told by otherwise excellent professionals that all it would need would be the occasional trip to Cardiff by a producer to brief himself.

From one perspective it was not surprising that the corporation should respond to changes in the external climate by seeking sharper central control. It is, after all, what all businesses, including governments, do when they perceive threats to their existence, particularly if they are strapped for cash. Tussles between centre and periphery are common in most large organisations, as was confirmed to me once in a long diatribe against head office from a man who ran half a continent for Hewlett Packard. But perhaps there is rather more at stake for a small culture than the make and model of photocopier it uses. Some degree of tension was, therefore, inevitable between the centre and Scotland and Wales, especially as rising devolutionary prospects drove in the opposite direction throughout the decade. It reached a peak in the aftermath of the devolution referendum. 1997 was a pivotal year.

The prospect of real democratic devolution for Scotland and Wales was tantalisingly close as the general election grew near, although it had been dampened by Tony Blair's unexpected announcement that there would be referenda in both countries. Those who remembered the 1979 referendum feared that the result in Wales would be repeated, even if by a less overwhelming majority. This was one matter on which my usual optimism deserted me. Opinions polls before the vote were rather more encouraging than in 1979 but even their relevance was thrown into doubt when the campaigning was disrupted by the lightning strike of the death of the Princess of Wales on August 31, 1997.

Elizabeth and I were returning from France that morning and caught the news on the radio as consternation spread through the early morning queue for the ferry on the quayside at Le Havre.

It became a week of frantic activity. Once it was clear that the referendum would still be held and that campaigning would be suspended for only one week, we had not only to redraft our campaign programming, but also to respond to the public reaction in Wales. We debated daily whether we were responding to it or creating it, although large news machines cannot easily be stopped dead in their tracks even had we been so inclined. However, more subtle changes were made.

Princess Diana's funeral fell on a Saturday when the BBC National Orchestra of Wales was due to perform the Poulenc *Gloria* at the London Proms that evening. The *Gloria* was dropped and Faure's *Requiem* substituted. Although not scheduled for television we offered it to Mark Thompson, then Controller of BBC2, who jumped at the chance to create a more reflective mood at the end of a febrile week. His swift acceptance gave our producer, David Jackson, a formidable challenge. Every camera in the corporation seemed to have been committed to the coverage of the funeral and David had to beg and borrow the necessary kit from every corner of the BBC to deliver the event. James Naughtie, who had been on air continuously since early morning presented the programme. He delivered a moving opening piece to camera then, exhausted, promptly fell asleep in his box.

The intensity, not to say hysteria of the mourning that week suggested that the country had momentarily lost any sense of equilibrium. How could Wales be expected to regain sufficient of it to be able to summon the courage to vote for radical constitutional change? All bets were off. My personal nightmare was that Scotland would vote Yes and Wales would vote No and I would have to attend the monthly meetings of the regional directorate and watch the corporate croupiers push all the winners' chips towards Scotland and, if the two sides in Ulster could ever settle their differences, to Northern Ireland. Even while talking to some of the staff in Wales I was often surprised that so many seemed not to understand quite how much was at stake. There was going to be a devolution dividend, in money and jobs, but it was depressing to think that they might not bother to vote to capture a share. It was not a BBC Controller's job to persuade them.

On the night of the vote I stood in the newsroom with Anne Sloman, the BBC's bustling chief political adviser – and, as it happened, the daughter of a Cardiff councillor – watching the No votes pile up in the early stages of the count. 'It's not looking good for BBC Wales,' she said, shaking her head, deepening my gloom and inadvertently confirming a belief in the political nature of some of the BBC's decision making. But then the evening changed.

The gap between Yes and No narrowed until, on the Welsh language results programme that we were producing for S4C, its presenter, Dewi Llwyd asked John Meredith, the reporter at the Carmarthen count, whether there was truth in rumour that the Yes majority there would be sufficient to decide the result in favour of the Yes camp. John Meredith, struggling in his mind with BBC guidance that reporters should not anticipate the result, paused, nodded assent and finally said Yes. Several hands in the newsroom including my own punched the air, prompting a sideways look from Mark Byford.

It was difficult to believe. Out of a total of 1.1 million votes cast there was a majority of only 6,721, but the swing since 1979 had been sensational. Then only 20.3 per cent of voters had said Yes, this time it was 50.3 per cent. Wales had changed. It was a different place. The grinding of tectonic plates had worn away industries that had defined us for a century. Language divisions had melted away. We had grown used to Europe. The temper of Thatcherism had both highlighted how different was our own, and perhaps, ironically, instilled the confidence to assert the difference. The young, in particular, had voted Yes twice as often as their parents.

But it was not a wave that swept all before it. Arithmetically, the majority was small enough to have been decided by an accumulation of chance events across 40 constituencies, also allowing every part of Wales to say it made a difference. In James Cameron's film *Titanic*, made that very year, there is a scene where muscled stokers scramble for safety from their doomed compartment as the icy water rises. To an orchestral crescendo an engineer dives out under the descending bulkhead doors with only inches to spare. Wales, too, had made it in the nick of time.

There was little time to savour the moment. Later that Friday morning the mood was punctured by a rail crash at Paddington where a south Wales train had collided with a freight train killing seven and injuring more than 150. Some of my London colleagues including Ann Sloman were on the train but luckily escaped injury. The following day, both expectantly and reluctantly, I left for five weeks at Wharton Business School in Philadelphia, and on the plane started to list the questions that the referendum result would pose.

What sort of Assembly would it be? Would its main work be done in plenary sessions or in committees? Would it be elected by a system of proportional representation? What difference might it make to the nature of political debate? Would our own deep-rooted habits as journalists push it into a template of our own making? What kind of daily service should we provide for Welsh audiences on radio and television? Should we ape the current coverage of Westminster or try to find new programme formats? Could we harness online technologies to generate a deeper dialogue? Should our coverage be mainly in the hands of political correspondents obsessed with party cut and thrust or with specialist reporters tackling individual policy areas and shadowing the subject committees? How would we handle the proceedings of a bilingual institution?

And further afield, how should the BBC's UK network programmes respond? Remembering the sad effects of the media's disregard of Stormont for half a century, how could we make Welsh issues interesting and relevant for a wider audience? Would London newsrooms care? What impact should the existence of the Assembly and of the Scottish Parliament have on the shape and content of the BBC's central news programmes?

It was these last questions that were to provoke the most fierce debate within the BBC, drawing the Broadcasting Councils to the fore again. The BBC was determined to be generous in its response, and Mark Byford, in charge of regional broadcasting, was earnestly thorough in marshalling the response. In Scotland and Wales teams devised detailed plans for new programmes and new staff, but there was an unbridgeable difference between us and the centre over the future of the six o'clock television news, a difference that conflated journalism and politics.

News people in Cardiff and Edinburgh could foresee that, when the new institutions were under way, policy differences across England, Scotland and Wales would create real difficulties in putting together British news programmes that would accurately reflect those differences without resorting to a clumsiness that would be irritating to audiences everywhere. We knew that promises of a new degree of care and attention to such sensitivities would wither away under daily newsroom pressures and the undeniable asymmetry of the British audience. We had all been to conferences designed to make editors aware of the need to report the whole of the UK and many remembered the howls of laughter at one such event when a senior radio

executive said they would tackle the problem by 'putting more producers out in the sticks'.

Promises of yet more 'sensitivity training' for London editors,
though sincerely meant, made us in Wales and Scotland as uncomfortable as London colleagues. It conjured visions of London staff put up
against the wall in Television Centre or Broadcasting House, with their
legs apart, while short, hairy Welshmen wearing miners' helmets and
kilted Scots with all sorts of menacing cutlery in their socks, applied
electrodes to various parts of English bodies. But there was no doubt-
ing the need to change perceptions, particularly of Wales, beyond our
borders.

However, the notion that Wales and Scotland should produce their
own six o'clock television news programmes became such a cause
célèbre in Scotland that the idea quickly came to be seen as a threat to
the British constitution. In Wales the issue was played out in a lower
key, largely because there were no competing newspapers to create a
howl-round of noise, but also because it was in Scotland that the issue
would be decided for the whole of the BBC. The story unfolded under
the banner of the 'Scottish Six', yet it was in Cardiff that the seeds had
been planted.

In 1994, during the BBC-wide Programme Strategy Review we had
put forward the proposition that, between six and seven, the division of
the hour between a central news and a regional news should be
abandoned in favour of one combined programme in which international, British and Welsh news could be woven together. We knew at
once that the idea caused jitters in London because we were urged
several times by our McKinsey minder not to include the idea in the
document. We remained insistent although agreeing to couch our
proposal in tentative terms. It was not done out of mischief or any
separatist impulse, but because we thought it was, journalistically, an
entirely natural path to follow.

In one sense, this was hardly new ground. In the 1940s my father
and others had brought news of the war daily to Welsh audiences in the
Welsh language from a BBC basement studio in Portland Place. In
1980 I had sat in several small television stations in California watching editors take network feeds of international stories from New York
to be integrated into their local bulletins. Early in 1982 I had led an
HTV team in piloting such an integrated format for S4C. In 1988,
while at Tyne Tees, I had discussed the notion with Stuart Prebble, head
of regional programmes at Granada, who was keen to provide just such

an hour with a northern slant. By 1994 BBC Wales had been providing S4C with a global and local blend, twice nightly, for twelve years. Radio Scotland, Radio Wales and Radio Cymru were and are doing the very job all day every day.

In the 1994 review we argued that there were technological, editorial and competitive reasons for change. New digital production techniques were making the distribution of sound and vision to multiple points easy and cheap. It was naturally decentralising. Not to use it was to justify central control of news production against the trend of technology. Editorially, the proposed fusion would allow us to report and analyse public policy initiatives and their effects, bringing the Welsh and UK dimensions together in a seamless way that would make them more relevant for our audiences. It would give added status to the Welsh news agenda and our presenters, eradicating any lingering provincialism.

It would also eliminate the duplication of stories in London and Cardiff news programmes on those days when a story from Wales made it into the six o'clock news. Right in the middle of the debate, we had the starkest example of that duplication as London and Wales pressed coverage of the sensational resignation of the Secretary of State for Wales, Ron Davies. We also thought that such a change would allow the BBC to differentiate its main early and late evening news programmes more clearly, as well as strengthening the BBC's early evening schedule at a time when ITV was highly competitive. We did not foresee the mess that ITV would make of their early evening schedule as an unintended consequence of their abandonment of ITN's *News at Ten*.

There were, of course, contrary arguments. There would be logistical problems to be overcome and satisfactory arrangements would have to be made for dealing with major national or international breaking stories. We also had to recognise that the BBC UK news brand was powerful and had a long history that resonated with the public in every part of the kingdom.

By 1998, although the proposed new constitutional arrangements had given added force to our journalistic arguments, they cut more sharply across the corporation's centrally-driven management culture, and exacerbated the increasing nervousness about the momentum of events in Scotland. As a result some paper studies of news agendas for a three-day period were undertaken in order to assess the proposal, but a full programme pilot such as HTV had done in 1980 was never attempted. The level of corporate anxiety became increasingly apparent as the Governors grappled with the issues, though its full extent did not become public until the publication of John Birt's autobiography, *The Harder Path.*

In a chapter entitled, *Holding the BBC together,* John made it clear that he foresaw a domino effect in which Scotland, followed by Wales and ultimately Northern Ireland would opt out of first the *Six O'Clock News* and then the other major news programmes until there was no UK-wide news at all left on the BBC. This would be followed by the decline of the BBC into a weak federal institution, perhaps even its break up, leaving a diminished English Broadcasting Corporation and low-funded sister organisations in the other nations. Such was his concern that he took the issue to the Prime Minister, Tony Blair, who agreed that Peter Mandelson, the minister without portfolio, would work with Michael Stevenson, the deputy director of regional broadcasting, on a plan of action directed at Scotland where, unlike Wales, there was a real and public head of steam.

Quite apart from what this said about the independence of the BBC, it was an apocalyptic vision that I have never shared, believing, to borrow Roosevelt's words, that the BBC had nothing to fear but fear itself. I was always perplexed by the corporation's capacity to gobble up the big strategic issues and deal with them with energy and imagination, and yet to be so nervous of devolution, as if its arrow was always aimed at the heart of the organisation.

My view may be coloured by the fact that Wales's communitarian ethos is instinctively friendly to public service broadcasting and the levels of satisfaction with the BBC's output have been traditionally high, but it is more than that. I have always felt that the BBC's positive credit balance with the public, based on its history and values, gives it great freedom of manoeuvre. Moreover, when it decides to give full backing to a programme idea it invariably does so with powerful effect. Even produced from Cardiff or Glasgow these programmes would have been unmistakably BBC products, embracing its array of authoritative journalists around the world.

Egged on by the press, the debate in Scotland reached hysterical proportions. A team of senior executives visited the Broadcasting Council for Scotland only to find their own faces on the front page of one newspaper under a huge, one word headline – 'Wanted'. Days later things were not helped by the publication of a report on the future of news by the BBC's news division. Despite the governors' assurances that they were consulting seriously on the 'Scottish Six', the report implied that the decision had been taken. Embarrassingly, it transpired that it had been prepared without any consultation with the regional broadcasting directorate. When the whole Board of Governors ventured to Scotland to meet the BCS they were, according to John Birt, 'exposed to an incessant tirade of bile, vitriol and abuse'.

Sir Christopher Bland's visit to Wales, was more polite though not without its spiky moments. The BCW had its own soft and hard cops. Sue Balsom, a businesswoman with a political nose, and Adrian Webb, then Vice Chancellor of the University of Glamorgan, gave a sophisti-cated account of the devolutionary imperatives. The formidable Edwina Hart, later the Assembly's finance minister and then health minister, jabbed solidly with straight lefts. At one point Sir Christopher apologised for interrupting the flow of one member's argument with the rather twee excuse, 'I don't have my note-taker with me'. Edwina Hart, a professional trade unionist, leant threateningly forward. 'It's very simple, you pick up your pen...' The council chairman, Roger Jones, always fond of the vocabulary of battle, but by now knowing the way things were moving around the governors' table, pressed the council's case though with care not to burn bridges.

In December 1998, the governors announced their decision. Though there was to be no opting out of the *Six O'Clock News*, the decision was dressed with a promise of a further review in a year's time. We assumed the issue was dead for the foreseeable future. But there were also more positive things to reveal. Wales would receive a £6m uplift in its annual allocation to fund a full-hearted journalistic response to the new institution. Within a few months we also managed to increase that figure to fund the direct broadcasting of the Assembly's proceedings, for which S4C provided space on its second digital channel. Scotland, under the BBC's informal and unstated Barnet formula, would receive £9m with £5m pencilled in for Northern Ireland against the time that its own Assembly would convene.

Some years later I calculated that that £6m, together with a further £11m granted to Wales in the early years of Greg Dyke's regime, and another £3m that HTV gained from a renegotiation of its own Treasury licence payments, meant that the Yes vote in 1997 had delivered a devolution dividend of £20m to the broadcasting industry alone – an additional, continuing annual investment greater than the then published cost of establishing the National Assembly itself.

By now the new democracy was less than six months away, and

while teams of people busied themselves with the serious business of journalism and the installation of our facilities in Crickhowell House, some of us turned our minds to giving the Assembly a start to remember. At the turn of the year it was alarming to find that although officials wanted a big event they had no real idea how to set about it nor what it would cost. In January we proposed to them that an open air event that the BBC was planning for June be switched to the day of the royal opening on May 26. We would take charge of the event and contribute those facilities if other support could be found. Michael Bogdanov sketched out a grandiose plan under the title *Voices of a Nation*.

On the night a roll-call of Welsh talents, from opera to rock, performed on two stages linked by a catwalk. So many artists wanted to take part that we had to limit even the stars to one item. Only a handful of the new Welsh bands were missing, some objecting to the profusion of royals. The composer Karl Jenkins, and Gwyneth Lewis, my always frank and perceptive chief assistant at the BBC, and some years later Wales's first 'national poet', wrote an anthem. Nearly 40,000 crowded the Cardiff Bay site where the Wales Millennium Centre would eventually be built. *The Scotsman* wrote an editorial asking why Scotland had not managed to celebrate in such style. It was heady stuff. The following night I stood on the steps of the BBC at Llandaff watching the biggest and longest electrical storm south Wales had ever seen, thanking my lucky stars it had not arrived a day earlier. It was time to leave the BBC.

9 Thinking about Wales

1985 was one of endings and beginnings. The collapse of the miners' strike in March was, in Wales, a cause of national grief, even if the mourners were split between those who believed it was murder and others who believed it was suicide. Even the Government's supporters had the grace not to cheer. This was an industry that had defined Wales in the eyes of the world, now it faced decimation if not total extinction, and a worse fate even than the steel industry where the past decade had seen the shedding of 50,000 jobs, three-quarters of its workforce. If the energy of the miners seemed spent, other confrontations beckoned and serious riots filled hot nights in Brixton and Toxteth. With unforgettably hard-edged oratory that made a nonsense of the 'Welsh windbag' jibe, Neil Kinnock, in conference at Bournemouth confronted the Militant Tendency, that had burrowed dangerously into Labour.

It was also a year in which several disparate strands of thinking came to the surface, all them presaging the revival of the 'Wales project': a television series on Welsh history from HTV/Channel Four, *The Dragon Has Two Tongues*, Gwyn Alf Williams's book *When was Wales?* and a book of essays, *Wales, the National Question Again*, edited by John Osmond. The two books certainly had a profound influence on the intellectual community. The year also saw the relaunch of the cultural magazine *Planet*, the publication of which had been suspended by its owner Ned Thomas less than a year after the 1979 referendum.

Less remarked upon was an address delivered by the secretary of state for Wales, Nicholas Edwards, to the Cardiff Business Club in March, only five days after the end of the miners' strike. It was a speech that had an unpredicted outcome that came to play a large part in my own life.

Nicholas Edwards, now Lord Crickhowell, had been the MP for Pembrokeshire since 1970, and secretary of state for Wales since the start of Margaret Thatcher's tenure in Downing Street. He would stay in that job until his retirement from the Commons in 1987, making him the longest serving holder of the post to date as well as one of the most productive. His public school tones and somewhat brusque manner of social exchange, not to mention his Government's policies, allowed his opponents to polish the Tory stereotype. Yet in economic terms he was regarded as one of the 'wets' in Thatcher's Cabinet, although that had not prevented Wales from having to endure the worst effects of the economic recession and industrial 'restructuring'. Despite this, even opponents acknowledged his intense application to his territorial brief. He left several marks on Wales – the Conway tunnel in the north, and the Cardiff Bay development and the National Museum's new galleries in the south.

Edwards chose not to concentrate on the strike but on some of the underlying weaknesses in the soft side of the Welsh economy, much of which echoed the government's central themes. He bemoaned a prevalent suspicion of change and felt people were energetic only in maintaining the status quo. Education establishments were remote from industry. Financial institutions had opted for safety, and there had been a lack of entrepreneurship in business. Less commonly acknowledged by other ministers, but emphasised by Edwards, was an intellectual gulf between the financial and the industrial world, and a physical gulf between the City of London and the manufacturing areas of Britain. Without any hint of irony, he worried that many thought Wales to be a decaying part of the country with no business culture. Although he was clear that the Government had to lead in responding to these weaknesses, it would do so as a catalyst for investment and participation by the private sector. The clear message was that the private sector, including the professional community, had an important role to play.

The theme became a regular topic of conversation between myself and my closest friend, Keith James, whom I had known since schooldays. He was then the chairman of a Cardiff law firm, Phillips and Buck. Keith has been one of the unsung champions of business in south Wales for four decades. He and another partner, Roger Thomas, had found themselves running the practice only days after qualifying in the late sixties and had driven growth hard. Perhaps more interested in business than in the law, Keith had become a shrewd adviser to countless successful local firms, helping them to grow and later, too often, to be sold. In the nineties he steered his own partnership into an alliance with a group of similar English practices in provincial cities to form Eversheds, becoming its chairman for nine years. It was largely through his influence that Eversheds, having taken over a Bristol practice, chose to concentrate their combined activities in Cardiff rather than across the Severn, as many other organisations had done. By now half its 700 staff are advising companies outside Wales.

We both shared a sense of frustration at the inadequacy of some of the older mechanisms for advising Government. The official body – variously entitled the Council for Wales, the Welsh Council and the Welsh Economic Council – had been fundamentally flawed since it had no independent research capacity and became little more than a stop on the circle line of civil service advice. When the Thatcher Government did away with it, nobody wept.

A new Welsh Industrial and Economic Committee had become a talking shop of representatives of key institutions and would soon peter out. The chambers of commerce were parochial in their outlook and capacity. The CBI too, had little research capacity in Wales and the IOD was still in an embryonic phase. I was conscious that the universities of Wales were culpably inactive in the policy field. Keith, fired by a visit the previous year to MIT and the Boston beltway, was as critical as the secretary of state of Welsh higher education's palpable lack of entrepreneurship.

In July Phillips and Buck lunched Nicholas Edwards at the Cardiff and County Club and, despite reservations about the creation of another organisation, floated the idea of a Welsh Business Institute that might channel the collective wisdom of the professional community through groups of experts focusing on particular issues. It was not dismissed but neither was it encouraged. Although senior civil servants would, from time to time, express to me their disappointment at the lack of intellectual challenge to their policies, it was clear there was no rush to organise such a dialogue.

Over the coming months we looked at other precedents: the Scottish Council for Development and Industry that had created a powerful capacity for independent research, and two English foundations – St George's House, Windsor and the St Williams Foundation at York – both established, in the words of the latter, 'to provide an independent forum where major and critical problems affecting contemporary life can be studied with a view to finding better possibilities for their solution'.

Eventually these ideas came together in a paper in February 1986 setting out a proposal for what we called a Welsh Economic Institute. We argued that 'the general failure to harness the intellectual and business communities to a common end...impoverished both debate and action...[meaning that] the shaping and sharpening of policies could become a dangerously private matter'. What was needed was 'a body that can provide a regular intellectual challenge to current practice in all those spheres of Welsh life and administration that impact on our industrial and economic performance'.

It would establish links with a range of institutions including government and the university but 'it must be truly independent of them, beholden only to the need for its work to be of quality and relevance and, above all, effective'. Most important of all was that as much as possible of its work should be in the public domain to extend debate, change attitudes and fight against a culture of private complaint and public silence. To that end it would have to be independent of party and not dependent on government finance.

In March Keith, a member of a Cardiff Business School advisory panel, put the paper to the panel to see whether any fish would bite. The reaction was mildly positive, but the one enthusiast was David Waterstone, the Chief Executive of the WDA, who had had some frustrations of his own in dealing with the Welsh Office. With his and the WDA's active assistance an organising group started to gel. But it was another eighteen months before it was finally registered as the Institute of Welsh Affairs. Its launch was delayed until August 1987 to avoid clashing with the June general election that, in defeat, proved to be such an epiphany for many Labour MPs on the devolution issue.

Under its first chairman and deputy chairman – respectively, Henry Kroch, president of AB Electronics, one of the largest private sector employers in the south Wales valleys, and Sir Donald Walters, a wartime 'Bevin boy' and barrister who had successfully mixed the law, business and Conservative politics – it produced a steady stream of work despite having no full-time staff.

Reports on the valleys, the problems of the rural economy, the requirement for new visual arts facilities, air services and a foothold for the Chancery Bar in Cardiff followed at regular intervals. Requests from Welsh Office civil servants to see the draft of the report on the valleys, seemed to confirm that there was a need for us. Despite the fact that the work drew on an exceptionally wide range of people, the prominence of business and the legal profession on its board allowed sceptics and wags, ever eager to pigeonhole the new organisation, to dub it, rather unfairly, as 'the CBI in drag'.

Henry Kroch and Donald Walters brought integrity and solidity to the organisation, and it was a remarkable feat to keep up the volume and quality of this output, especially since one of the disappointments was the reluctance of the business community to come up with cash rather than help in kind. Maintaining an organisation with scant financial resources is a common enough problem in the voluntary sector, but especially so for a charity that has intellectual rather than emotional appeal and, for the most part, long term rather than short term effect. Business also had a common nervousness of policy as something akin to politics and, therefore, to be avoided. Yet this was precisely the fracture that we had to bridge if we were ever to become a joined-up community.

Frustratingly for me, the family and I had left Cardiff for Newcastle three months before the Institute's launch in 1987, but two years after returning in 1990 I succeeded Henry Kroch in the chair. It was soon clear to me that although we had some administrative staff, and that Hugh Thomas, a former British Steel executive and walking contacts book, had been an unpaid part-time director, unless we could appoint a full-time director to provide daily drive and focus, the IWA would inevitably wane. Like most charities we faced a catch-22: without steady revenue we could not appoint staff, but without staff we could not easily find steady revenue. A proposed alliance with Cardiff Business School beckoned for a while but came to nothing.

Keith James and I finally made a series of pitches that, I hope, sounded less desperate than we felt, and landed £40,000 a year for three years from Hyder, £50,000 a year for three years from the WDA, and a gift of £50,000 from Sir Julian Hodge through the foundation that bears his mother's name. When we visited him he had just passed his ninetieth birthday, but was as sharp as a razor and still calling the Julian Hodge Bank from his home in Jersey every morning for a daily update on its balances. The letter stating our case had included some flattering remarks about his contribution to the business life of Wales. When we entered the room, the letter was in his hand. He put down his large pipe, looked at us schoolboys and said, 'Do I get the job?' Suddenly, we were able to move up a gear.

The director's job was tailor-made for John Osmond, who was appointed early in 1996, having already been a key motivating figure in the intellectual and political life of Wales for more than two decades. We had been close colleagues at the *Western Mail* and he had come to work for me at HTV on *Wales This Week*, after the premature collapse of the magazine, *Arcade*, which he founded and edited.

He had left the *Western Mail* to launch *Arcade*, a fortnightly magazine that effected a resurrection of political debate through writers, historians and poets, including Raymond Williams, Gwyn Alf Williams, Dai Smith, Ned Thomas, John Ormond and Nigel Jenkins.

The *Arcade* experience also brought John closer to the literary life of Wales, especially in the English language, and he became one of the founders of the Welsh Union of Writers and its chairman in the late eighties. *Arcade* existed for two years, until the controversial withdrawal of an arts council grant soon after an exposé that drew in Nicholas Edwards and Denis Thatcher and got rather more publicity in the London prints than is normal for Welsh magazines. The cover of the final edition read, 'Wales declared an *Arcade*-free zone'.

Like many a passionate believer in a cause, he came, in one sense, from the other side. His great-grandfather, Henry Osmond, had emigrated from Cornwall to Cardiff at the very end of the nineteenth century and opened a quarry just above what are now the ITV Wales studios at Culverhouse Cross on the western edge of Cardiff. Business success meant they lived in the Great House at Ely and Henry Osmond's monument stands in the nearby graveyard of Caerau's historic but now much vandalised church. His parents, both Cardiff born, were, in John's own description, intensely British and Tory, avid readers of the *Daily Express* who were still not disposed to dismiss Napoleon from the identification parade of Britain's arch-enemies.

A sense of Welshness would have come, as it did to another Abergavenny resident, Raymond Williams, in part from the surrounding landscape, but in John's case from the Presbyterian church where John's father was an elder. The Minister, Penry Jones from Llanelli, and his wife, Gertrude, from Bangor, were both Welsh-speaking, and imbued with the Christian Socialist tradition. They became, in effect, 'surrogate parents' to John, making him a son of the manse by proxy and ingraining the habit of political debate.

In an emotional speech on his sixtieth birthday in 2006, John recounted how, while at university in Bristol, he had surprised himself with the strength of his reaction to the Aberfan disaster in 1966, which he felt was a life-changing experience. He was not alone. Aberfan was as important a milestone in Welsh attitudes as the drowning of Tryweryn a decade before. It was also the time of Vietnam and CND. John discovered a capacity to keep several balls in the air at once, combining his studies in philosophy, politics and economics with editing the weekly student newspaper, a post he was offered after an interview with Sue Lawley, then the student president.

He arrived at the *Western Mail* in 1972, after four years on the *Yorkshire Post*, and we worked together on the devolution issue, the two general elections of 1974 and the referendum on Europe the following year. In all this he worked at speed, as he still does, one minute acutely alert and at other moments seemingly in another world.

During a briefing visit to Brussels with myself, Trevor Fishlock, and the then *Guardian* correspondent in Wales, Ann Clwyd, John was lost in reverie at the wrong moment. We boarded a train, realised he was still on the platform and shouted. Leaping on at the last moment, the sliding doors caught his jacket suspending him above the train floor like a butterfly caught by its wings. Although later he gathered extensive experience of television, he has always been, at bottom, a man of the printed word. Even in newspapers he hankered after the space for a deeper approach to policy issues, and as a result produced a steady flow of books to accompany almost everything he did.

He had produced the first of these, *The Centralist Enemy*, within two years of joining the *Western Mail*, seizing on the rationalisation of the steel and the gas industries to illustrate a running trend that, whatever the technological or economic pressures, was denuding Welsh society of a seam of senior decision makers. At the time the steel industry was only five years into its nationalised form, and the gas industry was responding to the advent of North Sea gas. Similar points were then being made by more established bodies such as the Scottish Council for Development and Industry, but John gave the issue a more polemical edge and tethered it to the devolution mast.

Four years later he took it a stage further in *Creative Conflict*, which was both more philosophical and more practical, pitching Aristotle against Plato, unity against pluralism, community against state, and using the argument to criticise the Labour Government's proposals for devolution to Wales and Scotland, that were then before Parliament.

If he has always wanted to go beyond journalism, it is as a practical, engaged intellectual rather than a denizen of an ivory tower, although his prodigious output would put many an academic to shame. He described the scale of the referendum defeat in 1979 as a 'personal, political, and even professional trauma'. He walked the streets of Cardiff in depression on the night of the result while his newsroom searched for him. It was also undoubtedly a turning point in the level of his engagement.

It was his particular talent as an editor, as much as author, that was one of many reasons that made him such an obvious choice for the IWA. Many of the volumes he had edited had been the result of seminars and projects that had drawn together widely differing views. Even before *Creative Conflict* was published, early in 1978, he had been

planning another volume on socialism, nationalism and international-
ism that, after the 1979 referendum, was changed into a quite different
book of essays, *The National Question Again – Welsh political Identity in
the 1980s*. This brought together writers, historians and politicians of all
parties to give an unmistakable early signal that the period of post-
1979 mourning was over, and that the battle was rejoined. The book
also gave us Denis Balsom's enduringly influential analysis of the
geography of Welsh attitudes. It divided Wales into *Y Fro Gymraeg* (the
Welsh heartland of the north west), British Wales (east Wales and the
south-east coastal strip and south Pembrokeshire) and Welsh Wales
(the industrial valleys, including south Carmarthenshire). It
overturned several tired stereotypes in ways that were crucial to the
restructuring of Welsh political debate. It would not be possible thereafter simplistically to equate identification with Wales with the strength
of the language in an area.

Shortly after the 1987 general election, just as the IWA got going, a
new Campaign for a Welsh Assembly was launched, with John as its
secretary. Although it did not manage to effect anything as powerfully
inclusive as the Scottish Convention, it succeeded in establishing
groups in nearly 20 towns across Wales. They began to relate devolution to practical policies and crossed party divides.

At the same time, with his friend and colleague, Robin Reeves, he
conceived of the St David's Forum, aiming to meet annually under
Chatham House rules to bring officials in Wales together with a wider
grouping. In setting up the IWA we had spoken to John about ensuring that the two organisations complemented each other. We wanted to
avoid the name 'forum' for ourselves, a word that I had always opposed
on the grounds that it smacked too much of a talking shop. The St
David's Forum was, in reality, a series of events rather than an organisation, and after John joined us it was subsumed by the IWA.

The seamlessness of John's work and interests was evident in the
fact that while keeping this campaign going, he was also producing a
10-part series for Channel Four on identity in the UK entitled *The
Divided Kingdom*. Inevitably, he was writing another book to accompany the series. It was directed by Colin Thomas, who went one better
than his own earlier series on the history of Wales by having not two but
five presenters: Kim Howells for Wales, Margo MacDonald for
Scotland, A.T.Q. Stewart for Northern Ireland and Julian Critchley
and Beatrix Campbell for England – the last two being more interested
in class than place. The series was particularly keen to explore the

English dimension to identity and it was no accident that at the same time John found himself on the founding council of Charter 88 that was opening up a wider constitutional debate in the rest of Britain.

The momentum of the constitutional debate in Wales increased after the 1992 election, given urgency by the certainty that the accident and 'bastard' prone Major government would lose the next election. By 1995 Labour, after some fractious internal debate – though less fractious than in 1979 – was committed to creating an Assembly, even if debates about precise powers and voting systems were not at an end. By this time the Campaign for a Welsh Assembly had transmuted into the Parliament for Wales Campaign, with John in the Chair, and it was this post that he relinquished in March 1996 to take on the work of the IWA.

In ten years John Osmond transformed the Institute, increasing its membership from barely 100 to more than 1300, filling out a branch network, editing a thrice-yearly journal that is still the only current affairs journal of its kind in Wales – with the possible exception of the Welsh language magazine *Barn* – and up to a dozen other publications each year. His prodigious workrate dipped marginally only once, when he slipped from a rock on the Pembrokeshire coast and broke a leg.

Professor Kevin Morgan once described him as a 'one-man civil society', but although solitary in his resolution he has also been a shop steward to the nation – a great convener and harrier of others. Even before the 1997 referendum he pulled together an IWA working group, including two retired civil servants to look at the desirable ground rules for the forthcoming poll. Crucially, it proposed separating the dates of the Scottish and Welsh referenda. The Welsh poll took place a week after the Scots voted. Another working group under a former deputy secretary at the Welsh Office, Ivor Lightman, to examine the initial Government of Wales Bill, foresaw the confusion between legislature and executive that the subsequent 2006 Act ended.

Most spectacularly, he organised a vast exercise to sketch out some of the issues and options facing the first Assembly Government in 1999, a project that drew more than 700 people into 21 study groups. They included some who would become special advisers to Cabinet Ministers in the new Assembly Government as well as the future Clerk to the Assembly. The dense 400-page volume that emerged from the exercise led to the most remarkable book launch. We had to book overflow rooms and a public address system in Cardiff's Park Hotel for a crowd of 500 that was addressed by the then Permanent Secretary, Rachel Lomax.

It is difficult to gauge the influence of the IWA. By 1999 the old jibe of the 'CBI in drag' had long gone, but the early nervousness of Assembly ministers and senior civil servants meant they rarely took a relaxed view of criticism or alternative proposals whether from the IWA or the media. Although John Osmond's own affinity with the 'national movement' was hardly a secret, his approach has always been resolutely ecumenical, which does not always win friends in the tribal badlands of politics.

The IWA's Board, too, has always been committed to a pluralist stance, containing, as it has done for most of the recent past, a former UK vice-chairman of the Conservative party, a former chairman of the Welsh Liberal Party's policy committee, a former Director of the Institute for Public Policy research – a London think-tank that had been a key influence on Labour in the run-up to the 1997 election, and the secretary of the Wales TUC. John's decision to stand as a candidate for Plaid in the 2007 election was a test for the board. It deserved some credit for concluding that an organisation that existed to encourage the growth of civil society should not debar an employee from aspiring to the ultimate democratic responsibility.

The Institute has managed some useful interventions, sometimes in the course of acting as a tool for others in sparking debate. Perhaps the most important was the publication of the academic paper that laid the statistical basis for obtaining the EU Objective One status that has been crucial in augmenting the development capacity of the Assembly throughout its first decade. More recently, our statistical study for the Assembly Government of the deprivation factors across the south Wales valleys and comparable areas of disadvantage in the rest of Britain provided powerful justification for a new initiative in the Heads of the Valleys. Some studies, of integrated childrens' centres and social housing, for example, have been commissioned by ministers.

Our report, *Bread and Roses*, that drew its title from the American phrase quoted by Jim Griffiths in his autobiography, kept the Cardiff opera house dream alive, in reconstituted form, at a black moment of despair. A deeply critical report on architectural standards, *Designing Success*, led directly to the creation of the Design Commission for Wales by the then Environment Minister, Sue Essex. A policy review prior to the 1997 election has also given birth to Academy Health Wales, a forum for cross-disciplinary discussion of health issues.

In time, however, it may be that the IWA's championing of the Welsh baccalaureate concept will be seen as its most important achievement. It became a central concern for us as a result of our 1993 report, *Wales 2010: Creating our Future*, inspired and driven by Dr. Gareth Jones, a retired management consultant who gave his fizzing energy to the IWA for more than 10 years. It argued for a Welsh baccalaureate that would cater for young people wanting to pursue both academic and vocational routes, and that it should be in place by the year 2000.

The work was taken up by a triumvirate comprising two heads of Welsh comprehensives, Eirlys Pritchard-Jones and John David, and a former Director of Examinations for the International Baccalaureate Organisation, Colin Jenkins, who had just retired as Principal of Atlantic College, an international sixth-form college housed in the exotic St. Donat's castle on the Glamorgan coast. Atlantic College had pioneered the International Baccalaureate in the UK, and I knew from the experience of two of my sons, who were students there, of the quality and breadth of the education. It became a long saga that illustrated the deep official and political resistance to the baccalaureate concept.

By February 1996, after a long process of consultation we published our curriculum proposals. Although many schools and colleges responded warmly, official reaction was more circumspect not to say hostile. Before the 1997 election it was no surprise that the Conservative Government should hold fast to the alleged 'gold standard' of A-levels. After all, when commissioning Sir Ron Dearing to look at the education of 16-19 year olds, it had tied one hand behind his back by insisting that the continuation of A-levels was a given.

With the election of Labour there was every expectation that things would change. A few weeks after the election I attended a meeting of the National Council for Vocational Qualifications in London, where the new education minister, Baroness Blackstone, announced confidently that 'we are going down the baccalaureate road'. Yet before the summer was out there was a screech of brakes and squeal of tyres as Tony Blair insisted on deferring to 'middle England' and the *Daily Mail*, making clear that the A-level examination was sacrosanct. The Bac was off the agenda.

This was a real setback, as it was clear that officials and ministers in Wales were reluctant to face the risks of Wales going it alone, despite the fact that we had persuaded the IBO to allow the International Baccalaureate to be a safety net qualification. One mandarin utterance will stay in the mind for ever: 'The problem with the baccalaureate is that it's about a transformation ... and we are not into transformations at the Welsh Office. We are into building on what is there.' We were undeterred. For every objection raised, a further piece of work was commissioned. We attempted to reassure by surveying the attitudes of business and of schools and colleges within Wales, and in order to scotch official belief that the Welsh Bac would not be acceptable at universities elsewhere in the UK, we surveyed them too – with highly encouraging results.

All in all we published seven pieces of work in seven years, allowing the University of London's Institute of Education to describe it as the 'the most thorough piece of curriculum development in the UK'. Yet at the beginning of our target year of 2000 it was still going nowhere. But then fortune smiled. In the early autumn of 2000 Labour and the Liberal Democrats began negotiations on a coalition. Dr Gareth Jones, who was also then Chair of the Welsh Liberal Democrats' policy committee, and had already helped stitch the Welsh Bac concept into his party's policies, was able to insist on a pilot as part of the coalition deal. Frustratingly, the education minister, Jane Davidson, was persuaded not to adopt the IWA's model and another, in our view inferior, was cobbled in a matter of weeks by a team at the Welsh Joint Education Committee. A-levels survived, but an important breach had been made.

There is a sense in which such interventions are less important than the fact that the Institute exists, gathering people together to listen and confer and share ideas. Unlike most other think-tanks in the UK, it boasts a wide and diverse membership that seeks no personal benefit from it other than that they should be better informed and that the society with which they identify so strongly should improve and prosper.

10 Who killed Hadid?

The building of an opera house for Cardiff has been one of the longest sagas in our cultural history, outstripped only by attempts to establish a Welsh national theatre. Numerous schemes have come and gone. There was a period when scarcely a building in the city with some semblance of gravitas had not been measured up for the role, though they were sometimes demolished before cultural planners could draw breath. A hoarder by nature, I still have some of the feasibility plans. It was, therefore, a rather exciting privilege to sit for a short time on the building committee of the Wales Millennium Centre, and pore over the plans of the one that would actually become a reality.

It was nerve-racking for all kinds of reasons: the inescapable funding issue, several redesigns, debates about procurement routes, civil service scepticism, political nervousness, a change of contractors and a change of chairman. The first chair, Sir Alan Cox, a Birmingham accountant who had spent a large part of his career in the steel industry, had bullied the scheme along for nearly six years, and had the imagination to draw into the centre's vision the Welsh youth movement, the Urdd, that immediately broadened the constituency of support beyond opera. He was followed by Sir David (now Lord) Rowe-Beddoe, who had been a force in Welsh life for more than a decade as chairman of the WDA, and was one of the few people with the business and political clout to overcome a crisis of political confidence after the fixed price contract with one contractor proved, not unexpectedly, rather less fixed than politicians imagined. He drove the project with flair not only to its opening but to its first realistic financing in 2007.

But hanging over the project throughout the years of planning was the shadow of a previous scheme that had divided the public and the politicians and whose collapse became, unfairly in my view, the dead albatross blighting the reputation of the Welsh capital.

For some years before the turn of the millennium Cardiff's most famous building was one that was never built – Zaha Hadid's Cardiff Bay Opera House. The formal rejection of the scheme was announced by the Millennium Commission on 22 December 1995, a grey morning lightened only too briefly by excited anticipation. In some quarters disbelief and anger were in the air. Stomachs knotted in disappointment. The announcement seemed a death knell for the city's cultural credentials, and brought down the wrath of architectural commentators on Cardiff's head. The city was lambasted as provincial and philistine, some even saw racism at work.

Even then Hadid was an international figure and by now she is a winner of the profession's most prestigious award, the Pritzker prize. Inevitably, she is much written about, and even a decade later few can do so without mentioning Cardiff in unflattering terms, while few can write about culture and Cardiff without mentioning Hadid. The damage was prolonged, though diminishing, but the hurt still runs deep, especially for those most closely involved. There are some who still do not speak to each other.

Mathew Prichard, a businessman, collector of art and philanthropist, who had chaired the Arts Council of Wales in the 1980s, was chairman of the Cardiff Bay Opera House Trust for its first six months, and even after a bout of ill-health forced him to step down he remained chairman of the selection committee for the architectural competition in which Hadid was chosen. Since he is also the grandson of Agatha Christie, it seems appropriate to gather all the suspects in the library and ask, who killed Hadid?

The list is longer than you might think: the trust itself, including Lord Crickhowell, its chairman for the remainder of its life, and the most passionate supporter of Hadid's work; Sir Geoffrey Inkin, the chairman of Cardiff Bay Development Corporation, and some members of his board; John Redwood, the secretary of state for Wales and his political assistant Hywel Williams (since converted into an ardent Hadid fan); Russell Goodway, the leader of Cardiff City Council; the Millennium Commission, including Michael Heseltine and its chairman, Virginia Bottomley, the secretary of state at the Department of National Heritage; the press and broadcasters; and, lastly, to lend tone and context to the gathering, the Prince of Wales. In this list of dramatis personae, everybody played a part.

It is often forgotten that the episode was played out during the rather rickety political era of the John Major government. Although a site for an opera house had been set aside in Cardiff Bay in 1988 at the instruction of the then secretary of state for Wales, Peter Walker, the Cardiff Bay Opera House Trust was not formally constituted until June 1993, a month before the Maastricht Treaty was ratified after, in John Major's own words, 'a year of gruesome trench warfare in the

Commons'. It was also scarcely a year following a general election that had surprised most of the Conservative Party and dumbfounded the Labour Party everywhere, but nowhere more than in Wales.

At the outset the trust was dealing with a secretary of state for Wales, John Redwood, who had become a figure of fun having broken a golden rule of television – if you don't know the words, keep your mouth shut – during the Welsh national anthem at the Welsh Tory conference. (I had had to sanction its rebroadcast.) Soon after he arrived in Wales, he attended a dinner that the BBC gave during the Royal Welsh Show. I asked him whether Wales had held any surprises for him. He replied tartly: 'Rumours of my ignorance are greatly exaggerated. I have been here before you know.' There was no small talk. A combination of powerful intellect, uncomfortable views, and limited social skills had alienated him from many in his own party in Wales, while already being regarded as disloyal by his own Prime Minister.

His approach to the job was also somewhat at variance with that of his predecessor-but-two, Nicholas Edwards, who, as Lord Crickhowell, now chaired the trust. Lord Crickhowell and John Redwood are not two people you can imagine having a gossip, least of all together. Redwood did not care for the Hadid scheme and his views were echoed by his assistant. During a phone call to Hywel Williams well before his master's resignation in June 1995 I raised the issue of the opera house. 'Ah!' he said, 'the beast in the Bay. I shouldn't worry your head about that.'

On the other side of the political fence, Labour was beginning to recover from the shock of 1992. In the May 1994 local elections, following a reorganisation of local government, Labour controlled the new Cardiff Council, and its leader, Russell Goodway, was wholly dominant within his group. Two months later Tony Blair was elected leader of the party and moved swiftly ahead in the polls. The party's shadow Welsh secretary, Ron Davies, was reviving the devolution policy and the party was warming to taking on the 'quango state'. It was a time when the edge to political life was at its sharpest. At a Labour party conference in Brighton one MP assured me there was no hope for 'Nick Edwards's opera house'.

Following the September 2004 announcement of Hadid as the winner of the architectural competition, all these factors impacted on the dynamic between the local authority and CBDC. Never short of personal confidence, Russell Goodway would undoubtedly have felt the political tide moving his way affecting his view of a large quango that was not only on his doorstep but squatting in one of the most attractive rooms in the house. Russell, knowing that the development corporation was time limited – it was wound up in 1999 – savoured his superior legitimacy and was determined to demonstrate his power and his deal-making skills. CBDC would have to learn to live with him, not least because he was on their board.

Though formally the sponsor of the opera house trust, the development corporation was far from a hotbed of support for Hadid. Its chairman, Sir Geoffrey Inkin, is a towering gentleman of military bearing and record. He served in Northern Ireland as Commander of the Royal Welch Fusiliers and carried the sword of state at the Prince of Wales's investiture in 1969. He had also stood for the Conservative cause in a general election at Ebbw Vale, where Tory candidates are sent to be shot at. The political connection as well as his brisk despatch of business, saw him successively into the chairmanship of the Cwmbran Development Corporation, the Land Authority for Wales and CBDC – the last two concurrently.

He was a highly effective advocate for the Cardiff Bay development and had a reputation for pragmatism and playing a straight bat. He was not opposed to Hadid, but neither was he an enthusiast, and would have been influenced by the extent of public opposition to the scheme as well as the vehemence of some on his board. His chief executive, Michael Boyce, who tended to make his points with expansive hand gestures as if about to produce a dove from his sleeve, had a reputation as a martinet, and the aesthetics of property development were never a priority.

The vice chairman, Jack Brooks, as well as being Jim Callaghan's agent, had been Russell Goodway's predecessor as leader of the pre-1994 South Glamorgan County Council. He was known as a cunning tactician, and is said to have avoided the embarrassment of having his own council vote against the development corporation's Cardiff Bay barrage scheme by lighting a pipe in the council chamber, setting off the smoke alarm and having the chamber cleared. Stories about Jack eddy around him like smoke, and largely from his own pipe. He is an engine of the Welsh oral tradition.

While leading South Glamorgan he was a powerful champion for areas of south Cardiff that for years had had a raw deal. His main passion was boxing and he was prone to claim, not unreasonably, just as many tangential social benefits for the sport as others would claim for the arts. A few years later, when the Centre for the Visual Arts in the city's Victorian central library – a centre that had been established with considerable assistance from Mathew Prichard's family trust – folded, he was influential in bringing to that fine civic building a sharply contrasting tenant, the British Boxing Board of Control. Jack liked a good scrap.

So did Brian (B.K.) Thomas, an insurance broker of such rabidly right wing leanings as to make Norman Tebbitt seem like Rowan Williams. He was quite aggressively against Hadid. Red-faced at a Cardiff Business Club dinner he leant across the evening's speaker – a bemused Bernard Ingham, himself no stranger to apoplexy – to harangue me on the continuing and supreme relevance of the classical orders of architecture. I doubt that B.K.Thomas was familiar with *De Architectura*, but he would certainly not have known that Vitruvius had fewer buildings to his name in his lifetime – i.e. none – than Hadid at that moment.

Given some of the opinions within the CBDC board, Russell Goodway's view was not decisive in relation to Hadid's fate, but it was crucial in giving priority to the millennium stadium project over the opera house. The council had no clear cultural policy – the European Capital of Culture bid was a decade away – and to the extent that it did, it favoured sport. In February 1995 its officers had largely written the WRU's bid for the 1999 Rugby World Cup, which then seemed as important for Wales as the Olympics became for London. The council was integral to the stadium project and the World Cup bid in a way that was never the case with the opera house project. The World Cup had a fixed date and a new stadium would be the clincher. It would have to jump the queue. Proponents of the opera house took to arguing that there was no reason why Cardiff should not have two millennium schemes, although the *Western Mail* was consistently sceptical of this assertion, but if Cardiff had to choose there was no mistaking which way the authorities were going to jump.

Hadid's scheme became the victim, in public at least, of an unfair and unwelcome contest between apples and oranges, in which the media played a depressingly predictable part. The media, both newspapers and broadcasters, will often take up stories because they fall into familiar, though unconscious, templates. The treatment will often depend on which template fits the bill. The approach to the two schemes was framed by fundamentally different assertions: the stadium by the positive assertion 'Rugby is our great national game'; the opera house by two negatives, 'We all hate modern architecture, don't we?' and 'Opera is for toffs,'

The first of the negatives seemed to have the endorsement of the Prince of Wales, though he never intervened directly on the Hadid issue. His first critical incursion into architectural matters in 1984 had struck a nerve with the profession and a chord with the public and gave the word 'carbuncle' a new usage. He later elaborated his view, attacking the exclusivity of the architectural profession and advancing the belief that architects should be in touch with the past as well as the future – although in practice he clearly preferred a far greater reliance on the former. His appeal for a reassertion of beauty in architecture gave voice to a deep public concern about the excesses of modernist planning and building in the sixties, helped frame debate on architectural issues, and may even have influenced the course of contemporary practice. But his view seemed also to exclude even the best modernist architecture, even in places that had no constraining reference points from the past.

Hadid's sharply angled building – which, in a different mood, the Prince might have seen as Islamic – gave new meaning to the phrase 'cutting edge' and was well beyond the royal pale. It did not help that Paul Koralek, who was praised for organising the Cardiff Bay competition and was a key influence on the selection panel, was from the Ahrends, Burton, Koralek practice that had designed the 'carbuncle' that the Prince had killed off. Things were coming full circle. One of the Prince's advisers, Marcus Binney, founder of Save Britain's Heritage, wrote to the *Financial Times*, accusing Hadid of representing 'the kind of absurd architectural arrogance that the public has long learned to distrust'.

The second assertion – 'opera is for toffs' – had the support of all tabloid newspapers, as they demonstrated so conclusively when giving the Arts Council of England a caning over its first £55m grant for the refurbishment of Covent Garden. The tabloid storm over that grant broke on the day of a WNO performance at the New Theatre in Cardiff. Michael White, *The Independent*'s music critic at the time, said, to me presciently, 'I guess Cardiff can kiss its opera house goodbye.'

The effect of the imposition of these journalistic templates was twofold. First, it posed entirely false choices, a familiar pattern when it comes to arguments about arts funding. To this day the WRU's Millennium Stadium website talks of winning its Millennium Commission funding 'after competition from the proposed Cardiff Bay Opera House'. One of the very few occasions when I was loudly critical of my own BBC Wales newsroom was when it ran a telephone poll within the evening news programme, *Wales Today*, asking people to choose. Telephone polls are notoriously unscientific and usually designed to confirm rather than confound prejudices. This was no exception. I thought they had no place in BBC news programmes, and instructed that they should not be repeated. A more acceptable methodology was used by the *Western Mail*, even if it still posed the usual false choice. It showed 26 per cent in favour of the opera house which, in the circumstances, was surprisingly positive.

The Hadid scheme had been in the public domain for almost a year, before anyone saw sight of the plan for the new stadium. For that time it was a contest between a dream and a scheme, something that was sure to disadvantage the latter. The journalists did their work. Hadid's plan was questioned to death, while the stadium plan, when it was eventually published, sailed through with only the lightest public examination, even riding roughshod over the legitimate concerns of the police – which BBC Wales did highlight – about the capacity of the city centre, and particularly the railway station, to handle crowds twice as large as any previously experienced in the city. The timescale for the stadium meant that there would be no architectural competition for a building that was going to dominate the centre of a capital city, nor any serious pursuit of alternative sites.

Though the stadium bid was submitted in a later funding round than the Hadid scheme, the Millennium Commission expedited its decision to take account of the time pressure created by the Rugby World Cup, announcing its £46m grant to the WRU only two months after it turned down the opera house bid. The commission's money was committed and building started even before the WRU had concluded the deal on the neighbouring BT telephone exchange that would need to be demolished, and, at the other end of the proposed ground, without securing agreement with Cardiff Athletic Club, owners of the neighbouring Cardiff Rugby Club ground. That last agreement proved stubbornly elusive, and the old stadium's carcass continues to stick out of the north end of an incomplete Millennium Stadium like a drunken rugby supporter mooning out of the rear window of the bus home.

While Cardiff has shouldered the blame for the demise of the Hadid design it is sometimes forgotten that it was the Millennium Commission itself that did for it, and that in two stages. First, it turned down all requests for amending its self-imposed rule limiting its maximum contribution to 50 per cent of the cost of any scheme, despite the patent inequity that this occasioned for any major project emanating from Wales. In the process it illustrated one of the financial disadvantages of devolution that has been too little studied and which was to assume greater importance following the creation of the National Assembly in 1999.

Just as the National Lottery was getting under way the Arts Council of Great Britain was being broken up into four national arts councils. As a result the arts lottery fund was similarly divided, and shared out on a population basis. This meant that the Arts Council of Wales was managing a fund that amounted to £15m in 1995/96 – the lottery's first year of operation – a sum that was dwarfed by the Arts Council of England's fund of nearly £300m. While the two figures represented a parity of funding in per capita terms, they did not and do not now produce a parity of effect. Einstein's theory of relativity is just as valid in public expenditure, as those who complain about the Barnett formula have belatedly realised.

Although both Arts Councils were willing to contribute up to 75 per cent of the cost of a scheme, ACE was able to handle large-scale proposals that were entirely beyond its Welsh equivalent. It was for this reason that Covent Garden was able to go to ACE and get 75 per cent, while in Cardiff the opera house trust had no option but to go to the Millennium Commission where it would get only 50 per cent. It meant that a part of the country that had the smallest pool of private and corporate donors had, proportionately, twice as steep a hill to climb as a comparable scheme from any city in England.

Crickhowell recounts that the issue became the subject of 'fierce correspondence' with Virginia Bottomley, although to no avail. As if to rub salt into this wound, the commission's chief executive, Jennifer Page, initially said that if the Arts Council of Wales tried to top up the public contribution the commission would reduce its own on a pound for pound basis, although it eventually relented on this issue. It was little wonder that the Millennium Commission found the opera house trust's fund-raising targets improbably daunting. But this only added to the hostility that some of the commissioners themselves felt about the proposed building.

It was not just aficionados of the Prince of Wales's theories that had doubts about whether the building would work in human terms. Walking around the exhibition of the eight finalists in the National Museum, with some members of the staff of the Welsh School of Architecture, was to hear some deep reservations, not least about the microclimate that the west-facing opening in Hadid's perimeter building might have created. In this informed group the vote seemed to go to the Japanese entrant, Itsuko Hasegawa. Manfredo Nicoletti's ocean of glass – that newspapers had tried to turn into the local favourite – was dismissed as tricksy and, more important considerations apart, unsuitable for a city that plays host to Britain's third largest population of seagulls.

Hadid was ill-served by the exhibition, and by the replacement of the original translucent, perspex model – that at least gave some credence to her 'crystal necklace' metaphor – by a lumpen wooden model that appeared unfinished and, according to Crickhowell, that she had never approved. That last fact attested to a naïve disregard for public relations that was especially damaging given the style of her perspective drawings, whose astonishing beauty lie in a complexity that borders on abstraction. Personally, I always thought the reference to a crystal necklace was a mistake; her scheme appealed to me more as a Welsh castle with the free-standing auditorium as its keep. Public relations was not the trust's forte.

After two years of intense controversy it was rather remarkable that the Millennium Commission's thumbs down on 22 December came as a total surprise – to the extent that at the BBC we discussed whether there had been a journalistic failure on our part. According to some of the opera house trustees the indications to them were positive right up to the meeting of the commission two days earlier. During the week of the announcement Nicholas Edwards and the Trust's manager, Mandy Wix, expressed their total confidence to anyone who asked. It was obviously misplaced.

The commission had always played its cards close to its chest, giving applicants very little indication of its early leanings with regard to their proposals. One commissioner later told me he thought that this might have been a mistake, as negative decisions tended to come as a bombshell. At the risk of mixing metaphors, Lord Crickhowell went off like a roman candle in front of the cameras, wounded not only by the decision but also by the fact that it had come at the hands of people he thought were political allies – Virginia Bottomley and Michael Heseltine. It began a period of debate, misunderstanding and sulphurous acrimony that I began to witness at closer quarters.

Following a meeting during the Christmas break with the MP Alun Michael, then vice-chairman of the trust, I discussed with colleagues at the Institute of Welsh Affairs what we might do to help. The result was a report by John Matthews, a locally-based arts consultant, on the application of various ceilings on lottery grants by the commission and the arts councils, arguing that 'inconsistencies identified appear to penalise the smaller nations of Britain'.

It was published in February and was carefully drafted so as not to sound like special pleading for a particular scheme. Matthews suggested a 'sixth good cause' that would 'commission an audit of Britain's stock of major buildings and building needs and set aside appropriate monies to facilitate, for example, the building of an English National Stadium or the Cardiff Bay Opera House without setting communities against each other and minimising charges of elitism in the choice of projects to be supported by the distributing bodies'. The report was titled *The Lottery of Lottery Funding*. I am not aware that it had an effect, but the sense of its approach was echoed almost a decade later in the arrangements for establishing The Big Lottery, where, despite the existence of devolved funds, a pot for major projects has been retained at a UK level.

The first month of the new year saw the trust and CBDC drift disastrously apart, based on two conflicting readings of the commission's position. The trust believed that the commission's objections were surmountable and that it would be amenable to the submission of a revised scheme. Crickhowell believed he had a commitment from Jennifer Page to that effect, albeit only by means of a phone conversation. CBDC were equally adamant that they had been told by the commission not to bring the Hadid scheme back to the table.

On 18 February I met with Alun Michael and the National Museum's director, Colin Ford, who saw a chance to move his own ambitious development agenda forward. Alun was keen to resubmit the Hadid scheme but recognised that the project might need to change its name to the Cardiff Bay Millennium Centre and that the substance and presentation of the business plan would need to be improved. Colin, impatient with Wales's disputatious habits, was keen to find a way of replacing his Industrial and Maritime Museum in Cardiff Bay, and saw the prospect of housing new galleries and an IMAX screen within the Hadid scheme by removing the car park that the planning authorities had insisted should be incorporated.

Both thought that the Millennium Commission would find it easier to deal with a new organisation to front the bid and that it should be more representative of the community than the opera house trustees. But the prime advantage was that the museum's involvement would draw the Heritage Lottery Fund into the funding equation. The three of us were also aware of rumours that CBDC's chief executive was tempted by a cut-price option that might be run by a commercial theatre operator. This would have been unlikely to result in any landmark architecture, or to allow for much community involvement and would certainly have been anathema to WNO.

We agreed that the IWA, as a neutral body that had not been involved in the initial discussions, should convene a meeting of all parties and that the agenda should be broader than simply the future of the opera house bid. Three matters would be put on the table: housing the performing arts in Cardiff, Wales's approach to the millennium celebration and joint working among arts organisations in the city.

No preparation would have been adequate for what transpired in the sombre, wood-panelled surroundings of the National Museum's Court Room at 4.30pm on 8 March 1996, under the gaze of the bronze heads of previous museum presidents. It was the worst meeting I have ever chaired, the meeting from hell. It was never going to be easy but earlier that afternoon Sir Geoffrey Inkin had circulated a letter to all the prospective attendees to the effect that the development corporation had concluded 'on the grounds of its high total cost, its apparent lack of support from the local authority and the public and the absence of backing from the Millennium Commission, that the Hadid scheme should be set aside'. The result was that as the various parties took their place the atmosphere was highly combustible. It may well have been a calculated pre-emption on Inkin's part, but it was based on a clear – if contested – reading of the commission's position and a very accurate reading of the local authority's position, something that was immediately confirmed by its leader Russell Goodway.

In opening the meeting, Gareth Jones, chair of the IWA's research panel, and I had both expressed the hope that, at the very least, we could agree that there was a need for a centre for the performing arts in Cardiff. Goodway leapt in to contest even this. He hadn't seen any evidence. 'No-one has persuaded me.' Alun Michael and Inkin crossed swords from opposite ends of the table. Goodway was determinedly rude to WNO's chairman and chief executive, Lord Davies and Anthony Freud, seated right opposite him. He didn't think they should be involved in any new scheme. 'After all, what's WNO bringing to the table?' His question brought a stunned silence, after which he confirmed that the local authority would put nothing into it.

Goodway's provocative philistinism proved too much for

Crickhowell who stormed out, slamming shut half a ton of oak like a clap of thunder. Alun Michael, conscious that reporters and cameras were waiting on the museum steps raced after him to avert disaster. Back in the Court Room I suggested that the IWA prepare a report setting out the case for a Centre for the Performing Arts. Russell Goodway promised he would read it. CBDC said they would be prepared to support a new scheme. An hour after the end of the meeting Geoffrey Inkin and Crickhowell hosted separate parties at the opera, either side of the central aisle in the dress circle of the New Theatre. There was much scowling and some words of abuse could be lip read. In the circumstances *I Pagliacci* seemed quite suitable.

Some of us stayed behind in Colin Ford's office to write a press release announcing that steps would be taken to establish a new project. In May the IWA published its report, *Bread and Roses*, setting out the case for a Millennium Centre for the arts in the Welsh capital. It was another eight years before the Wales Millennium Centre opened its doors. Another long, rock-strewn road, but over which all parties managed, in the end, to clamber.

11 To opera sideways

It was a spectacular introduction to opera. The night air was baking, and the street lights had failed to screen out a starry sky. We shuffled into our places, encircled by walls whose ragged tops were silhouetted high above us. Eventually, even schoolboys settled as the lights rose, pooling on the warm brickwork as well as the stage. Verdi's *Aida* was under way, with every circus trick in town, at the Baths of Caracalla in Rome. I remember little but the spectacle, the sense of visual and musical scale, and some great performances probably passed me by. After all, we had gone there in 1960, not for the opera or even the Holy City but for the Olympic Games, to cheer on British athletes then at the height of their glorious losers phase. For most of us, in our mid teens, it was not only our first opera, but our first trip abroad. First impressions were in crowded competition.

Some may have experienced an early Damascene conversion to opera but, in truth, many people come to it late, often at a time when they feel better able to make the investment in time than when the preoccupations of children and family dominate. I approached opera sideways. As a nine-year-old I had experienced the thrill of that first entry in *Zadok the Priest*, as one of the ruffed choirboys of Swansea's churches celebrating the Queen's coronation at the Brangwyn Hall. There was a closer teenage camaraderie to be had later in the Cardiff Aelwyd Choir, including a heady performance at the Royal Albert Hall in the annual lachrymose flush of sentiment on St David's Day.

At about the same time I had managed to see WNO's *Nabucco* from the exquisitely uncomfortable upper circle of the New Theatre. Elijah called upon God to destroy the temple of Baal. Stagehands rattled the thunder sheets vigorously and lightning flashed before the stage was plunged into darkness. When the lights rose again the whole chorus lay face down. A loud whisper was heard across the upper circle. 'Which one's Baal?'

A decade later my contact with the arts had started to ebb away under the pressures of working for a morning newspaper, though occasional theatre reviews for the *Western Mail* included having to avoid Peter Seller's fate in *Only Two Can Play*. During the second act

of Saunders Lewis's play, *Cymru Fydd*, at the national Eisteddfod at
Bala, the backdrop went up in flames. It was a rather larger fire than he
and his co-conspirators managed with damp matches in a vain attempt
to prevent a bombing school being built in North Wales in the 1930s.
Television offered more opportunities, though the arts were not
officially part of my own bailiwick at HTV. Nevertheless, with Sir
Geraint Evans on the board – as iconic in his time as Terfel today –
aided and abetted by the ever-mischievous, opera-loving journalist,
John Morgan, and the director of programmes, Aled Vaughan, the arts
had a secure place in the company's heart, and a surprisingly large
space in its schedules.

It launched a harp festival at St David's Hall – though it was short-
lived – and delivered a memorable Verdi *Requiem* with Margaret Price
and Gwynne Howell, conducted by James Lockhart. Geraint Evans
had struck up a partnership with the composer Norman Kay, who
became head of music. Kay had written one opera for the BBC, *The
Rose Affair*, based on a play by Alun Owen. At HTV he wrote a second
based on *The Christmas Carol*, with Geraint Evans as Scrooge and
Gwynne Howell as Marley and managed to carry off the Salzburg
Opera prize for opera on television. HTV had, in the 1970s, broadcast
Alun Hoddinott's *The Beach of Falesa*, that had been commissioned for
WNO and for Geraint. It followed up by commissioning another
Hoddinott opera – *Murder, the Magician*, with a libretto by John
Morgan. The rest of ITV, including the company's other half in the
west of England, looked on in bemused astonishment, not least when
the largest studio at the new headquarters at Culverhouse Cross was
designed on such an immodest scale specifically so that it could accommodate an opera production, complete with orchestra. While HTV
West executives headed for Los Angeles, HTV Wales board members
headed for Salzburg, though as ITV headed for the nineties, it was
increasingly clear that this was not a growth sector in the industry.

Tyne Tees Television, which also gave creditable coverage to the
arts, dipped its toe into the deep waters of sponsorship by backing a
Scottish Opera production of *Lulu*. It was not entirely to the board's
taste. 'Was it a sell-out?' someone asked at the next meeting. 'Yes, at the
beginning,' came the chairman's crusty reply. There was more enthusiasm for helping Northern Sinfonia, since it was, in effect, the national
orchestra of the north east.

These were the last of ITV's boom years before Margaret
Thatcher's auction of the regional franchises laid waste to the system

and particularly to regional loyalties. Tyne Tees was determined to knit itself into the region and I found myself on the boards of both the Northern Sinfonia and the Northern Stage Company, both of whom were going through a difficult period. The Northern Sinfonia was fortunate in having a young and able director, John Summers, who pulled off a coup by engaging the cellist, Heinrich Schiff, as artistic director. Schiff stayed for six years and not long after he left John Summers left to play a leading role in the revival of the Halle Orchestra.

At the time the redevelopment of both banks of the Tyne had not begun and the Sinfonia played in Newcastle's only sizeable hall, the City Hall, an old-fashioned unraked auditorium with a horseshoe balcony that would bounce alarmingly during Lindisfarne's obligatory New Year's Eve concert. The Sage, the Sinfonia's Norman Foster-designed new home on the Gateshead side of the river, was a distant dream in those pre-lottery days.

Cardiff had had its own purpose built concert hall – St David's Hall – since 1983, not only providing the BBC Welsh Symphony Orchestra, as it was then known, with a home base but also a good reason to increase its playing strength from 78 to a full symphonic 90, a crucial development that happened three years later. In 1990, arriving at BBC Wales, it was an extraordinary feeling to know that one's staff also comprised a symphony orchestra. The headquarters at Llandaff was not only a building charged with the driving hubbub of a newsroom and the creativity of other programme makers, but also a place where ninety musicians went about their daily business of rehearsing and recording and making musical magic.

It made for a decade of tense concert going, since any level of owner-ship of a performing company makes the witnessing of its performance a more nail-biting experience than that enjoyed by the average ticket-purchaser. It sharpens the moment. The pleasure of seeing other companies perform is made up, in part, by relief from that tension.

The Welsh orchestra was on increasingly good form, largely influ-enced by its principal conductor, Tadaaki Otaka, and its director, Huw Tregelles Williams. The change was noticed and John Drummond, the torrentially loquacious controller of Radio 3, increased its quota of Prom concerts. The number of annual tours to mid and north Wales was also increased. It was a period, too, when the orchestra was keen to show off its new-found form in other countries, tours that often had a significance beyond the music.

A tour to Vienna, Prague, Leipzig and Berlin during the week of the reunification of Germany could not fail to be a moving experience. In Prague we met the leaders of the Civic Forum that had been so instrumental in their 'velvet revolution', bringing back memories of 1968 and the premature ending of the 'Prague spring' that had affected so many of us. Our translator, a doctor who was struggling to make ends meet, in part because of her own past commitment to reform, wept as our orchestra played Sibelius's Second Symphony in a Smetana Hall still heavy with the dust of neglect. In Leipzig the historic, though not beautiful Gewandhaus, was our second venue, though history's focus that week was more on the city's Nikolaikirche, where the candles of the East German revolt were first lit.

A tour to Japan, that had long been Otaka's aspiration, was more problematic, and was on the point of cancellation for lack of funds. We had just announced more than three hundred redundancies, so this was not the moment for a BBC controller to discover hidden money in a back pocket. Otaka, clearly wielding a wand as well as a baton, suddenly produced a sponsorship cheque for £250,000 from Hitachi, one of the flood of Japanese companies that had come to Wales at the height of the 1980s inward investment boom.

Otaka is a deeply intelligent conductor, whose gentle, self-effacing personality is transformed on the rostrum, where he can be vigorous to the point of levitation. The self-effacement resumes once the performance is over. I have never seen a conductor more reluctant to take the plaudits that are his due, always putting the players first. He would tell the story that his father, one of the first Japanese conductors trained in Vienna, returned to Japan to conduct the very first concert in the rural town of Komagane. His father reached the podium and bowed to the audience, whereupon they all rose as one and bowed back.

Tadaaki, or Chu as he was known to his friends and colleagues, has a ready sense of humour. During a rehearsal in Japan he stopped to give a woodwind player an instruction, but got his name wrong. Apologising, he paused before adding nervously, 'All you Welsh look alike,' which produced gales of laughter. The orchestra always responded to him, and did so in no small measure during Mahler's fifth symphony at the final concert. Players from the Tokyo Philharmonic lined the entrance to the post-concert reception to clap our players in, much like a rugby team would do. It was a typically Japanese mark of respect and a touching climax to the tour.

Four years later, in Japan again, the economic climate was very different. Sponsorship was at a fraction of its level in 1991, and we again struggled to finance the visit. Eventually, on the basis that the arts and trade can go hand in hand, the Welsh Development Agency decided to support the tour, with the result that the final concert at the Suntory Hall was attended by the British ambassador and senior board members from an array of the largest Japanese companies. Later at a reception at the embassy, the WDA's Chairman, David Rowe-Beddoe, with his customary chutzpah, reminded the company that in 1905 the Japanese navy had been victorious in the Russo-Japanese war, partly because its fleet was fuelled by smokeless Welsh coal enabling it to be less easily detected than the larger Russian fleet. I was never sure what effect this tale had, but the ambassador, who happened to be on the same flight back to the UK, was insistent that it was the best high-level turnout from Japanese industry that he had seen and that the WDA had certainly got its money's worth.

Musically, the tour had been a great success, helped by having the cellist, Steven Isserlis, as soloist. The physicality of his performances belied an easy temperament. He played Elgar's Cello Concerto in the first half of a concert outside Tokyo, and after the interval quietly tucked himself into the back row of the cellos in place of a sick player for Brahms' fourth symphony. The final concert, brought even the reserved Japanese to their feet, with applause that went on even after the orchestra had left the stage, forcing Otaka to return entirely alone for one last retreating bow. By this time he was also Principal Conductor of a Japanese symphony orchestra, funded by the *Yomiuro Shimbun*, a tabloid daily newspaper. The day that Britain boasts a *Sun* Symphony Orchestra, will be the day the arts say to Rupert Murdoch, 'Gotcha,' – or vice versa?

In the same year the orchestra headed west as well as east, having been invited to play a concert in the hall of the General Assembly of the United Nations, to mark the UN's fiftieth anniversary. The concert was one of the toughest because the richly furnished hall, designed as a debating chamber, had the deadest acoustic anyone had experienced. A second concert, at the acoustically more helpful Lincoln Centre, made it a spectacular Welsh week in New York, since Bryn Terfel and Margaret Price were also appearing in *Figaro* at the Met. Silver petals showered down on the two Welsh *galacticos*, though the rapture could not stop the Big Apple's usual unseemly rush for the door.

It was not always easy to justify the cost of foreign tours. At the BBC it was, financially, a difficult decade and budgets were being cut and jobs lost. The accountants always reckoned that the BBC had one orchestra too many, with the result that at any one time, one of them was in deficit – a game of financial pass the parcel. In all the circumstances it would have seemed a mite insensitive to be spending spare cash on a 'trip'. Although we had increased the number of orchestral tours around Wales, we were also conscious of the potential accusation of using British licence-payers money to please audiences overseas. For both these reasons substantial sponsorship was a necessity.

For any arts organisation facing this dilemma – even ones that do not enjoy the BBC's high profile – it is important not to take too narrow a view. Looked at in relation to most arts budgets, the cost can seem disproportionate, but looked at in the context of the task of creating an international image for a single part of United Kingdom that has need of an active relationship with the rest of the world it seems much more modest. The arts can provide an effective platform for promoting all kinds of trade, including tourism, particularly when they can perform at the highest international standard. Over time, they can also begin to shape a country's image in more subtle ways.

For large ensembles that tour abroad infrequently, overseas visits can also have a powerful motivational effect that generates its own lift back home. In 1993, not long after the BBC Welsh Symphony Orchestra was renamed the BBC National Orchestra of Wales – in a move to shore up its defences against any possible BBC cuts – the orchestra was one of three invited to play in the Mahlerfest at Amsterdam's Concertgebouw. The other two orchestras were the Berlin Philharmonic and the Vienna Philharmonic. This was exalted company. Two nights before we were due to play, I was spellbound by the Berlin orchestra's performance of Mahler's ninth symphony, and held my breath as Claudio Abbado conducted both the audience and the orchestra through the final diminuendo and its essential aftermath of silence.

I confess that, much like a Welsh team manager before facing the All Blacks, I wondered how we would fare two nights later. It was to be Mahler's 'unfinished' tenth symphony, conducted by Otaka's successor as principal conductor, Mark Wigglesworth, a bold and exciting conductor, known to take risks. He and the players pulled it off in a manner that provoked the kind of superlatives usually kept for sports journalism. They brought the audience to its feet. It was an emotional moment.

Success in such company is important and has a lasting effect on an ensemble's self-esteem, something that is also true for smaller arts organisations who can find it easier to engage in direct artistic collaboration with artists from other countries. The one criticism that can be made is that, in Wales, we have not yet drawn all this activity into a coherent approach. The creation of Wales Arts International in 1997 – a joint venture between ACW and the British Council – was an important step forward, but another step change is now needed. Wales needs to match England and Scotland who have both developed international strategies for their arts, conscious of the 2005 Foreign Office review of the effectiveness of Britain's public diplomacy. This would need to embrace the Assembly Government, the Arts Council, the other Welsh cultural quangos, as well as two UK organisations – the British Council and Visiting Arts. This is one field where we would be foolish to let the devolution process prevent us from seizing the advantages of engaging in wider British initiatives. After all, the logic of devolution is the pursuit of the penny and the bun.

The media could also help by foregoing their knee-jerk parochialism when it comes to foreign travel by any public body. When the Freedom of Information Act came into force in 2004 the first and immediate request to the Arts Council of Wales came from the *South Wales Echo*. It wanted details of any foreign travel by any member of the council or its staff, complete with the cost of hotels and flights. There is nothing wrong with the public disclosure of such information, except that one knew immediately that the purpose of the request was to shape a large stick with which to beat us. We were fortunate, it had been a quiet year. I believe a similar request was made to other quangos and councils. In an era of globalisation, and in an enlarged Europe, this particular media obsession is perverse.

The truth is that our artists, our public officials and our elected representatives, do not travel anything like enough. During one discussion about the quality of the public spaces in our capital city, I recall trying to persuade Russell Goodway, then the council leader, to visit a list of exemplar cities in Europe to see how big a quality gap Cardiff had to close. The idea obviously had some appeal, but then he shook his head. Used as he was to a good media kicking, he thought he would be 'crucified again by the *Echo*'.

There is one event that draws artists from across the world to Wales – the *BBC Cardiff Singer of the World* competition. The competition was the brainchild of the entrepreneurial and chain-smoking Merfyn Williams, then head of music at BBC Wales, who created it in 1983 as a way of using the new St David's Hall. Since then, every other year, 25 singers are invited to Cardiff to sing their hearts out before a panel of greats – Marilyn Horne, Joan Sutherland, Christa Ludwig, Gundula Janowitz, Sherrill Milnes, Tom Krause – and a succession of opera house and festival directors, including Peter Jonas, Sir Brian McMaster, Matthew Epstein, Anthony Freud and John Fisher. Marilyn Horne and Joan Sutherland, always sparking off each other, came back time and time again, creating a real bond with the competition, Joan Sutherland eventually becoming the competition's patron.

Cardiff Singer was an important link with WNO, an essential partner in the venture. Julian Smith, using the company's network, found the singers. The WNO orchestra alternated with the BBC band through the five heats, although, for understandable reasons, the BBC always played on the final night. Successive general directors of WNO chaired the panel of judges and Anthony Freud always got a cheer for delivering the verdict not only in English but in impeccable Welsh. His successor, John Fisher, a considerable linguist as well as musician, followed suit *con brio*.

During the 1980s and the first three competitions the BBC often had to resort to 'papering' the house, despite Karita Mattila's win in the very first competition. But after the 1989 battle of the baritones between Bryn Terfel and Dmitri Hvorostovsky, the demand for tickets took off and through the nineties I received more desperate pleas for tickets for Cardiff Singer than for rugby internationals. Tiny tenors, tall baritones, petite and voluminous sopranos battled their way through arias, lieder and nerves. Winners and losers of heats glowed or wept. After his own heat the diminutive Chilean tenor, Tito Beltran, went further, did a handstand and walked down the backstage corridor on his hands for the cameras.

For four competitions in the 1990s, a large sponsorship deal with BP, £300,000 per competition, enabled us to launch a world-wide auditioning system, making Julian Smith, WNO's Head of Music, a veritable Marco Polo of opera. Anna Williams, an organiser supreme – and for many years a massive help to Brian McMaster at the Edinburgh Festival – mothered the singers for a week, encouraging and calming and occasionally wiping away tears. Sometimes she wasn't needed. One singer was rigorously chaperoned by her real mother, breaking out only on stage, though unfortunately with a vibrato that, as a reviewer of a famous Welsh soprano once wrote, 'you could drive a truck through without touching the sides'. Not all wine travels well.

The most common look of surprise during the week is always on the faces of the singers at the final when they suddenly face a full hall of Welsh people blasting out their national anthem. This is a discriminating audience. It is not everywhere that, as happened during the WNO's sixtieth anniversary concert in 1996, Carlo Rizzi could turn to the audience, without demur, and conduct 2,000 of them in their own rendering of *Va Pensiero*.

★ ★ ★ ★

The Johnson Buildings had seen better days. The name, inscribed in stone along a high parapet, had not crumbled entirely away, and could still be read. The windows leaked, noxious smells wafted from a basement that was below the level of the canal that passed behind, on its way to the Bute East Dock. Sticks of wild buddleia sprouted from an occasional chimney and gutter. Offices sprouted from narrow corridors or half landings designed to disorientate, horizontally and vertically. Four floors up – or was it three and a half? – the ceiling of a large room arched up from floor level, giving it the feel of a wartime Nissen hut. Only the acoustic tiles and a piano hinted that it was a rehearsal room. It was also where the board of Welsh National Opera met. If a room could suffer from schizophrenia, Room 301 would be it.

Like many an arts company, WNO, Wales's biggest, had no history of affluence. Its first offices were in the back rooms of a car showroom. For 20 years it squatted in the Johnson Buildings and managed to acquire along the way two warehouses, a disused stable block and, the newest of its buildings, the Princess of Wales Building, a big step forward but still stubbornly utilitarian and sharing none of the princess's physical attributes. For 58 years the company had no performance base to call its own. At every venue it was a touring company, including at Cardiff's New Theatre, a few hundred yards from its permanent encampment.

None of this stopped the company from dreaming, for dreaming had been a habit from the start: the dream of an indigenous opera company for the 'land of song', then in sequence the dream of a professional company, the dream of its own orchestra, a dreamt journey from provincial to national to international, and eventually the fixed dream that the company and its country deserved a fitting home for its art.

WNO's history underlines the truth that national institutions cannot be built overnight like a traditional Welsh *tŷ un-nos*. Under an old Welsh tradition tenants could claim land rights if they could erect a dwelling in one night. Historians now tell us that these houses were usually unsound and insanitary, and that a process that spoke of duress rather than opportunity did not deserve to be romanticised in any way. WNO was built over half a century not half a day, and is still a company where the institutional memory is very strong. That should not be a surprise. Even the largest opera companies are, on any other business scale, of middling size, and usually small enough to preserve a familial feel.

That was emphasised by the fact that for the whole of the last quarter of the twentieth century it had been chaired by one man, David Davies, Lord Davies of Llandinam, an heir to a tradition of entrepreneurship and philanthropy that had helped make modern Wales. His great-great-grandfather sank coalmines and built railways and Barry Docks – where my own grandfather worked as a coal trimmer – to break the Bute monopoly at Cardiff. His grandfather, the first Lord Davies, an active supporter of the League of Nations, was the moving force behind the building of the Temple of Peace in Cardiff's civic centre, also endowing the first Chair in International Relations at the University of Wales, Aberystwyth. His great-aunts amassed a wonderful collection of French impressionists and bequeathed them to the National Museum of Wales where they remain its central jewel.

David Davies presided over the growth of WNO to its full international stature, by giving it a steady compass bearing, and a steely judgment masked by a gentle touch. It should have been his lot to lead the company into its new home in the Wales Millennium Centre but delays, an illness and the sense of an impending new era as the National Assembly started work shaped his decision to hand over the reins. It coincided with my own retirement from the BBC, and with the new millennium only a few weeks old I joined the board as chairman designate, with a view to completing the handover the following autumn.

The history of the company is the story of the triumph of artistic ambition and achievement over the threat of financial disaster, in total disregard of the puritan ethic, as described by my Baptist mother, that 'ready cash is a check on the imagination'. The founder, Idloes Owen, like many a new businessman, began with a deficit, even playing a season at Porthcawl, the traditional home of the miners' eisteddfod, in an attempt to wipe out losses incurred in Cardiff. Financially, it didn't work. In the company's first decade deficits were cleared by public subscription and by individual board members, and the Friends of the Opera organisation was launched primarily to do likewise.

A succession of deficits through the 1950s did nothing to encourage a more positive frame of mind at the Arts Council of Great Britain, notwithstanding the fact that it was run by an eminent Welshman, Sir William Emrys Williams. Faced with his own shortage of funds, he became an advocate of 'regional retrenchment'. 'If an emphasis must be placed somewhere in that motto of "Raise and Spread" it seems wiser and more realistic to concentrate on raise', he wrote in 1952. AGCB's preference was to support the Carl Rosa company and Sir William, with a blithe disregard for the Welsh climate, suggested that WNO become a mini Glyndebourne. The then Chairman of WNO, Bill Smith, retaliated by suggesting that WNO take over Carl Rosa. By the end of the decade the company's financial state was parlous, with a widespread belief that, despite the support of the Welsh Arts Council, London, which had the bigger purse, would prefer to see WNO die.

Appeals were made to the local authorities. Not all were forthcoming, Newport Council declaring that 'Cardiff is not a convenient place for Newport to visit'. The late sixties saw a change of heart, at least at the Welsh end, with the Welsh Arts Council's grant to WNO increasing steadily until by 1968 it accounted for a full 36 per cent of the council's expenditure. In that year it was widely believed that the grant would be doubled – though it is not clear whether this was more than wishful thinking – and plans were laid to make the orchestra professional. When it became clear that there would be no increase of any kind, it became something of a national cause, and the occasion of the first ever appeal to the Welsh Office, then only four years old, the suggestion coming from the arch-fixer of the day, Lord Goodman. It was turned down, prompting a letter of complaint to Jennie Lee from no less than the Welsh Committee of the Communist Party, surely a unique event in the history of opera in the western world. Renée Short, a Labour MP who had been a theatrical costumier and ran her own stage design business, was dispatched to Cardiff to carry out a public inquiry into WNO.

According to the company's historian, Richard Fawkes: 'The outcome solved nothing. WNO was informed that only Manchester and Scotland had been designated for opera development outside London and that no additional help can be found.' In the early 1970s the pattern was much the same, with the addition of a national conference of local authorities called by the Lord Mayor of Cardiff in 1972, and the Welsh Parliamentary Party jumping on the bandwagon. Deficits were reined in at the start of the decade and again in the early 1980s, now in a very different political climate.

Profligacy was never the issue, more a case of artists pulling

Britain's notoriously low cultural expenditure up by its bootstraps, through the talents of the likes of Brian McMaster, Matthew Epstein, and Anthony Freud, and conductors, Richard Armstrong, Sir Charles McKerras and Carlo Rizzi. The Welsh MPs thought that 'the deficits were the result of success'. The notion that opera development outside London should be restricted to Manchester and Scotland, if true, was never one with which the Welsh Arts Council could agree, since it was arguing with some constancy that WNO was a company in which Wales should take pride.

The story illustrates the fact that, like the funding of the BBC Welsh orchestra, the funding of WNO has always been an issue for British as well as Welsh institutions. Stop-go funding of the ACGB by central government, changing priorities at ACGB itself, variable funding of the Welsh Arts Council first by ACGB and, after 1994, by the Welsh Office, all resulted in grants that could, quite unpredictably, be either zero or below or above inflation. There was seldom a consistent relationship between grant and required output. All in all, it was hardly a sensible way to fund and plan the work of a single company, let alone a sector.

In all this WNO was not alone. For most of the second half of the twentieth century opera, ballet and theatre companies, arts councils and governments were complicit in a ritual dance. Over a period of years – only the period was variable – a company would amass large deficits before declaring a national emergency and threatening closure. After a seemly delay, an arts council or a politician would ride to the rescue waving a cheque. This would be accompanied by a publicly acceptable mixture of admonition and mutual admiration, and the cycle could begin again. As in any threesome – and it was mostly a threesome – one party would feel out in the cold: arts companies would tear their hair out, governments would get irritated, and the public would look on with varying degrees of incredulity.

Early in 1996 a BBC2 fly on the wall documentary series on the Royal Opera House, *The House*, had gone disastrously wrong or wonderfully right, depending on your particular prejudices about arts management, adding fuel to the flames. It emphasised that arts organisations, too, had to look to the motes in their own eyes. By the end of the 1990s, it was dawning on all sides that this was not the best way to run the arts.

In this climate, in January 1999, the Arts Council of England launched the 'stabilisation' scheme, a new lifeboat, and it was to this that WNO was admitted in the first few months after I joined the board of the company. It was based on the supposition that large arts organisations with high fixed costs were operating at well below their optimal capacity. They were like large cars where the drivers had plenty of ideas about places to go, but not enough petrol to get there. The result was that the public were not getting the best return for the investment that had already been made.

Peter Boyden, who became the lead consultant to WNO for the exercise (and later carried out the review of English language theatre for ACW), had persuaded Gerry Robinson, the commercially experienced chairman of the Arts Council of England, that, as a rule of thumb, an increase of some 15 per cent in revenue funding for many organisations would produce a 60 per cent increase in output. Here was an opportunity for the development of a more rational approach to which both the funder and the funded could subscribe with some hope for longer term stability; an opportunity, too, for WNO to climb into the lifeboat and to test whether it held water. It was not before time. The company's accumulated deficit had reached £1.5m, the number of new productions in the year had dropped from four to one, touring weeks had been cut and solvency was a standing item on board agendas.

It involved two years of work by half a dozen working groups to examine every aspect of the company's operations. There was plenty of evidence that some other companies had regarded the scheme as just another new set of hoops through which they had to jump to get another funding fix. It was true that there were some at WNO who were, initially, sceptical about the process, but it quickly dawned on most that here was a positive opportunity to eliminate some of the deficiencies that had been holding the company back. At bottom it was simply a process of self-examination and change that is common in business, not least in broadcasting, and it was reassuring that there was unanimity across the company, the two Arts Councils and the consultants that we should protect those creative elements that, in Anthony Freud's words, 'allowed the company to fly'.

Outside the company there were mixed and contradictory reactions. Some London critics saw it as a further example of 'bean counters taking over' and assumed that it meant the imposition on an arts organisation of a regime of Taliban severity. Within Wales several other organisations were envious of what they saw as WNO's special treatment, ignoring the fact that it would almost certainly lead to the creation of an ACW stabilisation scheme for Wales, as transpired in

2002. One of the arguments that ACW advanced, successfully, at the time was that it wanted to give every one of its revenue clients the same uplift as was awarded to WNO. In that sense WNO made a break-through that benefited the whole of the Welsh arts sector.

The work also coincided with the Assembly education committee's review of cultural policy, where there were some signs of discomfort with WNO's size and scale. One member, reassuring me that WNO would not suffer from the review, perplexed me with this proposition: 'If we were starting from scratch, we wouldn't want to create a company of this scale.' 'What scale would you like?' said I. 'Well, smaller of course,' came the reply. Although I can understand the roots of the Welsh obsession with the small scale, in the case of opera it is hardly appropriate, and ignored the fact that it is WNO's scale that allows it to carry out an extensive touring function in England as well as Wales, justifying ACE's 60 per cent contribution to the total grant. In that sense the company remains a cross-border bargain for both sides – not unlike the BBC National Orchestra of Wales, that is effec-tively a deal between ACW, BBC Wales *and* BBC Radio 3.

The only downside of the stabilisation process was that we decided to make six orchestral players redundant. No-one took pleasure in such a change, but these were players called, on average, for only half the orchestral sessions across the year. Their positions would, in future, be filled on a freelance basis. It also involved tough box office and sponsorship targets which, in subsequent years, were very largely met. But far from 'falling victim' to the process, as some outsiders suggested, WNO ended up with a one-off investment of £4.25m and an increase of 15 per cent in its annual grant, the deficit cleared, new productions restored to their previous annual level, touring activity raised to its highest ever level, marketing equipped with the research and the tools that were so vital in filling the seats in the Millennium Centre three years later, and, perhaps most significantly, the transfor-mation of the nature and scale of its previous education and community programme. Some victim.

Given its roots it is not surprising that WNO should have one of the oldest education departments in British opera, although the patchwork nature of WNO's funding over the decades had meant that education had never enjoyed a settled place in the core funding of the company. Instead, it was funded in an ad hoc way, by a local authority, private sponsor, trust or foundation willing to support an individual project, usually spending no more than £50,000 a year. The new strategy changed that, creating the WNO Max programme. (Pepsi Max was the popular drink of the moment.) This was to embrace everything the company did away from the main theatre stages, backed by a core budget of nearly half a million pounds a year, and exploiting fully its remarkable ensemble of artistic and technical talent.

For the first time, the renamed education department was able to plan long term, to move beyond a series of excellent but rather disconnected projects to create a consistent and concerted link to new audiences and communities, to young people through primary and secondary schools and youth opera, through to a young artists programme for those early in their professional careers. This was not to be a van load of throwaway performances, or something done to tick an accessibility box, but a programme of work that would have artistic purpose: one that, gradually, would begin to complement and interact with the main stage repertoire and, importantly, start to connect WNO more effectively with writers and composers and the other resident companies in the new home that was only a few years away. Crucially, the planning of this activity, driven initially by Sarah Alexander, was integrated with the company's central planning function, giving it a new standing in the call on resources.

The Max concept raised the question of the relationship between an opera company and its community, a subject that some years later was debated at Opera Europa's annual conference in Cardiff. Public funders have many different motives for making an investment that, from one angle, can look disproportionate. Some of it is to do with prestige. Nations want opera companies in the same way that they want their own airlines. Cities want them in the same way that they want premier league football clubs. In a situation where economic competition in Europe is as much between cities as nations, these things can be outward signs of where you are in the league table, and at a time when civic leaders are busy reading Richard Florida and proclaiming that culture is their core business, opera companies are seen as flag carriers.

To this extent opera's community could be said to be defined by the funder – the city or the region or nation – and given the cost, public funders are entitled to ask a lot of opera companies. Although ACW provides only 40 per cent of WNO's total public grant, the sum represents 15 per cent of ACW's total grant in aid. ACW's next largest client, Clwyd Theatr Cymru, represents less than 6 per cent. In contrast, ACE's 60 per cent contribution to WNO represents only 2 per cent of its total English grant in aid. But it would be sad if the nature of an arts company's community were to be defined solely by the funding relationship. Community is not only about money. We have in Wales a paradoxical situation where Welsh National Opera performs more often in England than in Wales, and England, therefore, pays more than Wales does for the pleasure. Scottish Opera has suffered from not having such a cross-border deal, but that's another story.

The figures demonstrate that although the Welsh cash investment may be smaller, Wales's investment of emotional capital in the company is far higher, and emotional capital is not created by the funder, but by the public. Welsh National Opera is 'our company' – one that we want to share with many English cities and, potentially, with the rest of the world – but emphatically 'our company'. Where does that sense of ownership come from? It doesn't come solely or even mainly from the transaction of buying a ticket. It comes from the origins of a company and its affinity with a nation's more deep-rooted cultural history.

In Wales's case that stems not from the musical traditions of a royal court but from a democratic, religious and cultural history where music has played a crucial part: a choral tradition that was based on the chapel, the mine and the quarry, and a network of amateur endeavour expressed through a hierarchy of competitions in *eisteddfodau*. It was out of this amateur tradition that WNO grew, and the reputation of its amateur chorus still resonates long after that chorus went professional.

Of course, other European countries have their own distinctive musical traditions from Italy to Latvia, coloured by different histories, religious traditions, folk art, or patterns of patronage. The Welsh eisteddfodic tradition places the tiniest children onto stages before large audiences in their communities very early in their lives. I can still remember my quaking knees. Arguably, it is this tradition, this mechanism, that has given Wales a predominantly performance culture and explains the extraordinary roll call of singers to emerge from a small country of only three million people, the same size as Birmingham: Geraint Evans, Stuart Burrows, Gwyneth Jones, Margaret Price, Kenneth Bowen, Della Jones, Gwynne Howells, Robert Tear, Catrin Wyn Davies, Dennis O'Neill, Anne Evans, Rebecca Evans, Bryn Terfel – and one could go on. It is an extraordinary phenomenon, that is sometimes taken too much for granted.

There is a temptation to say that these historical roots are now no longer relevant, that the decline of traditional industries and their attendant social structures along with the decline of religion has severed the connection with the taste and habits of the past. Certainly, there has been change. People live their lives in different ways and technology has had a huge impact, but even together these things have not created a cultural tabula rasa. Choral activity in Wales might not be as ubiquitous as it once was, but the best choirs are more adventurous and eclectic in their repertoire than of old. The taste for oratorio is still in evidence, a side-effect being the rather different audience for WNO's deeply moving production of *Jephtha* than for the core repertoire. Of course there is change, but there is also a continuum into which national companies play.

In both Wales and Scotland debates about the governance of the arts have prompted people to ask what is the meaning of a 'national' company? What does it mean in a small country like Wales? What makes a 'national' organisation different from other arts organisations? Is it a title that a company can assume, or, in these days of accountability and compliance is it a title that has to be earned or, God forbid, applied for? There can be a tension between the outward, international orientation of opera companies, and their involvement with their communities.

Singers, composers and producers always were inveterate travellers, even before the invention of the aeroplane. One of the great names of the nineteenth century, Adelina Patti – remembered in Wales through the Patti pavilion in Swansea – was born in Madrid of Italian parents, grew up in the Bronx and carried a French passport. She sang in north and south America, and all over Europe including Russia, before deciding to build a small theatre of her own at Craig-y-Nos in the upper Swansea valley. Opera was a global business long before the word globalisation was coined. The stars of the opera industry – singers, conductors, directors and designers alike – are citizens of the world, the jet-setters of the arts, but there is something to be gained for any artistic company from having roots, and WNO is fortunate that its own are deeper than most. Out of those roots grow obligations.

The first must be cultural leadership, which implies a full-hearted engagement with the rest of the cultural community in any one place – with its writers and poets, with its visual artists, designers and photog raphers, with dancers, broadcasters and film-makers, but perhaps above all with its composers. That is not always easy to achieve, given the pressures that bear down on companies to fill large auditoria time and again. In relation to talent that surely means that, while needing to access the best international artists, a national company also has an obligation to nurture indigenous talent at every level – young people through education or youth opera, young artists schemes, and partnerships, where appropriate, with higher education institutions.

That can operate at other levels, too. It is some forty years since two of the great Welsh literary figures of the twentieth century wrote for WNO – T.H. Parry-Williams translating *I Lombardi* into Welsh and Saunders Lewis writing a light opera, *Serch yw'r doctor*, a free adaptation of Moliere's *L'amour medecin*. Both works were created respectively for the national eisteddfod at Ebbw Vale in 1958 and Cardiff in 1960.

WNO's new situation of cohabiting in WMC with seven other companies that include both the literature academy and Diversions dance company, holds renewed creative promise, as was evident in 2006 with the first of Gwyneth Lewis's contribution of two librettos to a trilogy of operas on environmental themes, and again in 2007 with the collaboration between WNO and the national dance company, Diversions, on Kurt Weill's *Seven Deadly Sins*. The scale of resources that any opera company commands also demands generosity in the way those resources are shared with the rest of the artistic community and the public. The bigger the sharing, the bigger return for the company creatively and in both public and political support.

Leadership also implies an obligation to innovate, and here the public broadcasting parallel is relevant. Throughout its history the BBC has been aware of its role as a standard setter, and, in recent years, particularly aware of its need to extend or enhance the public value of all that it does. Yes, there is a need for ratings some of the time, just as an opera company has to put bums on seats, but there is also an obligation to take risks – to know the audience well and to be alongside them most of the time but, at other times, a judicious way ahead of them: pushing into areas of challenge and experimentation. That is easier when there is trust between producer and audience, a trust that itself reflects community as well as creating it.

That said, the obligation to innovate and to take risks is not always easy to interpret in an art form that, in repertoire at least, has a reputation for conservatism. It's a clichéd comment by now that opera seems over-reliant on older repertoire for the main stages, with little new work that is sufficiently compelling and successful to draw reliable audiences. The question of why theatre responds more readily to contemporary events than opera is an intriguing one. It is easy to list the potential blockages: cost, musical idiom, financial risk, the longer lead times of opera, the affinity between music and allegory, the problems of marrying music with demotic speech or simply that opera companies can become boxed in by their very size. And yet works like

John Adams's *Nixon in China* and *The Death of Klinghoffer*, demonstrate that the effort is worth it. Audiences do respond.

Lastly, there is the obligation to break down barriers to the arts and to enlarge access, and there are plenty of signs of innovation in this area: Graham Vick's work at Birmingham, recent initiatives at Covent Garden – not least involving Music Theatre Wales at the Linbury – new music collaborations at The Sage at Gateshead, WNO's own Max programme. This work is defining opera's community in different ways as, too, will online developments such as WNO's pioneering podcasts of scenes from *The Flying Dutchman* with Bryn Terfel. It may even turn the education and outreach departments of opera companies into true research and development departments for opera, vital for the future health of the art and the audience.

It may also offer an escape from hoary accusations. Opera is the art form that most often faces the wearisome charge of elitism. It is true, historically, that in the nineteenth century theatre and opera-going developed social codes of dress and behaviour that were intended to define and thus exclude, and that there are hangovers. Images of Glyndebourne as a Brideshead with music, all black tie, champagne and hampers, are easy to conjure, and in that instance not inaccurate. But that is like condemning flying because of the existence of First Class seating, and who at the airport ever rejected an 'involuntary upgrade'. But in opera access has by now gone far beyond being a mere defensive shield, it is part of the mission, a pathway for future audiences, a route to long-term survival for opera companies.

The elitist gibe has rarely been so empty as in the case of Welsh National Opera, by now the least expensive place in the UK to see top class opera. The move to WMC allowed us to introduce £5 tickets for the first time. But it is more than a pricing issue. It has to do with the ethos. The company has its roots in the amateur musical traditions of Wales. Its chorus remained amateur for 22 years until 1968, even then retaining an additional voluntary chorus for another five years. The dearth of large theatres in Wales has meant the company has always been adept at small-scale productions in village halls and schools, and started touring in Wales in 1949, only three years after its founding. One of the first concerts was given in a hired marquee in Llanybydder, to which, it was said, 5,000 people came by coach and car and even horseback. They would have come, like much of WNO's audience in Wales, impelled by a parallel tradition rather than in search of social cachet. They still do.

12 A not so poisoned chalice

The fare was cheese and wine – 'a little wine and a lot of Kraft' – the white as warm as the red; a roomful of artists and suits gathered for the presentation of prizes and cheques to some lucky writers. Myself, merely the *Western Mail* reporter. The prizes were to be presented by the writer Saunders Lewis, an oracular figure, founder of the Welsh Nationalist Party and later to become a Nobel Prize nominee. He began to address the gathering in his characteristically scratchy, subversive voice – to the growing discomfort of the Arts Council's officers and members, and not a few of the supposedly deserving prize winners.

Lewis expressed amazement that a committee of expert people had sat down to discuss and decide who should be the recipients of these awards. It was all a waste of time. No committee, he said, could decide what new writing would be of lasting value. Posterity alone would decide and posterity would almost certainly disagree. A more logical approach would be for the Arts Council to place an advertisement in the *Western Mail* to announce that on a given day, at a given time, it would fling open a window on the top floor of its building and scatter several thousand pounds in new fivers into the breeze. This process would not only be quicker and cheaper, but also just as likely to find true talent and greatness as the more bureaucratic route. True to his principles, he delivered the speech twice, word for word, in both Welsh and English, prolonging the pain.

Working for an arts council requires a masochistic streak. When it became known that I was to take on the chair of the Arts Council of Wales I lost count of the number of people who used the phrase 'poisoned chalice', while giving me a look that suggested in none-too-subtle a fashion that anyone thinking of taking on the task must be mad. They seemed to suggest that it was a swift route to universal unpopularity on the simple basis that – a bit like commissioning television programmes – you have to say no to ten times more people than those to whom you say yes. While subscribing to the view that man's reach should exceed his grasp, many in the arts are obsessed with measuring the gap. Some friends of the arts can be more unpredictable than their enemies, believing that poking a friend in the eye does no lasting damage and is therapeutic for both the poker and the poked. Why would anybody wish to set up camp between the rock of government and the hard place of the arts sector?

Saunders Lewis was, of course, being wisely mischievous. The wellsprings of art are not bureaucratic, and posterity will have the last word. It is true, too, that processes and procedures do not determine artistic worth, but they and the money that flows through them do allow artists to live, arts organisations to survive, venues to be built and sustained, connections to be made between different arts and people of all ages, lives and communities to be enriched, children to be inspired and imaginations kindled. And if receipt of public largesse requires the filling in of a form, so be it.

That said, arts councils across the UK have been busy in recent years trying to pare down their bureaucratic side. The innumerable funding schemes that had mushroomed in the 1990s, partly fuelled by the new lottery money, were being sharply reduced before the lottery was a decade old. In Wales, funding schemes were reduced from no less than forty to three – individuals, organisations and capital – and a similar reduction had taken place in England, Scotland and Northern Ireland. Forms are also shorter. But it is not only the arts organisations themselves that rail against bureaucracy.

In my experience, few meetings of an arts council pass by without a council member pleading for more time to discuss the art. Despite strenuous efforts, the agendas of arts councils are too often dominated by the encumbrances of our compliance culture in a way that can affect a council's creative relationship with artists and arts organisations, unless it actively constructs a conversation that is separate and qualitatively different. One of the sad effects of the doubt cast over the Arts Council of Wales from July 2004 onwards was that it hindered the council's attempts to generate that conversation anew after the difficulties that assailed it around the turn of the millennium.

Those difficulties had their roots in the breakdown that occurred in the 1990s. This was charted in painful detail in a report by a retired civil servant, Richard Wallace, to the Assembly's education minister, Tom Middlehurst, in August 2000. Wallace listed a series of happenings that in combination 'would test the most robust and responsive management'.

It is a truly formidable list: in 1994, the creation of the Arts Council of Wales, spun out of the former Arts Council of Great Britain and involving the absorption of the three Welsh regional arts associations; in 1996-97, an internal reorganisation that, responding to the creation of the National Lottery, reduced the number of artform directorates and created an artform/access split; the emergence of a whole new range of clients as a result of the lottery; in 1996, the reorganisation of Welsh local government that affected working relationships between ACW and the local authorities; in 1998, a fierce public dispute about ACW's drama strategy, together with the appointment of a new chief executive who lasted only 18 months, and an unsuccessful defamation action against ACW staff; in 1999, the appointment of a new chair, Sybil Crouch, who had been strongly opposed to the drama strategy and now held a powerful mandate for change. Within a year she had, through no fault of her own, an interim chief executive, a management team beset by uncertainty, and a newly opened National Assembly already embarked on a review of cultural policy by its post-16 education committee. And all this against the background of four years of flat funding both for the council and for local government.

But that was not the end of it. Wallace reported in 2000, providing an unambiguous diagnosis, though some doubtful prescriptions for change. In reviewing what seemed to have been an implosion, he concluded that ACW had lost the confidence of the arts community and lost confidence in itself. A year later – in October 2001 – a new chief executive, Peter Tyndall, arrived, drafted in from the Welsh Local Government Association, where he had been head of education and culture. At the same time Anthony Everitt, a former secretary general of the ACGB, and another consultant, Ann Twine, had been engaged to put forward a new structure for the council, that was implemented in April 2002. This carried a commitment to a review, one year hence, that was completed in July 2003.

In April that year, I took the place of Sybil Crouch in the chair, appointed by Jenny Randerson, the Liberal Democrat culture minister, only a month before an election that saw the end of the coalition and the appointment of a new, Labour culture minister, Alun Pugh. In the summer of 2004 the Assembly Government announced its review of the quangos and, following the blocking, by vote of the Assembly, of its policy in relation to ACW in February 2006, a further review of ACW and its relationship to the Assembly was established under Elan Closs Stephens and her panel. It is not difficult to understand why the staff of ACW believe they have been subjected to a form of prolonged water torture.

One of the areas where it is possible to argue with the findings of the Wallace report is in the relative importance he attached to central management and regional offices respectively. Tension between the centre and the periphery is common to many organisations, and ten years at the BBC gave me more than enough experience of the arguments from either end of the spectrum. Often organisational change moves in cycles, centralising at one point in the cycle, and decentralising at the next. Wallace lamented both the weakening of the regional committees and what he saw as 'the lack of a strong and active central management'. But though his prescription wished to see both gaps plugged, his proposed structure would have made the council a creature of the regions.

He proposed that the regional committees should be distributing or executive committees, and that the council itself should be built up from those committees, with at least half its membership being their direct representatives. A similar proposal was put forward by the Stephens review in 2006. Everitt also toyed with creating four rather than three regions. Although this played well to the early obsession of the Assembly with avoiding the impression of centralisation in Cardiff Bay, it did not take account of the cost of such a heavily regionalised arrangement, or the lack of distinction between the national and regional roles of a significant proportion of the client base.

When examining regional structures in Wales, many have been too fond of looking over their shoulder at the fluctuating regional arrangements of the Arts Council of England, forgetting that Wales as a whole is smaller than many of those English regions. Neither did Wallace take account of the fact that the National Assembly was created to fill a *national* policy vacuum. His proposals would have seen the Arts Council squeezed between an Assembly intent on setting policy and regional committees handling budgets that would have been shaped by their own de facto control of the council. It put one in mind of the definition of a region preferred in despair by the chairman of a public authority in the Scottish Highlands, as 'an area larger or smaller than the last area for which we failed to find a solution'.

Thankfully, Anthony Everitt and Anne Twine were not willing to go that far. Although acknowledging the challenges of Wales's geography, and the probability that 'regional and local alliances will be best negotiated at a regional level', they also recognised fears that the balkanisation of the council might weaken art form expertise, while 'dividing its limited grant-in-aid could limit flexibility and might inhibit major regional developments'. If budgets reflected regional populations, they said, ACW would find it 'hard to cater for the lumpy distribution of arts practice'. They reported a 'widespread fear of fragmentation both of policy and administration and a corresponding inflation of ACW's running costs'. However, it was also thought that, politically, the regional dimension was 'a given'.

The Assembly had been anxious to counter any suggestion of over-centralisation, and had established its own regional committees, although, surprisingly, the education committee's review of cultural policy made no mention of the issue. Everitt and Twine proposed, and the council accepted, that there should be three regions, with their offices, staffs and committees, but, importantly, the committees would be creatures of the council not vice versa.

Again responding to this regional pressure they also went along with a proposal about which the arts community was much more sceptical – the dispersal of its senior art form officers around the three regions. The consultants thought that this process should be spread over ten years, as vacancies arose, but the council insisted on an immediate redistribution of several of these posts from Cardiff to Carmarthen and Colwyn Bay, a change that prompted more than one resignation. One effect of this pressure was to exclude from consideration the reintro-duction of specialist art form committees, whose loss in the mid 1990s had been much lamented by the sector, often forgetting the complaints about cronyism that those committees had often generated.

It is not a surprise that still the most persistent theme in the sector's pleas to the Council is for the further strengthening of art form expert-ise – and it was a key motivation in the creation of the post of arts director and David Alston's appointment to it. That necessity is not confined to Wales. It was one of the major themes of the peer review of the Arts Council of England in 2005.

Whatever caveats one might enter about the decisions of the council in relation to the 2002 restructuring, there is little doubt that Sybil Crouch and her team put the show very firmly and effectively on a new road, a task that required an extraordinary amount of time and commitment from its unpaid members. They were not helped by the immediate capping of the council's operational costs for a period of three years, before the true costs of the structure could be evaluated. It is not always easy to marry the endlessly messy preoccupations of politics – the short game – with the imperatives of organisational devel-opment that require long term detailed application, and the council was perhaps more aware than the politicians that the act of restructuring was the beginning and not the end of a process.

* * * *

To set against all this pain and angst, every member of an arts council has endless opportunities to relish the myriad expressions of the talent that abounds in society, whether in organisations or individuals. The public debate about the arts is so often concerned with the fate of organisations that the work of the individual artist can be easily ignored. And yet it is the bedrock of everything. So much of our vocabulary is in the plural or the collective: the arts, the performing arts, the visual arts, the creative industries, the sector, revenue funded organisations. Yet in the end they all depend on the singular imagination of the artist, even where he or she works with others.

It was perhaps significant, not to say chastening, that the two healthiest areas of the arts in Wales in the early years of the new millennium – literature and the visual arts – were the two fields that were least dependent on organisations. It was to counter this preoccupation with organisations that the council had established the Creative Wales Awards in 2002, and in its first year handed out the money – some £70,000 – electronically. Coming from the world of broadcasting, where a profusion of award ceremonies has honed narcissism into a fine art, I felt that these awards to artists needed a little razzmatazz that would gain them some public attention, in addition to a bigger share of the financial cake. In 2003 it was turned into an event where we handed out £204,000 amongst 20 artists. By 2006 that had grown to nearly £300,000 and been extended to include writers, despite the parallel literature bursaries. Much the same happened with the Book of the Year event, moving from an ill-attended session at the Hay Festival to a packed event at a Cardiff hotel, and with the added benefit that the Welsh Books Council was persuaded, not before time, to put a much bigger effort into marketing not only the winners but also the books on the long and short lists.

This was no bad time to be close to the arts in Wales, and they provided plentiful cause for celebration. Bryn Terfel, already a world star, was entering the years of his prime, and tackling his first Wotan. Importantly, too, he was using his talent and his leverage to create a large-scale musical festival on his home patch in north Wales, even if it was rather too often meteorologically challenged. The pianist, Llŷr

Williams, was proving to be one of the finest instrumentalists Wales has produced, provoking questions about why Wales has a much stronger vocal than instrumental tradition. The harpist, Catrin Finch, was also helping to redress the balance, at the same time taking on a missionary role for her chosen instrument with a younger audience. Any one of these three artists would suffice to create a memorable event; all three performing at the opening of Galeri in Caernarfon in April 2005 was an embarrassment of riches.

After a period of decline the Welsh choral tradition was showing new signs of life, with younger choirs and conductors finally exhibiting the verve and innovation, and wit even, that seemed to have been locked out for so long by a depressing uncritical conservatism. At one point I convened a meeting of choral conductors to discuss the situation, at which it was revealed that Wales was the one part of the country where the Association of British Choral Directors struggled to get conductors to attend their training workshops. Even in an area of already undisputed excellence, Donald Nally, in a few short years as WNO's chorusmaster, took the WNO chorus into new territory.

In a very different musical vein Music Theatre Wales, committed to contemporary chamber opera, cemented a relationship with the Linbury Theatre at Covent Garden. All this had a youthful emphasis, underlined not only by the biennial delights of the Cardiff Singer competition but also by the success of the best of the chamber orchestras, Sinfonia Cymru, made up of young instrumentalists – an orchestra shaped by Gareth Jones while a repetiteur at WNO and adopted enthusiastically by Terfel himself.

The visual arts were in pushy form, perhaps buoyed by the completion of Peter Lord's hugely influential historical survey of the arts in Wales, even if not always sharing his conclusions. In a single year, 2003, Shani Rhys James was awarded the Jerwood painting prize, and two other artists from Wales, Amber Hiscott and Alex Beleshenko – whose works in glass now adorn both the Wales Millennium Centre and Richard Rogers's National Assembly building – were shortlisted for the Jerwood craft prize. Six artist-makers made their mark at the international Sculptural Objects and Fine Arts exhibition at Chicago, and Wales showed up for the first time at the Venice Biennale. Early the following year, the first Artes Mundi Art Prize, another brainchild of Wales's most fertile cultural entrepreneur, William Wilkins, was awarded to a Chinese-American, Xu Bing, at the National Museum.

The awkwardnesses of post-devolution Britain were played out at

Venice where the Scottish and Welsh exhibitions were not permitted to have national pavilions because they are not, in the Biennale's eyes, 'sentient nations' – more specifically that they do not control their economies or defence. The event throws up a higher barrier than other cultural bodies such as FIFA and the International Rugby Board, partly because of Chinese objections to non-state participants. The Celtic presences also raised the question of whether the British pavilion was an English pavilion. The upshot was that Wales and Scotland were among sixteen included in a category entitled, rather unimaginatively, 'Extra'. By 2005 Northern Ireland had joined in – part of the increase to eighteen 'non-sentient nations' – this time under the even duller title of 'collateral events'.

In contrast, the bravura of the opening of Wales's first Venice show was wondrous to behold, with Cerith Wyn Evans's military searchlight beaming the eighteenth century *Gweledigaethau'r Bardd Cwsg* (Visions of the Sleeping Bard) by Ellis Wynne in Morse code high into the Italian sky – probably the first artwork to need permission from air traffic control. In a converted brewery on the Giudecca Paul Seawright's large photographic images of the Welsh valleys set them, literally, in a new light, much as Ernest Zobole had done in paint. Some Welsh artists – with a world view that Enver Hoxha would have been proud of – grumbled that Seawright was from Belfast, that Cerith Wyn Evans worked in London and that the film-maker Bethan Huws worked in Paris. The selectors, wisely remembering Joyce and Beckett, took no notice.

The Venice presence had been suggested and pressed hard by an architect, Harry James, who also chaired ACW's capital committee. It was a sound judgement, characteristic of him, and vindicated also by the wit of our second showing in 2005. In this, the more obvious appeal of Paul Granjon's copulating automata, was matched only by watching the faces of increasingly frustrated visitors as they endured the long, circling flirtation before the machines got down to the business. Some very august visitors could scarcely contain themselves. Alongside Granjon, Peter Finnemore's films, balanced between humour and threat, and Bedwyr Williams's startling Welsh-Italian montages also contributed to a rather zanier image of Wales than that with which we are familiar. Even in the heat of Venice, it was a breath of air.

The Welsh Book of the Year attested to the health of Welsh writing and publishing. The organisers started to issue long as well as short lists, and judges for both the English and Welsh sections ritually complained about the number of volumes they had to read. Increasing interest in Welsh authors from London publishers and the arrival of new energetic entrants on the Welsh publishing scene, were reflected in an equal split between the two in the short lists. If there was an issue, it was whether more categories should be introduced so that novels, poetry, history and biography would not have to contend together. In Wales it is rather more difficult to find the level of commercial sponsorship that would either allow that to happen or, alternatively, to ratchet up the value of the two main prizes. But prizes are not everything.

Gwyneth Lewis, Gillian Clarke, Owen Sheers and Sheenagh Pugh were carving a place for themselves in a wider poetry world, where the two Thomases, Dylan and R.S., had for so long been the default Welsh poets, despite Dannie Abse's self-effacing lifetime of gentle but incisive observation. Menna Elfyn, Grahame Davies and Gwyneth Lewis gave expression to the linguistic complexities of Wales by moving between the languages in their work. Poets vied for titles: Menna Elfyn became a children's laureate, and Gillian Clarke the Capital Poet for Cardiff's 2005 centenary, and Gwyneth Lewis became the first National Poet.

In fiction Stevie Davies and Trezza Azzopardi, and Angharad Price in Welsh, were in a line of talented women writers that is still being extended through Rachel Tresize and Jo Mazelis. The discovery of another world made Sarah Waters a star writer. Meanwhile, John Williams gave voice to a seamy side of Cardiff, a million miles from the boosterism of the city fathers, and Niall Griffiths beat a scatological path between Liverpool and Aberystwyth. Emyr Humphreys remained indefatigable and eternally relevant.

For the council there was a certain poignancy in all this activity, since literature was no longer represented in its small platoon of art form officers. At a purely functional level the Council had delegated its support for authors to Academi in 1998, having advertised a franchise for a national literature promotion agency. It was a highly successful initiative and Academi has since been run energetically by Peter Finch, an entrepreneurial poet who had, for two decades, run the Welsh capital's only decent arts bookshop – an institution that, alas, is no more, but should be revived. He is also unique in being in some ways a surrealist who yet manages to work with the system. Four years later, following a government review of the functions of the Welsh Books Council and an ACW review of its own support for literature, the arts council relinquished its role of supporting publishers to the Books Council.

In combination this was a remarkable change for a council that had, through the 1970s and 1980s, employed a Literature Officer, Meic Stephens, who was so personally industrious and pervasively influential that he was accused of running a state publishing house. I am sure that publishers find it easier to deal with one organisation not two, but the removal of one anomaly often creates another. The changes often now lead to the supposition that the council has no remaining interest in literature. That is not accurate. It still funds Academi and the Book of the Year scheme and the post of National Poet, and gives revenue support to the Hay Festival and Ty Newydd, the writers' centre in North Wales housed in Lloyd George's last home.

It is true that the council, partly because of outside pressures, was seen to have been distanced, albeit reluctantly, from something that is central to so many arts. To many on the council this was painful, simply because it is impossible to conceive of a national arts council that has no interest in the literature of its people, no interest in the flowering of both our languages, no interest in the words that fill our books – our poetry, fiction, criticism, or historical writing – no interest in writing that brings life and edge to our theatre, film and television, or inhabits our music in so many ways, and no interest in what shapes our critical discourse. Whatever the practical benefits, this was a qualitative loss to the council.

I had never been much of an aficionado of dance. I have found it easier to suspend my disbelief at even the most outlandish opera plot – and they can be very outlandish – than at the sight of a pair of clogged feet clacking their way round a besom brush or, especially, the jingling sight of handkerchief-waving Morris dancers. This last is the one smidgeon of racism that I allow myself. Yet, in recent years contemporary dance has been a revelation, and not only to me.

In the last few decades, dance has spread across Wales, led by a remarkably extensive network of community dance organisations, such as Rubicon and Dawns i Bawb, capped by Community Dance Wales, and inspired, too, by the leading professional company in Wales, Diversions, that has been running an extensive outreach programme for all of its 21 years. Contemporary dance has also benefited from the historical crossover with now vanished companies such as Brith Gof and Cardiff's Laboratory Theatre. This has given us a continuing line of individual performance artists such as Marc Rees, Sean Tuan John and Eddie Ladd, who, among her other achievements, broke the mould of arts programme presentation on television in the most outrageous androgynous fashion during her period with BBC Wales's *The Slate* in the 1990s.

The emphasis on contemporary dance was probably the unintended consequence of the absence of a national ballet company, and the missionary zeal of dance supporters has been fuelled by a feeling of being the funding underdog. The Scottish Arts Council spends three and half times as much as Wales on dance, excluding more than £3m for Scottish National Ballet. If that last figure is included the multiple is eight. The absence of a Welsh national ballet company is bemoaned by some, but just as many believe that the effort required to establish a classical ballet company of the highest standard in Wales would be massively more costly than the encouragement of contemporary dance of an equal standard. The latter is not only more economical of resources and, therefore, more capable of surviving in smaller communities, but also has a wider potential for participation.

That said, the audience for dance is growing and the situation may well change as the result of the opening of the Wales Millennium Centre that has suddenly given Wales a major platform for dance performance that it did not have before. One of the most significant successes of WMC's first year was the appeal, first of the Kirov Ballet, the quintessence of classicism, then Australian Ballet, with its more contemporary flair, followed by one of the geniuses of the contemporary genre, the Mark Morris Company. Here was a venue attempting to create a new audience for dance through consistent high quality programming, and slowly succeeding.

Theatre was in a more parlous state, and a house divided against itself. Over the decades theatre in Wales had had too many false starts – a longer running saga than the reform of Welsh rugby – and without the comfort of a past golden age. It had not had the benefit of consistent policies or consistent investment. Theatres had been built across the land, and some money had gone into new writing, but investment in production was woeful. In 2003 the wounds inflicted in the battle over the drama strategy at the end of the previous decade had still not fully healed, and yet the problems that that review had identified remained: an unsustainable but unchanging number of theatre companies – most of very small scale – constrained by years of stand-still funding, a precipitate decline in local authority grants following the 1994 reorganisation of local government and, from 1998, a steady decline in lottery cash. This had led to little new blood and, with some honourable exceptions, the erosion of artistic standards. The theatre sector had little confidence in ACW, while the council despaired of the sector's sectarian fractiousness and lack of self-criticism.

The previous drama strategy, robbing Peter to pay Paul, had brought the council to its knees, and the price of peace had been a new funding deal for the theatre in education companies. The reconstituted council, under Sybil Crouch, followed this with a swift determination to establish a Welsh language national company, Theatr Genedlaethol Cymru, and to constitute a new writing company, Sgript Cymru, based at Chapter. But though theatre funding had increased, no-one could look at theatre provision in Wales and say that it was balanced and rounded and likely to satisfy and grow audiences. In 2003/04 theatre in education and for young people accounted for 40 per cent of ACW's total spend on theatre, with Welsh language work taking another 20 per cent.

The only sizeable producing theatre working in the English language was Clwyd Theatr Cymru in the north east at Mold, whose polished productions had half an eye on the cross-border audience in Cheshire. The Torch Theatre at the south western extremity in Milford Haven survived, against all the odds and in spite of receiving no annual funding from Pembrokeshire County Council. When I visited The Torch soon after joining ACW, its artistic director Peter Doran showed me the dressing room shower cabinets that, for financial reasons, he plumbed in himself, raising the question of who was subsidising whom.

Across the urban belt of south Wales that accounts for two-thirds of the Welsh population the only significant producing company was the severely under-funded Sherman in Cardiff, a small 400-seat venue whose speciality had been theatre for young people. While that had its own considerable value, it could not be right that two million people, bounded by Chepstow and Llanelli, Cardiff and Merthyr did not have a single producing theatre company concentrating on the adult audience and comparable in scale with the The Abbey or even The Gate in Dublin, the Citizens or Traverse in Scotland or even the West Yorkshire Playhouse. Michael Bogdanov, struggling valiantly to create a viable company of his own, reminded the world regularly that there was no comparable urban area in the UK where mainstream theatre provision was so weak.

It was not difficult for Peter Tyndall and myself to agree that the development of English language theatre should be an urgent priority. In May 2003 I wrote to the minister setting out our intention to create a working group drawn from the sector and to appoint a consultant to work with them. Later in the year we engaged Peter Boyden, who had worked so effectively on the stabilisation programme at WNO and, more importantly, had done a review of regional theatre in England that had unlocked £25m from the Treasury. Depressingly, this was greeted with suspicion in many theatre quarters. Some regretted that the review was not to encompass the whole of theatre, in both languages as well as theatre in education, but though there was some tempting logic in this view we had no wish to fight recent battles all over again. Others saw it as an ACW plan to impose a national theatre, whereas we had no fixed outcome in mind and gave Peter Boyden total freedom in arriving at his conclusions.

Calls for the creation of a national theatre for Wales have been raised sporadically for at least ninety years. My own father had been involved in one unsuccessful attempt, with the actors Clifford Evans, Meredydd Edwards and others, in the fifties and sixties. Half a century earlier, in 1914, two months before the war began, George Bernard Shaw, who had himself forsaken Dublin for London, encouraged such attempts in an article for the Liberal newspaper, the *South Wales Daily Post*. Parodying the old rhyme about the Welsh he wrote:

> Taffy was a Welshman,
> Taffy was a poet.
> But as he had no theatre
> He never came to know it.

Commending the national theatre project, he added: 'Taffy, having no legitimate opportunities for the employment of his great gift of imagination and adventurousness, became the less reputable things that are mentioned in the other version of that popular rhyme.' In the same article he also laid down a suitable brief for any such institution: 'If it succeeds it will not be a place for ebullition of patriotic sentiment and flattery of local self-sufficiency. On the contrary, it will be rather a place of humiliation and penitence, relieved by laughter and tears.'

Peter Boyden, working quickly, may not have been faced with tears, but had to confront a cloud of grumpiness. The audience at an open session at ACW's annual conference at Llangollen was sullen and wary. When Peter asked the audience whether they could at least agree that there was a need for major producing theatre in south Wales, scarcely a hand moved as people calculated the possible negative effects on their own organisations, and, perhaps, worried about taking on Terry Hands who sat at the back. It was a low moment.

Clwyd Theatr Cymru, under Terry Hands, was the main centre of text–based professional theatre in Wales, and aspired to become the 'national theatre'. He had built an impressive ensemble of Welsh actors and the output was consistently polished and powerful, including one of the best productions of *The Crucible* that I have seen. His associate, Tim Baker, also had an enviable track record of adaptations, although the company as a whole was criticised for failing to encourage much new writing and being too dependent on examination texts.

Terry, with encouragement from Cardiff Council's leader, Russell Goodway, had taken advantage of the city's bid for European Capital of Culture to push his ambition of establishing a south Wales base for his company, with a scheme to convert a city centre chapel into a theatre. This was always a shaky proposition since, as the WMC building rose in Cardiff Bay, there was considerable political opposition to yet another new venue in the city. The rest of the sector, too, was adamantly opposed to any notion of a CTC monopoly, in a country where any notion of a national theatre would have to be a 'theatre of many voices'.

In Peter Boyden's view, shared by the working group, the essential pre-condition to success in contemporary theatre had to be the instinct to collaborate and, whatever the virtues of the Hands regime, that was not the most obvious amongst them. His penchant for leaving repertoire decisions to the last possible moment, consciously rather than carelessly some thought, was the despair of receiving theatres across Wales to which his company was committed, under its funding agreement, to tour. It created a widespread resentment in the rest of the sector that was, inevitably, casting envious eyes at Clwyd's funding. To obtain substantial direct funding from ministers for a mobile touring facility that bypassed the chain of theatres that had been built across Wales only rubbed salt in the wound. In all these circumstances it was hardy surprising that no-one was rushing to endorse CTC as the national theatre.

Another influential voice came from Scotland. Joyce Macmillan, the theatre critic of *The Scotsman* newspaper, addressed a conference of the Wales Association of the Performing Arts, and warned against the premature creation of a national institution. The Scottish Executive had just provided £7.5m to set up a national theatre for Scotland, but as a commissioning agency rather than a building-based theatre, effectively federating a top level of theatre activity. Macmillan thought the viability of the concept was based on the presence of an existing substructure of production that was much stronger in Scotland than in Wales. Wales, she thought, needed more time. It made one wonder whether Wales could learn from Czech history, and the formation of a 'Provisional Theatre' in 1862 prior to the formation of the Czech national theatre in 1883.

Boyden produced a sophisticated and perceptive report that addressed the fundamentals of the ecology of theatre in Wales, in a way that helpfully overrode the exclusion of Welsh language theatre and theatre in education from his brief. It confirmed that the production sector was 'under-resourced, under-valued and under-developed', and envisaged the development of CTC, the Torch and the Sherman as cornerstones of mainstream production, and as sources of work for touring, as well as the development of a building-based company in Swansea. In a nod to the Scottish precedent and initiatives in some English cities, he also proposed a 'creative producer franchise' that would commission work across Wales. In some respects, the report was, in fact, almost too elegant, in that it did not provide a clear and single peg on which a politician could hang his hat and a bagful of money.

The timing of the report was not propitious. Theatre development waited in a queue behind existing commitments, although it was able to take advantage of some of the 'Arts outside Cardiff' funding. A start was made by merging the Sherman and Sgript Cymru, to create a stronger company that could take fuller advantage of the redevelopment of the Sherman building that was already in prospect. A similar capital development at the Torch was supported and underpinned with additional revenue funding. Shortly after I left, Peter Tyndall shrewdly re-badged the creative producer franchise concept as a commissioning 'national theatre' with a bid for £2.5m. Alun Pugh came up with £250,000 to kick-start it, with another £500,000 to strengthen the producing companies. In its first budget the new coalition heritage minister, Rhodri Glyn Thomas, set aside £2.5m for its first three years. A national theatre was about to creep into being after all.

★ ★ ★ ★

For all the joys of visits to theatres and galleries, to witness performances or the shiny results of new money, or the tattiness resulting from its shortage, an essential attribute for any arts council is the ability to stand back and see the big picture. It seemed to me, on arriving at ACW in April 2003, that it was essential to build a more powerful strategic capacity that could become a trusted centre of intelligence about the arts in Wales, one that would be perceptive in its analysis, effective in its advocacy and at the service of the arts sector, the council and its regional committees and government at both central and local level. While having clear commitments to its client organisations, it should also develop a capacity to look at the arts sector in toto, regardless of whether or not parts of it were funded by the council. That needed to be done alongside the paring down of bureaucratic processes to an absolute minimum.

It was painfully apparent – particularly after the departure of Fran Medley, the deputy chief executive who had held the fort as acting chief executive until Peter Tyndall's arrival – that the chief executive was massively over-burdened. The only senior executive within hailing distance of his office was the Finance Director, while the only other people reporting directly to him were the three regional directors, far flung and so enmeshed in their important regional tasks that they had little time to spare for the central agenda. It was an unstable wheel, with a wide rim and electronic spokes but an under-engineered hub. It was this that led to a plan to replace the deputy chief executive post with two new posts: an operations director, to sharpen internal organisation and create a consistency of service across the three regions, and an arts director, to guarantee that artistic considerations would be at the heart of the process by building our artistic expertise.

It would be wrong to suggest that the council was doing nothing but contemplating its own navel. The state of the sector was always its biggest concern, and increasingly so, as the uplift in the council's funding came some two years later than in England, in large part due to Assembly finance division's lack of confidence in ACW, then in the throes of its own reorganisation. This had left a large number of the council's client organisations teetering on the brink of insolvency, testing even the most resilient boards and managers.

At WNO I had seen how much further ahead the Arts Council of England was in tackling these problems through its stabilisation scheme. ACW wanted to follow suit, but its lottery fund, grappling with the peak of its capital building programme, had much less money to spare. The result was a more modest sustainability scheme that tried to address the problems of individual organisations, including their deficits, but without generating a tail of increased annual revenue commitments. It says something for the commitment of arts organisations that when 14 of them were later admitted to the scheme they all responded positively, despite there being no prospect of a bigger annual grant as an incentive.

As a prelude, in October 2003 the arts consultant, David Pratley, produced the most illuminating survey of the sector that anyone had seen, shedding light on many of the deeper issues that underlay the surface problems. Of the Council's 120 clients more than half responded. 78 per cent were more than 10 years old, 41 per cent were more than 20 years old, and 51 per cent were still being run by their founders, in one case despite having had five chairmen of the board. More than three-quarters had no more than 10 staff, while 47 per cent employed fewer than five people. Half had only one or two employees with managerial responsibilities, resulting in many of them having to stretch themselves across a wider range of disciplines – marketing, finance and human resources as well as the artistic function.

The picture that emerged confirmed the evidence from Pratley's previous study of Galleries and Exhibition Spaces in Wales, of a sector with a low turnover of senior staff, lacking 'the stimulus and challenge associated with rapid job progression' seen elsewhere, coping with wider spans of managerial responsibility and 'more spatially separated from each other'. In these respects the sector seemed to have much in common with the independent television production sector in Wales in the 1990s. This emphasis on the human dimension of arts infrastructure was a useful corrective to the common mistaken assumption that infrastructure equals buildings.

Money was still a major worry, despite the 35 per cent increase in grant-in-aid over the previous two years. Only 8 per cent considered their financial position to be healthy, with 63 per cent believing there was a serious financial threat to their continued existence. Thirty-eight per cent claimed to be coping with deficits, with much of their time being devoted to managing creditors, raising funds and dealing with low staff morale. Arts organisations with deficits tended to be mature, with an average age of 27 years. More worryingly, only 57 per cent said that they produced cash flow projections during the year. Despite this problematic situation, 84 per cent wanted to grow their organisations over the next five years, presumably encouraged by the recent increases in arts funding. Unfortunately, their desire to grow was usually based on a projected increase in dependency on ACW, a combination that, said Pratley gently, 'would suggest a pattern of artistic activity that may be increasingly unsustainable'.

Many of the companies were also being boxed in by two other

trends: a greater dependency on lottery project funding to cover what was, in fact, a shortfall in core funding and the increasing hypothecation of ACW funding by the Assembly Government. Together these 'reinforced the culture of project funding', often obliging companies to increase their activity when the more sensible course might have been to stabilise their output and devote more effort to marketing. Overall, the report pulled into focus the importance of having a sustainable client base, less dependent, where possible, on ACW funding. This ran alongside a need to take account of the physical sustainability of venues, the need 'to stimulate a process of organisational renewal' and to place a far greater emphasis on cultural leadership.

Discussions with David Pratley also prompted me to do some research of my own, comparing our own client base in Wales with that in Scotland and England. It was surprising to find that Wales had more revenue funded client organisations than the Scottish Arts Council, despite the fact that Scotland's population is twice that of Wales. At the beginning of 2003/04 they had 104, we had 120. Wales also had more client organisations per capita than England. ACW had one client organisation for every 23,000 of the population, ACE one for every 38,000 and SAC one for every 48,000. The other side of this coin was that at that time, on average, each Welsh client was getting £150,000 a year, each English client £196,000 and each Scottish client £300,000.

The difference in the size of clients in Wales and Scotland was also striking, with 15 per cent of ACW clients receiving less than £25,000, while the corresponding figure in Scotland was 1 per cent. In Wales 70 per cent of our clients were receiving less than £100,000 each year against only 43 per cent of those in Scotland. At the other end of the scale only 12 per cent of clients in Wales were receiving more than £250,000, against 20 per cent in Scotland. This was happening despite the fact that the grant-in-aid spend per head in Wales had just caught up with and overtaken the similar figure in England and, in that year, matched the Scottish figure. This pattern has not changed markedly, although the unavoidable teeming and lading between grant-in-aid and lottery funding has meant that some of Wales's smaller clients have now moved back onto the lottery side of the fence reducing the client base by fifteen. Such figures can be a two-edged sword.

It was important that the council and, more importantly, ministers did not jump to the wrong conclusion. After all, the stark difference in the shape of the sectors in Scotland and Wales may have been fully justified by circumstances. Scotland, not Wales, might have got it wrong, or vice versa. Both might be right. The structure in Wales might represent a fine carpet of activity spread through every community, or it might be the result of unplanned ad hoc accretions.

The proper response to such data is not to conclude that we should be like Scotland, or that ACW should be spending £300,000 on every client in Wales – delicious prospect thought that would be – but to ask, how and why are the two situations so different? Is the pattern of spend in Wales a more appropriate pattern for us, or not? Is it different because it needs to be different? How did we get to where we are, by design or by accident? Is this shape of things the most effective way of delivering the benefits that we all want? Most important of all, how sustainable is this pattern of spend and organisation? What shape to its spend should the council be aiming for in ten years time?

I set out these questions and the data that lay behind them openly at the council's annual conference at Llangollen in May 2004. They were questions that the council had to face in implementing its sustainability scheme, in reviewing its portfolio of clients and also in shaping a scheme to spend effectively the additional money that had been earmarked by the Government for the 'Arts outside Cardiff'. The last of these – a £2m pot set aside to balance the government's investment in WMC in Cardiff – was a useful illustration of the problem.

The initial, considered response from the sector was that the 'Arts outside Cardiff' money should be distributed around virtually all the venues in Wales, nearly 50 of them. This would have spread resources so thinly that the public would have seen no noticeable effect from one of the Assembly Government's best initiatives. Not entirely mischievously, I suggested that we settle the money on six centres in a way that would create impact. The final settlement embraced 16 venues, but with many, such as the three theatres in the three valleys of Rhondda Cynon Taf, grouped collaboratively. It was a sensible compromise between the need to make a difference and the other need for geographical spread.

It also demonstrated that we often had to push arts organisations to ask themselves hard questions, suggesting new thinking about the sharing of resources and expertise or even mergers – a sharing that might release resources for the art itself. All this had an additional irony, since the questions we were raising anticipated the core theme of the Assembly Government's reform programme, *Making the Connections* – published later that year.

With a few exceptions the reaction was ultimately positive. By the middle of 2005 the three arts marketing agencies in south Wales had come together to form a single agency, Audiences Wales, that won the backing of every local authority from Chepstow to St Davids. If successful, it held the prospect of a single agency covering the whole of Wales. Merging the administrative and managerial function allowed more resources to be put into the front line, enabling it to mount, in its first year, a campaign aimed at increasing the engagement of 16-18 year olds in the arts across south and west Wales – something it would not have been able to do under the previous arrangements.

At the same time the Sherman Theatre and the new writing company, Sgript Cymru, had started the process of merger, intended to create a more powerful presence for theatre in the capital city. It now exists as Sherman Cymru. The two public art promoters, Cywaith Cymru and CBAT, the arts and regeneration agency, followed suit to create a new organisation Safle (place or location). In Powys, three community organisations – Celf o Gwmpas in Llandrindod, CARAD in Rhayader and Arts Connection in Newtown – although maintaining their separate identities, had instituted a system whereby their chairs and chief executives met as a de facto top tier board, that oversaw the sharing of expertise.

All this required a mixture of persuasion, resolution and negotiation by Peter Tyndall, Jane Clarke and other senior staff. The fact that these changes, sometimes painful for individuals, were accomplished, for the most part, without the public, defensive warfare so common in the arts said much about the confidence and competence of the ACW executive team, and not simply the logic of the proposal. It also gives the lie to any assumption of ACW passivity in relation to its client base.

It is, of course, easy to make the case that this task should have been attempted sooner. In theory the best window of opportunity for such structural change would have been the moment at which the taps were turned on in 2002/03. It is always easier to reorganise when there is sufficient money around to incentivise change. But it is not difficult to see why the council, at that stage, made a simple, even distribution of its cash: the memory of its almost fatal travails with theatre in education, as it tried to pursue its drama strategy in the late 1990s, was still fresh in the mind. The necessary preoccupation with the ensuing restructuring meant that it did not yet have in place a process for monitoring quality of output that would be sufficiently robust to withstand the inevitable challenges to tough decisions. A start on developing such a process began in 2003.

It is this kind of organisational development that sits ill with initiative-obsessed modern government. The development of the sector required – and will still require – the further development of the council itself. It is a long job. In April 2003 I did not know that a bigger government agenda would intervene in less than sixteen months to disrupt a process that, so the council thought, was already aimed at better government.

13 The bonfire lit

14 July, 2004

Some days are fuller than others. Today overflowed. At ten I met Anthony Freud, WNO's General Director, in the company's crumbling John Street offices to discuss the current problems over its young Music Director, Tugan Sokhiev. Anthony was in the mood to unburden all and took me, like the barrister he is, through every twist and turn. The news wasn't good. Despite Tugan's great musical gifts, he has not been able to create a relationship with the orchestra and chorus – some of whom have not exactly helped. Factions have apparently conspired. It's a besetting sin in groups.

Tugan himself is determined to go, though he and his agent are, not unexpectedly, arguing with the company over terms. It's not exactly a surprise. I told Anthony on the night Tugan pulled out of Traviata at the New Theatre that it would be almost impossible to row back from that action. It is a double tragedy. It will blot the record of a young conductor of prodigious talent, but it also leaves Anthony bruised and depressed just at the moment when he should be elated at the prospect of moving the company into its new home. He has even toyed with resignation. I told him that is a bad idea. Despite his tiredness – he has cancelled a much-needed sabbatical to deal with the crisis – he has already been busy, successfully persuading Carlo Rizzi to return. He said the Board would have to take some tough decisions tomorrow. If Carlo returns it could just avoid a public relations disaster at the very moment when everybody should be celebrating the move to WMC. It was a long confessional morning. I left at 1.15.

At 2.00 Peter Tyndall came into my office at ACW at an unusually urgent pace. 'Even as we speak Rhodri Morgan is on his feet in the Assembly announcing that ELWa, the WDA and WTB are going to be absorbed into the Assembly civil service.' The 'bonfire of the quangos' has been lit, under the three biggest. Peter had no information on our own fate, at least until we both dipped into the Assembly's quite appalling website and, after some swearing, managed to find the text of the statement. Sure enough, they are going to look at the other quangos over the coming months.

I rang Kevin Morgan, our most public academic, and the wittiest,

who is busy earning the enmity of his own party for being a 'critical
friend'. Only a few months ago at an IWA conference, he described the
'bonfire of the quangos' as 'a piece of loose talk rather than a thought
through policy'. I reminded him that he had also said it was prepos-
terous to think that the Assembly could digest ELWa in the morning
and the WDA in the afternoon. He saw the funny side of that, but
thought it was a 'black day for civil society in Wales', and recalled that
it was Bastille Day. The rest of the afternoon at ACW was all nervous
speculation. For the first time since joining ACW my stomach knotted.

The day started with opera and ended in truly operatic fashion.
BT was in town. The company had decided to hold its annual general
meeting in Cardiff and its chairman, Sir Christopher Bland, had
invited a dozen people for dinner at the St David's Hotel overlooking
Cardiff Bay. I was there with other colleagues from the company's
Wales Advisory Forum. It was a surreal evening, the only calm being
in the bay outside. Despite his fierce reputation I always enjoyed Sir
Christopher's brisk style during his days at the BBC. Tonight he was
energetically genial and it wasn't hard to see why he needed to be.

The guest list included Andrew Davies, the minister for economic
development, (standing in for the First Minister et al), presumably
with the used matches in his pocket. Andrew often has the look of a cat
with the cream, but tonight he knew he had a bucket of it.
Surprisingly, and pettily I thought, he made it clear that he felt the
greatest triumph of all was that the announcement had not leaked. I
suppose that is some sort of triumph in Wales. There, too, were the
chairs and chief executives of two of the three quangos he has helped
toss onto the flames. It was an evening of small huddles, frostiness and
nervous laughter.

Ann Beynon, BT's national manager, whose husband Leighton
Andrews is a Labour Assembly member, earned her salary twice over
carrying an invisible fire extinguisher. Graham Hawker, chief executive of the WDA, was puce with rage, his stubbly hair and beard
looking even stiffer and spikier than usual. Roger Jones, his chairman
was all bustle, wonderfully angry, but cannily ambivalent. Elizabeth
Raikes, chief executive of ELWa, was more composed, but still might-
ily pissed off, having taken up the chief executive's job only three
months ago 'clearly under false pretences'.

Roger, Graham and Elizabeth were furious that they had received
only a few minutes warning of the First Minister's statement.
Graham's indignation was fuelled by the fact that someone rang him
and refused to give him the news until he could speak to the chairman. 'I told him. I only bloody work here.' Rhodri Williams, chair of

the Welsh Language Board and I speculated about the future of our own organisations. Rhodri seemed more relaxed than me at the prospect of absorption.

Andrew D made the best joke of the evening, apologising for the absence of the First Minister and others. 'The Prince of Wales is hosting another dinner at Margam tonight. Never before have I seen my republican colleagues so keen to go to dinner with the Prince.' Sir Christopher said the obligatory things about his company's contribution to Wales, but no-one was listening. The extent of the nerves became apparent when Roger Jones, a former colleague of Bland's on the BBC Governors, got up and thanked BP instead of BT. We all laughed – Roger too – but Graham H underlined his poor relationship with his own chairman by rubbing in the mistake with a vengeance. After the meal the huddles were even tighter. Graham brushed past me as he made for the exit, spitting out the word 'bastards', in not so sotto voce. Steam was coming out of both ears.[1]

With Graham gone Andrew D let loose, attacking Hawker for failing to consult on his recent (and now aborted) management restructuring. Clearly, there is no love lost in either direction. The cabinet has managed to keep things tight but most are surprised that Graham has not seen it coming. Many quangistas have thought that in the case of the WDA it was not if but when. As far as I could see the first reactions to the day's news can be summarised as: ELWa – absorption overdue, even though unfair on Elizabeth Raikes herself; WDA – absorption inevitable, but not wholly desirable; WTB – better left outside, but paying the price of arguing its case publicly.

★ ★ ★ ★

Fortunately, the Arts Council was due to meet only two days later at Llandrindod. It was an early opportunity to test the water. The agenda was heavy and institutional – the annual corporate plan, the draft audience development strategy, the review of English language theatre, progress on our strategy for using the new 'Arts outside Cardiff' money. The input from the Council members was, as usual, valuably robust and I wondered whether all that would disappear if the Council became a civil service department.

No-one argued against the bonfire in principle and several could see reasons for change, especially in the case of ELWa and some portions of the WDA. Dai Davies, the one private sector buccaneer amongst us, made a general case for the whole reform programme, on the basis that it could get rid of a lot of bureaucracy. Dai, who in his record industry incarnation had managed The Stranglers and Lou Reed, was hot on the issue of intellectual property and his sweeping ideas for supporting the creative industries in Wales had made a big impression on Andrew Davies. Although I always had a lot of sympathy for Dai's ideas and his impatience with red tape, it was excessively optimistic of him to think that it can ever be got rid of when public money is involved. The music industry is unique, and as a result he had much less understanding of the way more conventional organisations worked.

All of us found it difficult to believe that absorption into the civil service would make anything less bureaucratic. For the arts, the council was solidly in favour of the arm's length principle. Nevertheless, I cautioned against knee-jerk reactions. It was early days. I thought our argument was winnable and our combination of grant-in-aid and lottery funding was also a strong line of defence. We needed to formulate a case that was well-researched and reasoned and to put forward positive ideas for improving the relationship with the department, though taking care that it did not come across as too critical of ministers.

The following day Elizabeth and I drove to Stratford with friends, one of whom had been heavily involved with the WDA for years. In the car there was only one topic of conversation. Corin Redgrave as Lear gave us three hours of throaty anger that tested the difficult acoustics of that theatre to the utmost. Mathew Rhys's powerful Edgar was, I thought, better than his Romeo that we had seen a few weeks previously. After the performance we met him for a drink. When we saw him in *Romeo and Juliet* the lid to Juliet's tomb had stuck and he had to rush to the wings and carry her on. On stage, he said, all he could hear as he tried to lift the slab in vain, were two technicians underneath hissing 'Shit. Shit. Shit.'

* * * *

23 July, 2004
The First Minister's meeting with Assembly Sponsored Public Bodies Chairs – all of us around a large square of tables in a windowless conference room in the security conscious marble bunker in Cathays Park that Alex Gordon designed during the height of the IRA bombings. I have been to only two of these meetings previously and found them to be polite and ritualistic, everyone shamelessly playing for 'brownie points' by claiming how enthusiastically our organisa-

tions are pursuing government policy. It had the feel of a medieval
court in mufti. This meeting was different. Suddenly, I sensed that
everyone round the table thought that they had nothing to lose. At
last, the forum has produced some honest dialogue.

The meeting was very revealing, both of Rhodri and of the govern-
ment's approach to process. Rhodri opened, spelling out the reasons for
Public Service Reform, the posh phrase for the bonfire. The most strik-
ing thing was that there was not much about outcomes – other than
for the civil service – and no acknowledgement of any potential
problems. He said the nub of the matter was that they had never been
able to use the quinquennial review system to amend the governance
of Wales, though he did not make clear why that is the case.

He saw this reform programme as 'a creative move'. He was really
talking about beefing up the civil service, 'to give us more policy-
making firepower' – growth by acquisition rather than organic
development, an organisational manifestation of covetousness. He
thought the current machine was 'unusually generalised', whereas
ASPBs are specialised. He wants the machine to have the advantages
of specialisation and better career paths for civil servants. The only
way to do this, he says, is 'by integrating the machinery'.

We are all free to make representations, but there's a presumption
that all bodies will be absorbed into the civil service unless there are
strong grounds for not doing so. Any submissions are needed early in
September – in other words he is giving us only August to get together
a decent plea of mitigation. Beyond that, not much that's precise.
Decisions have been taken on ELWa, WDA and WTB, decisions on all
remaining public bodies will be taken in October, November or
December with the aim of bringing everything into the civil service 'by
April 1, 2006 or, possibly 2007'. Jon Shortridge, the Permanent
Secretary, visibly blanched at this prospect, as well he might. It
confirms the impression that some of this is being made up on the hoof.

Rhodri tried to reassure everyone that these decisions are not based
on any prejudice against quangos. Given his record in opposition –
WDA, CBDC etc. – and the fact that he and some of his ministers,
when talking to the media, constantly refer to 'the quango state' or
'quangoland', with a distinctly pejorative edge, this was taken with a
very large pinch of salt.

Paul Loveluck, President of the National Museum, and of impec-
cable civil service credentials and manner, thought it was unrealistic
to expect to absorb so much change in only eighteen months and
reminded us all that quangos had been established partly because
people felt that the civil service and local government were not deliv-

*ering as they should. Some of the civil servants present winced at that
one. I wonder whether any one of them has given Ministers such blunt
advice. Phil Evans, chairman of WTB, who does not like to beat about
the bush, asked whether the government had the competence to do
what WTB had managed to do in recent years. Rhodri said he
accepted that remark as a challenge. Brian Connolly, chair of
ACCAC, and a solid Labour trade union man, warned that they
would face poaching of staff from the English regional development
agencies that were becoming more competitive.*

*Only David Jenkins, not long retired as secretary of the Wales
TUC, raised a laugh. He chairs a body called Health Professionals
Wales that was established only four months ago. 'So far we have had
an induction day for board members. When we have our first full
Board meeting the main item will be whether we are going to be
wound up!' But he also made the most important point of the meeting,
asking how it is proposed to engage with wider civil society under the
new dispensation. He hoped it would not be on the lines of the
Business Partnership Council that, he said, was a failure.*

*Everyone feels for Elizabeth Raikes. She was enticed from a senior
job in local government to head up ELWa only a few months ago, when
ministers must have had this reform firmly in their sights. Not only
does she have just cause for personal grievance, I guess she has grounds
to sue. She was very controlled and mainly anxious to minimise the
period of uncertainty. She asked when the Assembly Government
would be consulting on the new structures. He said they would consult
'all the way through to April 2006' – and this in July 2004 – an
answer that gave comfort to no-one, least of all the staff of ELWa.*

*Rhodri said they would not be able to consult on structures until the
necessary secondary legislation had been passed by the Assembly. I
flagged that we would raise a different set of considerations in relation
to the arts. I also pointed out that, as a member of the Radio Authority
that had been rolled into Ofcom with four other regulators, I was aware
that two years of intensive preparatory work had been done by half a
dozen working groups drawn from the five existing bodies and assisted
by the consultants Towers Perrins, even before the Communications
Bill was enacted. Rhodri's way will, I suppose, be cheaper.*

---

1. Those two valves clearly couldn't cope with the mounting pressure. He resigned the
following afternoon in real time' while appearing before the Assembly's Economic
Development Committee. It was unheralded. He had not even told his own Chairman.

14 Grappling with Government

Otto von Bismarck famously said that there are two things in life one should never see being made: sausages and policy. I shall have to wait for the sausage experience. The progress of the bonfire of the quangos during 2004 and 2005 had a strange fit with the common Blair disposition to announce initiatives first and only then to engage in debate. Blair, of course, had had the benefit of resounding mandates – majorities of 179, 167 and 66 during his three terms of office. To that extent we may call his approach evidence-based hubris.

The Assembly Government has not been in that happy position, Labour governing first as a minority government, then in coalition with the Liberal Democrats and then, in the Assembly's second term, with a majority of one based solely on the fact that opposition parties provided both the Presiding Officer and the Deputy Presiding Officer. Peter Law's defection after a row with his own party in 2005 even removed that de facto majority until his death in April 2006. The election of his widow, Trish Law, prolonged that situation.

After the 2003 election one Labour member told me to expect the slap of firm government because 'the people had spoken'. Most objective observers thought that the people had rather mumbled something and seem likely to maintain their preference for such *sotto voce* responses for a while yet. Even some within Welsh Labour felt the party and the government was having difficulty in coming to terms with the continuing implications of even the current limited degree of proportionality in the Assembly's electoral system. The 2007 election seemed to complete a rite of passage.

The justification for tackling the quangos was based – at least in 2004 – on the fact that the promise and prospect of a bonfire of such bodies had had some resonance during the devolution referendum in 1997. Despite Kevin Morgan's assertion that it was more 'a useful slogan than a worked through policy', there is some truth in that claim, although I suspect it resonated more with the party than with the public. However, the mandate theory is dodgy at the best of times and often the last resort of governments that have failed to convince on some issue or another. In this instance the promise was more than seven years old, and there had since been the debates during the passage of the Government of Wales Act 1998, resulting in considerable changes to the accountability of quangos, not to mention two elections to the Assembly itself, each with their own manifestos.

The Labour manifesto of 2003 actually contained no reference at all to the quangos. The only mention of institutional change was contained in the commitment to take note of the recommendations of the Richard Commission that had been established 'to examine the powers and the electoral system of the Assembly... based on a detailed examination of how our new devolved institutions have worked'. The manifesto went on: 'Any proposals for change will be judged against the only criterion that matters to Labour – the ability to improve the quality of life of people in Wales.' In the event, the application of this last criterion in the field of the arts became very hard to spot.

Strangely, the other parties were more forthcoming on these issues. The Liberal Democrats made a specific commitment in the field of culture and sport, promising 'a National Assembly led review of the functions and effectiveness of all ASPBs and bodies associated with the arts, culture and sport in Wales to examine the extent to which greater integration of those organisations can be achieved to promote greater joint working and cooperation.' Plaid talked of 'enabling the WDA and ELWa to concentrate on delivery' but did promise to merge the Environment Agency, the Countryside Council and the Forestry Commission into one body. In the cultural field it also promised to 'revitalise' Cymru'n Creu, the culture minister's forum, by providing it with its own secretariat. It favoured the transfer of as many functions as possible from ASPBs to local government, but doubted whether 'the current pattern of local government could cope with these additional responsibilities'. Welsh Conservatives made no mention of reform of the quangos other than to say that they valued the work of the WDA and the professionalism of its staff, though adding that it would benefit from 'streamlining'.

It was five months after the Assembly elections, in autumn 2003, that the first signals of a more radical approach became evident. The IWA had been publishing a series of papers under the title *The Gregynog Papers*. Two of these had looked at the future of political parties. In 2002 Jonathan Evans, in a paper on *The Future of Welsh Conservatism* argued for a more autonomous Welsh Conservative Party, urging it to embrace the devolution process. The following year Phil Williams, Wales's only polymath politician of recent times, had written a paper, *The Psychology of Distance,* which emphasised that the gap between the prosperous and the poor in Wales was more important than the distance between north and south. Sadly, he died before it was published.

We had asked Carwyn Jones, a Cabinet Minister much touted as a future leader of Welsh Labour, to address the future of his own party. He had been invited to write the paper before the election, but we did not receive a draft until the autumn. On 11 October, as was the pattern with all the Gregynog Papers, a group of people met at Gregynog, the University of Wales's extramural centre near Newtown, to discuss the draft.

In addition to Carwyn Jones and myself, the group included the IWA's director, John Osmond, the political scientist, Denis Balsom, the AM for Preseli, Tamsin Dunwoody, Delyth Evans, an able Assembly deputy minister who had stood down at the time of the 2003 election because of family commitments, Jon Owen-Jones, Labour MP for Cardiff Central and a former Welsh Office health minister in pre-Assembly days – who had been something of a thorn in the Assembly Government's side on health issues – and Geoff Mungham, a journalism lecturer at Cardiff University, who had thought much about the future of Labour, his own party, and had written a book – jointly with Kevin Morgan – *Redesigning Democracy, The Making of the Welsh Assembly.* Geoff died suddenly while working in Holland some months later.

We spent some time discussing the future of the quangos and, in retrospect, I should have taken more note of Carwyn's disregard for any contrary arguments, even though some thoughtful and cautionary comments were coming from sympathetic people. It is almost certain that his final paper, published in January 2004 and little changed from the first draft, had been seen by Rhodri Morgan. In a section entitled *The Quango State* even Carwyn had to confess to the paucity of debate: 'We are now in a devolved world, yet there has been no serious debate about the future of these bodies.' Although he acknowledged that scrutiny of the ASPBs had greatly increased, that the relationship between ASPBs and ministers was now much closer and that appointments procedures were much more open, it was not a particularly deep examination of the issues and was couched very much in party terms.

On the subject of appointments, that had rightly loomed large under the Conservatives in the pre-Nolan 1980s and early 1990s, he confessed that 'there are many in the party who believe that the system is far too generous to our opponents', adding that 'there is no doubt that the new system is fairer and much more open, *at the expense of the governing party*'. (My italics.) There seemed no need to clarify whether this was despite or because of Nolan.

On any reading of these short, no-nonsense, two pages, there is little doubt that the key issue was control. The partnership rhetoric that the Government was wont to use so liberally, was dispensed with swiftly: 'There is often much discussion of partnership between them and the Assembly. Yet all ASPBs rely on the Assembly for their existence and their finance. It must be remembered that ASPBs are subordinate to the Assembly, not its partners.' He acknowledged that there should not be a policy of 'blanket abolition', and thought there might be a case for keeping the Countryside Council or the Environment Agency and for reconstituting some of the present boards as advisory bodies to assist ministers.

Although one would have to concede that there is something to be said for not allowing past practice to dictate future policy, neither royal charters nor the Government of Wales Act 1998 was allowed to cloud his vision, despite his legal background. He concluded that the 'present structure of many ASPBs is superfluous' and insisted that 'the debate over their future must begin soon so that the re-structuring of government, begun in 1999, can continue' – though not, as it turned out, in that order.

His complaint that some ASPBs had been reluctant to acknowledge their subordination was taken up in more forthright terms by the economic development minister, Andrew Davies, at the Welsh Labour conference. On 29 March 2004 the *Western Mail* carried the headline 'Quangos fired warning shot to toe the Assembly line.' In an attack, seemingly aimed at the WDA, on the issue of the dispersal of economic activity across Wales, he complained that 'there are those who feel that they are somehow independent and free to do as they please regardless of Government policy and priorities ... those who feel that they have the authority and right to set the agendas and priorities for their quangos', and warned that 'if anyone in the delivery agencies thinks they can keep the old Wales, the comfortable status quo, then they had better think again'. Yet, even then, many felt that this was more to do with a specific battle between the minister and the WDA, rather than presaging the sweeping change that was unveiled less than three months later.

That is not to say that anyone at the Arts Council was unaware of a much spikier relationship with government. After a difficult year between Jenny Randerson, the first culture minister, and my predecessor, Sybil Crouch, our chief executive, Peter Tyndall and I were anxious to mend fences with the culture department. At official level this seemed to work well. At a ministerial level it was more difficult. Only a month after I took office, the Assembly elections ended the coalition and Jenny Randerson, made way for the Labour AM, Alun Pugh. Pugh, understandably anxious about his small majority of 436, put a lot of time into his constituency. As a result Mondays, Tuesdays and Wednesdays were the only days when he could be guaranteed to be in Cardiff. Diary pressures meant the chair of ACW, along with those of the other cultural bodies, was rationed to a meeting every six months – about the same as Mathew Prichard enjoyed when he chaired the council in the 1980s, when Nick Edwards was the sponsoring secretary of state.

This might have sufficed in days when quangos were run on a relatively loose rein, but is far from adequate in a period when they are subject to long and detailed remit letters from sponsoring Ministers, as well as regular appearances – up to 2007 – before an Assembly culture committee. Without a closer relationship, that needs both formal and informal interaction, it was impossible to develop the kind of personal rapport and synergy that would have oiled wheels and avoided unnecessary misunderstandings. Our one private dinner together ended awkwardly, when the hotel at which we met managed to give away the minister's coat, containing all his keys, to a total stranger. I dropped off a shirt-sleeved minister at his overnight hotel, and worried that it did not seem a good omen.

It is in the nature of political appointments that ministers are handed portfolios to which they bring no prior specialist knowledge. In the case of the culture portfolio, with its mixing of the arts and sport, it is not luck which half of the job captures the minister's heart. Jenny Randerson had exhibited a real interest in the arts and been responsible for putting in place a cultural strategy in the wake of the policy review by the then education committee, under Cynog Dafis. She was constantly seen at events and, according to some, the steady stream of positive publicity on the arts contributed to her chalking up one of the largest increases in majority in any seat in the 2003 Assembly elections.

Alun Pugh had very different priorities and made little attempt to disguise the fact when talking to people in the arts field. His passion was for the mountains, whether on foot or on mountain bike, and he had the unhappy knack of always drawing on sporting analogies when talking to people in the arts. It betrayed an odd lack of self-awareness. This was particularly evident when he met nine new members of the Council over dinner during two days of induction in May 2004. Although he made his customary profession of a passion for the arts, he constantly came back to the sporting sphere. It did not go unnoticed by anyone.

Although in many ways personable and affable, his business style could be nervously brusque. At one point during the session I tried to make a helpful, not to say obvious point that it was in everyone's interests for the direction of the council and the government to be fully aligned. Stressing that we were keen for the closest relationship, I tried to reinforce the point: 'If they were not aligned it would...' He cut across the sentence sharply, 'You'd lose.' Dai Smith said to me afterwards, 'I take his point, but he needn't have been so brutal about it.'

★ ★ ★ ★

ACW now had only the holiday month of August 2004 to prepare its submission. We were fortunate in having available to us one of the most experienced arts consultants in the country, David Pratley, who had only recently put flesh on our own sustainability programme and went on to be instrumental in effecting some of the important structural developments that ACW wanted to achieve. A lawyer by training, he always chose his words carefully, the clarity of his thinking based firmly in the precision of his language. He agreed to start work immediately on pulling the relevant information together.

In 2002 he had completed a review of comparative mechanisms for funding the arts as part of the Scottish Executive's quinquennial review of the Scottish Arts Council. In it he had examined the operation of the arm's length principle across the UK and identified the Assembly Government's annual remit letters to ACW as 'quite unlike any other document between government and a UK arts council in over-stepping the mark'. He had also identified the direct funding of Welsh chamber orchestras as a cardinal breach.

Meanwhile there was work to be done with the political parties, since the July 14 announcement had caught them on the hop and they had given the announcement a surprisingly favourable reception, one which Kevin Morgan has since interpreted, with some justification, as a failure of the function of opposition.

There is no better place for seeking out politicians in the summer in

Wales than the National Eisteddfod. That year's event took place in the
mature grounds of Tredegar House at Newport, giving the festival a
more urbane air than usual. The public and politicians of all parties
tour the eisteddfod field each year, looking in on the caravanserai of
pavilions that had been dubbed 'quango alley' and which, in their very
number, made an unfortunate case for some reform. Not that the
Welsh Assembly Government could complain, since it was camped in
its own pavilion, quite separate from that of the National Assembly of
Wales – a constitutional nicety that managed to escape the punters
rather more easily than its expense.

All the opposition parties seemed receptive to our case and even the
Labour chair of the culture committee, Rosemary Butler, in whose
constituency the eisteddfod was being held, spoke publicly in favour of
our independence, along with the Assembly's Presiding Officer, Dafydd
Elis-Thomas. I hovered in the background counting our support across
the parties. Less comforting was the minister's visit to ACW's own
pavilion, as much for its brevity as for anything that he said. He had
agreed to only a short visit, to launch a £500,000 injection into the
council's Collectorplan art purchase scheme by the Principality
Building Society. He then rushed off to announce the appointment of
Meri Huws, a Labour party member, as chair of the Welsh Language
Board. He was clearly anticipating a row, which duly broke.

It was not the job of the Arts Council to take a view on the ASPB
reform programme as a whole, rather to seek to establish, if necessary,
that the arts required a different solution. Our official line at the time
was that the review gave us 'an opportunity to examine the principles
that govern the relationship between the arts and government as well as
the practical arrangements that enable us to deliver the best service to
both. Our understanding is that the Government is looking for
arrangements that will deliver the best outcomes'.

I sought out Sue Essex, the Assembly's finance minister and a better
listener than most. We shared a deep interest in the built environment
and she had, as environment minister, acted swiftly on the recommendations of an IWA working group that, building on a paper from the
architect Jonathan Adams, had proposed the creation of a Design
Commission for Wales. She was now taking a leading role in the ASPB
review and I established that there was no intention of adopting a one-
size-fits-all strategy. Solutions would be tailor-made to individual
circumstances.

One of the concerns at the time was that the Scottish Executive had established a Scottish Cultural Commission, under the chairmanship of James Boyle, who had slipped out of the post of chair of the Scottish Arts Council to undertake the work. James was a former BBC colleague. He had been both editor of BBC Radio Scotland and controller of Radio 4. At one point in 2003 all four arts councils were chaired by ex-broadcasting people, three of them from the BBC: myself in Wales, James in Scotland and Rosemary Kelly in Northern Ireland, while the Arts Council of England was chaired by the former Chairman of Granada, Gerry Robinson. The Scottish Cultural Commission's task was to 'look at the cultural furniture' in Scotland and decide what needed shifting.

I knew from his record as controller of Radio 4 that James was not a man to leave something alone if it could be changed. He could be quite radical and attracted, rather unfairly, a deal of opprobrium from Radio 4's Home Counties audience for his meticulously researched changes to its programme schedule, most of which stood the test of time. Despite his connection with the Scottish Arts Council, there were worries inside that it could be for the chop. My conversations with him were more reassuring. He believed that the arm's length principle was still important, though he wondered whether it could be achieved in different ways. But it was clear that the main thrust of the commission's work would be around the 'entitlement agenda', building on a visionary statement about the role of culture right across government in Scotland, delivered by its First Minister, Jack McConnell, in April 2003.

In framing our own submission in Wales we had been encouraged by the terms of a letter sent to all ASPBs at the beginning of August by the permanent secretary, Sir Jon Shortridge. This stated that each decision would be made case-by-case on the basis of an evaluation that matched the functions of each ASPB against a set of common principles. The government's presumption would be that 'where such bodies undertake functions which are essentially governmental in character, in that they set or lead on an aspect of public policy or policy delivery, they should be merged with the administration'.

There would be three exceptions: where bodies audit or regulate Assembly Government business or are quasi-judicial in much of their work; where bodies take decisions which are better kept at arm's length from the government; and where such bodies undertake functions or exercise professional judgements which are clearly non-governmental in character.

At this stage most of us were keen to give the government the benefit of the doubt, and were comforted by the fact that we seemed certain to qualify as an exception on the last two of the three counts. Our main case was based around two propositions: the continued relevance and value of the arm's length principle and the enormous gain deriving from the integration of our responsibilities for distributing the Assembly Government's grant-in-aid with our role as a lottery distributor, for which we were technically responsible to Whitehall's Department of Culture, Media and Sport.

The submission was signed off at the council meeting on 10 September and sent to Ministers. That it was also published openly was, apparently, a cause of irritation to some of them, but it was hardly a document that could have been kept under wraps. We owed it to the sector and to the public to publish. If the council was going to be sent to the knacker's yard, it was not right that it should happen in the dead of night without public debate and without one peep of protest.

The document conceded that much had changed since the arm's length principle had been developed, but while it was not possible simply to restate it in quite the same unambiguous way as in the mid-twentieth century, it was equally out of spirit with the times to write it off solely on grounds of age. Like the rather younger BBC licence fee, not everyone loves it, but few can think of anything better to put in its place. There is now an expectation that the arts will contribute to the attainment of broader political goals in return for taxpayers' subventions, and the cultural agenda is also affected by the activity of departments other than the culture ministry. But that did not abnegate the primary reason for the maintenance of arm's length arrangements in individual funding decisions. We set out our core case:

'*Respect for individual artistic endeavour*' – a principle re-affirmed by the Welsh Assembly Government in *Creative Future* – requires acceptance of the artists' role to question issues of state and to offer critiques of public policy and public attitudes – to challenge both rulers and the ruled. Arguably, this is particularly important in Wales where visceral issues of identity and language are contested matters. Throughout history, literature, plays and exhibitions have offered an alternative view to issues on which there was a prevailing political orthodoxy. Even in the former Soviet bloc, these forms of public dialogue, often the only ones permitted under law, changed patterns of governance and democracy. In the USA, too, where freedom of expression is a constitutionally enshrined right, exhibitions and films which promoted moral values at odds with prevailing political and public opinion have facilitated critical points of debate and change.

Any move towards a system in which directly elected politicians become answerable to their assemblies for the decision to finance works of art at odds with prevailing political or public opinion will run the danger of compromising the independence of artists to raise such questions. The artist, of course, is no more free than the general citizen from the proper constraints of the law, and is as answerable for acts such as defamation or incitement to racial hatred as anyone else. But such accountability is defined by statute, is exact and is known in advance. A system which created direct political patronage in the absence of any enshrined rights protecting freedom of expression – and in which control might be exercised in ways that were not defined, exact or known – creates a fundamental democratic deficit. All other practical considerations of the impact of integrating public patronage of the arts into Government are of secondary importance to this cardinal issue.

Should funding for the arts become the direct responsibility of the Assembly Government, it would have certain parallels with an alternative model – sometimes known as the 'Architect' model. It is represented by those democratic European states – notably France, Germany and Austria – where government acts through a department of state, whether a ministry of culture or an umbrella department embracing culture. In this model government is able to ally its cultural policy with wider social policy objectives since there are no intermediary bodies through which it makes policy and grants. In such states as this model operates, freedom of expression is often enshrined in basic law. The economic status of artists also tends to be enshrined in law and artists associations tend to have an enshrined right to consultation or participation in public policy. None of these basic laws exist in the UK.

Although our arguments were designed to counter the idea of absorbing the Arts Council fully into government, many of them were just as applicable to the lesser proposition that emerged a few months later of taking direct control of six of the council's largest client organisations. In particular, we advanced the notion that direct ministerial control would lead to a diminution of accountability rather than its enhancement – the substituting of the Arts Council's carefully defined processes with a culture of lobbying, abetted by pork barrel pressures from Assembly members. As well as plaudits for their largesse, ministers would have to deal with brickbats resulting from the much more frequent refusal of grant applications.

We also worried about whether direct ministerial control implicated the government as a 'shadow director' of arts organisations and affected the role of boards in their capacity as independent trustees of charitable organisations. We did not imply that this last issue was insurmountable, but it would need to be resolved.

Lastly, anxious not to seem complacent about existing arrangements, we set out a number of ideas for improving the working relationship between the council and the government. When I first joined the council I had discussed this issue with Peter Tyndall. It was clear to me that nothing had been done since the creation of the Assembly to examine the relationship between quangos and their sponsoring departments. Although all accounting officers worked to the Financial Statement and Management Memorandum, these documents have more to do with technical compliance than with working relationships at the policy level. No new protocols had been developed to recognise the new political dispensation and to introduce clarity into the relationship.

Long before the lighting of the bonfire I had suggested that we try to develop a set of protocols to govern our own relationship with the culture department. Although sympathetic, Peter cautioned that if we raised the question at that stage we would probably get an answer we didn't want. At that point he was probably right, but I still wonder whether history might have been a little different if a range of public bodies in Wales – either individually, or better still collectively – had begun to think through the possible substance and implications of such protocols during the Assembly's first term, and particularly during the period of the coalition government. Now the issue had to be addressed in more adversarial and defensive circumstances.

* * * *

Quite how wrong we were in placing reliance on the exceptions listed in the Permanent Secretary's letter became evident later that autumn when internal papers relating to the process were released to Sybil Crouch under the Freedom of Information Act. The very first paper, written *before* ACW submitted its own document, was remarkable for its lack of rigour. In a paper that was almost wholly descriptive it made the unequivocal statement that 'the functions of the ACW are essentially governmental in character' without acknowledging that the Jon Shortridge letter also envisaged an exception where bodies 'exercise professional judgments which are clearly non-governmental in character'. There is no sense in this paper that the proposition might be, at the very least, debatable.

It did note that the Assembly had no power to abolish the council, other than indirectly through primary legislation or through the council's consent, and informed us that the office of the Counsel General had given advice that the Assembly could not legally assume the role of lottery distributor. However, it concluded, without further argument, blush or caveat, that 'there is a strong case for merger into the Assembly'. This was then repeated in equally bald form in a briefing for a meeting between the First Minister and officials on 22 September.

Prior to this meeting officials had compiled an overview of the submissions made by the cultural ASPBs. Although Professor Kevin Morgan and Steve Upton later wrote, in an academic paper, that it was 'difficult to imagine more robust arguments for the arm's length principle' than were contained in the submissions of ACW and the National Library of Wales, the overview produced by officials was distinctly sniffy about the ACW document. They viewed some of our claims as 'overstated and didactic' – perhaps influenced by their view that 'its [ACW's] understanding of the contemporary Assembly civil service is atavistic'.

They dismissed ACW's worries about a possible loss of specialist expertise as a result of merger, by quoting the experience of the merger of the social housing organisation, Tai Cymru, some years before – a comparison that is not testimony to official imagination. They did, however, concede that the issues of artistic independence and lottery funding were real and thought it would probably be necessary to establish an independent panel of experts along the lines of the Welsh Industrial Development Advisory Board.

So, despite the clearest advice about the government's lack of powers to abolish the council, at the meeting on 22 September it was decided to continue work on the basis of merging both the Arts Council and the Sports Council into the civil service 'subject to further work on how lottery funds would be distributed'. The note of the meeting acknowledged that 'consideration needs to be given to the timing and content of the announcement for these bodies given the need for new lottery arrangements, Royal Charter surrender or new primary legislation'. At a cabinet meeting twelve days later these conclusions were brought forward, having been 'tested with the relevant portfolio ministers'. Quite what those tests entailed we do not know, but we can take comfort that ministers are not in aircraft production. The issue put to the cabinet was not whether to merge ACW and SCW with the Assembly, but how to do so.

The First Minister had agreed to my request for a meeting, and I arranged to take Dai Smith with me, as he still had purchase with the Labour Party and had just been appointed by Alun Pugh to edit the

Library of Wales series. The meeting, on 20 October, went rather better than Dai and I had expected. Rhodri was, as usual, warm and genial, Alun a lot stiffer. Despite warnings no-one raised the issue of the publication of ACW's submission. I did the necessary in professing our active sympathy with the general aims of public service reform, before setting out ACW's stall once again: arm's length principle, integration of grant-in-aid and Lottery money, and holistic management of the sector.

Understanding that Ministers never relish the thought of backing off, we both tried to get over the point that making an exception of ACW would not be a mark of failure of the policy, but rather the exception that proves the rule – proof of the integrity of the review process.

Judging reactions was difficult. Alun made no interventions, and neither did any of the civil servants present. Rhodri did all the talking. He seemed reasonably receptive, but hung up on the fact that for the big projects like WMC or WNO it is the Assembly that has to stump up. We both felt reasonably pleased at the end of the meeting. Dai, who doesn't hand out plaudits easily, thought I was on form. He thought that if it was 70/30 in favour of abolition going in, it was 60/40 against abolition coming out. We confirmed these lines of argument in a letter which also set out how we had already been addressing some of the Government's other 'citizen-centred' themes for reform of the public sector that had just been launched as an initiative under the title, *Making the Connections*.

Officials put together a further appraisal of the cultural ASPBs, dated 27 October. This raised questions about some of the arguments in the ACW submission, though occasionally misrepresenting them. For instance, it attempted to counter the case 'that direct Government control would stifle innovation and creativity'. But we had not argued this. It is true that we had alluded to that fact that some had alleged this of practice in European countries operating to a different model, but our case was, explicitly, based on ensuring freedom of expression, pluralism in taste, protection from inappropriate policy pressures and a focus on quality, 'without extraneous considerations'.

The rather shallow counter offered to this argument was that the Assembly 'had already directly funded a number of successful arts projects', citing, maladroitly, amongst others the Clwyd Theatr Cymru mobile theatre and the chamber orchestra scheme, both of which had caused disagreement between the culture department and the council under successive ministers. The chamber orchestra scheme had been a classic unplanned intervention that proved unsustainable three years later when the Assembly handed responsibility for the orchestras to the Council, but without the previously attached funding. Clwyd's mobile theatre scheme was highly controversial in the cash-strapped theatre sector on grounds of questionable effectiveness in delivering both access and value for money – two arguments that were overridden by ministerial whim, shaped by the persistent, though no doubt charming, direct lobbying of ministers by Clwyd's artistic airector, Terry Hands.

Earlier that week I had been in north Wales at the announcement at Oriel Mostyn of the chosen artists from Wales for the next Venice Biennale, before heading that same evening for Theatr Clwyd for the premiere of Ed Thomas's new play, *Stone City Blue*. Buoyed by a powerfully written and deftly choreographed tour of Ed's head, I went for a Chinese meal with the cast and crew, including Terry Hands. It wasn't long before the issue of the council poked its way through the mountain of spare ribs. 'I'm sorry, Geraint, but the council has got to go,' said Terry. 'It's of no use. What has it ever done for us?' I could only blink in the face of such extreme monocular vision. The council had virtually committed *hara-kiri* to save Clwyd. Its attempt to switch money from theatre in education to bolster Clwyd's finances had brought it to the edge of abolition.

For most of the following month I endured the added frustration of trying to keep in touch with events from a distance, having gone on a long planned holiday to India with my wife and friends. International dialling in some parts of southern India is still in its infancy, so not only were the phone bills high, but my index finger was worn out endlessly dialling and re-dialling on old fashioned dials at outlandish hours of the day.

Outside official circles, the arts sector, which had initially been disturbingly quiescent, started to stir. Early in November the visual arts galleries, the performing arts and the presenting venues – which together represented almost every major organisation in Wales – each went public in our support. More importantly, all four Labour members of the Assembly's culture committee were on our side in resisting abolition. Rosemary Butler, the committee's chairman, and Leighton Andrews were powerful allies, at some personal sacrifice in terms of their own influence and perhaps advancement in government. Both had made their views known directly to the First Minister.

In a debate on 11 November both Leighton Andrews and his party colleague Lorraine Barrett spoke in our support, though not in support of a Liberal Democrat motion for which the ground had not been properly laid to gain full cross-party support. During a bout of stomach cramps in India, I worried down a crackly line with colleagues that the debate might have been premature and counter-productive. We were wrong.

Leighton argued strongly against merger on grounds of 'principle, pragmatism and politics', citing Jennie Lee, the first ever arts minister in the UK, in his support. On the arm's length principle he had some fun, attempting to scare his colleagues with a vision of a Tory Wales:

> Suppose they had a culture minister who was extraordinarily right-wing, who might be opposed to abortion, might be critical of mutli-cultural-ism, and might want Victorian values taught in schools. Suppose that this Tory culture minister learned that Spectacle Theatre [a theatre in educa-tion company], for example, was to stage a play in which a son killed his dad and slept with his mum – an everyday event in Cwmderi, if you watch *Pobol y Cwm*. You can almost see this Tory culture minister, fulmi-nating in his or her office, thinking "I'm not having this. I do not care who this Sophocles bloke is, we cannot have these damn people coming over here and corrupting our morals." The grant to Spectacle Theatre would be slashed. A bit far-fetched you may say, but it is the extreme cases that test the principles. If you can give powers to a Labour culture minister, you cannot argue if the same powers rest with a Tory culture minister.

Several speakers referred to the way that the council had recovered its poise and influence in recent years, and now needed time to settle and develop after 10 years of continuous reorganisation. Lorraine Barrett pleaded with the minister to take on board her concerns and those of Rosemary and Leighton.

Then came a sharp change of tack, presumably based on the fear that some of its own members of the culture committee would vote against ACW's absorption. On 15 November, in a cabinet paper under his own name, Rhodri Morgan suddenly stepped back from subsum-ing the council within the civil service. Although he stuck with the line that 'ACW's grant-in-aid functions are essentially governmental in character' he was 'not yet persuaded that we have come up with a credible alternative'. Indeed, he advanced one conclusion that, had it been properly acted upon, would have saved his own party, as well as everyone else, much trouble. 'The qualitative nature of the judgments which underpin arts funding and the deeply rooted sensitivities about the risk of politicisation of the arts,' he said, 'point in the direction of continuing the arm's length relationship.'

His inclination was to leave ACW as a distributor of both grant-in-aid and lottery – the one-stop-shop we had been trying to preserve – but asked officials to come up with proposals 'to rebalance our relationship with the council so that its role is more clearly about delivering on strategic policy and framework [*sic*] we have set'. He rightly put his finger on the issue of the lack of clarity in the relationship, but the language was significant – not 'improve' or 'clarify' the relationship but 'rebalance' it – much more than a hint of a zero sum game.

One of the great ironies of all this was that while the civil servants beavered away to satisfy ministerial appetites, across the road from the Assembly people were bracing themselves for four days of celebration to mark the opening of the new Wales Millennium Centre. It is a prosaic name for a building that blazons its artistic purpose so brazenly on its steel helmet with two different thoughts in both our languages in letters ten feet high. 'In these stones horizons sing' jostles with the Welsh *Creu gwir fel gwydr o ffwrnais awen* (Creating truth like glass from the muse's furnace) to mark the building's civic credentials unmistakably. The concept had come from Jonathan Adams, the words from poet Gwyneth Lewis, while the lettering was as close an approximation of David Jones's calligraphic art as you can get in steel plate. Although I had been inside the building several times, many of us who had lived with the project along its bumpy path were choking back tears now that we saw it inhabited for the first time.

As if unable to wait for the scheduled opening night, Sir David Rowe-Beddoe, who had bullied the Assembly Government into making it happen, (albeit with the additional bulldozing support of the finance minister, Edwina Hart), laid on a glitzy event to present lifetime achievement awards to Dame Gwyneth Jones, Shirley Bassey and Alun Hoddinott and – since this was not the kind of occasion to be pernickety – to the late Richard Burton. It reminded me of the no doubt apocryphal story of the Irish art purchase scheme: 'It has to be work by a living artist, but we are willing to stretch a point.'

Over the celebratory champagne friends close to government were nudging and winking as if they had St Vitus' dance, reassuring me that everything was alright, that the council was safe. It felt almost unreal, as if these events were happening on another planet. Nothing could have punctured the elation of that opening weekend. I would not have believed that any government would wish or even dare to snatch defeat from the jaws of such a victory.

The following night the red carpet was out for the first time,

Elizabeth and I sat in the stalls. Across the aisle, the architect Jonathan Adams sat tensely still, seemingly within himself, savouring the enormity of his achievement in shared space and joy. Alun Pugh and his partner, Mary, herself a music teacher, were a few seats away. As we returned after the interval, the safety curtain jammed and caused a long delay. Alun leant across and jested loudly, 'I'm holding the chairman of the Arts Council personally responsible for this.' Jonathan Jones, chief executive of the doomed tourist board, was sitting behind him and tapped Alun on the shoulder. 'If you take them over, Alun, you'll be responsible yourself.' As we waited, such was the good humour that no-one dreamt of a slow hand clap. Instead, strains of *Calon Lan*. Only in Wales could such a gala audience have started to sing quietly to pass the time.

The euphoria of that weekend was to last for less than two days. The senior team at ACW had always been clear that, in management terms, there would be no practical difficulties in dealing with full independence for the council or with full merger with the civil service. What they dreaded was the worst of all worlds, a fuzzy half way house in which managers would never know from one day to the next or from one issue to the next whether they were working to their chief executive and council or to officials and the minister. This is exactly what the charge to 'rebalance the relationship' threatened to create.

In less than a week officials cobbled a paper that canvassed four options. The government could assume responsibility for all strategic planning OR for revenue funding key strategic clients OR it could set up a Culture Board for Wales to set the overall strategic direction OR it could tighten controls through the remit letters and new directions on lottery spending. It may be that officials set out the paper in this way in the belief that ministers might choose one or two of the options. If so, they did not anticipate that, such was the appetite to get as close to merger as possible, ministers would eagerly grasp at all four without any amendment or heed for the practical questions that had been only sketchily listed.

And so, on 30 November, 2004, with no further consideration, let alone consultation, and with only one short phone call from Alun Pugh to myself fifteen minutes before the plenary session started, the hastily assembled package was unwrapped by the First Minister. The Government was proving itself a gourmand not a gourmet.

15 Suspended animation

The list of changes announced that November were extensive, although the application of the permanent secretary's grounds for exception was, arguably, not always consistent. While the central bonfire of the WDA, the Wales Tourist Board and ELWa continued to burn merrily, a new brushfire was to be started to clear the surrounding undergrowth: twelve agricultural advisory committees rolled into one, nine health advisory committees rolled into the existing Wales Centre for Health. Health Professionals Wales was to be abolished before it had met – giving new weight to the notion of 'giving birth astride the grave'. NHS Trusts and local health boards were encouraged to merge 'where there is co-terminosity'. The Curriculum Authority – ACCAC – would be abolished 'although retaining the integrity of its professional judgment covering all of its regulatory functions' – dismissing two of the permanent secretary's exceptions succinctly in one sentence. The Countryside Council for Wales was in the 'can't touch list', though it lost control of the successful agri-environment scheme *Tir Gofal*.

Among those who made it to future's shore, the Environment Agency was saved by being part of an England and Wales regulatory body, and the Care Council for Wales by being non-governmental and regulatory. While it could hardly be argued that the functions of the Higher Education Funding Council were non-governmental, it was saved by Parliamentary assurances given at the time of the 1998 Act along with the need for, in the First Minister's words, 'maintenance of the arm's length principle'. That irony was not lost on some of us. The National Museums and Galleries of Wales and the National Library of Wales were also, and rightly, untouched. The Royal Commission on Ancient and Historical Monuments of Wales, too, was adjudged non-governmental and to be kept, although it was to be subjected to a re-branding exercise along with other built heritage bodies.

Much of this made sense and created little fuss, which made it all the more perplexing that the government seemed so unperturbed by the prospect of an unnecessary row or two on the culture front. All controversy was to centre on two of the three remaining cultural quangos, the Welsh Language Board and the Arts Council.

Although the Sports Council had much in common with ACW – a royal charter and a lottery distribution function – unlike the arts and the Welsh language sport is not a politically contentious area. With no issues of principle at stake SCW chose, understandably, not to resist the proposals but to seek the best organisational arrangements. The Welsh Language Board was quite another matter. Always a contentious area, there were strong grounds for keeping the board's promotional and regulatory functions outside government. Its chair, Meri Huws, whose appointment had been criticised as an example of party political favouritism, now mounted just as robust a defence as the Arts Council.

Many people were mystified that so many bodies were put through a process that threatened abolition when the Government knew from the outset that, in many cases, it did not have the necessary legal powers to carry out the threat. If you discount the charge of incompetence, two possibilities offer themselves: either the Government was making a declaration of future intent, to which it would return when the necessary powers were available to it, or it was simply bidding high so that less radical, but nevertheless painful change, would seem conciliatory. The truth of the former will be revealed, if at all, in the fullness of time, the latter tactic worked more quickly. Some of our supporters breathed a sigh of relief that we were not for the scrap heap, even while others claimed that we were being emasculated.

For my own part I felt very supportive of the creation of a Culture Board to bring together the chairs and chief executives of the cultural quangos, since the wider ministerial forum – Cymru'n Creu – had not proved a very good investment of people's time. I had myself suggested to officials that the latter should be reorganised, with an inner grouping to monitor the implementation of the cultural strategy's action plans and a wider group meeting less frequently to debate issues as needed. There was also every reason to support a stronger culture department. The council would benefit from it being better equipped to develop policy and to make the case for the arts within government, particularly in the annual budget rounds.

The only problem was that the government's way of achieving this seemed to be the decapitation of ACW's organisation by transferring its strategic and planning functions into the department. This was particularly worrying since one of the council's prime concerns at the time was the need to strengthen the top of the organisation. Peter Tyndall had not had a complete management team since his appointment, some three years before. Since mid-2003 we had wanted to create two senior posts, director of operations and director of arts, the first to drive improvements in the organisation, including its developmental capacity, and the second to deepen and sharpen our art form expertise.

We had managed to create and fill the first of these, financed out of savings, appointing Jane Clarke, someone whose experience as an accountant with KPMG and heading business affairs at the Arts Council of England, eminently suited her to build the developmental role. But the recruitment process for the second had been delayed nearly 12 months by the bureaucratic impediment that all changes in posts that report directly to an ASPB chief executive have to be cleared by the Assembly Government. Now, in July 2004 the announcement of the ASPB review forced yet another postponement.

During 2005, despairing of certainty, we felt we could wait no longer. David Alston was appointed and took up the post in September of that year, two years late. As a former keeper of art at the National Museum of Wales who had also had a period as acting chief executive of the Lowry Centre at Salford, David had impeccable credentials for the role. He and Jane Clarke, allied to Peter Tyndall's shrewdly pragmatic managerial gifts, promised to make a formidable team.

There was no doubt that the biggest problem was created by the government's proposal to take control of six of the council's largest clients: Welsh National Opera, the BBC National Orchestra of Wales, Clwyd Theatr Cymru, Theatr Genedlaethol Cymru, Diversions Dance and Academi. Not only did it drive a coach and pair through the arm's length principle, at a stroke it threatened to take away 43 per cent of the council's budget. More worrying was a sense that this would not be the end of it.

Citing the precedent of the government's direct funding of WMC and Artes Mundi, the First Minister said, rather starkly, in answer to the previous culture minister, Jenny Randerson, 'It is simply an extension about which you are trying to make a distinction in principle, but it just does not exist. We are already doing it and we will do it twice as much from now on. The Arts Council will do less of it and it will also advise on it.'

This clear and unsophisticated statement rather confirmed the view that the proposals were not founded on any principle, or underpinned by any artistic or financial logic. As the old saw has it, there are times when one must rise above principle. In their paper to ministers, officials had advised that criteria for selecting directly funded companies would need 'to be clear, robust and easily communicated'. Yet the six companies chosen had no particular coherence, other than being lead organisations in their field.

The rationale offered was that they were all 'national remit' companies, but if that was to be the criteria there were many others, among our 120 clients, whose remits covered the whole of Wales in public art, film, dance, and music, not to mention national support agencies in areas like arts training. WNO and Theatr Genedlaethol Cymru had both taken the word national into their titles, yet one had an established track record of 58 years standing, while the other was a young company that still needed careful nurturing having been set up by the council only two years previously. Clwyd Theatr Cymru had always wanted to be recognised as the national theatre company, but the council's own review of English language theatre had, in common with most of the theatre sector in Wales, resisted the notion. If the development of English language theatre went along the lines we were recommending, it would actually strengthen CTC itself, but would reduce its relative dominance in the theatre ecology as whole, and rightly so.

Neither was there a financial trigger. The government's chosen six were not the council's six largest clients. Chapter Arts Centre and the Sherman Theatre, not scheduled for transfer, were both in receipt of bigger grants than Diversions. Chapter's grant was also larger than that of Academi. Five of the six were performing arts companies, but Academi was a literature promotion agency that also represented writers. Academi also distributes bursaries to individuals, which seemed to fly in the face of the First Minister's statement that they had 'left the issue of grants to performers outside the ambit of Government'.

A fundamental concern for the council was the prospect of creating a two-tier system for the arts in Wales. In the previous four years the council had striven successfully to rebuild itself. It had sorted out the unglamorous processes of grant applications, reducing the number of funding schemes from 40 to three, and was trying to shift the emphasis of the organisation towards the core issue of artistic quality. If that could be addressed effectively, through a sensible system for monitoring quality, then at least it might have a sounder basis for pushing change, for taking necessarily difficult decisions more readily, and for making them defensible. We believed that such a system would have more credibility if it were applied in each art form fairly and across the board. The transfer of the six companies threatened to derail that strategy. Worse than that, when seen against the increasing propensity of culture ministers to make other direct grants, it would, we thought, create a climate that would ultimately subvert the role of the council, even in those areas ostensibly left to it. It proved impossible to persuade government of these organic connections.

The connection between the two strands – the transfer of strategic and planning functions and the transfer of the six companies – was identified succinctly by Leighton Andrews, by far the most incisive interrogator of his own government's proposals. While searching for some clear criteria for choosing companies for transfer to the department he pinpointed a key consequence: 'There is a danger, in some respects, that if the Assembly Government takes over major companies in every art form, it is essentially setting the strategy for every art form.' He immediately linked this to a second question to the First Minister: 'When you talk about strategy planning and policy staff moving into the Welsh Assembly Government, does that include the specific art form experts within the Arts Council, or do they stay with the Arts Council?' The First Minister was moving onto thinner ice.

The options paper put to Ministers had had only this to say: 'The Assembly Government would need to acquire the expertise necessary to carry out these functions and ACW's running costs would be reduced proportionately. The small ACW resource engaged in these activities could be transferred to the Assembly Government.' In the First Minister's response to the question, on the day of the announcement, this was translated into 'we are probably talking about a handful of staff, around half a dozen…It may be subject to detailed consultation'. The art form issue was left unaddressed. Significantly, in the following twelve months we never once received any indication that these issues had been analysed with any degree of precision. We saw not even the roughest draft proposal for consultation.

★   ★   ★   ★

When the council met at Newtown, three days after the announcement, the mood was glum. Two-thirds of the members had been there for only eight months. They were a knowledgeable, experienced and deeply committed team, eager for progress and development, a quality they retained throughout the coming difficult year. But now they were quite deflated by the tone as well as the substance of the announcement.

Although the First Minister had said, routinely, that the proposals were not a comment on performance, from the council's point of view his opening words had been essentially negative: 'The Arts Council of Wales and the Sports Council of Wales will continue in existence as the Government cannot be a lottery distributor.' Neither he nor the culture minister offered any public endorsement of the council's performance, role or value that day or in the ensuing weeks, something that was deeply felt, particularly by staff, at all levels.

In the council meeting one chink of humour penetrated the gloom. Peter Harding, the culture department's head of arts arrived just as the discussion began. As he came through the door, Dai Davies shouted, 'Hello, boss.' The laughter was a release, but it could not the hide the anger of some. Naturally, resignation was in everyone's mind, though as part of the struggle between head and heart, the choice between the half-full and the half-empty glass. People placed themselves at different points in that spectrum, though not even those unfazed by large bonfires spoke in favour of the government's proposals. Equally, even those most disposed to resign gave weight to the Monty Python line thrown into the debate: 'The time has come for a really futile gesture.'

Our problem was that there was so little detail available, though at the time we assumed, wrongly, that it existed. The First Minister had said that there would be detailed consultation on many of these issues. What did direct funding of the six companies mean? How exactly would the strategic interface with the Council work? Where would artform responsibility lie? In the announcement was a statement that we would still be asked to advise on the six companies. How meaningful and systematic would that be? Most important of all, was there a will to make the relationship with the Council work? If not, there seemed little point in the Council pursuing the course of the living dead. If, on the other hand, the answer to this and other questions was positive, the Council could still be a powerful force for good in the arts.

I had hoped to see the First Minister and the culture minister before the council, but it could not be arranged before the following Monday. In the meantime officials had been able to tell us very little. The upshot was that we convinced ourselves that immediate resignation would avail little. We had been advised that the government did not need a vote in the Assembly to push its plans through – in any case, it had a majority. Resignation would simply result in our replacement by more compliant people. Better, it was argued, to play it long, and try to maintain a good relationship with the government in the hope of a sensible discussion of what would work. We would give this a chance before deciding on a more public course.

Given the impending meeting with the First Minister after the weekend we issued a muted public statement welcoming the establishment of the Culture Board, flagging 'serious concerns about several aspects of the proposals' but saying that we wished to meet ministers to gain more clarity. That proved much more difficult than we then knew. It may, or may not have been the right call.

There followed a frustrating year that appeared to pass in slow motion. When Peter Tyndall and I met Rhodri Morgan and Alun Pugh and no less than six officials the following Monday, the First Minister seemed not only relieved by our restraint, but genuinely grateful, and anxious that we got down to detailed discussions with the department. But, as it turned out, speed did not seem to be on the agenda. One of the signs of dysfunction between organisations is the existence of different concepts of time. Unlike people, organisations do not own watches. Most have calendars, but some take an agricultural view of time, working to seasons rather than weeks. We now entered this Welsh farm time zone.

Alun Pugh's meeting with the Council at the end of January left the council in a worse mood than before. People were depressed at the absence of any rationale for the changes, or any clear vision for the arts other than a sincere commitment to social justice on which we needed no persuading. He could not have mistaken the strength of feeling. Dai Smith was particularly robust with him. After that there was radio silence from the department. By early March not only had nothing happened, but it was clear that nothing would happen this side of the General Election in May. The situation was further complicated by the apparent intent to reorganise the culture department, thus destabilising and preoccupying the department's own officials.

It was not until 18 May that we had our first formal meeting with officials – talks about talks. We did not meet again until 15 August – more talks about talks. Eventually, a workshop meeting was arranged for 15 September, above a bar in Park Place, more than nine months after the announcement, nine months during which the council's frustration grew monthly. The workshop started to get down to business, though it was not helped by the presence of a consultant who was also working on the WDA merger and seemed to think this was going to be a carbon copy.

On the obligatory flipcharts we worked out a SWOT analysis – the strengths, weaknesses, opportunities and threats for the council and for the department. It was embarrassingly one-sided, which probably explained why, weeks later, when we were sent notes of the meeting, only the opportunities and threats were listed. If proof was needed that this was not a serious effort to find common ground, this was it. We would soon be facing the second winter of our discontent. Rather than waste any more time, we decided to put all our ideas on paper and submit them to the Minister.

These had been formulated back in February 2005, so that we could go into any discussions with a coherent view and some positive answers. I had presented them to the council that month at Gregynog, but we had held them back in anticipation of discussions in which, I had then hoped, they could have emerged from an examination of practical issues rather than being seen as a competing Arts Council proposal. We had fed some key elements into the preliminary discussions in May and August, but at subsequent meetings got no indication that they had been floated with the minister.

The proposals attempted to recognise the political realities of our situation, the real need to strengthen the culture department and our own need for clarity of role and purpose. We wanted and needed a constructive relationship with the minister and his department, to be collaborators not rivals and to have a relationship that was clearly understood by the public and the arts sector. Progress for the arts would come only when the objectives of the council and the department were fully aligned. If it was to continue in existence and to handle a complex client portfolio effectively, as well as to take the difficult decisions that we knew were on the horizon, the council had to possess a necessary authority based on knowledge and expertise, transparent and fair processes, and the declared and consistent support of government.

On the other hand the minister, we thought, had to be able to demonstrate our enhanced accountability to him and, pragmatically, we could see that this would have to involve some kind of special recognition of the larger 'national' companies. He also needed to build greater strategic capacities within his own department, so that it could be seen to be the fount of policy. Both sides should be able to count on consistent behaviours and openness. The council believed the circle could be squared, that bringing the two sides closer together was not incompatible with the maintenance of the arm's length principle, and that the 'direct funding' of the large companies could be defined in a way that should satisfy both sides. We thought we were offering a win-win solution.

On the strategic front, we put up more than half a dozen ideas, the

first of which was that we should abandon the notion of separate strategies, in favour of a single joint arts strategy, drawn up by the council and
the department in full collaboration. There was little purpose in the
Assembly Government having its own glossy strategy, *Creative Futures*,
and the council having a separate, equally glossy five-year strategy of its
own. Having one document, jointly prepared, would be the clearest
manifestation of the 'bringing together' of policy and strategic planning.

To underpin this work we thought the research officers of the
cultural quangos should be brought together with the relevant culture
department staff to form a research sub-committee of the minister's
new culture board. Since the department was usually represented at
the council's meetings, we suggested this should be reciprocated by
allowing ACW's chief executive to attend the minister's policy board.
The minister, we thought, should also be more closely involved in the
formulation of our lottery fund capital strategy. Regular secondments
of staff in both directions, more direct access routes for advice from the
council to the minister, the possible co-location of ACW and culture
department staff completed the picture. All we asked in return was
recognition of ACW as 'the primary (although not exclusive) source of
external advice on artform development'. If I had any worries at all
about these proposals, it was that they might be going too far.

The biggest challenge was the proposed 'direct funding' of the six
large companies. Could we find a definition of the policy that both
conformed with ministerial statements while avoiding all the drawbacks
of splitting the sector, a solution that would be politically defensible?
Bowing to the realities we acknowledged that 'there would be a benefit
in recognising a tier of companies that, because of their scale and remit,
have both a leadership role within Wales and a disproportionate impact
on the perceived success of Wales in the arts beyond its borders'.

We did not specify the companies, since we also proposed a process
for reviewing the criteria for national company status and the obligations that should flow from it. We were conscious that no-one had
addressed the issue of whether such companies might fall out of the list
if they did not perform well, or how others might be added. We thought
there was sense in 'accommodating the possibility of change over time'.

But how to fund them? Our suggestion was that ACW's grant-in-
aid from the Assembly should be divided into two blocks – one for the
'national remit' companies, however defined, and one for the rest. The
size of both blocks would be determined directly by the minister, but
within each block the grants to individual companies would be deter-

mined by ACW. In our paper to the minister we were realistic enough
to admit that in the case of the 'national companies' block, this would
leave the council with precious little flexibility, but at least 'it would
preserve a common relationship between ACW and all client companies and a consistency of managerial and monitoring practice by the
public funder, even while separating out the national companies, as a
group, for a more direct and discrete decision by the minister'.

The paper had not been a rush job. Its content had been mulled
over for a long time. It was studiously non-confrontational. It strove to
take account of the political needs of the minister as well as observing
organisational principles. It attempted to create mechanisms and
conditions that would be a real rather than imagined improvement of
the status quo. It recognised that effective working relationships are
often 'more dependent on daily practice and contact than on formal
constitutional arrangements'. It tried to take account of the best interests of all parts of the arts sector. Whatever its merits or its deficiencies
it stood in stark contrast to the total absence of any detailed proposals,
or even counter arguments, from the parent body.

No reply was received but ten days later, on 14 November, Peter
and I met with the minister and his officials for one of only two regular
yearly meetings. There was scarcely any discussion of the paper. 'We
are not going to do that,' was all Alun Pugh said with reference to our
proposals on the six companies, clearly wanting to move on to another
issue. I tried to draw him back to the other part of the paper on strategic issues, but got no clear response. He wondered why I wanted to talk
about these issues rather than access. Towards the end of the meeting
he agreed to my proposals for criteria for recruitment of four new
members of the council. This cheered me since the previous recruitment exercise two years previously had drawn 60 applications and
given us nine stimulating new members.

The one remaining uncertainty was my own position, so I asked for
a private conversation and all but one of the officials left. I told him that
I would welcome the opportunity of another term, but that I hoped we
could work more closely together than we had so far managed. We
needed to meet more regularly to get a much better understanding of
each other. Ominously, he said that he had not made up his mind, but
promised me a decision before Christmas.

The Council met on 2 December and resignation was again in the
minds of several members, together with some regrets that we had not
gone head to head with the government on the issue a year ago. Even

so, we decided that we would exhaust all avenues before doing so. It was agreed that I should to try to set up one further meeting with ministers. I rang Alun's office. He did not take the call, but his secretary rang back and asked me whether I could see Alun on 23 December. It was the only date he would be available in Cardiff.

Two days before the scheduled meeting, in the pre-Christmas period when the press are supposedly too busy compiling end of the year quizzes, a crumb of comfort came from over the border, although not one likely to shake the resolve of my own minister: the DCMS's peer review of the Arts Council of England, chaired by Baroness McIntosh, which gave the arm's length principle a fresh endorsement.

The English review team had been a strong one. Jenny McIntosh had been an executive director at the Royal National Theatre and chief executive at the Royal Opera House. She had also been a valued colleague on the board of Welsh National Opera. It also comprised two government officials – one from the Department for Education and Skills and the regional director of the Government Office for the North East – a former head of culture at the Greater London Authority, Baroness Young, and two outsiders, a fashionable theorist of the creative industries, Charles Leadbeter, and the chief executive of Creative New Zealand, Elizabeth Kerr, who ran a lively arts council in her country, and one whose title the Scottish Executive were later to crib for their own newly truncated council.

There had been some speculation that ACE was for the chop, largely fuelled by some hostile speeches from the junior minister, David Lammy. The review team's report took a different view, and one which could have been applied almost word for word to the situation in Wales:

> ...there will always be attractions for any government in strengthening control over its sponsored agencies. But supporting and developing the arts in England is a multi-faceted, wide-ranging and difficult task: there are no simple solutions to the challenges it presents. We believe that government, the public and the arts community benefit from the focus, authenticity and reach that an arm's-length body can provide. We are not convinced, however, that the relationship between DCMS and Arts Council England is presently underpinned by sufficient commonality on respective roles, or by the necessary mutual respect to enable these potential benefits to be realised.
>
> We think it is worth the effort to get this right. Although there are currently imperfections in the way Arts Council England operates, it is nonetheless a national asset: a significant repository of knowledge and

expertise which the team believes should be developed and used more effectively. Energy needs now to be devoted to improving the systems and relationships already in place....

It set out a list of actions that both the DCMS and ACE should take 'to create a more nuanced and cooperative relationship', stressing that 'arm's length should not mean independent to the point of avoiding opportunities for joint working' and that 'the most effective NDPBs have been able to expand the imagination of government'. It was a thoughtful document that did not skirt around the difficulties of the relationship, but also gave due weight to the worth of the Arts Council and the core principle on which it was based.

★ ★ ★ ★

At 9.10 a.m. on 23 December, the last Friday before Christmas, the Assembly building was empty apart from the receptionist and a security man. Politicians of all parties have an unmannerly habit of keeping you waiting, but this was longer than usual – to the extent that the receptionist rang Alun's office twice and warned me, apologetically, that it might be another half hour or more. This was not a good omen. If he was having to have a discussion with his senior official about what to tell me, it was hardly likely to be good news. A secretary came down to get me at 9.50 a.m.

In the coming months Alun was to deny that he had sacked anyone. While that was correct in the technical sense, there was no mistaking it on the day. Having been in the sacker's chair on several occasions, the signs were easy to see: the stiff manner, the hesitation, the clipped sentences, the lack of eye contact, the common avoidance of the central objection, the desperate wish to get the meeting over. He did not beat about the bush. He said that he was going go through a full appointment process. Apparently, his main concern was that he had been shocked by the results of our opinion survey that, he said, had 'confirmed what I expected and feared about the difference between the classes'. 'This is going to be my major focus and I want someone to lead on this,' he added. It was a handy screen around the real disagreement on governance.

It was also a great irony. My pitch when appointed was that I wanted the Arts Council to become a recognised centre of intelligence. Now he was using the results of our most impressive piece of new intelligence to hang me. Neither I nor any member of the council would have had any problem with developing the access agenda, but if he did not have sufficient confidence in me after the last three years, I told him, I would not be applying. Without that confidence between minister and appointee, it would not work.

He said he did not plan to say anything until the New Year and that he hoped that when an announcement was made there would not be 'a slanging match'. I said that I would have no intention of slanging anybody, but that I would have a view, as would others who would read his actions in a different way. He shrugged. I asked him whether he would be willing to meet with the ACW working group. He said no, he would prefer to meet with the whole council. There would be no further debate on the six companies. 'That decision is taken, done and dusted.' I was back in my car by 10.05 a.m.

Eighteen months after the lighting of the bonfire, and thirteen months after the announcement of the government's plans for the Arts Council, a time during which the council had, with much effort and many misgivings, been a model of restraint, it could contain its anger no longer. It met on 3 January 2006, deciding to write a letter of complaint to the First Minister and to go public with a three-fold complaint about the ASPB Reform issue, lapses in the process for appointing new members, and my own position. The letter, from Janet Roberts, the vice-chair, complained that this accumulation of issues 'compromises the independence of the council and is damaging to the relationship that needs to exist between the council and the government'.

There followed a most extraordinary outburst of support for the council's position, aided and abetted by a vociferous campaign by the *Western Mail*, that had its own beef with Alun Pugh over rude remarks he had made about the paper when it appeared before the Assembly's culture committee. I often thought the paper's support for myself was by way of recompense, since the previous October they had carried a damaging feature in their arts section, in which they listed fifty 'movers and shakers' in the arts in Wales. Unfortunately, they had me in pole position, with the minister an embarrassing ninth. Although it was a frivolous journalistic exercise, designed to amuse, it was extraordinarily unhelpful. When I next met the editor, Alan Edmunds, I told him he could buy me a long lunch if I lost my job.

He had often wondered whether the council had the support of the arts sector, but told me later that any doubts he had were allayed at the Creative Wales awards in January. These awards, designed to assist individual artists, had become something of an event in the last three years. When I stood to speak I was astonished when the whole room rose with a loud roar of support and prolonged applause. Whereas a year before we had worried about the quiescent nature of the arts sector, it had now clearly found its voice. There was a real sense of unity in the room. Rosemary Butler, said some kind words and, given her own government's position, bravely presented me with a red rose.

Although it had been clear that the government's proposals would not have gained a majority in the Assembly on a free vote, such freedom was never in prospect. Indeed, throughout the last year we had assumed that, despite its slim but effective majority, the Government did not need to have a vote at all. Now the opposition parties scented blood and on 10 February challenged the government's business statement, demanding a full debate on the issues.

In the first of a series of depressingly fractious exchanges on these issues in the Assembly, Alun Pugh shrugged off all criticism and dead-batted like Geoffrey Boycott of old. The access issue was used to muddy the water, not least through an exuberant class-warrior parody by Huw Lewis attacking 'the bleating of a middle-class Cardiff and rural-Wales-based crachach'. The result was a tied vote, and under the rules the Presiding Officer, Dafydd Elis-Thomas, declared the motion lost. A few days later the government announced that there would be a debate in government time on 1 February.

The fact that the Labour rebel Peter Law had voted with the opposition meant that it was possible to defeat the government on the substantive issue, but as with so many votes in the Assembly at this stage it was on a knife-edge. I had, by chance, shared a taxi with Peter Law, in London, just before Christmas and it was clear that he was unwell. The opposition was concerned that he might not show, and the two days before the debate added some unexpected twists.

On the Monday I received a call from John Marek, the deputy presiding officer, to say that Peter Law's sister-in-law had died and the funeral was on the Wednesday afternoon, the same afternoon as the debate. There was talk of postponement that I did not relish. It was not until the following morning that it was confirmed that a car, with minder, would be sent to pick Peter up. He might not be there for the debate, but it was hoped that he would get there just in time for the vote. Then just to ratchet up the tension again came the news that John Dunwoody, father of the Labour AM, Tamsin Dunwoody, had died in France. It was not certain whether she would return to this country in time. I wondered what else the great scriptwriter in the sky had in store.

Suddenly, fourteen months after its announcement, the government had discovered a reason to reform: it was because 'we have a real problem with access', though most of us were mystified as to what effect government control of the six larger companies would do to solve it. After all, access was a word that had not surfaced once in the internal papers that had led to the decision. A second new thought popped up. We need reform so that organisations 'become more developmental in nature'. What did this mean? It sounded as if the issue was, suddenly, one about policy and performance, although at the outset of the process the First Minister had denied that any of the proposed changes reflected on those things.

Strangely, Alun Pugh himself put up no organisational arguments of any kind to defend his proposals. No mention of strengthening the civil service that had been at the heart of Rhodri Morgan's announcement, no mention of unifying strategy, no mention of accountability. Instead, heat not light was the order of the day, with such anger on both sides that Dafydd Elis-Thomas had to reprimand speakers from both government and opposition, including the leader of his own party. He was clearly exasperated and said despairingly to the whole chamber at the conclusion of the debate, '... as a former member of the Arts Council, I am ashamed of you'. Shortly, before the end of the debate Peter Law had slipped quietly into his seat. The government lost by one vote.

Under the terms of the motion all preparations for transfer of responsibility for the six large companies were to be halted and the issues remitted for consideration by a independent panel that would be asked to consult widely. The government was asked to do nothing before bringing another motion back to the Assembly in December. The Arts Council of Wales was intact, but facing its fourth review in a decade.

★ ★ ★ ★

Elan Closs Stephens has been a key player on Wales's cultural scene for some decades, although better known following her appointment to the chair of S4C – the first appointment to a public body in Wales as the result of open advertisement following the introduction of the Nolan rules. She brought to her broadcasting role acute critical faculties and real knowledge of the media, as befits someone who has a personal chair in communications and creative industries in the Department of Theatre, Film and Television at Aberystwyth. For almost a decade she dealt with the Assembly Government and the DCMS in defending and promoting S4C's role, and was thus no stranger to government. She had also advised on the 2002 restructure of the Arts Council. She was, therefore, well-equipped to lance this particular boil.

Nevertheless, it was difficult to predict the outcome from studying the panel membership. Three were, in their own ways, direct clients of the Assembly Government: the President of the National Museum, the chairman of the Welsh Books Council and a board member of the Wales Millennium Centre. On the other hand, there was also considerable experience of the value and operation of the arm's length principle in different spheres.

The two broadcasters, Elan Closs and Roger Lewis, had long experience of the tricky relationships between public service broadcasting and government. Lewis, who had run Classic FM very successfully for many years was managing director of HTV Wales when appointed but, by the time the report was published, had moved to be chief executive of the Welsh Rugby Union – some might think a bed of sharper nails even than the Arts Council. But he was also a board member of the Wales Millennium Centre that was directly funded by the Assembly Government in both capital and revenue terms. Paul Loveluck had been a well-regarded civil servant in the Welsh Office before moving out to run first the Wales Tourist Board and then the Countryside Council for Wales. Since retiring he had taken on the presidency of the National Museum and had had to work out his own organisation's modus vivendi with the Assembly Government.

Professor Wynn Thomas, a distinguished writer and critic, headed a department at Swansea University studying the literature of Wales in both its languages. The higher education sector in Wales had put up a strong resistance to the possibility of absorption of its funding council into the civil service. He had also been a member of the ACW's literature committee as well as chairman of Academi, the organisation that had had most difficulty with the direct funding proposal. However, as the then chairman of the Welsh Books Council he was in a direct funding relationship with the culture minister. Vicky Macdonald had been a curator of the Royal Cambrian Academy in Conwy, as well as an advisor to the Arts Council and a long-standing member of its north Wales regional committee. Alan Watkin, a second member from north Wales, was chief leisure and library officer at Wrexham, and had in his care a substantial and active municipal art gallery.

These were certainly independently-minded people and the more optimistic saw a clear, if sub-conscious, indication that the government had no wish to replay the same row again. The independent review is a well-used mechanism for getting governments off hooks. The fun lies in predicting just how it will be done. The worry lies in the parallel knowledge that it is not in the nature of such panels simply to endorse the status quo. Change for change's sake is always a danger. The nature of the compromise that would emerge was, therefore, difficult to foresee, guaranteeing some suspense.

Appointed in April, the panel had been set a deadline of reporting in December 2006 and worked with commendable speed. In this it was helped by the near unanimity of opinion on some of the issues from the arts sector itself – expressed in 219 written submissions. This unanimity was enough to scotch any temptation to kick for touch until the May 2007 election. It delivered its short and crisp report on time. Sensibly, it did not attempt to go over the rights and wrongs of the dispute between the Council and the Government, describing the situation as the inevitable after-effect of the relationship between a devolved government and an ASPB' in which there was confusion about who sets strategy. It was, they said, time for clarity. In its essentials it turned out to be remarkably close to the alternative proposals that the Council had submitted to Alun Pugh a year earlier.

ACW had proposed the creation of a single, joint strategy, and a more direct route for advice to ministers. Stephens recommended a 'dual key' board that would oversee the development of strategies and which would also be a transparent forum for the Minister to take advice on unforeseen issues. ACW had proposed a joint approach to research. Stephens agreed, recommending that this should be dealt with jointly through the strategy board, for good measure asking for £750,000 of 'free money' in a new research and development fund to act as a lever for change.

ACW had suggested recognising the special needs of 'national companies' and a review that might consider extending the list beyond the big six companies that the Minister had put in the frame. Stephens suggested further work by the strategy board on the role of national organisations and what constitutes a national organisation and its wider responsibilities to the nation. The panel was firm that national companies should not be directly funded by Government.

Beyond this, the panel envisaged a charter for the arts promulgated soon after each Assembly election, and including a declaration on artistic freedom; a greater concentration by ACW on its developmental role; a further strengthening of ACW's art form and arts management expertise; the designation of 'beacon companies', recognised for their excellence. These beacon companies and beacon individuals would have access to a 'merit pot' of £2.5m per annum as a reward for their excellence. Responding to the Beecham Report, *Beyond Boundaries*, which recommended collaboration across Wales's small local authorities, the panel also suggested the creation of regional strategic partnerships with consortia of local authorities, but going hand in hand with the introduction of 'a mandatory requirement for all unitary authorities to facilitate arts opportunities and activities'.

Inevitably, given that the terms of reference were framed as a review of the Arts Council rather than a particular issue, there was a listing of what they saw as shortcomings in the council's approach and performance, although these were all issues of which the council was more aware than anyone, and ones from which it had been diverted by the prolonged uncertainty first over its existence and then over the extent of its role: the strengthening of its art form expertise, and its advocacy and developmental roles. Most thought that some balancing flak for the council was inevitable, given the unequivocal, though low key, rejection of the notion of direct funding of companies. The downside was that it gave the reader a snapshot of the council, rather than a description of the council as a work in progress.

Nevertheless, the council felt obliged, in its response to remind people not only of long standing schemes such as Collectorplan and Night Out, and the development of the network of galleries and theatres, but also of its work in brokering collaboration and mergers in the sector. The council had a long track record on development, and was already intent on moving further in that direction. What it needed was support and space to carry it out, since it would involve continuing internal change and the augmentation of its business skills as well as difficult decisions which could be guaranteed to be resisted by those whom it did not benefit. The same need for time and space applies to the development of art form expertise – an issue that had also surfaced in the peer review of the much larger and more generously staffed Arts Council of England.

There was perhaps more substance in the criticism that there was an absence of strategic papers, e.g. a strategic paper on social inclusion, and what it saw as a culture of management not strategy. But it was right in thinking that this was another result of the lack of clarity, as between ACW and the department, on where strategic responsibility lay.

There was another aspect of this issue that the panel did not remark upon. Some of ACW's art form strategies had been compiled during the Assembly's first term, on the too optimistic assumption that the upward trajectory of growth would continue. In that sense the council had shared in the euphoria of the Assembly's first term, and some of the strategies were unashamedly aspirational. While the Stephens panel was wanting the council to embrace 'ambition, challenge and innovation', the council itself was in the process of revisiting all its plans to take a more realistic view of future funding. While the panel was mildly critical of decisions it saw as being taken on the basis of financial size rather than strategy (e.g. a decision to drop most revenue clients receiving under £20,000) it missed the point that this had been a first step, to start clearing the ground to make room for just the strategic approach that it was advocating, as well as to ensure that the council had the funds to safeguard the panel's other priority, excellence.

There were two areas in which the report was over-optimistic. The difficulty of separating strategic from operational issues does not disappear when you establish a strategy board. If anything the difficulty increases, particularly if, in other areas of government, the integration of strategy and operations is the norm. The panel itself conflated the two aspects as when it proposed that 'the Strategy Board should set the strategy *and viability* (my italics) of the WMC, as a holistic entity including the resident companies'. If the panel had, instead, followed its own logic, it would have recommended that the WMC cease to be a direct client of government.

The other issue that the report did not fully resolve was advocacy. It proposed that ACW should act less as a gatekeeper body and more as an advocacy body for arts organisations at the strategy board and in other arenas. Advocacy for the arts in government should remain with the minister; advocacy for companies and organisations and their development more generally should remain with ACW. While this seems eminently reasonable in itself, it represents an incomplete picture of the advocacy problem.

The whole episode had confirmed what had been increasingly evident, namely, that there are severe limitations on the advocacy role of the Arts Council. While it is free to advocate the value of the arts in general, it will get short shrift from government if it advocates particular developments in public. In a situation where special advisers were, at one stage, seeking right of approval over every press release issued by the council, its freedom to advocate publicly on behalf of the arts sector is severely circumscribed. If that constraint is accepted, it is bound to affect the relationship between the council and the sector. It is asking the arts sector to take the strength and effectiveness of the council's private advocacy largely on trust. My own conclusion is that while the council will always want to do everything to ensure that that trust exists, the sector now needs to develop an advocacy capacity that is quite separate from both government and the council.

But these are only minor reservations, when set against the panel's achievement. At the strategic level the long-term importance of the panel's report will rest on four recommendations. First, the re-affirmation of the arm's length principle. Second, the conviction that one of the culture minister's prime tasks is to champion the arts within government with 'particular emphasis on developing co-operative strategies with fellow cabinet colleagues'. That said, it is not quite true that the culture minister is the 'only person capable of a joined-up approach to the arts at cabinet level'. That leaves the First Minister out of the equation, and there is an interesting precedent in New Zealand, where the Prime Minister is also minister for culture. Third, the promulgation of a cultural charter at the beginning of each four-year Assembly term. Fourth, the suggestion that the arts should become a mandatory rather than a discretionary responsibility for local government.

The one danger that remained was that the wide acceptance of the report by both Government and opposition would turn out to be simply a successful kick into the long grass, rather than a template for action.

REFLECTIONS

16 The arts in a young democracy

There is always a danger in writing a detailed account of events in which you have been involved, that you can lose perspective and exaggerate their importance. The heat of the moment soon cools. Today's headlines are soon beyond recall, and sometimes rightly so. I have set out the story of the dispute between ACW and the Assembly Government at this length for four reasons.

First, the issues are important for the arts, and may arise again, as the new powers given to the Assembly, and particularly to its executive, in the Government of Wales Act 2006 may place fewer constraints on government in this field in the future. Second, because it fills out the Welsh dimension of the arts governance issue that is being played out differently in each of the countries of the UK. Already a Conservative Party taskforce on the arts in England, led by John Tusa, has recommended direct funding of national companies, to the consternation of many of those companies. Third, because I believe that the story says something about the development of political decision-making in Wales's young democracy. Fourth, because it relates to wider issues in our society.

It is easy to dismiss this whole episode as a spat between one of the smallest public bodies in the land and one of the smallest departments of government. The Arts Council of Wales's grant-in-aid is, after all, little more than an accountant's rounding in the Assembly Government's £14 billion budget – 0.2 per cent of the total. The culture department is its smallest portfolio. And yet, an entirely unnecessary and avoidable row was allowed to distract both the government and a government-sponsored public body for a long period, dominating the headlines to an extent that was extraordinary for the arts in Wales.

The government created for itself a barrage of criticism and adverse publicity and, eventually, a public defeat. It could not have been unaware of the dangers. They had been pointed out to the First Minister and his cabinet colleagues and to special advisers on more than one occasion by myself and other council members. The government proceeded against the overwhelming weight of opinion in the arts sector itself, against the unanimous view of all opposition parties, against the advice of several of its own backbenchers and in the face of the misgivings even of some cabinet ministers, for what could only ever have been a marginal gain. It was a mystifyingly wilful piece of self-harm.

At the same time, an Arts Council that had been steadily and successfully rebuilding its competence, expertise and reputation since 2002 – following the most torrid period in its existence – was threatened with an unenviable choice between, at best, a further prolonged, distracting review of its role, purpose and operation or, at worst, a perceived emasculation. It had come out of probation, only to be threatened with permanent electronic tagging.

A public body fully respectful of a government's democratic mandate, eager to create a productive relationship with its sponsoring minister and department, and which had constantly sought intelligent dialogue, had been presented with deficient proposals based on the most meagre analysis and been pushed, slowly and reluctantly and against all its instincts, into open conflict with that government. Moreover, it had obliged the council to struggle against a major distraction from its prime purpose at a time when social and technological developments were generating an agenda for change, both for the council and the sector it served, more formidable than ever.

The course of the argument itself made the case for the arm's length principle. In a country where the public sector is overwhelmingly dominant and sources of private finance for cultural purposes are scarce, I lost count of the people who said they supported the council fully but could not go public as they were chasing government grants of one kind or another.

Academi, one of the six organisations scheduled for transfer, became locked in a bitter internal dispute that divided its board. Many were horrified at the prospect of being a ministerial client since it represented writers as well as promoting them. But as time dragged on through 2005, those who counselled either silence or accommodation – by then a majority – became even more cautious, on the sole premise that they were concerned for the organisation's funding, thus making ACW's case. A senior person in another of the six companies was cavalier in his honesty: 'To hell with principles. I'm a whore. Show me the money.'

It exemplified the gulf of understanding between, on the one hand, a professionalism that claimed some understanding and knowledge of the arts and arts organisations and, on the other hand, an urge for control widespread in contemporary government throughout the UK and allied to the more depressing, self-induced imperatives of the political process. Here was a public body trying its best to take a rational approach to the issue of good governance in a particular field, even to the extent of trying to create a rationale for government actions where none was offered by government itself, and faced with a ministerial power, empowered by the act of election to override, apparently without the need for justification, a separate legitimacy of knowledge or professionalism. This was one corner of life to which the 'respect agenda' did not apply.

The episode also confirmed the capacity of cultural issues, be they the arts or language, to touch sensitive spots, generating reactions out of all proportion to their call on government resources. This was the other side of the shining coin that delivers benefits for society and for government also quite disproportionate to their cost. Nevertheless, as council members we had to ask ourselves whether our resolve in this matter was simply a misplaced amour propre, an automatic defence of vested interest. I, certainly, did not think so, for it also raised questions about our society and government that are not only germane to Wales's hesitant, young democracy but also touch on issues and debates that are live throughout the UK.

This is a period of great tension between the demands of security and of civil liberties, and of a growing fundamentalism in all religions with their increasingly strident demands for safeguard from offence. On 19 December 2004, less than three weeks after the First Minister announced the Assembly Government's proposals for the Arts Council of Wales, hundreds of Sikhs in Birmingham protested against Birmingham Rep's production of *Bezhti*, a black comedy that depicted rape and murder in a Sikh temple. Their protest was so violent – bricks were thrown, and several policemen injured – that, after discussions with the police, the theatre cancelled the production. The play had been written by a young Sikh woman, Gurpreet Kaur Bhatti, who had felt 'imprisoned by the mythology of the Sikh diaspora' and was carrying out a traditional provocative role of theatre in attacking institutionalised hypocrisy.

The theatre had, in fact, consulted with the Sikh community, although the theatre's artistic director, Jonathan Church, later admitted that it had been a mistake to give it the impression that the theatre was willing to negotiate the content of the work. It was, reportedly, not thought offensive by many younger Sikhs, though many religious leaders joined Sikh elders in urging a boycott. Some of the cast and the author went into hiding for a time after receiving death threats.

Birmingham Rep was not alone. At a conference of theatre managers a few months later the *Guardian* reported that the manager of a Belfast theatre complained of being regularly picketed by Free Presbyterians objecting to any discussion of homosexuality. Hamish Glen, from the Belgrade Theatre in Coventry, who had been a member of the steering group for ACW's review of theatre in Wales, said he had been forced to resist calls from his local authority to eschew plays of a religious or politically controversial nature. An arts council officer from the Midlands said she had been contacted by one local authority wanting to know whether arts council funding agreements forbade works that might cause religious offence. Janet Steel, who had directed Bezhti, confessed that the violent reaction to the play had created a pressure within her to censor works she was directing.

Only weeks later, and before *Bezhti* had fully faded from the headlines, the BBC broadcast *Jerry Springer: the Opera* in the face of the largest 'viral e-mail' campaign it had yet suffered, despite being one of the world's most popular websites. This was undoubtedly a new phenomenon – a coincidence of heightened sensitivity to offence coupled with a new potential for magnification through technology. Before and after the broadcast the BBC were contacted by no less than 65,000 people, 96 per cent of them complainants, although many of their complaints were in similar form. In contrast, little more than a year before, Martin Scorsese's *The Last Temptation of Christ* had prompted only 1,554 complaints to the Independent Television Commission, while a *Spitting Image* 'image of God' puppet had drawn only 341. The complaints against *Jerry Springer* also had a more sinister side. Several senior BBC executives claimed they had received death threats after the campaigners published their home telephone numbers.

The opera had been launched at Battersea Arts Centre before a hugely successful run, first at the National Theatre and then at a commercial West End theatre. On television it attracted BBC2's largest ever audience for opera – 2.4 million. On stage it had attracted little protest, but the move to television, and in particular to the BBC, gave the protesters a national cause and a purchase on publicity that they used to the full. Once achieved, theatre did not escape lightly. A proposed tour of regional theatres was truncated when thirteen of them pulled out. One of those that stayed in was the Wales Millennium Centre where it played to good houses in June 2006, despite a call from the Roman Catholic Archbishop of Cardiff for it to be banned.

On *Jerry Springer*, Alun Pugh's stance was, at one level, exemplary, despite revealing that it had generated the largest mailbag on any issue in his political career. He stated publicly on several occasions that it was not a matter for him but for WMC, although, equally significantly, it had been a matter for discussion at one of his regular business meetings with the centre's chief executive. The direct relationship between minister and venue raised the crucial question: what if the minister for culture, rather than being a modern cycling secularist had been more in the mould of the late George Thomas, a combative Labour secretary of state for Wales and president of the Methodist Conference or, to come back to the present, in the mould of a Ruth Kelly, a member of Opus Dei? These are not far-fetched comparisons given the cultural and religious make up of Wales or the certain prospect of regular coalitions. In the Labour-Plaid coalition that followed the 2007 election, the culture brief was given to a nonconformist minister.

The concerns raised by both *Bezhti* and *Jerry Springer* had been heightened by the Westminster Government's determination to introduce an offence of 'incitement to religious hatred', which it attempted on three occasions: first, in the Anti-Terrorism, Crime and Security Bill in 2001, when it was dropped from the bill after objections in the Lords and then in 2004 in the Serious Organised Crime and Police Bill. Again it was dropped, not because of a change of heart, but in order not to hinder the passage of the rest of the bill before the May 2005 General Election. In June it emerged for the third time, in a free-standing measure, the Racial and Religious Hatred Bill.

It was energetically opposed by writers, comedians, actors and theatre workers, who all saw in it a real threat to freedom of expression, not least to comedy and satire. English PEN mounted a vigorous campaign with the open support of Monica Ali, Rowan Atkinson, Howard Jacobson, Philip Pullman, Nicholas Hytner and, not surprisingly, Salman Rushdie and Gurpreet Kaur Bhatti. As in Wales, ministers were adamant that freedom of expression was safe in their hands. Any threat, they said, was exaggerated. The Home Office minister, Fiona Mactaggart, attempting vainly to reassure, said there would be few prosecutions. The bar, she claimed, had been set high.

The writers, in response, were equally adamant that nothing as solid as a high bar existed. They said it would be 'a grave folly to rely on the views of a minister to safeguard our fundamental freedoms'. They did not back down and they kept up a constant pressure. On 25 October the House of Lords passed amendments that required the 'intention', and not just the possibility, of stirring up religious hatred. The government was undeterred and sought to overturn their Lordships wishes in the Commons. On 31 January, 2006 – ironically, the night before the Welsh Assembly voted down the plans to weaken ACW – the Westminster Government, too, was defeated. Both issues, in Cardiff and Westminster, were decided by only one vote.

Of course, some will not wish to see a connection between these matters. Wales has been spared religious strife so far. Racial tension has not generated large-scale riots, as in English cities, although individual racial incidents in many Welsh towns have been rising. Our multi-faceted complacency on these issues is misplaced: complacency about our approach to race and ethnic communities, encouraged by their longevity and relatively small scale, and air-brushing from history the tensions that did erupt; more generally, a great willingness to think that difficult issues can be spirited away by a belief in the good intentions that dominate our idealised view of Wales; and too great a readiness to limit the parameters of our domestic political debate, leaving non-devolved issues to be debated out of earshot in Westminster. We have had our own tensions. Issues of language and identity have been hotly contested, generating civil disobedience and episodes of violence, the latter thankfully rare. It is not impossible to imagine them re-emerging.

In a period of burgeoning global tensions, it is perfectly possible that one day the considerable Welsh capacity for self-satisfaction could be blown apart in unpredictable ways. That is why it would have been be shameful for the organisation that represents our writers – writers in both our languages, guardians of a tradition and traditional speakers of truth to power – to be the client of a government minister. That is why it was right that we should have been concerned at the prospect of two theatre companies, based in the quiet rural market towns of Carmarthen and Mold, becoming direct clients of ministers. What might have happened if either company decided to try their hand at the kind of documentary theatre that, in England, has tackled the privatisa-tion of the railways, the Hatfield train crash, the Hutton inquiry and the Iraq war? That is why it was right that we should have been concerned that the BBC, the organisation that delivers more information to our eyes and ears than any other in Wales, might, through its National Orchestra of Wales, have become a direct client of government.

These things are not unconnected. They all impact on the arts. If civil liberties have to be constrained in the interests of security, all the more reason to ensure that the arts are truly and visibly independent, not least in a small national community like Wales where honest debate is already blunted by our very closeness. Mature societies and mature governments should want it so. The arts should want and demand it.

There is a wider issue, too. If the arts, like broadcasting, are a contributor to our democracy, and not merely a refinement of our social existence, then the dispute between the council and government is emblematic of a greater question. In setting the mood music for the 'bonfire of the quangos', some ministers had tried to portray the issue as a simple battle between the new democratic order in Wales and an old unaccountable order. This was rooted in a justified indignation at the undeniable excesses of political patronage during the Conservative years, but in over-simplifying the problem, the keepers of the new democracy also over-simplified the prescription.

As someone who had voted Yes in the 1979 referendum as well as in 1997, I still share, to the bemusement of many friends, an enthusiasm for the new institution, even when I disagree with some of its actions. But it is disappointing that the new, and perhaps inevitable preoccupation in Wales with novel levers of government, albeit limited in scope, has crowded out a wider reflection on our new Welsh democracy, as has happened for other reasons throughout the United Kingdom.

David Marquand has written eloquently about the broader phenomenon in his book, *Decline of the Public*. It is a book about the public domain, a domain outside party politics, 'the domain of citizenship, equity and service' that he sees as essential to democratic governance and social well-being and which he regards as 'both priceless and precarious – a gift of history which is always at risk'. He argues that that domain is at risk now from a combination of 'market mimicry, populist governance and central control', all of which are linked and feed each other.

To be fair to our new Welsh democratic institution, the most powerful source of these debilitating trends within the UK has been central government, and not just of one colour. The Assembly Government would also argue that it has done more than most to eschew market mimicry and that populist appeal is not easily achieved in Wales. But the habit of central control is infectious, and set against the logic of the public domain which is 'quintessentially pluralist'. Marquand makes a powerful argument for self-confident and powerful intermediate institutions 'not just to protect the public domain from market and private power, but also to protect it from an inherently over-intrusive central state'.

In further reforming our institutions in Wales, perhaps we should take greater account of the downside of enfeebling the intermediate institutions that populate this public domain. We should give more thought to the qualitative aspects of democracy, to that part of a democracy that lies beyond elected government and beyond party, to the necessarily layered nature of any civil society and the needs of those layers, and to the benefits of deeper debate rather than the distraction of superficial disputation.

17 Appetite and access

People tend to remember only the benign manifestations of chaos theory, the unpredictable effect of the beat of a butterfly's wing down serendipity's chain. My parents had bought me a bicycle, rather reluctantly, when we lived in Swansea in the early fifties. It was a liberating gift. It opened up to sandy exploration all the glories of Gower, a peninsula as regularly indented as my cycle's sprocket. But within three summers we had moved, tearfully, to a Cardiff that, in the days before the development of Cardiff Bay, seemed more like an inland city.

There was here no choice of handy bays, no Mumbles lighthouse to wink at me nightly, nor even the sound of the foghorns that had punctuated winter nights earlier in my life when we lived a stone's throw from Barry Docks. New cycling challenges were needed. So, at the suggestion of a schoolfriend, one day we set off from Cardiff to cycle to the home of his relatives near Stratford. They did me a lifelong favour. They booked tickets for this fifteen-year-old and his friend to see Laurence Olivier as Coriolanus at the RSC. A year later, again bikeborn, we were back at Stratford to see Peter O'Toole as Shylock.

At the time I was only dimly conscious of Olivier, and Peter Hall meant nothing at all. O'Toole was a different matter. Earlier that year he had turned up at home to discuss Dylan Thomas with my father. It being a Sunday afternoon and my mother having had a good Baptist upbringing, he oozed all his Irish charm in asking her for a glass to help with the half bottle of whisky he had brought with him, and by the end of the afternoon was recording folk songs on our bulky Grundig tape recorder.

Even now I can feel the power of those Stratford performances. I can hear the audience's intake of breath as O'Toole literally rent Shylock's garment with a great ripping sound. I can hear the loud, collective gasp as Olivier, in the assassination scene, pitched himself from a perilously high platform, and, surreptitiously caught by the ankles by two of the Volsci, was left hanging, upside down, facing the audience, blood dripping from his fingertips – a brilliant and famed, physical *coup de théâtre*. I would defy any young person to be unaffected by the power of these plays, by the thrill of live performances or, indeed, by the shared response of an excited audience. It left me with an ineradicable sense of expectation every time I enter a theatre, concert hall, or opera house.

I know of no-one in the arts who does not want others to have access to such magic, no-one who does not want young people, in particular, to be taken through such promising gateways. They desire that not because they want to reduce crime or drug-taking or to increase the nation's gross domestic product, though they may want all those things. Neither do they believe that the arts guarantee to make saints out of sinners. They simply want to share something beautiful. They do not want people to miss out on experiences that they regard as important, enlarging and enriching. The instinctive wish of all artists is not only to share their art, but also to make the arts part and parcel of the lives of more people. That is as true of those in the so-called high arts as it is of artists who have dedicated themselves to working in the community. Their commitment is acted out daily across Wales.

From a modest building that was once a convent in Cardiff's Adamsdown, Rubicon Dance has, over 30 years, offered a range of courses with attendances rising from 65,000 in 2004 to 84,000 in 2006, representing about 1500 people a week – from youngsters to pensioners, and of both sexes – spread across the most disadvantaged areas of Cardiff and Newport. Ruth Till, for 20 years the director of the company, combines a dancer's poise with an earthy laugh, both of which are handy in the front line of community arts. Having trained as a dancer before moving into community work in Leeds in the late seventies, she built Rubicon into the pre-eminent community dance company in the UK, also winning an international reputation for its work in the United States, Australia, Eastern Europe and Scandinavia. On a summer's weekend in 2005, more than 400 of her followers – aged from eight to 93 – created a sea of dance in the Oval Basin outside the Wales Millennium Centre to celebrate the capital's centenary.

Is all this art? 'At the very beginning I loved dance,' she says, 'and simply wanted everybody else to enjoy it. You have got to do this, it's wonderful. Yes, sometimes you do feel it's social work. Sometimes it's something else, sometimes pure art – so it's along a continuum. What pegs it to art is that we tend to work from people's own abilities to dance, their own ideas and ways of doing it. It may not always be the greatest artistic creation, but when it happens, those are great days.'

The company has had its share of Billy Elliotts, young people who have gone on to dance professionally, but it's clear that that is not its only measure of success. She cites countless examples of people whose lives have been changed. A one-time truant, assailed by domestic problems, started to come to a weekly course and found herself sufficiently inspired to move on to a full-time one. 'She won't be a professional dancer, but she is going to college, and she's leading a youth group. She has become an attender rather than a non-attender,' says Ruth.

Another young woman whose life was salvaged is now doing a degree in philosophy. 'She won't dance professionally, but she will love dance for the rest of her life.' Sometimes less spectacular results can be no less meaningful, she says, citing a housewife with more than her share of problems. 'She thought her session with us was the best hour in her week, not because she is experiencing great art, but she is being and working with others, dancing and enjoying it and feeling good afterwards. Isn't that enough? Does it always have to be more?'

Fifteen miles away in Penygraig, in the Rhondda, Margaret Jervis has presided over Valleys Kids since 1978 when she and her husband, Richard Morgan, set it up in a whitewashed coal cellar as a community arts organization to be run by local people. They swiftly pulled in Hywel Edwards, a probation officer who wanted to work with young offenders in a different way, and now chairs the company. Valleys Kids began, under a different name, with a grant from a job creation programme, but is now housed in Soar chapel, on which lottery money has wrought a sympathetic but unmistakably modern transformation of real quality. It lights up the surrounding square just as effectively as it lights up the lives of those who pass through its doors.

I guess Margaret Jervis's crisp Scottish accent has been softened by thirty years in the Rhondda, but it retains that no-nonsense timbre that generated a 'respect agenda' long before it became a Blairite mantra. Like Ruth Till, she believes fervently that the arts are a truly effective way of 'engaging the disengaged', and emotion comes to the surface whenever the tales of individuals are told. 'Someone told me at the start of one session that I had changed his life. I could hardly speak. It was difficult to carry on,' said Margaret at the beginning of an eloquent catalogue of hope. 'I know we are making a difference. There was the mother who said to me, "You have stopped my son going to prison." There's C. who, when she had successfully finished her A-levels, said that had it not been for the youth club and the youth theatre, she would have ended up as a single mum, and probably on drugs. There's seeing J. going off to a conference in Italy with real confidence. His parents had been involved in drugs, he hadn't been succeeding at school and was in a terrible situation, but he got involved in the drama workshop and then the youth theatre. To see him get to the point when he could go away on his own amongst all those foreign students and be able to hold his own in a work camp – that was a golden moment.'

Valleys Kids has begun to spread beyond Penygraig to the rest of the valley. Margaret again: 'The Penyrenglyn estate at Treherbert was a no-go area when we started there with some money from Children in Need. We had no base until we were given two houses in a run-down block of four. Look at Penyrenglyn now – an estate that looks nice, the housing has been renovated, the drug dealer has gone, and there are no kids on the risk register, where there used to be nine. It's not a no-go area anymore. That estate has been turned around and the arts played an important part in that.

'I won't claim it's just the arts, but they played a major role in changing people's perceptions of themselves, and their community. If you are living on a run-down estate, in poverty, and your children don't succeed in school, you don't have very good health and everything in your life seems to be wrong – how do you help people out of that? You have to give them a different image of themselves. And we try to do that by using film, music, singing, theatre, the visual arts, the arts class for adults. They now have a gallery on the main street in Treherbert. They're saying we've got things that are good enough to go on show in a gallery. Isn't that wonderful?'

What marks both organizations is the commitment to quality and the beneficial side of longevity. If there is a value in the instrumental effects of the arts, then it is not always won quickly. Ruth Till: 'I get upset when people thrust money into your hand and tell you to regenerate an area. True access is a long haul. If we are really going to address access we have to develop long-term relations with an area or a group. It's a slow process. For instance, you might work with a group of kids who can be quite difficult. They might be kicking a ball around outside. Somewhere down the line you bring it inside and kick it around in the hall, and at some point the tape will go on and suddenly the ball goes away and they are running, and then they are jumping and again, somewhere down the line, they are dancing, and now you begin to develop a dance group. That can take months. It's not a magic wand – have some money for six months and do access – we are talking ten years.'

The undoubted truth about the value of long-term commitment is sometimes used by the community arts sector, though not by Ruth Till or Margaret Jervis, to diminish the value of shorter term outreach programmes that are now the stock-in-trade of most of the major performing companies. During the years of flat funding in the nineties, when arts organisations in Wales fought like ferrets in a sack with rather more energy than they directed at government, the battle for resources threatened to lead to a sterile division of the arts community into two camps: the community camp questioning the expertise of the large companies in education and the handling of disadvantaged groups, and the large companies, usually by implication, questioning the artistic value of community arts. Although in some circumstances there may be validity in this mutual suspicion – good practice is never universal – more generous government funding in the first five years of the millennium nipped the dispute in the bud, and there is now a chance of greater understanding.

Part of that understanding is that the large companies are attempting a different task: not always the provision of regular services in any one place, but an attempt to engender the excitement that their art form and their substantial artistic resources can create, in a way that smaller scale work may not always achieve. That is not to be dismissed, though its value is greatly enhanced by follow through.

The very first project carried out under the banner of WNO Max was a case in point. The *Katerina* project – an exploration of Janacek's *Katya Kabanova* – involved four primary schools in Merthyr, a town at the wrong end of most league tables of deprivation. Merthyr kids and Janacek? Well, why not? They visited WNO's workshops to see costumes and wigs being prepared and sets built and painted. Then they worked with the local writer Alan Osborne and composer Ruth Byrchmore to explore Katya's story but also to tell their own, rooted in their own environment and to construct and perform and record their own opera.

Alan Osborne's libretto – writing of *Katerina* trapped in her mother-in-law's house – contains these poignant words: 'my hair is knots, my jewellery rust, the cover of my bed is dust,' lines directly inspired by the words of a young girl in Goetre Primary School. She wrote them, saw them shaped in print, heard them rehearsed and sung and applauded. We can only guess what kind of epiphany that was. One young lad from Gwaunfarren school wrote his own definition of opera: 'A story told by singing with lots of fun, even though it made me deaf in one ear.'

At one stage in the project Anthony Freud and I sat in the circle at the New Theatre with 250 of these children to watch a full dress rehearsal of *Katya Kabanova*. In truth I was sceptical that this number of children, en masse, would be engaged by two hours of Janacek. I was wrong. They were transfixed. And when Suzanne Murphy, playing the mother-in-law from hell, took a curtain call they booed her as loudly as if she had been a pantomime villain. Something was working.

No-one has put the case better than the author, Philip Pullman: 'Children need to go to the theatre as much as they need to run about in the fresh air. They need to hear real music played by real musicians on real instruments as much as they need food and drink. They need to read and listen to proper stories as much as they need to be loved and cared for. The difficulty with persuading grown up people about this is that if you deprive children of shelter and kindness and food and drink and exercise, they die visibly; whereas if you deprive them of art and music and story and theatre, they perish on the inside, and it doesn't show.' It applies to adults, too.

★ ★ ★ ★

Are all these things beautiful and beneficial only in the one eye of the beholder? Are we kidding ourselves when we claim particular effects or powers for the arts? John Knell, one of the most stimulating and provocative analysts of the current cultural debate talks of the 'profound weakness of instrumental arguments for the arts – nothing serious, just the complete absence of theoretical and empirical causality'. It is true that arts data is notoriously patchy, that many arts organisations regard the gathering of data as a chore, and that the longitudinal studies beloved of social scientists simply have not been done.

Though good data is necessary to give some measure of the effectiveness of public spending or of public support, if we think that some scientific study will ever provide a politically incontrovertible case for the arts we will be chasing a chimera. It is easy to dismiss anecdotal evidence, but as one academic researcher reminded a recent international conference, 'organised anecdotal evidence is data'. Perhaps we should just put more effort into organising it. Our daily observations and insights matter. Some measurement is inescapable, but advocacy is more than measurement.

Are these mere oases, insignificant in a wider desert? Yes and no. In 1999/2000 ACW gave core funding of £464,554 to 14 community arts organisations. By 2006/07 this had risen to £1.75m spread across 24

organisations. The average spend per organisation had risen from
£33,000 to nearly £73,000. When the council gave evidence to the
culture committee's review of arts and sport in regeneration in 2004,
these 24 organisations were providing sessions for 414,000 participants – equivalent to 14 per cent of the Welsh population at a cost of
only £2.53 per head. Voluntary Arts Wales claims to represent 1,600
organisations in a country of only 2.96 million people, i.e. one organisation for every 1,812 people. Many of them are also raising other
funding from local authorities, local businesses, and charitable trusts.

The figures are in one sense encouraging, but they do mask voids.
As with so much in the arts, the distribution of these organisations is
the product of the varied accidents of history: the drive and interests of
one individual, the presence of an inspired artist-teacher or teacher-
artist, the coming together of like-minded volunteers, the insight of a
single local government official, influential councillor or council leader.
A happy combination of any of these can make the difference between
a community where green avenues can open and one that sees only an
eternal vandalised cul-de-sac. Being accidents, there is no uniform
pattern, no guarantee that opportunity will beckon everywhere. Only
the seed is ubiquitous, and so much more of it could flourish if more
effort were devoted to nurturing it.

It is easy to object that this is a view from some plush, middle-class
eyrie – easy but wrong. In 2001 the Assembly Government embarked
on its Communities First programme, designed to tackle the 100 most
disadvantaged wards in Wales. Edwina Hart, then minister for finance
and local government, was the minister behind the scheme. Her blunt,
combative style hides a former viola player in the National Youth
Orchestra of Wales. At the outset the public in these wards were asked
what new initiatives they would like to see in their locality In Rhondda
Cynon Taf, an authority that accounts for 23 of the 100 wards, the
partnerships set up to run the scheme across groups of wards, specifically requested arts development officers resulting in a formal 'creative
communities' project, jointly funded by the Assembly and European
Objective One money.

The existence of this widespread grass roots support for the arts
was confirmed by an ACW survey of 7,000 people across Wales – the
most detailed survey of its kind undertaken in any nation or region of
the UK. It showed that attitudes to the arts in Wales are overwhelmingly
positive. Three-quarters of the Welsh adult population (76 per cent)
attend arts events at least once a year. One in five (20 per cent) across

Wales actually participate in some arts activity. Three-quarters believe
that the arts and culture make Wales a better place to live. Public
funding of the arts is supported by 78 per cent, while no less than 95
per cent think that all schoolchildren should have the opportunity to
learn a musical instrument or take part in other arts activities. Nearly
seven out of ten think their communities would be poorer places
without art and culture. Comparable figures have been recorded
elsewhere in the UK. There is, surely, less need to worry about public
support for cultural investment than politicians or tabloid newspapers
might think.

Even in the more esoteric realm of contemporary visual art, the
public does not always conform to the tabloid stereotype. Tate Modern
has broken all records. It is not alone. In 2004 Wales launched the Artes
Mundi International Art Prize. The exhibition – which contained a
substantial ration of the sort of conceptual art that a government minister, Kim Howells, had famously rubbished when visiting the Turner
Prize exhibition – drew more people to our National Museum through
the months of March and April than in any comparable period since
the Museum was opened by George V in 1927. Some of us wondered
whether that was a flash in the pan. It was not. Two years later the
figures were 20 per cent higher, with twice as many school visits – 200
of them filling every available slot in the museum's timetable. While
seeking publicity for the prize, the organisers were told by one London
'quality' newspaper that it would help if they rubbished the Turner
Prize. Artes Mundi declined to do so and nothing appeared in that
newspaper.

It was around the issue of social equity that debate on the results of
the ACW survey concentrated. It confirmed that the arts were no
different from almost every other feature of life in the UK: namely, that
the better off access services of all kinds – educational, social and
cultural – more regularly and effectively than those lower in the social
scale. This general pattern has rightly been a primary concern for the
present governments in Westminster and Cardiff, although the
evidence since 1997 has been that these social disparities are extraordinarily resistant to policies geared to reduce them. Evidence of the
positive effects of policies such as Communities First in Wales and Sure
Start in England, have been disappointing. Investment in education has
not yet produced a significant reduction in the numbers leaving school
without qualifications or in the incidence of functional illiteracy. That
is not an argument for giving up on any of these policies, but simply to

say that changing society is not a simple matter of pulling levers.

It could be argued that the world of the arts in Wales has been more successful on this score than other fields of policy. Comparisons between the 2005 survey and the last major survey of its kind in Wales, in 1993, were encouraging. They showed that arts attendance had grown by nearly 40 per cent during that period and, surprisingly, had grown more strongly amongst the C2DE groups where the increase was 60 per cent. If any other field of public policy had been able to demonstrate such a positive change it's fair to suggest that the public would have heard a lot more about it from the spin doctors. But it was not convenient for the argument at the time, since ACW was in bad odour with the government as a result of the dispute over the council's future powers. In any case, it would undoubtedly have been used to accuse the council quite unfairly of complacency. The council's past and continuing commitment to access and outreach policies among its client organisations as well as its commitment to the strengthening of the community arts sector is demonstrable and outstanding, and the social disparities evident in the new data will rightly spur the council and the government to go further.

In deciding on future action there is a danger that governments will push to do the wrong thing. The more interesting message of the survey lies deeper in the data. The survey had been commissioned specifically to identify some of the barriers to attendance and participation in the arts. It was in this area that it produced the most surprising results. We had expected cost and transport, or even the potential for social discomfort that some can feel at arts venues and events, to be at the top of the list of barriers to attendance and participation. But that was not the case.

Far and away the most commonly cited factor for non-attenders was that the respondent was 'not really interested'. It accounted for 47 per cent of them. That was the case whether you asked about attending theatre events (34 per cent), art galleries and exhibitions (44 per cent), or festivals and carnivals (38 per cent). In comparison, those saying it 'cost too much' amounted to only 15 per cent for theatre events, 6 per cent for art galleries and exhibitions and 5 per cent for festivals or carnivals. Transport was cited by 7 per cent, 5 per cent and 4 per cent respectively. Those believing that they might feel uncomfortable or out of place at these events amounted to only 1 per cent across the board.

In short, seven out of ten of those in Wales who never attend an arts event are in the C2DE social groups and three-quarters of them say that they are either 'not very interested' or 'not at all interested' in the arts. Since a quarter of these are defined by social scientists as 'families struggling to get by in an otherwise affluent Britain' it may be unrealistic and even patronising to expect them to put attendance at the ballet higher up their list of priorities.

Even allowing for the fact that to some extent 'lack of interest' may stand proxy for other reasons that a respondent might not wish to disclose, to my mind the message of these figures is clear. The challenge of achieving greater social equity in arts participation and attendance has two dimensions – *opportunity* and *appetite*. The Arts in Wales survey data demonstrates conclusively that if we want to improve the situation for disadvantaged groups in this and future generations, it is vital that we put the issue of developing *appetite* at the top of the agenda.

Of course we should also continue to devise new and practical ways of increasing opportunities to attend and participate, but if we do not tackle appetite at the same time we will waste money, we will not achieve a more socially equitable outcome, and the lives of thousands will be less rich than they might have been. If, on the other hand, we manage to enlarge and extend that appetite, it will not only benefit disadvantaged groups more effectively than anything attempted to date, but will also benefit the whole of our society. That is a task for a whole government, not simply a culture department.

18 What are culture ministers for?

It was the opening night of John Metcalf's Vale of Glamorgan Festival. History and the contemporary came together in the setting. It was Ewenny Priory, the church immortalised by Turner, fresh from its careful restoration: cool, white walls setting off the solid and confident Norman stonework under a plain limed-oak ceiling, but the old rood screen now topped with an ethereal glass screen by Alex Beleshenko. Beneath the latter's watery shimmer the faint, square trace of large pixels underlies a bold cross set in a cloud of butterflies, and glowing through it all the eastern half of the church, as if giving a priest an option to cast his net on another side.

The Latvian Radio Choir rises to the magical setting, giving a flawless performance, fully mastering the complexity of music and soundscapes by an array of living composers, including the Latvian Peteris Vasks, who is there for a premiere of a new work. It was a moment to savour a balance between collective endeavour and individual artistry, symbolically different from the more monolithic sound of the traditional Welsh choir, as well as to sense the springboard to artistry provided by high technical competence. Also that knowledge is to creativity what a note is to music, an ingredient.

The same might be said about the arts within culture, the latter being a word capable of wide definition, as well as having an historical capacity to make British people uncomfortable. (Contrary to Wales's self-image, it would be a mistake to assume that Welsh people are immune to that discomfort.) Traditionally, the discomfort is often reflected in the political class, more obviously at the local level than the national; but even at the national level the word 'culture' is most often avoided. The German *kultur* has a muscular feel too it, *culture* in French sounds elegant, but in Britain 'culture' sounds more like something you would find at the bottom of a flagon of rough cider. Under Thatcher the relevant department was the Department of National Heritage, conjuring images of castles and stately homes. Only in 1997 did a British Government feel free to create a Department of Culture, albeit throwing in the words Media and Sport to dampen the effect. Chris Smith, its first incumbent did honour to the job as well as to the word. In his words, 'culture is what you grow people in.' It was sad, therefore, that the coalition government in Wales after the 2007 election reverted to the title Heritage, a backward step, even if the Welsh word *treftadaeth* has a more ancestral ring.

Yet talk of equipping ourselves for the knowledge economy is a cultural as well as economic shift. 'Clear red water' or a 'citizen-centred' approach to public reform is a cultural as well as managerial choice. Glib encouragement to Welsh people to be more confident is a cultural as well as psychological aspiration, just as Tony Blair's 'respect agenda' inevitably has a cultural as well as behavioural dimension. Different groups, of course, use different language and in the context of a narrower definition of culture, many politicians and business people, unfamiliar with the company of artists, fear their lack of fluency in the language of the other. It is small wonder that there is often a sense of disconnection that is damaging to the fulfilment of the aspirations of both parties. It is a disconnection that can also short-change the public.

Over the last few years John Holden, head of culture at the think tank Demos, has tried to explore ways of creating a more constructive triangular conversation between the politicians, the professionals and the public. Their current conversation, he argues, has become bogged down in a sterile struggle between those concerned with the intrinsic value of the arts and culture, art for art's sake, and those concerned with instrumental value, a requirement that the arts should be a kind of Swiss Army knife capable of solving every social problem, not to mention taking stones out of horses hooves. He argues that neither approach, on its own, has found the key to a new pro-culture way of thinking or to a fundamentally new place for culture in the pecking order of spending priorities.

While the politicians care most about instrumental economic and social outcomes, the professionals and the public are more concerned with intrinsic values, though the public might define that value 'at its simplest as a good night out, at its best a spiritually moving experi-ence'. The result of these divergent concerns is that 'the relationships between the public, politicians and professionals has become a closed, ill-tempered conversation between professional and politicians, while the news pages of the media play a destructive role between politics and the public'.

He argues instead for an emphasis on a wider concept of 'cultural value' that also embraces what he describes as 'institutional value' that 'relates to the processes and techniques that organisations adopt in how they work to create value for the public'. This sees the role of cultural organisations 'not simply as mediators between politicians and the public, but as active agents in the creation or destruction of what the public values'. This is not unlike the concept of 'public value' that formed the basis of the BBC's bid for a new licence fee settlement in 2006 and involves seeking, again in Holden's words, to 'achieve such public goods as creating trust, mutual respect among citizens, enhancing the public realm and providing a context for sociability and the enjoyment of shared experiences'.

Quite apart from advice for government and arts councils, he also seeks to place an obligation on cultural organisations themselves to find a new level of engagement with their publics in order to avoid a crisis of legitimacy, on the pragmatic basis that 'politicians fund what the public demands'. The trick here, it seems, is to get the public to find a language to express cultural value, rather than allowing either the cultural professional or the politicians to fix the language, giving the arts and culture a democratic mandate that is much deeper and direct.

It is not clear that creating a demonstrable public consensus of this kind is going to be any more realistic a goal than persuading politicians of the case for culture. It could simply be an alternative holy grail. But it is certainly worth a shot. After all, it is not as if we would be tilling barren ground. Cultural activity and consumption is already substantial. More books are sold and published than ever before. The enjoyment of music, both popular and classical, is constant and ubiquitous. The modern Adam and Eve have bitten the Apple and been left dangling from a pair of white wires. Technology has sharply reduced the barriers to entry for activities such as film-making, design and sophisticated electronic production.

Difficult though it would be to imagine or define a tipping point in advance, the process could not be other than beneficial, not least because politics and the arts have this in common: both suffer from a low level of engagement with their audiences and both politicians and arts organisations need to show some imagination in devising better ways to connect. For this reason, although Holden places a particular onus on cultural organisations, it would make sense if the cultural world and the politicians both understood the purpose of the project.

It would need several parties to take a positive view of a new continuing process, since this would not be a simple initiative with a neat beginning and end. The Assembly Government and its culture department in particular would need to develop their understanding of the subtleties of the proposition and to forego the defensiveness normally associated with it. It would also require it to give the arts council and some of the other ASPBs the resources necessary to continue the process of building and deepening their intelligence about public perceptions of cultural value as well as their responses to particular cultural offerings.

Cultural providers would need to graft onto their standard marketing practices, already commonly under-resourced, a new spirit of inquiry in relation to their audiences. It will be difficult enough to engineer this kind of constructive and opened ended conversation between three parties – Government, ASPBs and providers – but we cannot afford to leave local government out of the equation, a field where arts organisations endure the most common level of incomprehension, sometimes amounting to the theological concept of invincible ignorance.

The prospects are, however, not bright. While Holden's thesis has obviously carried some weight with ministers at the DCMS, Tessa Jowell's attempt, in a published address in 2005, to rebalance the argument in favour of the intrinsic value of the arts, rang few bells at the Treasury. In March 2006, the then junior Minister, David Lammy, the Minister for the Arts, while launching Holden's essay at a London theatre, spoke of trying to establish a settlement and a public consensus for the arts that could be as enduring as that which supports the NHS, but he offered no clear sense of how it might be achieved. Undaunted, Gordon Brown's new culture minister, James Purnell, has taken a similar line, and even commissioned Sir Brian McMaster to undertake a review of 'excellence in the arts'.

There had been more encouragement from Scotland following a ringing declaration from the then First Minister, Jack McConnell in 2003, influenced, many thought, by his wife who was running the arts in Glasgow at the time. McConnell had said he wanted culture to be his society's 'next great enterprise'. It was this that launched the Scottish Cultural Commission that took eighteen months, cost £500,000, and produced an ambitious, some said over-ambitious, vision. When it came to the crunch McConnell's Cabinet colleagues were less than enthusiastic about signing up to culture as an organising principle, although throwing an extra £20m a year at the arts seemed to most people ample compensation.

For some reason the debate seemed to pass Wales by – perhaps another sign of the wider disconnection from intellectual debate in the rest of the UK that has afflicted some areas of policy in Wales post devolution. In recent years no Welsh culture minister has attempted to paint a coherent picture of the place the arts and culture in society or in the priroities of government. It is often crowded out by the language discourse. Although the Welsh Arts Review, commissioned to resolve the dispute between the Welsh Assembly Government and the ACW, briefly endorsed the cross-cutting approach to culture, it did not manage to kindle a debate on that proposition. This is sad since Wales, with its relatively small-scale political and cultural framework, seems peculiarly well-suited to tackling the issues in a coherent way. Not to do so would be to miss a substantial opportunity.

Even if such a process were set in train and were, in time, to alter the content and tone of much of the debate around arts and culture, it would not entirely supplant more familiar arguments. The intrinsic and instrumental value of the arts cannot be hidden in the thickets of intellectual debate. Placing an onus on arts organisations to conduct a more creative conversation with their audiences does not let politicians off the hook. At present there is a lack of reciprocity.

If Government requires that the arts take a broader social mission to heart – and there is little reluctance on the part of the arts – surely the corollary is that we must draw in a wider circle of government actors not only into the policy discussion but also into the funding equation. A culture minister or a First Minister who managed to do that would have broken wholly new ground in the cultural debate in Wales. The arts are as worthy of the cross-cutting approach as the Welsh language. This would effectively reverse the usual instrumental argument. Instead of approaching it as a one-way and heavy-handed insistence on a social return on arts investment, the task would be to win a cultural return from as many areas of public investment as possible. It would also help redefine what culture ministers are for: policy leaders of a cross-cutting cultural agenda for a government, rather than signers of ad hoc cheques in a desperate search for the short-lived adrenalin rush of a more limited patronage.

What is the value of seeking social gain from the margins of the smallest department of state compared with seeking to knit culture into the agendas of the government's biggest spenders? What is the value of sporadic exposure to the outreach programmes of arts organisations compared with embedding the arts into the curriculum of our schools – not just as discrete lessons in art or music, not necessarily always as additions to the curriculum but as a tool for delivery of a greater part of the curriculum, a spur to creativity in all education, and perhaps an imaginative route to engaged citizenship?

Sadly, it is an area where Wales is beginning to fall woefully behind other parts of the UK. The 2007 review of the Welsh national curriculum contains no reference to the arts or creativity, despite specific references to such things as diet and health, money management, sustainable living, first aid and active citizenship. The Institute of Welsh Affairs, in its study of policy options for the Assembly's third term, post 2007, pointed out that Wales had no equivalent of England's well-funded schemes for encouraging the arts in schools – the Artsmark scheme and the Creative Partnership projects – both jointly funded by the DCMS and, significantly, the Department for Education and Skills. Neither have we seen the heavy investment in music education that Scotland has enjoyed.

This is not just a question of creating more rounded citizens, or generating larger future audiences for the arts, though both are highly desirable objectives. We are enjoined to be part of the 'the knowledge economy'. We are told our economic salvation is to lie in innovation, ideas and creativity. Exactly. If Wales needs an innovative, knowledge-based economy – or even innovative public organisations – how do we create it without nurturing imagination, challenge and creativity in every way? And what better way than through familiarising young people in their most formative years with the challenging imagination of artists, the invitation to the lateral leap?

The Welsh economy, it is said, suffers from not having sufficient highly-paid jobs. Too many companies seek high value services elsewhere. All governments are keen to develop the creative industries. One industry that fits the bill on both counts is design in its myriad forms – a function that is all-pervading in a consumer driven economy. How can Wales make a bigger contribution to an industry in which Britain is a world leader, if the visual arts do not have sufficient space and time within our schools, or if we do not maximise, through better collaboration, the potential that exists in the higher education sector? If we are to have thriving creative industries, they will, in large part be seeded in the arts. There is no film industry without the writer. There is no music industry without the young musician. It is often artists who have explored new media first. The arts, education and the economy are intertwined.

The issue also insinuates itself into both the economic development and environment portfolios. The Wales Tourist Board, not long before it was subsumed into the short-lived Department of Enterprise, Innovation and Networks, promulgated a strategy for cultural tourism. Admittedly, its definition of culture was wide enough to include food as well as festivals, but the starting point for most tourists is our natural and built environment. Famous visitors – Gilpin, Borrow, Turner – have marvelled at our landscape in Wales, but they have usually been less impressed by our cities, towns and villages.

Yet if we want to create a distinctive image for them to mark out our quality against competitors, it is our ambition and our cultural values that will determine it – exhibited in architecture, and fine urban and landscape design. That requires design quality to be a central objective of our planning systems, not an optional extra. And how do we nurture a public culture that values the quality of our physical environment if the fabric of our schools is decaying or their playgrounds are sterile or our streets are devoid of stimulating art and architecture? The arts, the economy, education, and the environment must be interwoven in our thinking and our actions.

Inevitably, such thinking must draw in local government. If the cross-cutting approach is necessary at the level of the Assembly Government, then it surely has even greater validity at the local level. Local government is potentially the prime actor, despite the fact that culture is still a discretionary spend rather than a statutory responsibility. But it should worry us all that so many people believe that it is the steepest hill that the arts have to climb. There are many local authorities in Wales that can be proud of what they have achieved on the cultural front. The best have shown vision and commitment and have been prepared to back words with action and money. However, the majority are a long way behind the best. And all this is in the context of local government in the UK giving a far lower priority to cultural matters than its counterparts in many of our European partner countries. And it is still cutting back.

We do not yet have comprehensive and reliable statistics about local government spending in this field. In 2003/04 the Audit Commission in Wales attempted a survey of local authorities to try to get to some baseline data, to compare not only spend but also the ways in which local authorities managed the arts and culture. Unfortunately, the price of local authority collaboration in this exercise was the Audit Commission's agreement that the information on each local authority should not be disclosed to any other party.

In 2005 ACW, at its annual conference at the Wales Millennium

Centre, signed a Memorandum of Understanding with the Welsh Local Government Association in the presence of the culture minister. Yet, only months later, when the WLGA's draft strategic document was published, culture was barely mentioned. Sports development officers in some authorities outnumber arts officers by more than 10 to one. Despite this ACW had to offer some authorities 75 per cent of the cost of employing an arts development officer in order to get them to appoint their very first one. In one case it had to offer 90 per cent. Conversations in some local authorities remind you of Sinatra's line, 'If you have to ask the question, you ain't going to understand the answer'. For instance, why is it that one can walk into the new offices of Pembrokeshire County Council, in Graham Sutherland's adopted county, one with more artists per square mile than any other in Wales, and see not a single work of art on the walls?

It is little wonder that a common refrain from local government arts development officers across the UK is to question why they have to argue their corner afresh each year, why it seems so difficult to attract consistent support and to create mid or long term plans for cultural development. It is true that, in Wales, the reorganisation of local government in the mid 1990s did not help by creating smaller authorities that were not easily able to carry the same burden as was shouldered by their larger county predecessors. Some significant arts organisations – Theatr Clwyd and the Sherman Theatre, for example – suffered badly from the fallout.

The internal modernisation programme in local government has also produced structures that are often opaque and where responsibility for the arts floats in a way that often makes both forward progress and accountability difficult. Ironically, some of these structures were devised to encourage people to break out of professional silos. In many instances all that has happened has been the devaluation of professional expertise, with few of the hoped-for compensating benefits. Most arts officers – and they are relatively new appointments in many authorities – sit at a third or fourth tier level, answerable within portfolios that can range across tourism, regeneration, libraries, lifelong learning or sport and, in one instance, even crime and disorder, but never with any sense of integration within a larger picture.

In the arts the partnership between the Assembly Government and ACW, on the one hand, and local government on the other, is the most important that we have. Where it works, the arts thrive and the public gains. Where it doesn't, the arts and the public suffer. It needs to work better than it does at present. It requires understanding and commitment from elected leaders and chief executives. It demands that responsibility for the arts and culture be clearly and unambiguously located at a senior level – and in Wales that may be a responsibility wider than a single local authority. It also requires an end to situations where those with authority have no knowledge, and those with knowledge have no authority – and an insistence on appointing professional arts expertise that is properly respected, trained and rewarded, and holding identified budgets that have some realistic relationship with that which they are expected to deliver. We must also end the situation where effective planning by arts organisations is often hampered by the reluctance of local authorities to match the arts council's own three-year funding agreements. Lastly, it needs clarity and consistency in the reporting of cultural expenditures that will enable robust benchmarking of performance.

Even if we were about to achieve the most thorough cross-departmental approach at the level of Assembly policy – grafting a cultural dimension onto existing mainstream areas of spend – the benefits could not be fully realised without similar action in local government. Money will always be in short supply, but it is in that very situation that the cross-cutting approach within local councils becomes the most sensible and efficient way forward. The task of encouraging local government in these directions must fall to ministers. Exhortation by an arts council will be of little value unless it is publicly supported by the words and actions not only of culture ministers but also of ministers who control the local government purse and can shape its approach to education and planning. This is one area where the democratic mandate is both necessary and shared.

In 2004 the Independent Television Commission in a rush of activity in its final year commissioned research into the nature of news. The authors, both from the Cardiff School of Journalism, Ian Hargreaves and James Thomas, observed that today, instead of making an appointment with the news at six o'clock or ten o'clock on a radio or television, we now live in era of 'ambient news'. It is all around us, 24 hours a day on radio, television, mobile phone or computer, ubiquitous screens in hotels and airports and ferries. Surely it is not unrealistic to dream of 'ambient arts', in the workplace, school and hospital, on our streets and in our public buildings? After all, to an extent it is there already, though not often enough, and too often token, marginal and cheap.

We live in an age when we are being urged to get beyond simple calculations of gross domestic product to more sophisticated measures of quality and even contentment. The demands of climate change are also forcing us to reassess our values alongside our behaviours. In this situation culture should sit alongside sustainability as the two defining characteristics of the quality and creativity of our society, guarantors of a civilised and caring community as well as its survival. This is what will change the 'texture of our living' that the Assembly Government's forgotten first cultural strategy sought to affect.

19 Anywhere but Cardiff

'Davies, write out one hundred times, I must not import my Swansea manners into Cardiff.' An instruction to a thirteen-year-old transgressor who had just transferred from Swansea's spanking new parkland grammar school, Bishop Gore, to Cardiff High School for Boys, an older urban pile set in a lake of tarmac, and the nearest thing Cardiff had to a boys' public school. The school and the city had pretensions. Cardiff had been named as Wales's capital only two years previously, much to Swansea's chagrin. Cardiff High, too, was intent on the high road.

Supposedly gifted with the city's brightest, via the indefensible 11-plus, it was a jewel in the grammar school system, and yet apart from it. The headmaster joined the public school club, the Headmasters' Conference, and to differentiate us further from other schools in the city, Tuesday and Thursday afternoons were given wholly to sport, with a full academic timetable on Saturday mornings. This played havoc with family life, and made several of us ask Jewish classmates whether we could become Jews – they were excused this irritating extension of the week. The rugby team fixture list included, rather reluctantly one gathered, the city's other schools, but prided itself rather more on playing private establishments further afield – Brecon, Monmouth, Hereford, Clifton, Oxford and Cambridge.

It is not difficult to see why Cardiff is tolerated rather than loved by the country of which it is capital. The seeds of its economic success have lain to the north and west, although culturally it has preferred to face east. Too often in the past it has preferred a provincial role to a national one. There is a perception that it has taken more from its capital status than it has put in. In this it is not alone. The ambivalence of capitals to their provinces, is everywhere reciprocated.

London is not much loved in the north of England, nor Edinburgh in the north of Scotland. Paris attracts the scorn of many in southern France. It is not only a question of capital envy, it happens on a more local scale. Cities everywhere generate passionate loyalties, and jealousy: Newcastle and Sunderland, Glasgow and Edinburgh, Liverpool and Manchester, Belfast and Londonderry, Cardiff and Swansea. Parochial grumbling and teasing is an ineradicable seam in community life, just as a gossip or a whinge drives much of our daily conversation.

This tension between capital and country was very evident in the early years of the National Assembly. Even on the day of the Assembly's royal opening there was squabbling about precedence between the Lord Mayor's office and the county lieutenancy, the arbiter of protocol. In that same year Cardiff Bay Development Corporation, that for some had symbolised the city's capacity to soak up investment, was wound up with few tears other than in the business community who thought the job was not yet finished. The need to secure funding for the Wales Millennium Centre, so hard on the heels of the Millennium Stadium, provided an additional focus. Neither, at the outset, did the locus of the new government in Cardiff Bay help the new institution as it sought to earn a deeper loyalty and legitimacy, while both urban and rural Wales grappled with huge economic problems.

But there was a deeper issue. The debate was in danger of becoming dysfunctional, not because of any peculiar intensity of feeling but because it was not rooted in any experience or understanding of cities and their role. Few in Wales seemed able to understand, or were willing to admit publicly, that an effective nation needs an effective capital both as a source of internal focus and as a face to the outside world. Such a capital is not just desirable but an economic, social and cultural necessity. Likewise, too few of the capital's leaders understand that the concept of a capital city is a concept of *relationship*, not merely *primacy*.

An awful lot has been written in recent years about the failure of urban Britain to understand the problems and plight of the countryside. This lack of understanding may not be as evident in Wales because so many our urban dwellers are a few generations closer to the land than many in the metropolises of England. In Wales the boot is on the other foot. The dominant failure of understanding concerns urban development, and the nature and role of cities in particular. It is a discourse that has passed us by. And why should that surprise us?

Historically, we have never been under any pressure to engage with it. There was no history of large-scale urban development in Wales before the industrial revolution, although the rash of castle building provided one focus. Power resided variously at Chester, Shrewsbury, Ludlow or London. We had no centre or internal focus of our own. Our language and culture has been essentially rural. The industrial revolution brought together our own people and an inward migration bigger than anything we are witnessing today, but that rapid concentration was into topographically separate valleys that fashioned a 'big village' culture rather than a city culture, rich though it was. The Licensed romantics like Jan Morris, when idealising a Welsh future for London newspapers, regularly paint a fairy tale picture of a 'centrifugal Wales', the physical development of the country through the nineteenth and twentieth centuries wished away as by a magic wand. It continues to strike a chord with Welsh romanticism. We are uncomfortable with cities.

In 1992 Meic Stephens, an indefatigable Welsh anthologiser and taxonomist, published a book of quotations about Wales and the Welsh under the title *A Most Peculiar People*. In it there are 30 references to Cardiff. Only four are positive, eight are neutral, but eighteen are thoroughly negative. There is a little praise and much acid criticism, well stirred in a bucket of condescension. What is intriguing is that much of the criticism comes from within Wales, from Welsh speaker and non-Welsh speaker alike.

It is no surprise that in the Victorian period while Lloyd George was complaining about the 'morbid footballism' of the *hwntws* (the south Welsh), a no less morbid nonconformity was complaining of Cardiff's 'growing reputation as the most immoral of seaports'. Since the charge came from a Merthyr newspaper, pots and kettles come to mind. In the 1920s, J.O. Francis – with particularly bad timing – wrote of 'Cardiff's dreadful distinction as the city with the largest percentage of million-aires'. At the time Cardiff's coal trade and many individual fortunes were collapsing. In one year alone, 1920-21, British coal exports dropped from £137million to £43 million. But Cardiff, according to the writers, could do nothing right. From the vantage point of the valleys Gwyn Thomas called it 'smug and philistine', before moving to Peterston-super-Ely.

Those migrating to the city from rural Wales, too, have paraded their discomfort. In 1936 W.J. Gruffydd, in *Hen Atgofion* (Old memories), a title with a strongly elegiac resonance, crystallised the rural incomprehension of an alien place, demonstrating in the process a refusal to imagine a plural experience of community. He wrote, 'The truth is that I have never lived in a community since I left Llanddeiniolen for Cardiff a quarter of a century ago. Here I simply reside – sleeping, working and eating; I do not *live* here…no-one round me speaks my language or thinks the thoughts I think; they are all rootless people, and none of them will be buried with their fathers… how sad it is that a Welshman should be an exile in Wales, for every Welshman living in Cardiff or its suburbs is an exile.'

What is sad about this rather curmudgeonly statement is that it was made despite the fact that he could count amongst his neighbours in Rhiwbina's Garden Village, Iorwerth Peate, later the founder of the Welsh Folk Museum, the historian, R.T. Jenkins and Ffransis Payne, a colleague of Peate's at the National Museum. Four scholarly swallows did not, apparently, constitute a Welsh summer. And yet, Gruffydd must have sensed the urban future, and been in touch with current architectural movements, since he made a positive contribution to the physical development of Cardiff as one of the founders of the Cardiff Workers' Cooperative Garden Village which created modern Rhiwbina, and was responsible for choosing its Welsh street names.

The city has fared better at the hands of writers more recently – notably Peter Finch, but John Williams, too, albeit with a bite – but a degree of linguistic, political or social discomfort often remains. Yet the truth is that Cardiff has never been the wholly alien city that some in Wales have sought to portray, something that is also true even of the period before the coal boom. There is, therefore, a need to counter the image of Cardiff as some late accretion to Wales, a gold-plated barnacle stuck to Wales' bottom.

Cardiff has been a participant in our history from the beginning. Its geographical position astride the rivers Taff, Ely and Rhymney and its proximity to the sea has meant that it has always had to engage with the world outside – the Romans, the Irish, the Danes, the Normans, and the Butes and their development of a cosmopolitan port. It has been a focus, too, for both the farmers and seafarers of south Wales through its markets and, from the fifteenth century onwards, its responsibility for the collection of dues for all 'ports and creeks' from Chepstow to Worm's Head – Swansea muscling in on the act in 1685.

It shared in the pain of the reformation with its own martyrs, and in the dilemmas and bloodshed of the civil war. Its people, too, suffered hugely in the depression years of the 1920s and 1930s. The awful poverty that afflicted so much of Wales – nowhere worse than the south Wales valleys – was also visited in no small measure on the people of south Cardiff. Even today some of the worst deprivation in Wales is found there.

The city has also had its own relationship with the language, whether in specifying, in 1838, that the clerk to the market had to be a Welsh-speaker, in the cultural enthusiasms of the Bute family, or the development of Welsh language broadcasting from the 1920s and Welsh language education in the city from 1949 onwards.

John Davies, in his study of the Butes, records how the second marquess supported the language – admittedly, as a means of encouraging the extension of religion – and that both the third and the fourth marquess spoke Welsh fluently. The second marquess, in 1828, asserted that 'the Welsh language is called for in almost every piece of patronage I possess'. At the very moment that the authors of the infamous 'blue books' were scouring the country for evidence that the Welsh language was 'an obstacle to the moral advance of the Welsh people', he was insisting that, in all the schools that he founded or aided, 'Welsh children should be taught to read in the Welsh language'. He also urged the Privy Council to ensure that at least one schools' inspector should be 'a gentleman familiar with colloquial Welsh'. The third marquess, says Davies, gave his livings to Anglo-Catholics who were Welsh enthusiasts partly from a familiarity with the problems of a bilingual church on the Isle of Bute.

It was even claimed that 'his passionate advocacy of the Welsh language at the Cardiff National Eisteddfod of 1882 led to the formation of the Welsh Language Society of its day, the body responsible for obtaining a measure of recognition for the language in education'. That said, it is fair to say that these views on the language were not shared by many of his estate officials, Cardiff Corporation or what was called Cardiff's 'shopocracy' – a term that more than hints at the essentially service nature of Cardiff's economy, then and now.

Despite the efforts of the Butes, Cardiff never grew to a size that generated the self-sustaining economic diversity of a Birmingham. It was there to service an extractive industry rather than be a manufacturing community. Some have even argued that the Bute's iron grip on land in the city prevented its industrial expansion and created a sectoral imbalance that remains a problem for the city even today. There is little doubt that Cardiff's retained wealth diminished sharply with the decline of coal. The city lapsed into a faded gentility that lasted almost fifty years, before getting a second wind with capital status in 1955, the creation of the Welsh Office in 1964, and the opening of the Severn Bridge and M4 in 1966.

Since then it has become an incomparably better city than it was, building on the huge expansion of Welsh administration, higher education and communications and of retail, the last owed mainly to the absence of serious competition elsewhere in south Wales. In a Wales that has a predominantly public sector mindset as well as a public sector economy this has seemed like an unalloyed benefit, particularly as the location for the bulk of Wales's policy community. But it has masked a downside, namely that the drawing of boundaries for grant-giving purposes, however necessary or equitable, has severely constrained the development of its economic base, to the extent that there is now less manufacturing in Cardiff than in Bournemouth.

It is not mere envy that leads people to contrast the relative success of the city with the enduring plight of some of the poorest communities in Europe a few miles further north. The needs of these communities are unarguably great and their call on our resources and imagination pressing. But the argument does not benefit from partisan distortion or from a belief in the zero sum game – the belief that some can win only if others lose. We must constantly remind ourselves that the most chilling and relevant comparisons are with the world outside. Internal relativities are less significant.

The common approach in current debate usually neglects some key facts. First, that despite its recent rapid growth in population Cardiff is still not a large city. To listen to some of the wilder political rhetoric, you might think that Cardiff was the size of Los Angeles. It is actually about the size of Nottingham. Second, it has its own very large areas of extreme deprivation: the Ely area of Cardiff has a population of 30,000, not far short of the population of Wrexham, while the Butetown ward is the poorest in Wales. Third, that Cardiff has the largest influx of daily work commuters from outside its boundaries of any urban centre in Wales – 70,000 people a day, equivalent to 11.5 per cent of the city's population. It is as if an international match at the Millennium Stadium took place every day. Fourth, like most cities it is a net contributor to the public economy, through the uniform business rate. The city will generate £144m in non-domestic rates in 2007-08. This goes straight to the National Assembly, from which the city will then receive back £77m. So £67m raised in Cardiff will be distributed to the rest of Wales. In this way Cardiff retains 54 per cent of its non-domestic rates, which compares with the 67 per cent retained by a much richer Edinburgh.

Of course, non-domestic rates are not the beginning and end of any cost benefit analysis. Many will point to the considerable benefits that Cardiff receives from housing the National Assembly and a host of other public and private organisations as well as the effects of the Cardiff Bay development, the Millennium Stadium and the Wales Millennium Centre. The location of the National Museum in the city has masked the absence of a city museum for a whole century. Suffice it to say that there are two sides to the question and, more importantly, that a relationship between capital and country based wholly on arithmetic would be a very sterile relationship indeed.

There are many reasons why Wales needs a successful capital city. The very fact of Wales's polycentric character increases rather than diminishes the need for the capital. It is the same paradox by which John Redwood, an arch opponent of devolution, created in Wales the sort of small-scale local government system that most needed an Assembly – one of the more delicious applications of the law of unintended consequences. There are powerful centrifugal forces in Wales, and those are not always unhealthy, but there is a need, too, for a physical, multi-faceted focus outside the governmental apparatus that can assist in creating the cohesion on which a successful society and government depends.

This is not to ignore the importance of Swansea, Newport and Wrexham or to argue against their development. Indeed, the failure to give Wrexham the same encouragement of city status as was given to Newport in 2002 was certainly a strategic mistake in terms of the development of north Wales. But for many functions the capital is and will continue to be the only Welsh city with the necessary scale to do what is necessary for Wales, although it will need to act in concert with others as a city region.

Regionalism throughout Europe varies hugely in form, but its one consistent feature is the presence of successful cities: Barcelona for Catalonia, Lyons for Rhones-Alpes, Milan for Lombardy, Stuttgart for Baden-Wurttemberg, Edinburgh or Glasgow for Scotland, Dublin for Ireland. That will remain true for as far ahead as we can see. It will certainly be the case in England where, because regionalism is so patchy, economic competitiveness will be substantially defined by the relative competitiveness of cities. It is a factor that we cannot ignore, not least since the Westminster Government has decided to support the development of what it calls 'core cities' in England, having seen that their competitiveness lags behind European competitors. The Scottish Executive has also carried out a review of Scotland's cities to emphasise their importance.

Cities are commonly, although not exclusively, centres of education. Any knowledge-based economy – existing or hoped-for – demands a concentration of high quality educational institutions with their research base. That tends to happen in cities. In the 1990s Cardiff University's vice chancellor, Sir Brian Smith, a lover of musicals as well as a chemist, with cheque-book in hand emulated a top football manager buying academic stars. The result of the subsequent research assessment exercise vindicated the strategy and lifted his university into the elite Russell group. The award of a Nobel prize to Sir Martin Evans, recruited to Cardiff in 1999, was the brightest feather in Cardiff's cap.

We should not forget, however, that its success in this regard is less spectacular when seen in a UK context rather than against the performance of its sister institutions in Wales. Though everyone lauds the number of top-rated research departments in the university, we forget at our peril that Bristol University has twice as many, and more than in all thirteen Welsh higher education institutions in Wales put together. Manchester's new university, formed by the merger of two institutions, is larger than the whole of Welsh higher education. These crucial facts should curb the drag anchor of envy.

In the era of globalisation successful cities are often a key to effective engagement with the rest of the world. They need not and should not drown out the wider appeal of the countries or regions that they represent, but they can raise and focus a country's profile. Their gateway function can convey a wider benefit. In Wales's case it may well be that it is the Assembly Government that takes the lead in developing international policy, but it is the capital city and its assets that are often the most useful tool of that policy. That is particularly true in a cultural context, where a sizeable and successful city is also going to be crucial to our national development.

It would be a terrible mistake to pose this argument as a denial of the polycentric element of Wales's existence. Our geography and topography are unalterable, although we could do a lot more to mitigate their effects. The arts provide a perfect example of the complementarity of the central and the dispersed. On the one hand, we have a chain of theatres and galleries that give expression to our geography as well as our arts. We also have two extraordinary peripatetic festivals the National Eisteddfod and the Urdd Eisteddfod that are both champions and a symbol of an amateur culture in the best sense of the term. But not even those most wedded to their dedicated nomadism would dream of extending the argument to embrace all artistic provision. They are not a suitable template for a more professionally-based performance culture in which, because the public's benchmarks of quality are international, Wales must compete.

In this professional field all the evidence is that we are strongest in those areas where we have created the firmest central bases: Welsh National Opera, needing substantial population as well as public funding for its viability, but also performing in Cardiff, Swansea and Llandudno and taking its orchestra and chorus to countless smaller venues in schools and communities across Wales; the BBC National Orchestra of Wales, again needing the sort of base which St David's Hall gives it, not to mention the support of BBC Radio 3, but using that strength to tour Wales, often to provide the core events of music festivals and to generate its outreach work; the National Museum, which has used its strength to extend its reach to every part of Wales. It is surely significant that the one cultural field where our pan-Wales provision has been weakest, save theatre, has been the area where we have invested least in production for the urban mainstream audience.

If we do not understand the role of cities and of a capital, and the potential fruits of a sound relationship between that capital and Wales, then we risk stunting our cultural as well as economic development, as well as the perpetuation of the politics of envy. We will risk a Wales that is no more than the sum of its localism, rather than a nation that is greater than the sum of its parts. That necessary understanding requires a positive and continuing act of exploration, one in which we can not only engage each other but also the remainder of Britain, as well as the cities of Europe and the world. That debate should encompass the role of cities and their communities, the planning of cities and the urban and rural landscape and the relationship between them, the role of architecture and every aspect of culture in our lives, the interplay of cultures, art as purposeful dreaming about every aspect of existence – an implicit and explicit debate from which people and government at every level can draw inspiration.

Such a debate could have taken place under the banner of European Capital of Culture, had Cardiff's bid succeeded. Sadly, it did not. Even more sadly, the momentum created by that bid throughout the cultural community was dissipated, and the bickering about money between the Assembly Government and the city council left the city's centenary celebrations in 2005 with none of the scale, imagination and verve that was implicit in the proposals for 2008. The fact that the castle was shrouded in scaffolding for its centenary year, even if unavoidable, carried an unfortunate symbolism.

Such a debate would serve an interest that is wider than any one city. It would help us get to know each other better as a nation. I had thought that it was no longer possible to talk any more of Cardiff, on the one hand, and Welsh Wales – that awful phrase – on the other, as separate places? No longer could anyone ask a Cardiff waiter about the weather and receive the reply, 'It's fine outside, but its raining in Welsh Wales.' Look at the way thousands of young Welsh men and women now migrate to Cardiff rather than to London as they did decades ago. Consider that 10 per cent of Welsh speaking people now live within its boundaries; a full quarter live in the diocese of Llandaff.

Yet only a few years ago I went with a group of about 20 Cardiff friends for a weekend of hill walking around Cader Idris. We had been meeting regularly for walks in various parts of south Wales. This time we stayed on the shores of Talyllyn. To my astonishment it became apparent that, for more than half the group, this was an adventure into the unknown. Despite being inveterate international travellers, within Wales they had not previously been north of Brecon. West to Newport, Pembrokeshire, yes. But north, no. As for knowledge of distant Snowdonia, this was more dependent on the ubiquity of Kyffin Williams' paintings than on journeys up the A470. And these people are not unique. A large proportion of the people of north Wales have not ventured south of Aberystwyth, prompting the question how can this be. How can we have left this gap in the education of so many? How can we create a sense of common citizenship, an emotional engagement between all corners of Wales, and between capital and country, without knowledge and familiarity?

Three highly visible developments are already making a contribution to greater familiarity between capital and country: The Millennium Stadium, the Wales Millennium Centre and the new National Assembly building. Their cumulative potential over time is great. For decades Cardiff Arms Park was synonymous with Wales, but it was a venue associated with one game only, rugby. The Millennium Stadium embraces both football codes, giving it a wider appeal that includes north Wales, while its roof has allowed it to provide a stage for the biggest music gigs, making it increasingly a place of pilgrimage beyond sport.

Even in its bland and utilitarian first setting in Crickhowell House, the National Assembly drew visits from all kinds of interest groups and from schools. The new Richard Rogers building has given a magnificent physical expression to the constitutional significance of the institution, enhancing its magnetic pull. In this there is an interplay between the building and its neighbour the Wales Millennium Centre. Attention has tended to focus on the latter's auditorium, but potentially as important is another part of the building – the 120-bedroom residential centre for the Urdd, a symbolically important development in the education of the youth of Wales. For three-quarters of a century the Urdd has drawn young people from the urban south, as well as other parts of Wales, to its rural camps at Llangrannog and Glan Llyn.

I attended Llangrannog in my youth, when the boys camped in tents rather than the present plusher facilities. It was an opportunity to lay early foundations for understanding between north and south, urban and rural. The WMC centre is the Urdd's first city-based camp, an opportunity to play to a different element in youth culture, to understand capital and country, indigenous and immigrant cultures, and to experience performance arts on a scale that is not always possible elsewhere in Wales.

With all their promise, the existence of these three important buildings also highlights an unfortunate fault line between the city and the National Assembly – a relationship whose dysfunctional side has been symbolic of Cardiff's relationship with Wales itself. You can, according to taste, blame this dysfunctionality on inescapable institutional rivalry or on personalities, on Assembly Ministers or on the adversarial approach of the city's leader, Russell Goodway, in the Assembly's early years. That the relationship has been a little fractious should not surprise anyone, since there is always a tension between city governments and the tier above: Ken Livingstone and Gordon Brown; Barcelona and the Generalitat of Catalunya; Paris and the Elysee.

Life would be a lot simpler for everyone, even if less interesting for the *South Wales Echo*, if the city and the Assembly Government worked towards a concordat that would begin to codify expectations the one of the other – not only the minor sensitivities of protocol, but also the role of each in relation to national interests. Such a concordat might also serve as a template for the relationship of other Cardiff-based national bodies with the rest of Wales. For we must remember that the capital is much more than its local authority: it is the whole of its civil society and its people. The process might also make Cardiff more conscious of the creative possibilities of its obligations to the rest of Wales, of the need for two-way traffic, as well as being a way of exploring a more focused vision for our connection with the rest of the world.

We are at a point in our history of understandably intense introspection, a moment when it is especially important to keep our windows wide open. In recent years the physical development of our capital has, give or take a barrage, reconnected us to the sea. It is a reminder to the city both of its hinterland and its international past and future role. How should that develop? I can think of no better exemplar than the plan devised for the largest city ever to be founded by Welsh people – Philadelphia – and with whom, inexplicably, Cardiff is not twinned.

The plan was developed by one of the gurus of globalisation, Dr. Howard Perlmutter, and his colleagues at the University of Pennsylvania's Wharton Business School, exactly a quarter of a century ago. I had the good fortune to be taught by him during a brief stay there immediately after our own referendum in 1997. The plan was based on his belief that, however small you may be as a country or city or community, you are now in a relationship with global trends. You can choose to be passive or to engage, but you cannot choose to be unaffected.

The high-sounding preamble, natural to the city of liberty, talked of people's right 'to re-conceive the meaning of the piece of earth on which they live as a beachhead to a better world'. It was a consciously international strategy. He wanted to reposition the city, to create a just and humane place through the integration of its economic, social, cultural and intellectual resources. Naturally, he saw the city's university as a driver.

He envisaged Philadelphia as seven international cities in one: an international city of health, of education, of partnership, of neighbourhood, of service and trade, of technology, and culture – a place intent on making itself a crossroads. He believed that a regional approach and an international perspective were both essential, and he did not underestimate the challenge. He warned that 'it is a role that will require an expanded way of thinking about ourselves and the world around us, and a bold commitment to pursue excellence at world class level'.

There is no reason why Cardiff and Wales, together, cannot aspire in the same way. There are plenty of signs that they have both chosen not to be passive but to engage: an Assembly Cabinet Committee on Wales and the World, the Assembly Government's formal links with other small legislatures across Europe, Wales's record on inward investment, and, on the cultural front, the *BBC Cardiff Singer of the World* competition, the Artes Mundi international arts prize, WMC's international aspirations, and the beginnings of the development of a cultural tourism strategy. We need to develop a clearer recognition of this pattern and purpose, to create a stronger framework of ambition and action. Perlmutter's strategy for Philadelphia may not be transportable in every detail from one city to another, but it is the sort of imagination that Wales and its capital city should strain to unleash.

20 The cities we deserve

Pompeii is a world heritage site. As we know today it is the result, quite literally, of seismic change. A town of 25,000 people with two wonderful theatres – one capable of holding 5,000, the other 1,000. They are next door to each other. They might even have shared the same box office or the same artistic director complaining about his budgets. The city fathers obviously had a sense of humour (and a sense, no doubt, of how tiresome artists can be) and put the theatres next to the gladiators' training arena. Nice touch that. But we can assume that the theatre was in demand. At home, too, the hands of artists and sculptors were everywhere to be seen, though metropolitan Romans might well have regarded the painted walls of the houses of Pompeii's merchant class as provincial kitsch rather than the height of fashion.

The people of south Wales have this much in common with the people of Pompeii: they, too, were given no choice about what happened to them. The valleys may not have suffered a seismic change, but it was a bewilderingly rapid erosion, that left a physical legacy as far above the high water mark of its economic success as Pompeii was left below the tide of Vesuvius's lava. Both have been successful candidates for World Heritage Site status. In 1984-5 the mining communities resisted that erosion because they were offered no alternative and they could see that none would be forthcoming. It was in sharp contrast to the events in Eastern Europe only four years later where people demanded change.

Post-industrial societies spend a lot of time trying to commemorate the past: to give status and pride to something that society, at another level, has seemed to cast aside. No-one should disparage those acts of artistic commemoration in any way, especially if they are well crafted. Among the most simple and moving pieces of public art in Cardiff Bay are two iron pillars by Stefan Gec, titled Deep Navigation. The steel for the seaward column was salvaged from Tower Colliery, that for the landward column from a bollard found during the excavation work on the Oval Basin. Both are ringed with brass collars, one carrying the names of all the collieries that sent their coal to Cardiff, the other listing all the world's ports to which that coal was shipped. It is a piece with a relevant contemporary message about the city-region and globalisation as well as being an act of commemoration.

Loss of community memory is a terrible thing and anything that fights that amnesia is surely to be encouraged. But we must get beyond nostalgia; circumventing Gwyn Alf Williams' infamous nightmare of Wales as 'a nation of wine waiters and museum attendants'. It is not only about remembering to remember but also about remembering to dream. One role of the arts and artists – and architects should be included in these categories – is to enlarge our capacity to dream, to foster imagination where it exists and to rekindle it where it has died, and to do so at the level of the community as well as the individual. That is why a place like Merthyr needs an arts centre as well as a vision for its heritage and the quality of its public spaces.

In Wales, we have lived with the impact of the depression of the 1930s on our collective psyche for three-quarters of a century. It has provoked some fine literature and painting but, on a wider front, it has too often constricted both our imagination and our capacity for action, and it has eroded our ability to be shocked. They say that familiarity breeds contempt, but it is an unconvincing proposition. Familiarity doesn't breed contempt; contempt is far too active a word. What familiarity breeds is weary acceptance, resignation, apathy, blindness. Too often these are the things that characterise our response to our physical environment. These are the enemy, and artists and architects should be front line troops in fighting them.

They say that children inherit the cities that their parents deserve. What will future generations in Merthyr or Swansea or Cardiff or Caernarfon say about the kind of towns and cities we are creating for them today? They will surely accuse us of selling them short. Sporadic passion will not convince them of our success. You have to use passion to shape an alliance of thought and imagination, ambition and expertise, organisation and money. Lack of imagination can diminish the potential of our assets. Lack of ambition can lead to complacency about quality and standards. Lack of expertise can make people nervous about seeking out the best. And without organisation and money nothing happens. Too often in Wales, and in many other places in the UK, the gap between rhetoric and reality is just too large.

That gap is usually most obvious in the documents issued by our local authorities, where the line between civic promotion and realisable strategies usually disappears under the glare of shiny paper and the false sparkle of the PR man's promised land. From the 1970s we all looked forward to a futuristic year 2000. Cardiff had a civic society called Cardiff 2000. A few years later, the word 'millennium' spattered everyone's corporate prose, swiftly ceding the ground to 'the 21st century': organisations fit for the 21st century, art for the 21st century, homes fit for the 21st century, 21st century cities. 2020 will be the next port of call. This obeisance to an endlessly recalibrated future that constantly recedes is worse than meaningless unless we can define what we want without devaluing our critical vocabulary, without calling the bad acceptable, the average good, and the slightly better than average excellent. It is this devaluation that sustains the tyranny of the mediocre beneath the public relations mask and postpones real progress.

Urban legacies are not always old, we are creating new ones daily, and in every community across the nation. Around Cardiff Bay the public flock to a new promenade and piazza where they can walk for pleasure, although it is noteworthy that it was created by a development corporation not a local authority. But all too often the result is disappointing: an insensitive road cutting Caernarfon in two; the grey slab of the Oldway building in Swansea, whose total absence of redeeming features is visible for miles around and an insult to the town's spectacular topography; the sad, misplaced suburbanism of Cardiff's Lloyd George Avenue; the linked Callaghan Square that could have been a treasured public space but is, in fact, a rectangular, furnished roundabout. All these have occasioned deep and obvious disappointment amongst citizens.

Such developments are the antithesis of urban design. Design assumes an end, a pre-arranged purpose, an implication of intent. But what was the end or purpose or intent in building Lloyd George Avenue as it is? Was it really intended that this long boulevard be devoid of any life-giving feature along its whole length, intended that the street furniture should be purchased from a catalogue rather than designed by artists? Was the stranding of Callaghan Square's public space in a ring of traffic purposely conceived? The answer to all these questions is no. There was an exciting masterplan drawn up by the David Mackay architectural practice from Barcelona, a city that has consciously reclaimed and extended its public spaces. The practice had played a major part in reshaping that tingling city for the Olympics, but its plan for a boulevard to Cardiff Bay was ditched in favour of a private finance initiative competition, instigated by the old Welsh Office, where the lowest bidder won.

Similarly, was it anyone's purpose or intent to pour the Millennium

Stadium into Westgate Street down three different ramps all at different gradients? Was the building of a cinema multiplex, devoid of any
car parking space, of doubtful commercial viability and poking itself up
the nostrils of the stadium, a pre-arranged purpose? Was it intended
utterly to destroy what might have been a dramatic piazza? This is not
urban design, it is wholesale urban accident.

This is not meant to single out particular professionals, or councillors or authorities, but rather to argue that we do not spend enough
time as a society, and as individual communities, debating and deciding what we want – our ends, our purpose, our intent – as opposed to
arguing about what rules we should apply in order to stop some things
happening.

Academic experts have their own explanations for the vagaries of
the British planning system and its results. John Punter and Alan
Hooper of Cardiff University recently published a powerful indictment
of the tensions between civilised planning and raw boosterism in the
Welsh capital. Behind this is an increasing cry for a greater sense of
ownership of the public realm. Much of the crticism is directed at local
authorities where the confidence of planners had been severely dented
by the mistakes of the 1960s, long before being battered again by the
laissez faire spirit of the 1980s, and the devaluing of professionalism
through the internal local government management reforms of the
1990s. This has left the public realm in towns and cities everywhere in
the UK as mere sweepings of space – the leftovers when the developers have finished – with the funds to make a difference dispersed
between transport and traffic engineers.

Some detect signs of positive change, and if that is so we need to
think about how it can be encouraged, how we can refocus our public
authorities on the primacy of the public realm, rather than allowing the
development process to be driven by a crude deal-making mentality.
We could redress the 'professional deficit' that Punter and Hooper
describe. As a boy in Cardiff, I and every other pupil knew the name
of the director of education – Robert E. Presswood – it was printed on
every exercise book. In my days on the *Western Mail*, every reporter
and a large proportion of the citizenry knew that the authority on
planning was the chief planning officer, Ewart Parkinson. Today, such
postholders are unknown to the populace, the planning and development functions divided and the old public, professional accountability
fudged by portfolios of disparate responsibilities and the often bogus
ministerialism of local government cabinets.

We could, as in Germany, give architectural design disciplines a more central place in the planning process than the non-visual land use disciplines that dominate today. If planning is a blighted word, is it too whimsical to think that an architect or landscape architect could be a city's 'director of fabric and feel', in charge of creating the right visual and psychological environment, not just in city centres but in smaller shopping centres, suburbs and estates, reining in the crude traffic-dominated tendencies of highways departments and providing opportunity for the invigoration of the public realm in a society that has become too private?

It is not only a matter for the professionals. Many wonder what can be done to reawaken interest in the democratic process. Where better to start that engagement than with the fabric of our villages, towns and cities – their centres, their suburbs and their streets – something in which all citizens have both an individual and a collective interest. The opportunities are legion, and ought to tempt an alliance of artists and architects and of professional and community organisations.

For instance, if citizen-centred government is to be the new watch-word, there is an unfulfilled potential in the Civic Trust movement that has achieved many useful and significant things, particularly in education, but has too often been characterised by hand-wringing nimbyism. The Civic Trust is a neglected asset, perhaps ripe for reinvention and revitalisation, and one that could look for imaginative alliances as well as exploiting more fully the potential of online communication.

There again, we have now in Wales a remarkable range of arts centres, often in new buildings: the Wales Millennium Centre, Richard Murphy's new building at Caernarfon, Austin Smith-Lord's Riverfront Theatre at Newport, the redeveloped Theatr Mwldan at Cardigan, not to mention the extension to the arts centre at Aberystwyth opened a few years ago, where Alan Hewson, its director, has been an enlightened client to good architects. These centres have an undoubted capacity to foster the connection between art, architecture and the public realm, as long as they consciously build that into their agendas. The bigger centres could also bring our civic societies into the arts family, enriching both in the process and soldering a connection between the arts and the physical fabric of our communities. And if arts centres, either because of location or available space, are not always the most appropriate place, could we not inject democratic engagement with art and architecture into the mix as we reinterpret the role of our public libraries?

The public art movement, too, could play a bigger role in bringing art and architecture together – especially now that Wales's two agencies have merged to create one of the UK's largest agencies of its kind. Public art's engagement not only with the creative community but also with local authorities and, more importantly, with the public through its participatory processes, gives it a potential to act as a bridge between all three.

As the name implies, it is the most accessible of all art, witness the chain of artworks that has begun to spring up alongside the A470. For years, British motorways – and I think especially of the M4 and A55 – have, uniquely in Europe, been devoid of artworks or any use of colour. A motorway journey through France is a richer experience, notwithstanding the tolls. In the UK Anthony Gormley's Angel of the North alongside the A1 in Gateshead has broken new ground, but it was two decades behind Ricardo Bofill's spectacular pyramid – an allegory on Catalan history – on the border with France at Le Perthus, or Els Limits, depending in which half of the village you are standing.

One is tempted to cheer the plans to emulate this at three gateways to Wales, but nervousness comes only from remembering that masterpieces cannot be ordered up in job lots at a boosterist's whim. The Angel of the North has been such a success because Gormley is a great artist, and because the idea was worked through over a period of years, supported by a bold local authority that had a twenty-year track record of enlightened patronage of public art.

If theatre and literature and the visual arts are there to challenge us so, too, are architects. Away from our cities, the urban fabric of the valleys has seen far less radical change than the landscape within which it sits. What future do we foresee for the valleys as communities, as settlements, as landscape? After all, from the air the area seems to be more of a national park. Is it possible that that landscape might have as great an impact on the future of the area as the urban-industrial history of the last two centuries?

As the extension of the south Wales motorway network proceeds, as rail recoups a few miles of the routes lost in the 1960s, and as new technologies change the nature of employment, new patterns of work and living are certain to emerge. They may alter the self-image, culture and aspirations of this dispersed city. The future could be driven by a desire to recreate the past or by unimagined new horizons. If the architect Will Alsop can see in the hills of Barnsley an echo of the hills of Tuscany and can imagine a San Gimignano of the north, how should we imagine the linear towns of the valleys of south Wales in 50 years time? If architects can vie to rethink the South Bank of the Thames, what about the admittedly more intimate and ravaged banks of the Rhondda, the Cynon, the Taff, the Rhymney, the Sirhowy and the Ebbw?

Anyone interested in the built environment in this country is in danger of becoming an incorrigible curmudgeon. Yet the climate is more favourable than we sometimes believe. The concept of the public realm, after some decades of denigration, is beginning to be loved again. There is a burgeoning public interest in design, as evidenced by the success of stores like IKEA and Habitat and the popularity of makeover programmes on television. Only the speculative house-builders seem stubbornly oblivious to the zeitgeist.

Government is much more sympathetic, even when it can't always find the money. The Assembly Government has created the Design Commission for Wales, even if it is still underfunded for the size of the task it faces. The technical advice notes issued by the Assembly Government's planning division have given local authorities the neces-sary tools to enforce higher design standards, although, inexplicably, too many councils remain dilatory or cowardly in their use. The Welsh Housing Quality Standards promulgated by the Social Justice Department have included the public realm in ways not attempted in England.

The cause of architecture in Wales is being fought more energeti-cally by the Royal Society of Architects in Wales, and notably through its journal, *Touchstone*, edited by our busiest architectural commenta-tor, Patrick Hannay. There are more, but still not enough exemplars of quality building to be seen across Wales: Foster's glasshouse, Adams's Millennium Centre and Rogers's Senedd. Thankfully, the National Assembly recovered its nerve in time to sanction the last of these – a superlative building that ought to have a positive, declaratory effect both at home and beyond. These are all open or, at least, half open doors and it is the duty of artists and architects and all their allies to push hard at them and to engage a potentially sympathetic public in the cause.

21 Voices on the edge

Wales has always had to fight for a voice. Its newspapers have always been local or regional rather than national, despite the *Western Mail* appropriating to itself the title of 'national newspaper of Wales'. Launched by the Marquess of Bute in 1869, five years before work started on the Severn railway tunnel, a geographically ambiguous title was chosen for the paper with the unlikely intention that it would also find a readership on the other side of the Bristol Channel. It remained a paper of south Wales.

North Wales relied on the *Liverpool Daily Post*, launched more than a decade earlier. Although the paper long ago dropped the word Liverpool from its title, it did not settle editorial offices in north Wales until 2000, becoming an entirely separately managed newspaper for the north in 2003, four years after the opening of the National Assembly.

In broadcasting engineers have been unduly influential. Wales struggled to win a radio station technically separated from the West of England throughout the 1920s and 30s, to the endless irritation of the peppery Scottish visionary and founder of the BBC, Lord Reith. His Scottish blood did nothing to make him better disposed to Welsh demands. His diaries are a study in exasperation, with references to the 'perfervid Welsh', the 'everlasting Welsh problem', and, after the appointment of a Welsh MP to a committee of inquiry, a protest that it was quite unnecessary because 'I settled Wales last Thursday'.

The same pattern emerged again in television, in both the BBC and ITV. The BBC's Wenvoe transmitter outside Cardiff broadcast to Wales and the West from 1952 to 1964. ITV did likewise from its St Hilary transmitter in the vale of Glamorgan from 1958, although, it has to be said, enraging the people of Somerset and North Devon rather more than the people of south Wales. West country anger did as much to secure new and separate frequencies, channel 7 and channel 10, as any protestations from Wales.

Further north Sidney Bernstein's hugely creative Granada served north Wales for six years until 1963 when the short-lived Wales West and North (WWN) was born. Half a century later older aerials had rusted into their chimneypots still pointing to Granada's Winter Hill transmitter. A national ITV service for Wales was created almost by accident when WWN collapsed only a year after its launch and was rescued by TWW on the mistaken assumption that it would guarantee the renewal of TWW's own more lucrative franchise. This engineering-led transmission pattern was reinforced by the Independent Television Authority's insistence on a Wales and West franchise, a linkage that it and its successor bodies have always thought too troublesome to undo, just as newspaper owners have never found it practical, i.e. affordable, to change the title of the *Western Mail*.

Even in the first decade of the National Assembly for Wales, one heard a senior official of the outgoing Radiocommunications Agency tell a broadcasting conference in Swansea that the Welsh border was immaterial since his organisation's only concern was 'to deliver a good signal'. In 2006 the new 'converged' regulator, Ofcom, though proud of being 'evidence-based', advertised a single radio franchise for Herefordshire and Monmouthshire, allegedly, without consulting its Cardiff office. I was involved in an unsuccessful bid that would have tried to solve the problem by providing separate services for each county, allowing the news service in each half to reflect the different news and politics either side of the border. The licence was awarded to a Hereford-based company, whose chairman thought the border was 'irrelevant'.

Does any of this matter? After all, such issues surface elsewhere in this jostling island. Before they merged and were then subsumed into one ITV, Yorkshire Television and Tyne Tees Television argued over the rural area south of the Tees. To the south, Yorkshire and Anglia fought over Lincolnshire. Border Television was what it said on the tin. In the BBC's structures Cumbria sometimes joined hands across the Pennines with the North East, at other times across Lakeland to Manchester. But the issues in Wales throughout the twentieth century were of a quite different order to those that emerged in England or even Scotland.

With the much lower key exception of Northern Ireland, nowhere else in the UK did anyone perceive broadcasting to be a threat to a language, or to a regional identity, let alone a national existence. Sub-national identities within England are more rooted in county and city loyalties, the latter enjoying a renaissance while county loyalties were being disrupted by several rounds of local government reorganisation. Scotland, presenting a short neck, rather than Wales's long flank to its larger neighbour, has proved less porous to external media, although the decline of indigenous Scottish newspapers has become a cause of much hand-wringing recently.

The issue of the Welsh language was, undoubtedly, the key driver of Welsh broadcasting campaigns both in the early days of radio and television, and later in the century when they culminated in nearly twenty years of civil disobedience between the bookends of the Saunders Lewis radio lecture in 1962 and the launch of S4C in 1982. But there was more to it than that – a national as well as linguistic aspiration. Wales became a separate region within the BBC on 4 September 1935, when the engineers – setting a pattern for themselves for the rest of the century – suddenly found a solution to a problem that they had earlier deemed insoluble. The fact that this happened not long after stonemasons, labouring on wooden scaffolding, had put the finishing touches to the National Museum in Cardiff, was no less significant for being coincidental.

This was the era of pre-democratic nation-building, and the campaigners were determined that broadcasting would be part of it. Cultural politics has impacted on the media in Wales for more than eighty years, whether the issue has been with print, radio, television or new technologies, or with public or commercial entities. It was important during the growth period of modern media. It is a dimension that is also important during the decline of some services. But it is in the last ten years, since the devolution referendum of 1997, that complaints about shortcomings in the media dispensation in Wales have begun to focus on the consequences for the new democracy.

Democratic institutions need bridges to the public. There is a need to connect the public to the institutions and to each other. Without these connections democracy atrophies or, if the institution is new, struggles to build its legitimacy. In Wales these bridges are weaker in the print media than in broadcasting, and the difference matters. Broadcasting deals well with the concrete and the human, less well with the abstract. Radio, diverse but targeted, finds more space than television for discussion and exposition, and holds its audience because, more often than not, people listen at the same time as doing other things, like shaving or driving or cooking. Television demands one's singular attention, hence the television commissioner's primary fear of boring the audience even for a minute. The portability of print, that needs no batteries, means that it can be ever ready for those few oases that arise, in the midst of the bustle of daily living, for the investment of time and concentration.

The diverse political colouring of newspapers aids and expresses our democracy, despite the capitalist nature of newspaper ownership. An intelligent, plural press is better able to act as a platform for the trading of information and contending ideas – facts, exposition, informed opinion. This not only has a broad public purpose, but it also sustains and enlarges the active policy community. Wales does not enjoy this facility. The result is that, to a greater degree than is desirable, that latter community is either left talking to itself within silos of expertise, or is engaged in a debate between consenting adults in private. Even the polemic on which limited circulation magazines rely, is less well-informed.

In 1999, Ian Hargreaves, head of the Cardiff School of Journalism, and now a senior executive at Ofcom, asked me to write a paper looking at these issues in relation to the National Assembly that was embarking on its rather rocky first year. The picture was grim enough at the time. Daily morning newspaper readership in Wales was dominated by London, accounting for about 85 per cent of daily sales (before the short-lived experiment of the *Welsh Mirror*). The comparable figure in Scotland was around 10 per cent. the *Daily Mirror*, the *Sun* and the *Daily Star* accounted for approximately seven out of ten morning newspapers sold in Wales.

This was and is analogous to the transmission overlap in radio and television, and underlines the porosity of Wales, in media terms, compared with Scotland and Ireland. The percentage of the population reading, rather than purchasing, a regional or local newspaper regularly in Wales was 80 per cent, the lowest figure of any part of the UK, except for Greater London.

In the subsequent eight years things got no better, although the gap between Wales and Scotland narrowed, largely because of a steep decline in the sales of indigenous Scottish newspapers. Weekday sales of the two Welsh morning newspapers – the *Western Mail* in the south and the *Daily Post* in the north – taken together, dropped by 24 per cent, from a combined 103,268 to 77,526 – the *Western Mail* by 30 per cent, from 57,035 to 38,865 and the *Daily Post* by 16 per cent, from 46,233 to 38,661. Weekday evening sales headed in the same direction, down by 20 per cent, from 304,586 to 244,698. Only weekly newspapers bucked the trend, recording an increase of 4 per cent, up from 260,651 to 272,026.

London newspapers outsell the two Welsh morning papers by more than six to one. Yet these British papers contain no consistent coverage of the devolved administrations (other than in Scottish editions), or much else from either country. In the last two decades of the twentieth century, London newspapers gradually withdrew all their full-time correspondents, leaving their editors devoid of any regular local intelligence. John Christopher for the *Daily Express*, Ken Rogers for the *Daily Mirror*, Ann Clwyd for the *Guardian* (later an MP) and Robin Reeves for the *Financial Times* were the last of their kind. Not that one should take too romantic a view of the past. Even in their heyday London correspondents struggled to get Wales into their papers.

The best known and most effective was Trevor Fishlock, who cracked the problem by offering his editors at *The Times*, through the late sixties and seventies, a stream of engaging and insightful feature material as well as hard news copy. It was the foreign correspondent rather than regional reporter model of coverage. He paid Wales the compliment of treating it as seriously as he later treated Delhi, Moscow and New York, and in the process produced a more rounded picture of Wales than that seen in any metropolitan medium before or since.

Wales is now dropping off the mental map of editors, just as the island of Anglesey does not appear on the maps of careless graphic artists. We are even getting used to seeing a new shape: England displayed as an amputee without its northern and western appendages. It is rarely possible for Welsh, Scottish or Northern Irish readers of London newspapers to compare the performance of their own country or locality, a health trust or a school, with English data. Shrinking staffs, even on London broadsheets, have even less time today to hunt out information which is not delivered on a plate.

This disinvestment has, of course, been more general, driven by fierce competition and sharply increased stock market pressure. The disturbing side-effect has been the air-brushing from public view of much of the UK outside the south east. The result is that in daily and Sunday newspaper terms Wales is becoming invisible not only to the English and the Scots but also to ourselves.

The worsening situation was never more evident than during the 2007 election and its unprecedented aftermath. There was almost no coverage of the Welsh election campaign in the London newspapers. On 12 April, in the middle of the election campaign, the *Guardian*, was moved to write a leader under the heading 'The forgotten election'. This attempted to give a potted version of the Welsh political scene, presumably because the election had also been forgotten in the *Guardian*'s own news pages.

Coverage of the result was little better. On Saturday, 5 May, the first morning that newspapers could report the result, the *Sun*, the largest selling morning newspaper in Wales, carried just thirteen words on the Welsh election: 'Labour lost control of the Welsh Assembly as its devolution policy fell flat'. This trenchant piece of political analysis was buried in a story about the results of the Scottish Parliament elections under the headline 'Jocks sock it to Gord'.

It has to be said that the *Western Mail*'s coverage of the Assembly election and the two months of manoeuvring to create a coalition, while not deeply analytical, was fulsome.

In this sense hopes that the existence of the National Assembly would lead to an improved print media dispensation for Wales have been exposed as a chimera born of frustration and envy of other countries. We have not seen the creation of a Welsh equivalent of the *Guardian*, of Scotland's the *Herald* or even the *Irish Times*. There is a further salutary irony in the fact that even in Scotland the decade following the establishment of the Scottish Parliament has been one of decline for indigenous Scottish newspapers. People complain that they are becoming more like English regional papers than true national ones. Interestingly, in the same period in the Republic of Ireland, the *Irish Independent* has held its circulation steady at 162,000, while the *Irish Times*, significantly, owned by a trust, has increased its circulation by more than 5 per cent to nearly 118,000.

If salvation is not going to come from some *deus ex Wapping*, is there any more hope closer to home? Since 2002 a group led by a Welsh author and academic, Ned Thomas, has been planning a daily Welsh-language newspaper *Y Byd* (The World) that would publish only on weekdays. It has painstakingly tried to assemble sufficient capital to launch the product by public subscription, an upmarket version of the nineteenth century creation of the University of Wales on the 'pennies of the poor'.

Its publication, much postponed, is scheduled for spring 2008. The group is not without newspaper expertise, and will be targeting a community renowned for its activism. But it is an ambitious plan that, to succeed, would need an eventual level of daily sales, about 15,000, that outstrips any other current Welsh-language publication by a factor of three. Even if hoping for its success, conventional business wisdom will no doubt slot it into the category of 'brave' ventures. It will also be the biggest ever test of the commercial viability of a Welsh-language product.

Surprisingly, the group's task is seen by many as no more difficult than starting a new title in English. In 2005 a group of former Trinity employees began the search for capital to launch a new 'quality' title into the Welsh market. They were no doubt encouraged by the fact that despite the decline in the *Western Mail's* circulation, its profitability had risen by leaps and bounds, to the current heady profit margin of more than 35 per cent, that far outstripped margins in its UK newspapers.

This financial performance, that can have been bettered by very few throughout the regional press, was no doubt the result of Trinity's astute commercial management. But it rested on a reduction in staff of close on 30 per cent combined with a substantial increase in public sector 'situations vacant' advertising, generously sized to take account of official bilingualism and equal opportunity requirements. Until very recently on Thursday mornings a thick supplement of job advertisements would appear where public bodies, enjoying a period of growth, set out their needs in two languages and, in the case of the Assembly, in an unusually large type. Now the Assembly is making more use of online advertising, although those pages still paint an unnerving picture of public-private sector imbalance in Wales.

The increasing concern about the effect of this print media shortfall on the democratic process seems paradoxical when set against the dominance of broadcast media over print in terms of consumer attention. Free of the shackles of balance and impartiality – rightly imposed on public service broadcasting – newspapers are often setters of agenda and mood despite the structural decline in their sales. They provide at one end the loudest part of the national conversation, and at the other the most thoughtful or opinionated, depending on one's prejudice. Alongside radio and television they embed our democratic institutions – but not all equally – into the narrative of people's lives. Everyone subscribes to the proposition that they are essential to the working of a democracy, whatever one's view of the deficiencies of newspapers or of democracy.

To the extent that such deficits impact on the much-lamented disengagement of the public from politics, it could be said that English regions suffer just as much as Wales. Research across the UK, done for the Independent Television Commission in 2002, demonstrated that in an age when news is ubiquitous, described by the researchers as 'ambient news', and where we can be told of disasters a world away in minutes, the place about which people are least informed is their own locality.

The public is denied the knowledge it needs, and civil society lacks the toolkit to sustain an intellectually healthy democracy below the UK level. This may not be of such immediate import in the regions of England, given the intense centralisation of English government, but it is an important gap in a part of the kingdom able, from May 2007, to frame its own primary legislation. The print media deficit in Wales has a qualitative dimension to it. It is not just facts that we are missing, nor merely an understanding. It is, rather, that we do not have sufficient competing understandings of our circumstances.

This concern about pluralism, or rather a lack of it, naturally raises sensitivities at Trinity Mirror, owners of both the Welsh daily morning newspapers, Wales's only weekend paper, *Wales on Sunday*, and 24 other Welsh titles, thus commanding more than 40 per cent of all newspaper circulation in Wales. When Trinity merged with the Mirror Group in 1999 it had been obliged to sell off the *Belfast Telegraph*, at the behest of the Competition Commission, partly to maintain a range of unionist opinion amongst the province's newspapers.

The commission's examination of the impact of the merger in different regions did not include examination of Wales as a whole, only a consideration of south Wales. Although it found that, in market share, the combined group would be less dominant in south Wales than in either the north west or north east of England, it remarked that 'Trinity itself referred to its operational areas as franchise areas which it sought to protect'.

Trinity Mirror's dominance in Wales and their ownership of the *Western Mail* and the *Daily Post* guarantees them an inordinate and, in many ways, unfair amount of attention. They will argue, with some force, that it is only the middle market that provides a platform for a viable newspaper in Wales, and that the Welsh AB market is too small to be able to deliver profitably a product that will stand comparison with Scotland or Ireland's best. That has not been an unreasonable conclusion in recent decades, but it is a stance that will always guarantee a level of discontent in the political community that can claim that no alternative approach has been tested. More recent trends towards niche products may open up new avenues.

With this as background the late James Thomas, of Cardiff's School of Journalism, in evidence to the Assembly's culture committee, referred to fears of homogenised output as journalists are asked to produce content for more than one newspaper in a group. It is a legitimate fear that has also been raised in the context of local radio. But there is a contrary argument. The fact that the two Welsh morning papers operate in separate and discrete areas means that they do nothing to add to plurality in the other's area. In theory, therefore, there would be no loss of plurality within Wales if Trinity were to combine the *Western Mail* and the *Daily Post* into a single title, suitably editionised, drawing on journalists in both north and south, to create a newspaper that could more reasonably claim to be a national newspaper in both geography and focus. As long as there was a genuine editorial gain, and a reinforcement of serious editorial purpose, we would be no worse off for the reduction in the number of titles.

Unfortunately, I suspect it may happen only at the point when the current profit margins start to slip and when the savings will go to shore up the share price. It is easy to see why, for journalists and for many in civil society, the trust ownership model of the *Guardian* and the *Irish Times* has a powerful appeal.

★ ★ ★ ★

These issues go beyond newspapers. One of the many ironies of the last decade, the first half of which encompassed the great technology-driven stock market bubble of the late nineties, is that some newspaper owners in Britain spent £6.8bn on buying regional newspapers that were, according to some, about to be put out of business by the very technologies that were boosting world stock markets and their own share prices. No such irony attended the parallel consolidation of the ITV, which had all the appearance of wagons being drawn into a circle. By the finish, as Granada and Carlton came together in 2002 at a cost of £2.6bn, there were echoes of the Goon show script: Secombe: 'Draw the wagons into a circle.' Sellers: 'But we don't have enough wagons to form a circle.' Milligan: 'Well, form a semi-circle.'

The 2004 merger, which consolidated ownership throughout England and Wales into one ITV wagon, only confirmed what viewers had seen on screen since 2001. It was then that Carlton and Granada had removed all regional logos under their control, to be replaced by an ITV logo of symbolic blandness. Only Scotland, Ulster and the Channel Islands stood outside the new ITV.

The Scottish Media group (SMG), owners of the two Scottish licences, went back to Scottish Television's roots and branded ITV in Scotland as STV instead. UTV remained UTV. Channel, owned by Huw Davies, who had run HTV Wales for many years, cutely insisted on being paid by ITV to give up its own brand in favour of the new behemoth. At the same time the regulators had, rather too helpfully, lightened the public service load by substantially reducing regional programming obligations in England, with a lesser reduction in the other nations. The regional impact of these changes evoked scarcely any comment by media commentators, blessed as the developments were by the magic word 'inevitable'.

At one level the arguments seemed irresistible. Within a few years analogue television signals would be switched off. Analogue frequency scarcity was already being replaced by digital profusion from earth and sky and underground cable. No longer would it be possible to impose obligations on broadcasters in return for a carefully rationed slice of precious bandwidth. Those owners would now be able to purchase bandwidth cheaply elsewhere. But there was another logic operating alongside this technological determinism.

It is a story worth reflecting on, but in so doing it is necessary to put sentiment aside. For the truth is that, contrary to the rhetoric of decades the regionalism of the ITV system was only ever one of its many facets, and a subsidiary and vulnerable one at that. The benefits and distinctiveness of its regionalism were balanced, particularly in the eyes of some of the larger companies, by its contribution to the system's very obvious disunity. It is often forgotten that regionalism was never part of ITV's founding purposes, and would always be vulnerable to the endemic centralising trends of all aspects of British life and government and, particularly, the drift of cultural power to London and the south-east.

Like the Empire the regional system was 'acquired in a fit of absent mindedness'. When independent television was created in 1955 the overriding objective was to ensure competition to supply programmes, and the only available means of preventing the emergence of a monopoly was geographical. According to ITV's historian, Bernard Sendall, members of the new Independent Television Authority fully expected enough frequencies to be available to allow for more than one commercial channel in each area, and felt that only government restrictions on frequency allocations frustrated that aim.

The section of the Act that required each station to provide a 'suitable proportion of matter calculated to appeal to the tastes and outlook of persons served by the station', was inserted only on a Government amendment at the committee stage, agreed without debate or division. It may, as Sendall, argues, have been crucial in determining one of the most distinctive features of ITV, but it was an unintended consequence.

Unintended or not, at one level it became a very real phenomenon. For 35 years, between 1955 and 1990, the date of the first franchise auction, even if share ownership lay for most part outside any one area, board and management identification with the region or nation could be intense. In many regions the ITV company was usually amongst the very few firms headquartered there. They may have been big fish in small ponds, but in the face of rampant centralisation in most spheres, they represented an autonomy of sorts. They were courted, both for coverage and cash. Their very names made them, automatically, regional champions, and for the most part they were rich champions too.

When at Tyne Tees Television, I commissioned the Centre for Urban and Regional Studies at Newcastle University to carry out a study of the company's overall impact. Beyond the calculation of monetary benefit it described a television company that tried to reflect every facet of the region's life, and which was a tool to be used by the region itself. Here, too, was an indigenous plc, most of its board and senior management living locally, stitched into its business, social and cultural fabric and, albeit in a limited way, informally accountable within its society.

It is, of course, possible to take a more cynical view. Identification with the region and increasing hours of local output became key cards to be played during the beauty parades at franchise time – 'IBA brownie points' as they were called – as well as during the passage of Broadcasting Acts. Chairmen and chief executives basked in civic applause as they made speeches extolling their commitment to regional economic and cultural aspirations at public meetings. Less was said about the inherent profitability of their monopolies or, in the 1980s, about the operational profligacy that often flowed from it.

Although the system had, quite soon after its birth, solidified into a federation, apart from encouraging the amassing of non-financial credit with the authority, there was no drive to build on the regionality of the system. On the contrary, much was made of the fact that the breakfast television contract, advertised as part of the 1980 round, would be the UK's first national ITV franchise. Advertisers had long been complaining about the lack of a one-stop shop to buy advertising. The breakfast service contained no provision for any opt outs to accommodate regional news, and since its advertising was sold quite separately from the rest of ITV, it did not need to match the regional-isation of ad breaks. In fairness to the IBA, the ITV companies themselves, lumbered with outdated ACTT union agreements that would have made the cost of localised breakfast services prohibitive, were themselves discouraging. Similarly, Channel 4 was also conceived as a national service, with the singular exception of the independent Welsh-language service, S4C.

Through the 1980s other realities began to press. There had always been a tension between the commercial and programming ambitions of ITV companies, but the balance started to swing towards the former. The key reality was that, for two-thirds of the ITV companies – the five mid-size and five small regional companies – what they made was not what they sold. They sold advertising, but they made programmes that were specific to one place and, there being no secondary market for this output, the cost came off the bottom line. This reality was masked for a quarter of a century by high profits and the fact that franchises were won or lost at regular intervals by the relative enthusiasm displayed for regional obligations.

The influence of the City was also becoming much more evident, putting managements under more pressure. A de facto division between voting shares and non-voting shares, which some argued had depressed the share prices of some companies, had disappeared. More companies were now separately listed. Like their bigger brethren, even the smallest ITV companies had to explain themselves at six-monthly intervals to ever younger analysts, many of whom had known no government other than Thatcher's and had not experienced a single downturn in ITV advertising revenue in their working lives.

For nearly nine years, with only one blip in 1985, advertising flowed in, as if on a golden escalator, increasing by an average 15 per cent a year, although it also had to finance Channel 4 with the proceeds. With this level of income anything was better than being off air, so trade unions were bought off on a regular basis. But the tectonic plates were moving more quickly than they normally do.

In 1980 Michael Checkland, then in charge of planning and resources at BBC Television, had started to worry publicly about the true cost of programmes. In 1982 John Birt, then Director of Programmes at LWT, did the same for ITV's programmes, an approach he was to pursue with some vigour at the BBC a decade later. In 1986 a Scottish economist, Professor Alan Peacock, was asked to look at the funding of the BBC. He threw his fellow Scot, the market prophet Adam Smith, at the ITV system, proposing that ITV franchises be tendered and sold to the highest bidder – although also proposing a quality threshold that Adam Smith would have approved of rather more than did Margaret Thatcher.

In September 1987 she famously lambasted ITV at a Downing Street seminar, with some justification, as 'the last bastion of restrictive practice', and the following year television advertising began a major downturn. In February 1989, Rupert Murdoch took a bet on the future by launching the UK's first satellite broadcasting system, and by the end of the decade a new Broadcasting Act had been passed. It administered a lethal auction of franchises, ensuring the lingering death of ITV's regional system and programming and the larger part of its immense public value.

The auction, which produced hugely disparate results across the system, hit Wales particularly hard, and much harder than Scotland or Northern Ireland. Aspirants had to cross a quality threshold and then stake all on a cash bid, that would be an annual index-linked sum to be paid for the privilege. In Scotland STV, pursuing a high-risk strategy, underpinned by the canny tying-in of key independents through programme contracts, were sufficiently sure of themselves to bid only a nominal £2,000, as did Central Television in England. Ulster Television, a little more nervously, bid just over £1m. Though outbid by two competitors, one of them failed the quality threshold while the other bid unrealistically high.

HTV was in a different position. The Welsh broadcasting scene was both active and fractious. Since 1982 Wales had had one more public service broadcaster than any other part of the UK – S4C. HTV's handling of its relationship with the newcomer meant that it was even less loved than ten years previously, both by S4C and some independent producers. Its forays into other businesses – fine art and diary production – had not been a conspicuous success. There were rumours of a diary published without the month of July. An air of vulnerability hung over it, attracting many easily spotted birds of prey. The *Guardian* thought it saw prospective bidders rushing around Wales looking for 'Welsh broadcasters with three names'.

I myself had had discussions in early 1990 with Roger Luard, then forming a very profitable media vehicle called Flextech, that got behind the only one of HTV's competitors adjudged to have surmounted the quality threshold – C3W, chaired by ITN's Sir David Nicholas. I would probably have joined them, had the prospect of joining the BBC not arisen unexpectedly. C3W's two competitors failed the quality test, despite being chaired by a former vice chancellor of Lampeter University, Lord Morris of Castle Morris, and a former British Ambassador to the United Nations, Lord Richard. A clue to the emotions surrounding HTV lay in the fact that Lord Richard's deputy was none other than Lady Harlech, widow of the man who had given HTV first his name and then its initial.

As ever in Wales, little of this was a secret. But it meant that HTV had to bid high, in fact so high that the Independent Television Commission's own business evaluation said it was 'uneasy about this application'. So where Scotland was to pay a mere £2,000 a year, HTV, representing this odd alliance between half an English region and a nation, and a poor one at that, would pay more than £20m. Between 1993 and 1998 HTV paid no less than £142m in cash bids and a percentage of its revenue, against Scottish television's £9.7m. Nothing like it had been seen since Gladstone ended the newspaper tax – the infamous 'tax on knowledge'. The connection between measured public service objectives and funding principles had been severed.

It put the company onto the back foot at the beginning of a decade that was bound to be a difficult one for the whole system. At one point it threatened HTV's very existence and, despite a painful recovery, left it vulnerable to takeover. It was passed like a rugby ball through four owners: United News and Media in 1996, Granada in 2001, Carlton only months later, coming under the newly merged ITV company in 2004.

* * * *

So, alongside the latest phase in the consolidation of newspaper ownership, we have seen the consolidation of ownership in ITV and of media regulation under Ofcom, and challenges to the concept of public service broadcasting, founded on the new super-abundance of frequencies and convergence of electronic media resulting from digital technology. The free market is on the front foot, loading the burden of proof onto public service providers. The citizen is fighting a rearguard action against the consumer.

In the face of these inexorable pressures, how will the local voice – and the Welsh voice in particular – be sustained? In an era where technologies are converging, where barriers to entry in the private sector in conventional print and broadcasting are severe, and where ownership and control of most media will remain outside Wales, how will a small, national community of citizens stand against the clamouring armies of the aggregated consumers?

If the last decade has been a story of the decline of regional newspapers and of the regionalism of the ITV system, on the face of it the next decade could be just as gloomy for cultural pessimists, of whom Wales is never short. However, the weakness of the media debate in Wales is that it is at this point that the debate usually stops, with much wailing and gnashing of teeth as the body of public purpose is lowered into the grave by recently consolidated undertakers with shiny limousines. It is an approach that will not get us very far as the world rushes by at speed beyond the graveyard wall.

Optimists in search of a new agenda may well have reason for some cheer, since there will also be opportunities to address these issues of 'voice' in new ways. But Wales needs to be more purposeful in seeking effective answers to its media needs. Although these are usually not matters that fall neatly into functions devolved to the National Assembly, there is a need to equip ourselves rather better to participate in the debate. An Assembly oversight function should not become an overlooked function. Rather than bewailing our powerlessness, we should seek to increase our influence.

A start might be made by writing the word 'media' into the title of the Welsh culture minister and his department. Far from being a case of 'cultural cringe' by copying the DCMS, it would remind the Assembly and the public that there are issues here that shape the cultural context in which Welsh people live and work and go to the heart of the effectiveness of its democratic institution, even if this particular responsibility is not devolved. It would also be an assertion that the totality of media regulation need not necessarily reside in one place. It is already spread between international agencies and European and UK legislation. Of the UK's three broadcasting regulators – Ofcom, the BBC Trust and the S4C Authority – one already exists solely for Welsh purposes. But a more public adoption of the media remit should, as convergence moves on apace, also go hand in hand with a recognition that an oversight function can roam well beyond broadcasting.

Ofcom, the powerful new kid on the regulatory block, is headed by Ed Richards, a creative chief executive, married to a former member of the National Assembly and, therefore, no stranger to Welsh issues. His organisation is charged with undertaking regular reviews of public service broadcasting, and its second such review began late in 2007.

But if past practice is any guide, there will be little public debate in Wales on these issues, other than in small coteries of the self-interested and the slightly artificial public meetings arranged by the broadcasters themselves, quite understandably, to try get their own messages across.

The fact is that in Wales public debate, as opposed to the private interplay of institutions, has struggled to keep up with the relentless flow of research publications and consultations that Ofcom generated in its first years, even in those areas of media policy with which we are most familiar. If that is to change the Assembly Government needs to be more active, and an increased monitoring capacity will have to be created. In addition, Ofcom's Advisory Committee for Wales and the BBC's Audience Council for Wales will have to play a more independent and public role in seeding debate, as the BBC Broadcasting Council for Wales did during the campaign to create S4C – rather than acting merely as internal and private sounding boards.

There is no shortage of distinct Welsh issues in this field. To begin with Welsh topography creates a significantly different set of problems for transmission than is faced in England. In terrestrial television Wales, with 5 per cent of the population, has required 25 per cent of the UK's transmitters. As we move to digital switchover in 2009 – and we are very near the front of the queue – viewers will find that many Welsh transmitters will carry fewer multiplexes – the groupings of frequencies – than English transmitters, thus delivering fewer programme channels. Inevitably, Welsh people will tune out of Wales just at the point when, according to Ofcom's own research, that longstanding problem was diminishing.

In radio transmission, Wales has been a second class country from the very start, and that is likely to persist in digital radio. When digital radio was introduced I remember suggesting, while wearing my BBC hat, that forcing Welsh radio services to share a digital multiplex with commercial providers would be like mixing oil and water. And so it proved.

Some years ago, when Kelvin MacKenzie's The Wireless Group owned both the Swansea stations and Valleys Radio, he was asked whether he intended to apply to operate a multiplex in the valleys. 'I would rather cut my f.....g right leg off' was the reported reply from this brilliant and notorious former editor of the *Sun*, having, no doubt, carefully balanced the interests of the citizen and the consumer. It captures colourfully and emphatically a harsh commercial view of terrestrial transmission realities in Wales. Ofcom has now made a move to extend the digital network, but Radio Wales and Radio Cymru will get to many parts of Wales in digital form more than a decade after all the BBC's main UK services, and the geographical coverage will never reach the levels planned elsewhere.

Commercial radio in Wales has grown without any coherent strategy to guide it, partly because the radio licensing processes would militate against its implementation even if it existed. Those processes are now more random in their effect than they were under the old Radio Authority. Increasingly, in such decisions, pluralism is now defined in relation to ownership of media rather than their content, to the consumer rather than the citizen, and in radio, to the range of music rather than to speech. Paradoxically, this has increased the BBC's overwhelming dominance of radio in Wales.

The ecology of local radio is also more fragile than in most regions of England, making the relationship with community radio more sensitive. Community radio itself may have a greater relevance, a view clearly shared by the Assembly Government, which has set up a fund to support it. Yet, in this situation, in the early summer of 2007 Ofcom published a report on the future of radio that foreshadowed a easing of radio regulation that many might regard as premature and could easily become a self-filling prophecy of the decline of local service quality.

The BBC and S4C will come more squarely into the firing line. Completion of digital switchover with the consequent total separation of S4C and Channel 4 programming, will expose the costs and benefits of S4C as never before. The size and make-up of its audience, its relationship with the BBC and even its very existence, will be scrutinised. One of the options that Ofcom touted for S4C – becoming a Welsh language content provider on other people's platforms – may have more legs than we think. The development of video on demand will fundamentally alter assumptions about the provision of Welsh-language as well as English-language television, putting a premium on marketing as never before. Although the Welsh language may begin to pop up on Sky, some BBC services and perhaps even the broadband BT Vision service, Wales will need to be alert to ensure that its voice is not lost in these new systems.

If the ultimate test is 'what is best for the Welsh language' the current institutional arrangements may survive, but they should not necessarily be a given. These will not be easy paths to negotiate, not least because of the amount of emotional capital that the Welsh speaking community has invested in one channel. Plurality and the fact that

S4C is Wales's only autonomous media institution will be important cards for it to play.

The BBC will have its own battles to fight. The 2007 licence fee settlement coming on the back of the short, but rashly high-spending Dyke era, will create internal pressures in which regional services and their development will, if old BBC patterns are maintained, have to be defended. More fundamentally, lumbering the BBC with the task of paying for the final stages of digital switchover – during which people will learn that those second or third sets, old analogue sets in the kitchen or bedroom, will suddenly become obsolete – will attract a degree of odium to the corporation just at the point, around 2011, when it will be having to defend itself against a more serious assault on the licence fee than anything seen hitherto. At that point the corporation will face a pincer movement between commercial interests intent on undermining the licence fee and other public service broadcasters determined to share its proceeds.

The financing of digital switchover through the licence fee may prove to have been an important breach in the inviolability of the fee that will be used to powerful effect as people advance the notion of 'contestable public service funding', the licence fee becoming a pool of money which the BBC, Channel 4, ITV and Channel 5 and even radio stations might bid for. Several permutations of this concept have been advanced including an 'Arts Council of the Air', the auctioning of specific franchises, and competition to run what are now BBC services.

The ramifications of any of these for regional or local services are not difficult to judge even at this distance. Channels 4 and 5 will have no interest in creating a regional or local dimension as that has never been part of their function. Theoretically, it might become possible for ITV to dip into the licence fee to shore up the last vestiges of its regional service, but it is difficult to believe that this is something ITV would want, as it has already spent so long negotiating this obligation away. Even were it to do so, it would be but a flimsy emergency shelter from the earthquake that would be rocking the whole of the BBC as the result of the fragmentation of its traditional funding.

Despite its potential for rousing the more sleepy cohorts in the BBC's army of supporters, the notion will have an easy appeal within and beyond Ofcom, partly on the basis that competition amongst public service providers is inherently desirable, since it encourages both quality and plurality. This can all too easily override any argument about serving nations, regions or even cities.

It is a common feature of many Ofcom documents that local and regional provision is labelled expensive and something which, though desirable, is regrettably unsustainable for financial and technological reasons, except perhaps in some attenuated form. The notion of local or regional programming as being expensive is deduced by multiplying what is usually the cheapest form of programming known to mankind by the number of separate areas to which it is provided, and setting it against the background of overall declining revenues. The expense is not always evident to the viewer or listener. This then becomes the staple justification for more minimal regulation. Thus is continued decline in the status quo managed, and 'realism' triumphs over public purposes.

There is, however, a more positive agenda on which Wales should concentrate and make common cause with other parts of Britain. Some of this agenda does not run directly counter to the grain of Ofcom thinking or of technological change. It would embrace such things as spectrum trading – the buying and selling of bandwidth – technological developments such as video on demand and Ofcom's own pet concept of a future Public Service Publisher and, underlying it all, the potential of online journalism. These are areas where we need to develop our expertise and our thinking in order to assert influence.

In attempting this, the angle of approach is all important. For decades media policy as it relates to Wales has been a process of amending British policy, with great difficulty and varying degrees of reluctance, to meet Welsh needs. Wales usually ends up as the final square on the Rubik cube that will not fit. It is surely time that we approached it from the other end in order to devise a media policy that is specifically designed for Welsh circumstances and only then to address what adjustments may be unavoidable to take account of the wider context, including the possibility of legislative change.

Such a policy would have to have considered the needs of a young democracy. It would embrace public, community and commercial services, and take print and online media into account, even where Ofcom may not have powers to intervene. It seek would bend engineering to the citizen rather than the other way round. It would also take into account the different ecology of production and commerce and the possibility of different ownership models. Most importantly, it would need Ofcom's assurance that it would not let go of the bird in the hand, before it has netted the two in the bush.

In all the uncritical wonder that has surrounded digital developments – and I can be just as captivated as the next man by the online sales pitches of Apple's chief executive, Steve Jobs – it is possible to observe two things: that the technology advances more quickly than you ever thought possible, but also that some elements of the status quo ante are more durable than you thought likely. More will change than you think, but more than you think will stay the same.

Just as television did not eclipse radio, the arrival of multichannel television has not totally subverted the main terrestrial channels. The decline of ITV has had as much to do with a failure of management as with the arrival of Sky. The ubiquity of the personal computer did not do away with paper, in fact we use more than ever. The growth of new media has occurred at a time when the sales of books are increasing. Chat rooms are busy, but so are book clubs. Online news has not yet killed off newspapers, nor do I think it likely it will do so in the near future. The almost infinite capacity to personalise services, made possible by the digital revolution, will not eliminate the time-saving mediation of the middle man. The blogger will not make the editor redundant – see the *Guardian*'s 'Comment is Free' website. The arrival of video on demand will not do away with the concept of a television channel as many have prematurely predicted.

This is not to argue for complacency or to be content to depend on survivals from the past, but to make the obvious point that we have to continue to maintain our voice on the legacy services, as well as engaging with the new, and seek ways of harnessing the two together.

Currently, it is impossible to foresee a point at which Wales will not require the survival of the present resources of the BBC and S4C, even if greater collaboration between the two will be needed to provide the best possible service to both linguistic communities. If S4C discovers that, even to maximise its Welsh speaking audience, it needs to float its service on a bed of English language programmes, as it has done in analogue for two decades, some will look to a marriage with a more expansive version of the remnants of BBC's 2W service. Though this might seem logical and cost effective in both money and spectrum, it carries the danger of relegating Welsh output for the majority audience to a minority niche.

The paucity of news sources in Wales also means that we should not lightly let go of the programme services, particularly, but not only, news, of ITV 1 Wales. If increasing spectrum availability has been the reason or excuse for removal of a large part of ITV's regional obligations, cannot the advent of spectrum trading be used to recreate the leverage necessary to restore it? The principle of public service will also need to be maintained in the world of video on demand to ensure that Welsh programming is both available and marketed, and does not suffer from the same weakness in distribution that has hampered the sale of Welsh books. The same can be said of the online environment, as Ofcom has recognised by backing the Public Service Publisher (PSP) concept, funding content across 'all communications platforms and technologies to achieve reach and impact ... [but not taking] traditional broadcast as its starting point'.

Much of the debate about new media is couched in terms of a move from passive to active consumption, from 'lean back' to 'lean forward', from serving 'the undifferentiated mass' to 'the personalised experience'. Exciting though that may be – and one has not only to acknowledge but also to embrace its creative potential – it is pertinent to ask where this leaves the *differentiated* mass called Wales that comprises only 5 per cent of the UK? What level and quality of shared information will persist to allow our society and our democracy to function more effectively and cohesively? An interesting template is provided by *OpenDemocracy.net* led by the founder of Charter 88, Anthony Barnett, although it has to be said that it has depended on charitable funding despite having a global reach and remit.

The way forward will not be found by pitting the old media against new, but by forging a creative connection between the two. I remember the days when the *Western Mail* was reluctant to carry stories about television, seeing it as competition. It was not alone. Now television dominates acres of newsprint. In the same way, the new media may find that they need the old media to signpost and to endorse as well as to connect with at least some part of their audience. Old media may need the new to pull them towards greater interaction with their audiences, but we may still need the older media, radio, television, print, to reinforce an identifiable geographic dimension for new online communities of interest.

The elevation of journalism in Wales in a way that encourages our development as a small, intelligent society may now depend on exploiting online as a starting point, rather than as just the extension of existing media. It might be that the Public Service Publisher will be a means of reintroducing an investment in public value at least equivalent to that lost through the reduction or ending of current broadcast public service obligations. It could also be a bridge to a new business model that will sustain professional journalism in Wales at a higher level. It might prove possible to turn the current model on its head and create, online, a core of serious journalism that would interact with user-generated material and comment, but which surviving newspapers might wish to buy into in order to be part of a wider national conversation.

There has been much hand-wringing recently about the state of journalism, both conventional and online: not least the culture of celebrity and a cynical approach to politics. Professional journalists worry about the threat from bloggers and the speed with which untruth and half-truth can spread around the world. But there are signs of a fightback, as seen in the increasing number of organisations that are now examining and debating the nature of journalism.

In America in 1997 the Project for Excellence in Journalism was established at Columbia University. In the same year, in a related initiative, the Committee of Concerned Journalists, a consortium of journalists, publishers, owners and academics, was set up, concerned that 'journalism was disappearing inside the larger world of communications'. The latter has received benefactions of more than $4m. It has proved a more uphill battle in Britain, although a new organisation, the Media Standards Trust was established in 2006 to foster higher standards and rekindle public trust. The battle is not yet over.

At the time of its 150th anniversary, on 15 October 1972, *The Sunday Times* – then under Thomson ownership and Sir Harold Evans's editorship, and investing heavily in the Insight team – published an editorial under the heading 'How we see ourselves.' In the light of subsequent history, of both the paper and its editor, it was a brave, idealistic claim. It examined the purposes of a newspaper.

It read: 'A newspaper ought not to be judged by circulation, though it cherishes its readers. It ought not to be judged by profit, though it needs profit to survive. It cannot easily be judged by influence either, for that is a complex and subjective question. It can be judged only by its purpose, and the purpose of a newspaper must be to find and tell the truth in society. Advocacy is not enough.' Creating the means to sustain a journalism that reflects that sense of purpose in a relatively small market should be a priority task for Welsh society. The new media are likely to be at its heart.

22 If you can't be big, be smart

There is a tendency when travelling abroad for people to covet for their own country every good thing that they see, and immediately lament its absence at home. Why don't we have trams like this, we say in Amsterdam. Why can't our waiters be as cheerful as this, we say in restaurants across North America. Why don't we have Mercedes for taxis, we say in Germany, especially if Cardiff's thankfully short-lived Lada taxi period still lingers in the memory. The advent of the Assembly created a new breed of tourist, searching for institutional or policy souvenirs to put on the new constitutional mantelpiece. People headed for Catalonia, the Basque country or Finland, but top of the list of destinations was our neighbour Ireland.

Wales has always had more of soft spot for Ireland than for Scotland and in the policy community it had been everyone's favourite ever since a Brussels-based taffia in the 1970s managed, with suspicious regularity, to arrange conferences on European regional policy on the eve of Ireland v Wales rugby matches in Dublin. In the early years of the new Assembly the attraction was obvious. Ireland had proved that basket case economies can be turned around, albeit not quickly. Wales needed that reassurance, not least as BSE, foot and mouth, and steel closures started to sound like a concerted artillery barrage against the new institution.

The interest was two-way. The Irish Government was taking a keen interest in devolution in Britain, and not only because of its relevance to the situation in Ulster. It had established consuls general in Cardiff and Edinburgh, and while in other countries they were answerable to the Irish ambassador in that country's capital, these two reported directly to the Foreign Office in Dublin. Irish research institutes were more intent on modelling the Scottish and Welsh economies than researchers within Wales itself. The Irish Institute of European Affairs had launched its own study of devolution in the UK, chaired by a former Taoiseach, Garret FitzGerald.

It was to this last body that the Institute of Welsh Affairs looked. It was rather envious of its financial resources, not to mention its elegant Dublin headquarters, as well as its wide political support including funding at one stage from nine Government departments. It was from the IEA that the IWA received a valuable and encouraging nugget. Its chain-smoking chairman, Brendan Halligan, who had once been general secretary of the Irish Labour Party, said simply, 'If you can't be big, you better be smart'.

Halligan also warned us that solutions created in and for one country could not always be transplanted into different cultural and political soil. The enthusiasm of the growing band of Welsh Erinophiles – amongst which I am happy to include myself – had to take account of the fact that the sets of levers given to a state and to a non-state region, even with a high degree of devolution, are very different. But that does not make Irish experience irrelevant. The more important lessons lie in the longer history of Irish institutional development over the last four decades of the twentieth century. It is less to do with the allegedly magical effects of European money, although as a final brick in the wall, Objective One funds undoubtedly helped, than with a transformation of attitudes and actions. Not the sudden emergence of the elusive confidence that too many public agencies and Welsh politicians of all parties preach about, but the recognition of the need for change in ways of thinking. The Irish long ago realised that the direction of change has to be plotted not in the turbulence of windy rhetoric, nor in the chance results of slugging matches between vested interests, but by the deliberate application of a critical mass of intellectual resource and independent analysis.

One of Ireland's foremost historians, Joseph Lee, writing in 1989 before the turnaround in the Irish economy manifested itself and in the aftermath of a catastrophic period in Irish public finances, bemoaned the fact that despite independence, it had taken the country more than fifty years to begin marshalling properly its intellectual resources. In the late 1980s Lee still felt frustrated that the process had not gone far enough. He compared Ireland unfavourably, in the organisation and application of academic knowledge, with Scandinavian countries where 'thought was not the hobby of esoteric coteries of leisured savants, [but was] directly relevant to the quality of national performance'.

Even so, he did chart elements of real positive change in Ireland from the mid-1950s, and characterised it as a growth in the demand for ideas that, naturally, led to an increase in the supply. And it was in that act that the real transformation of Irish society began. There is an obvious lesson for Wales. Intellectual openness, expressed in the form of consistent demand for analysis and ideas and the tolerance of critical debate, not least among both civil servants and politicians, is an essential pre-condition for Wales's success. Although the timing and timescale of that mindset change in Ireland confirmed warnings about judging the workings of our own National Assembly prematurely, it also suggested how far Wales had to go.

In 1945 an Irish finance official, Patrick Lynch, bemoaned the lack of adequate statistics for Irish economic analysis, a complaint that led three years later to the formation of Ireland's Central Statistics Office. The beginnings of Welsh statistics, for the most part, waited on the creation of the Welsh Office two decades later. Born in 1974, the Welsh Development Agency lasted for 32 years before being absorbed into the Welsh civil service, but it is worth remembering that the Irish Development Authority was established in 1949, a quarter of a century earlier. Indeed, the IDA had its powers extended in 1969, some six years before the creation of the WDA. It was as early as 1973 – again before the WDA's creation – that the IDA decided to concentrate on electronics and chemical sectors in its search for inward investment.

The 1956-66 decade had been a watershed for Ireland. There is now a consensus that the wellsprings of her recent success had lain, fundamentally, in the change during that period from an inward-looking society – the testy political defensiveness of a young state steered by Eamon de Valera, a cultural conservative – to an outward looking society under his successor, Sean Lemass.

In 1956, a year before Lemass became Taoiseach, an Irish census had produced chilling evidence of the continuing high rate of emigration. It was losing 43,000 people a year, most of them young. Seeing a country haemorrhaging young people, Lemass deliberately chose to put aside protection in favour of free trade and began to face up to the competitive challenges of that openness. Shrewdly, he did not think there was any need to choose between America and Europe but, rather, played both cards for all they were worth.

In 1956 too, T.K. Whitaker, a new breed of civil servant, was appointed to head the Department of Finance. Within two years he had directed the publication of a Government report, *Economic Development*, sometimes referred to as the 'Grey Book', now regarded as the key moment of change in Irish economic and industrial policy. Two years later, in 1960, the Economic and Social Research Institute was established, not to challenge the civil service but, consciously, to reinforce it. For its first five years ESRI was funded by the Ford Foundation, and then directly by the Irish Government. It has been a prime source of the high quality analyses on which consensus among all parties to Ireland's effective social partnership has been built. The growth in the number and influence of economists in the university sector, from the 1970s onwards, was a by-product of the establishment of the ESRI, rather than its precursor.

Currently, ESRI has more than 90 staff, 60 of them full time: economists, sociologists, geographers, even a psychologist, sustained by an annual income of more than 12m, less than a third of which is grant-in-aid from the Irish Government. It cherishes its independence, despite the fact that the secretary general of the government's department of finance is traditionally elected to its council. The remaining two-thirds of its income comes from commissioned work, much of it at the behest of other public authorities, including the European Union. Following the May 2007 elections its director, Professor Frances Ruane, was appointed to the Scottish Executive's Council of Economic Advisers.

Departments of the Irish government commission work through a tendering process, where ESRI is often in competition with university departments or international consultancy firms. It is organised in five research divisions: education and labour market, health services, macroeconomic and resource economics, social policy and a survey unit that works on a commercial basis and, among many other tasks, maintains a health database for Ireland. However, relatively little income is derived from the private sector, because of ESRI's rule that all its work has to be in the public interest and published openly in a refereed form.

These external sources of knowledge have been of major assistance to Ireland's structured national conversation. For nearly thirty years, until 2002, the country's social partnership approach had been embodied in the National Economic and Social Council that grew out of the National Industrial and Economic Council founded in 1963, in that crucial decade of change. NESC's function was to analyse and report to the Taoiseach on strategic economic and social issues. It had its own independent secretariat, comprising economists and sociologists as well as administrative staff, and could initiate work on its own account or at the behest of government. The NESC secretariat delivered its own substantial analyses of internal and external factors, but usually drew on external research. It also serviced Ireland's more recently created National Economic and Social Forum, that brought the community and voluntary sectors into the social partnership. In 2002 these two bodies were brought together into one National Economic and Social

Development Office attached to the Taoiseach's office, but still able to act on its own initiative.

No system in the world can abolish conflict or error, but there is considerable evidence that the Irish policy-making process, particularly in the crisis years of the 1980s, was greatly strengthened by the combination of NESC and ESRI. Together they provided a foundation of analytical rigour that constrained the clash of sectoral interests, prevented the negotiation between those interests drifting towards the lowest common denominator and provided a growbag for shared understanding.

Now that so many elements of Welsh public life have been incorporated into the state, it is worth asking whether a version of these arrangements, some source of independent expertise, might leaven Welsh corporatism by putting a wider range of tools at the disposal of that part of civil society that lies beyond party. The Assembly Government's arrangements for connecting with the rest of its community look pretty thin against this Irish backdrop.

However, this is to take a narrow view of a country's intellectual resources. Joseph Lee was equally critical of the lack of a market for ideas in the business and farming communities, political parties and even in Ireland's universities. He savagely characterised the response of business in the 1960s not as anti-intellectual but as 'sub-intellectual' on the basis that 'anti-intellectualism is too intellectually demanding'. This began to change slowly after the formation of the Irish Management Institute in 1953, despite the fact that the IMI had to rely on the support of a handful of big businessmen in the private sector and on the enthusiasm of the chief executives in the state sponsored sector.

In Wales, it was clear from the first year of the National Assembly's operation that the statutory provision for liaison with business was much less effective than hoped for, partly because of deficiencies in the organisation of business itself as a result of the size and nature of our corporate sector. Comparatively few in business seem comfortable in the world of ideas or of politics, and few owners of small and medium enterprises can afford to give time to public policy issues, even where they relate directly to business interests. On the other hand, most of the managers of larger businesses are running branch operations, likely to be in Wales for only a limited period. They do not always believe that such policy issues need be within their purview.

The most obvious intellectual resource for a small country is its university sector. Lee contrasted the lack of involvement of the Irish university sector with public policy, particularly in the field of social thought, with that of Scandinavian countries. He did not imply that Irish academics were inferior to academics elsewhere, rather 'what was and is inferior is the mobilisation and organisation of that intelligence at national level'. For our purposes in Wales, it is less important to judge whether he was right or wrong in his criticisms than to assess the relevance to Wales of that concept of the mobilisation and organisation of intelligence, and of his assertion that 'no small European state has achieved significant socio-economic progress in the twentieth century without developing a firm intellectual infrastructure in the human sciences'.

He traced the involvement of academia in the public affairs of several small European countries including his own. If he had included Wales in his survey, he would not have found much to cheer. Although there are some notable exceptions, the university sector in Wales has not covered itself in glory, though talk of a 'third mission' for universities together with the advent of the Assembly has shamed it into belated action. There are, of course, academic centres of expertise relevant to public policy: Cardiff University's departments of city and regional planning and social studies, its Wales Governance Centre, Centre for Advanced Studies, and its business school's Welsh Economic Research Unit; Aberystwyth's Institute of Rural Studies, and Institute of Welsh Politics; Swansea's National Centre for Public Policy; Bangor's Welsh Institute of Social and Cultural Affairs and Glamorgan's Welsh Enterprise Foundation. Cardiff and Aberystwyth also collaborate in a Welsh Rural Observatory.

This sounds an impressively long list and does indicate a welcome new focus, but many of these developments are quite recent, sometimes involving only a new label for one or two individuals. You are often left with a sense of opportunistic, academic packaging in the search for funds. There has not been a step change in capacity. While we have more expertise in social sciences today, we now have, arguably, less expertise in modelling the Welsh economy than we had in the late sixties when the late Professor Ted Nevin did his pioneering work. Wales would be hard-pressed, for instance, to match the Scottish network, Scotecon, that draws together economists in eleven Scottish universities and was created by a four-year funding council grant specifically to stimulate research into the Scottish economy.

Whatever encouraging developments there have been in Wales – and there have been some – it cannot be said to amount to a systematic mobilisation of our intellectual resources. Further development may depend not only on the Assembly Government's view of the practicality or desirability of such an approach, but also on ameliorating the effects of the quinquennial Research Assessment Exercises that have deterred many academics in higher education from studying Welsh issues by placing a premium on international publication.

When, in 1996, the IWA convened a weekend conference on Wales-focused research at a Newport hotel, it drew more than one hundred academics from very different disciplines. It was the first conference of its kind that anyone could recall, and we were left wondering why, in a nation that apparently enjoyed the benefits of a federal university, it had taken a small voluntary organisation to arrange such an event.

The reluctance of many of the participants at that conference to focus on Wales in their research work was palpable and blame was liberally bestowed on the influence of the RAE. But it did not sound a wholly convincing excuse, and I certainly had not found the same reluctance to engage with local concerns in universities in the north east of England. It was significant that, a decade later, when the University of Wales canvassed public support for its survival, while running scared of the National Assembly's review of higher education, its glossy publication gave pride of place to its work in Celtic studies while failing to mention the Welsh economy once.

That said, this is not to argue for an exclusively inward focus, since one key value of the academic sector should be its capacity to link Welsh concerns, perspectives and expertise to relevant research and thought throughout Britain and beyond. To some extent, the same can be said of the potential of international consultancy firms represented in Wales, another underused resource.

The issue here is the connection between government and sources of intelligence outside government circles. The world of ideas and creative research is just as subject to the laws of supply and demand, as Lee suggested. Five elements of our new democracy – the Cabinet, the civil service, Assembly committees, backbenchers and the wider civil society – each have a need for quality information, for the formulation of policy options, for decision-making and for the assessment of policy performance, in macro and micro terms. The extension of the Assembly's powers into primary legislation and the tightness of its financial corset also argues for the creation of new research capacity in the area of legislation and policy and in the management of public finances. Without it, as the IWA argued before the 2007 election, our politics will seem amateur.

The prospects for greater interest in research have certainly improved. In the early years of the Assembly there were encouraging developments. Before the Assembly opened its door, a central policy unit had been created within the Welsh office, although it is remarkable that a territorially-based, multi-functional department waited for 37 years before doing so. Even now it is relatively small and embryonic and focusing more on today's rather than tomorrow's issues. In the Assembly's first year the Permanent Secretary convened a group to discuss links with academia and a series of seminars were held. Many attenders from both camps were surprised that they did not already know each other.

Two years later, in April 2002, the Economic Research Advisory Panel was formed. While there has undoubtedly been an acceleration of research activity, and an improving intimacy between the players, there have been only small improvements in research capacity. The final element in ERAP's remit – 'to develop the capacity and expertise of Wales-based institutions to contribute to this research agenda' – is the area that it addressed last of all and in which it has done least. The creation of two PhD studentships, co-funded by the Assembly Government and the Economic and Social Research Council, would be thought by most people to be somewhat short of the mark.

The notion of the systematic mobilisation of our intellectual resources, despite the rather Soviet ring to the phrase, is a route to obtaining the maximum value from our investment not only in the governmental process but also in higher education. It should also result in accelerating the maturing of our civic society, ensuring that we remain outward looking even at a moment of internal focus unique in our history. And, of course, it may lead to a better Wales. But it must be based on diverse sources of commissioning as well as production of research. In that context it is worrying that one consequence of the absorption of quangos into the Assembly Government has been the effective nationalisation of research commissioning, that is potentially inimical to the healthy biodiversity of knowledge that an alert nation needs.

That development actually increases rather than decreases the need for a critical mass of specialist and multi-disciplinary research far greater than we have currently assembled. It must be able to generate a sustained and holistic focus on economic aims and performance, and have sufficient independence to think beyond immediate political agendas and horizons. Ideally, it should be connected to government, but not sit within it. It needs to be sufficiently free to challenge government policy from time to time, and both politicians and civil servants should be big enough to remain relaxed about that. It would provide an external benchmark for policy making, and could have as great an impact on Welsh public confidence in our economic management as did the granting of independence to the Bank of England.

For the Assembly and its civil service the creation of such a body would be a sign of strength and confidence, not of weakness. It would also ensure a balanced dialogue between pools of knowledge within and beyond government. The lesson from Ireland, as from many other states and regions around the world, is that if the primary policy aim is to create a knowledge-based economy, knowledge-based government and a knowledge-based society is as good a starting point as any.

23 Politics one can touch

The ease of modern living in western democracies was brought home to me many years ago when I heard a radio interviewer ask an old farmer what had been the most important transformation in his own lifetime. He did not mention the green revolution, fertilisers, pesticides, penicillin, tractors or automatic milking machines. Instead, and without hesitation, he referred to the invention of the rubber wellington boot. Dry feet marked out farming in the twentieth century from any previous period more clearly than any other phenomenon. He thought himself outrageously blessed.

Like that farmer I, too, could never be tempted to swap the present with any other period in history. It is a remarkable privilege to have lived in an advanced portion of the western world, through a period of prolonged European peace and during the most prosperous period in the history of mankind. That it should have coincided with that historic moment when Wales took a coherent, unified democratic form for the very first time in its patchwork existence, was an extraordinary bonus. Mine is a privileged generation.

Not everyone has shared equally in that good fortune. The inequalities in our society are pervasive and growing, within Wales, the rest of Britain and the world. At times during the past three decades it has seemed that the safety nets that had been conceived by the creative compassion of Lloyd George, William Beveridge and Aneurin Bevan were no longer to be cherished. Perhaps, in Wales at least, that moment of crisis has passed, although ensuring that these crucial countervailing forces retain their effectiveness as social and economic circumstances change remains a task without end. Poverty is now described as relative rather than absolute, even if no less destructive of the spirit than before, and our wealth makes fatalism in its face less and less justifiable.

Paradox is everywhere to be seen. It is by all accounts the age of cynicism, of the triumph of vacuous celebrity over substance, of the consumer over the citizen, the end of ideology, the death of party politics. Yet it is also an age when voluntarism still flourishes, where a new interest in matters of the spirit can be detected. This fills some churches, while its assertiveness splits others and its excesses make atheism a more active force. It is a time when the passions stoked by the information age and its global awareness have given birth to myriad causes, where even the arts and media are seeing a shift from consumption to participation, and where the stubborn grass of civic life still survives on meagre and sporadic nourishment.

In Wales a microclimate has developed to feed that grass in a way that may yet create a virtuous cycle of change. The 1997 referendum may have been won by a mere whisker, but the turnround in Welsh sentiment since 1979 was large, and much greater than in Scotland. The turnout at the three subsequent elections for the Welsh Assembly may not have reached 50 per cent, but it is at least higher than for local elections, confirming a correlation between turnout and media attention. The public may take a dim view of the general calibre of the members of its new Assembly, but polls also tell of an acceptance of the new institution. Wales's underlying economic circumstances may not have improved, but the same polls still accord the Assembly a relevance, rightly or wrongly, above other institutions.

Seen from a Welsh perspective it has been a democratic assertion of self and of control, a demand to own one's own problems and, to the extent that it is possible in this globalised world, to attempt one's own solutions. Sceptics may claim that its roots are shallow, that it has been an exercise by a portion of the political class, but in the fashionable phrase of the day, that class has made its own weather. At one level it has been a natural response to the reordering of global affairs, and a more intelligent one than Britain's grudging response to the development of European institutions. It has been about much more than flag-waving, though that has increased greatly as has the number of companies listed in Welsh telephone directories with the word Dragon in their titles – an interesting barometer of emotion though not one that will have any effect on turnover.

From a wider perspective it has been the first effective counter to the unremitting centralisation of British governance that has persisted unchecked for a whole century. This has been accelerated by the necessary controls of two world wars in the first half of the twentieth century and the desperate management of withdrawal from Empire and relative economic decline in the second. For decades, resistance to the modernisation of our industrial structures by unions and management locked in a nineteenth-century adversarialism ran alongside a similar resistance to the modernisation of our political structures. Even when Margaret Thatcher began to tackle the former, a deep British conservatism pushed constitutional reform to the sidelines of political debate. An excessive rhetorical regard for the sovereignty of Parliament persisted in the face of the parallel diminution of Parliament's practical power over the executive. Meanwhile local government was regularly restructured as a distraction therapy from its emasculation.

Eight years into the new system it is possible to look back and understand better what one hoped for from the change: an end to the possibility of periodic disenfranchisement represented by the Thatcher years, a barricade against a perceived threat of cultural oblivion for a small people, but above all an opportunity to blow new life into the grey embers of civic vitality, a chance to engage, in the hope that we might, together, just do things better. Civil society's debilitating lack of purchase on day-to-day government may not have been confined to Wales, but it has been much more keenly felt by a people conscious, if sometimes hazily so, of both their historical identity and economic weakness.

The return, at one level, has already been positive. If there have been some fumbles, there have been no spectacular dropped passes. The new Assembly Government, like all the devolved administrations, has proved perfectly competent, as one would expect given the long-standing British gift for administration. The pillars of the temple have not fallen. There have been good and bad policy ideas, successes and failures of execution – but that is the lot of all governments. The Assembly has had fewer administrative and policy alarums in its first eight years than the Westminster Government in the same period despite, or perhaps because of, the absence of decisive majority.

People will take sharply differing views on policy according to their own political persuasion, but consensus support has grown inexorably. It is true that the distinction between the Assembly Government and the Assembly as a deliberative body is blurred in the public mind, but that is hardly a surprise since it was blurred in the 1998 Act that set it up. It is also true that the scrutiny function of the Assembly has been the least well performed of all its roles, partly because of the narrow base of experience of its members. But abolition of the body is now close to unthinkable. Those who continue to argue that way find themselves in a box marked 'eccentrics' for people who write in green ink and copy their fulminations to sundry heads of state and the Pope.

Less than two years after the Assembly was created I found myself in a position to observe how powerful its very existence could be. The episode involved the future of Welsh Water, then part of Hyder, the multi-utility company that was struggling financially. Two young and very talented Welsh Water executives, Nigel Annett and Chris Jones, the former with a background in investment banking and the latter having been at the Treasury during the privatisation of the water industry, put forward a novel scheme to detach the water business from the electricity operation and turn it into a not-for profit company.

They had been given permission by Hyder to work on the plan behind Chinese walls, and had persuaded no-one less than Lord Burns, a former Treasury permanent secretary, to chair the embryonic company, under the title Glas Cymru. I joined the group, shortly after leaving the BBC, as somebody with some knowledge of politics in Wales. Meanwhile Guy Hands, a buccaneering private equity merchant, seemed to be the most likely buyer – creating the prospect that control of Welsh Water would be passed around the marketplace regularly like a parcel, while Wales and Welsh Water managers waited for the music to stop.

Neverthless, the Glas Cymru scheme made regulators nervous and aroused opposition in several government departments in London, wedded as they were to equity-based companies in privatised industries. It was particularly unpopular at the Treasury, largely because the plan to finance the purchase of the company through a substantial bond issue was uncannily similar to what Ken Livingstone wanted to do with London Underground, rather than adopt the public/private partnership that the Treasury eventually forced on him. While Terry Burns was immensely effective in neutralising some of this opposition, the existence of the Assembly and the fact that Glas Cymru had won the support of all four political parties in Wales, was crucial in persuading even the most sceptical to hold back from blocking the plan. They recoiled from crossing swords with a democratic institution, especially a unanimous one. It made me wonder how differently the landmark events of twentieth-century Wales – the depression, Tryweryn, Aberfan, the miners' strike – might have played out had the Assembly existed then.

You would be hard-pressed to find anyone to argue for a return to the old system of government in Wales since, in retrospect, it has the appearance of a bleak cul de sac, rather than an open-ended avenue for change. The frustrations of democracy are infinitely preferable to the corrosive frustrations of impotence. Instead, the parameters of argument now focus on the form and method of further legislative devolution rather than its desirability. The rapidity with which this logic has asserted itself has been truly surprising.

Few people in 1997, contemplating the narrowness of the referendum result, would have predicted that a commission to consider the future powers of the Assembly would have been established within three years of its foundation, or that it would have achieved a cross-party consensus amongst its members in favour of more clear cut primary legislative powers, or that a new act would have been passed in 2006 granting de facto legislative powers, albeit by a convoluted route. The speed with which the compromises of the 1998 Act demanded resolution will surely be repeated in relation to the undesirably labyrinthine qualities of the 2006 Act.

Paralleling this momentum, the Welsh public domain, hollowed out over the years, is beginning to take on a fuller form. My friend Patrick Hannan used to observe that in the golden age of Welsh rugby there was no shortage of parties in Cardiff on match day, only a shortage of guests. The same cannot be said of the current profusion of events in the Welsh capital aimed at a mixture of enlightenment and networking.

The Cardiff Business Club draws several hundred business people to hear prominent speakers address its fortnightly events through the winter months. The Institute of Welsh Affairs arranges regular lunches through the year for the same purpose. Several breakfast clubs do likewise. A firm of local solicitors arranges evening forums where issues are subjected to formal debate. Lectures on matters of current public concern, arranged jointly by Cardiff University and BBC Wales, are well attended. The CBI and IOD have their own programmes. Business in the Community has a thriving membership. All-party subject groups have begun to grow out of the Assembly itself to connect with the rest of society.

The realisation of the potency of Assembly Government has forced all manner of organisations to think harder about policy, as the steady stream of consultative documents has required a response. Lobbyists in Cardiff Bay have multiplied to the extent that they have now formed an association. At election time business organisations issue detailed manifestos of their own. The Welsh Local Government Association, for so long the creature of one party and a handful of warhorses who regularly bridled at the powerful new kid on the block, is now a more plural and thinking organisation. Wales's thirteen higher education institutions have had to concert their views through Higher Education Wales, appointing full-time staff for the first time in 2000. UK organisations have had to reconsider their representation in Wales. The Wales Council for Voluntary Action is now a large organisation with 120 staff, almost wholly funded by the Assembly Government, although some also see that as one of several signs of an incipient new corporatism in Welsh life.

It is this last feature that has given rise to disquiet, particularly amongst those who have had to connect on a regular basis with the Assembly. The overwhelming dominance of the public sector in Welsh life can be seen, from the other end of the telescope, as simply a function of the weakness of the private sector, but the effect is the same: an under-capitalised society is too dependent on the bank of Government, certainly financially, but also to a large extent intellectually. In Wales nearly 64 per cent of gross value added is attributable to the public sector, compared with Scotland's 56 per cent and London's 36 per cent. Only Northern Ireland is higher than Wales. Even these figures leave out of account a third sector that is not often talked about, the quasi-private sector – not least, ironically, the industry of business advice – that is nominally private but almost wholly dependent on public sector commissioning.

Apart from the economic consequences, there are also cultural consequences. The inter-connections of civic life, inevitably multiplied and intricate because of the small scale of society, often mean that in some form or another an alarmingly high proportion of supposedly independent people are in some way beholden to government. When combined with an historically well-attested aversion to direct confrontation, it is little wonder that Wales is too often the land of the pulled punch.

It explains the frequent mutual incomprehension between the Assembly government and other sectors over all manner of issues, most particularly in the world of business. For instance, during the second term of the Assembly, business routinely, and from my experience unanimously, despaired of government rhetoric and policy that was hostile to market-based solutions in the public sector, and criticised the dominance of the public and voluntary sectors in the maze of partnership bodies administering the European Objective One funds. Yet Ministers often professed to hearing no complaints, and not always disingenuously. Both sides were as ships that pass in the night.

Welsh society's necessary engagement with a democratic institution that is inside its own doorstep – rather than a very expensive train fare away – has also prompted a degree of self-examination. Many organisations dating from the nineteenth or early twentieth century – the University of Wales, the National Museum, the National Library, the

National Eisteddfod, even the BBC – had been able regularly to bolster their self-regard by emphasising their value as national symbols, proxies for the absent democratic forum. Once the Assembly opened its doors, however, those bodies have had to be judged more clearly on their functional value, and some have responded better than others.

Both the National Museum and the National Library have recently been marked out by energetic management. The National Museum has benefited from the policy of free entry to museums and galleries and the wider political support arising from the geographical spread of its seven locations. Meanwhile the National Library has attracted support for its enthusiastic embrace of digitisation and a more outward facing stance. But governance has been a live issue. Their respective Courts of Governors, that had already begun to lose their early twentieth-century gloss as a gathering place for national elders, now have more sensibly sized boards, although both lost their battles to appoint a majority of their own trustees. That is now done by the Assembly Government. They both escaped the bonfire of the quangos on the grounds of their charitable status.

The University of Wales has had the most torrid time, caught between a token and ineffective federalism (similar to the University of London) and the uncompetitive small scale of all but one its constituent parts. Following its meteoric rise into the elite Russell Group of British Universities, Cardiff's departure from the University of Wales in 2004 threatened to bring down the whole edifice, but since no volunteers could be found to play the part of executioner, it limped on. Although two other colleges, Bangor and Swansea, quietly let it be known that they were flirting with a similar assertion of autonomy to that of Cardiff, the University of Wales rather surprisingly appointed its first ever central vice-chancellor in 2007, with the unenviable task of breathing life into a parent whose children had only recently been debating switching off the life support mechanism and arranging a funeral.

The vigorous handbagging of vice-chancellors during the Assembly's second term by the long-serving education minister, Jane Davidson, robustly seconded by the chairman of the Higher Education Funding Council, failed to effect the mergers that many saw as neces-sary to compete in the British university market. Localism constantly trumped the still novel concept of national objectives. Merger talks between the University of Glamorgan and UWIC, between UWIC and Newport, between Bangor and NEWI between Aberystwyth and

Lampeter, and – more bizarrely – Lampeter and Newport, all foundered as the result of differing mixtures of academic snobbery, geography and misdirected ambition. Only Cardiff's merger with the College of Medicine got to the finishing line, to be followed almost immediately by sadly predictable demands from Swansea for an independent school of medicine of its own.

Higher education provided a salutary example of where the proper defence of the arm's length principle was not followed through with a reciprocal obligation to autonomous reform, despite all the funding pressures for change. The proper locus of the planning function for higher education in Wales – the Assembly Government, the funding council, the quasi-federal university, or the individual institutions – has yet to be resolved. Meanwhile the funding gap between Welsh and English universities continues to grow.

It is not easy for small and close societies to escape from a limited comfort zone. There are plenty of tales, from health waiting lists, higher education, to private sector entrepreneurialism, that could give credence to the notion of a general Welsh crisis of under-performance. Equally, there are pockets of excellence that warn us against excessive self-flagellation. Our difficulty is that our national penchant for self-criticism is often exuberant when generalised and aimed at others, but wonderfully muted closer to home – what a former head of the Audit Office in Wales described as a culture of 'apologism'.

In the early years of the Assembly it was not easy for government to acknowledge shortcomings when every criticism of public services was seen, quite unrealistically, as a sign of the failure of the new institution as a whole rather than the government alone. The defensiveness of conventional politics that obliges all governments to put a positive gloss on our circumstances, does not allow the mobilisation of society by the invocation of a Dunkirk spirit that a pessimistic reading of Wales's economic situation might justify. We have lacked any galvanising rhetoric. It was 2005 before the Government felt brave enough, or worried enough, to commission a report into public services from a team headed by an English local government luminary from the North East, Sir Jeremy Beecham. A year later it put its finger very publicly on fundamental issues of 'culture and capacity', in overcoming some of the inherent weaknesses of small country governance.

Not before time it provided some challenge to that enduring Welsh myth that small is always beautiful. To question this is heretical in Wales, where the communitarian ethos is strong. Legions of writers and poets have lauded their own square mile. At eisteddfodau the name of a winner's village is given as much emphasis as the winner himself or herself. If villages had anthems and flags, like the Olympics, the national eisteddfod would last a month. It is no wonder that E.F. Schumacher and Leopold Kohr took a liking to the place.

There is often power and strength in the small scale, but, as Beecham found, there is also weakness. Conversely, while bigness has its own drawbacks and is by no means a panacea – even London can be parochial – the large scale does have a capacity to deliver things quite beyond the small. In many cases there is sense in going with the grain of our localism, but the National Assembly has been created not only to support it, but quite specifically to go beyond it.

There are other small nation myths that need to be challenged – not least the complacent assumption that we are an especially cultured nation and that the English are philistines – two separate propositions that, in the heat of argument, are often conflated. These conjoined beliefs are often paraded as at the core of our identity and usually entail comparing apples and oranges – *cynghanedd* against Morris dancing, chaired bards against 'page three' models, rather than apples with apples – for example, university performance or the Welsh and English choral traditions. Government in England and Scotland has paid far more attention to the encouragement of the arts for young people, both in and out of schools, than has Wales.

Whatever may be said about the past, it is harder to see a qualitative difference in popular culture today on either side of Offa's Dyke, even where that is expressed through the Welsh language. If there is a strain of anti-intellectualism in English culture, it is today just as evident in Wales. Many of the things that excite my own curmudgeonly instincts can be found in equal measure in both places: dreary commercial architecture, badly designed domestic housing, fragile old centres carelessly ruined, rural housing problems, and local authority philistinism. In many of these fields Wales, sadly, has its nose in front. Even on the positive side, the present vibrancy of some cultural activity in Wales is paralleled in both England and Scotland.

This should be a reminder of the propensity of all small nations to exaggerate their distinctiveness. It would be stupid to deny the reality of Welsh difference or not to laud it – it is after all the essence of oneself – but there are dangers in over-egging it or becoming over-reliant on it. Where it exists it can be useful but, equally, in the policy field, it can be limiting to imply that the only rationale for policy divergence is a difference in circumstances. This is what tended to happen under the old Welsh Office, when areas of policy where Wales's special needs were not as plain as a pikestaff were usually subjected to mere badge engineering – Whitehall policy, Welsh Office logo.

The enlarged autonomy means we no longer have to prove that our needs and circumstances are demonstrably different before giving ourselves permission to take another policy course or simply to do something better than is done elsewhere. Rhodri Morgan's espousal of 'clear red water', the introduction of a Children's Commissioner or Welsh baccalaureate, and the ending of testing in primary schools, were all an assertion of this freedom as much as a response to differences on the ground – a *right* to seek the same or different ends by a different route.

Our belief in a special relationship with the rest of the Celtic fringe is another that needs some qualification. It is true that Scotland, Wales and Ireland have a strong sense of fellow-feeling that springs largely from the fact that we are all in a relationship with a larger neighbour. The Welsh and the Irish are closer in spirit, just as the Scots, though they may deny it, are closer to the English. But we should not use our delight at Irish *craic* or the camaraderie of Edinburgh's Princes Street on a match day, to deny our practical day to day affinity with the English – which is of a high order through proximity, marriage, co-habitation, law and language, and not just patterns of consumption.

The inter-penetration of populations between north-east Wales and north west England has been intense, so that no-one can plan towns or hospitals or universities on one side of the border without taking into account what is happening on the other. In the south the two Severn bridges have changed travel and shopping patterns on either side of a swirling channel, though perhaps less than some imagined when they were built. If a further Severn Barrage is built Weston-super-Mare will suddenly find itself closer to Cardiff than to Bristol.

Alongside the multifarious commonalities, one of the defining differences between the Welsh and the English, at the collective level, is our relationship with power. But however that changes, whatever degree of autonomy Welsh governance achieves in the coming decades, the real underlying affinities and interactions are certain to persist. Union of a kind will always exist. The interweaving of life in these islands is too close for that not to happen. The issue is the form and balance of that union, an issue that nationalists, devolutionists and unionists alike will have to address in much more detail as the devolution process rolls to a misty destination.

Another much-used circumvention of the English connection is Europeanism. The potential of the European Union as a means of affirming our identity in a wider context and enlarging autonomy without mediation by London, has great appeal in Wales. It helps explain a rather warmer feeling towards Europe than you would find in the *Sun*. But our engagement with Europe will have to become much more profound and constructive if it is to be more than a glib means of excluding England from our mental map, or a cover for a careless disengagement from English or British organisations that can prove counter-productive.

Europe and the rest of the world, particularly other small countries, have insights and experience that Wales should draw on much more than it does, but one cannot escape from the fact that our own circumstances have, in most regards, greater similarities with England than with any other country. Those similarities still make England, or its regions, the most frequently valid comparator. Its scale also makes it a collaborative resource on which we can fruitfully draw, for instance, in shared research, in ways that eke out our own limited funds and allow us to enjoy both the penny and the bun.

The relevance of these matters increases rather than decreases as the new system develops. Just as the creation of the National Assembly and the Scottish Parliament in 1999 was a pivotal moment in British constitutional development, it is possible that the 2007 election will be seen as a pivotal moment in its politics – a moment when politics in Scotland and Wales took on a continental rather than British paradigm – Scotland perhaps mirroring Spain, and Wales closer to Germany. In 2007 the political system in Wales seemed to catch up with the breakdown of other traditional monolithic structures in the rest of Welsh society.

It was a moment when three of the four parties had to address their internal fault lines as much as their differences with other parties: Labour, with its fast and slow lane devolutionists, not to mention those who would prefer to park on the hard shoulder and wait for the AA; Plaid Cymru, with its left-wing and centrist divisions, more evenly divided between their visceral distaste for Tories or for Labour than conference votes suggested; Liberal Democrats, discovering anew that the middle of the road is a very dangerous place, particularly without the policy focus or organisational discipline to deflect its members from looking in opposite directions; and the Conservatives, the Welsh party most altered by devolution, unusually finding an easy poise that the party has not enjoyed in England since the eighties.

The wider implications of this have been almost entirely missed by the British press. One might have thought that the existence of a minority nationalist government in Scotland, a labour-nationalist coalition in Wales, and a unionist-nationalist power-sharing government in Northern Ireland, taken together, would have prompted some considerable thought and comment. Instead it has been greeted by a remarkable silence. To the extent that that silence has been broken at all, it has been to comment on the end of strife in Ulster and the prospect of Scottish independence.

Few have bothered to distinguish between the consequences for the union and the consequences for the British unitary state – two quite different concepts, even if they are related. The inability or unwillingness of political commentators to grasp that difference explains why they felt able to ignore totally the 2007 election in Wales and its astonishing aftermath. Wales presents no present threat to the union, nor does it have a significant potential for violent breakdown, nor is it in a contested relationship with another state. Yet, arguably, the Welsh situation speaks more eloquently and precisely of the condition of the British unitary state, and its future course, than either of the other two countries.

This silence is emblematic of the current state of the union, whose key present characteristic is its laziness. The lazy union manifests itself in different ways. First, the emotional, excessively historical, British approach to constitutional debate that contrasts with the rationalism of a more European approach – our love of muddling through. Second, the failure of British media, but most of all newspapers, to report on the whole country, including the north of England, assiduously and intelligently. On the rare occasions that they do, Scotland and Wales are usually lumped together despite radically different constitutional and financial deals. Editors might reflect on the consequences of failing to report and scrutinise the misgovernment of Ulster in the decades before 1969, a failure that allowed Stormont's manipulation of government for sectarian ends to provoke disastrous and costly consequences felt for more than three decades after that date.

Third, there is the lack of serious discussion of the geographic dimension of economic development, in sharp contrast to the sixties and seventies when government at least talked about regional policy. There is a growing awareness of the distortion of Britain by the untrammelled growth of London and the south east, with all its economic, social and cultural consequences. It has been given a new twist by both the property market and the scale of the 2012 Olympics project. But there is little evidence of concern in government, of whatever hue, only a wringing of hands and some palliative gestures.

This may be the consequence of a market driven approach, but it is rather dispiriting to think that even professedly progressive governments do not regard this distortion as a market failure that the government, as the principal and overriding regulator, should address more urgently, forcefully and imaginatively.

If the response is to say that such unbalanced development cannot be tackled through central planning in this market-driven age, then the decentralising logic of markets should be mirrored in a more radical decentralisation of government, if for no other reason than to encourage what the economist, John Kay, has described as 'disciplined pluralism'. The inadmissibility of central planning does not mean that government is impotent in the face of this problem.

One feature of this blindness to the geographical dimension to policy is the crude level of discussion of public expenditure. A rash of studies published in 2007 described the deepening economic division of Britain between the south-east of England, including London, and 'an archipelago of provinces' to the north and west. The distinguishing factor in all of them was state spending as a proportion of economic activity. Much of the accompanying commentary took the form of magisterial lectures about 'the payroll vote', about the 'south-east paying for the rest of the country', 'the public sector crowding out the private' and 'subsidies keeping you poor'. There was little appreciation of the way in which economic policy has exacerbated the drift to the south east and privileged the financial sector over manufacturing.

One of the few to take a more sympathetic line was the historian, Tristram Hunt, chronicler of the rise and fall of the Victorian city, who pointed to the risks of London leaving the rest of the country behind. He compared today with a period of 'Edwardian excess' at the beginning of the twentieth century when, he said, London, then the epicentre of Empire, first broke away from the rest of the country. The outflow of investment, while undeniably profitable, contributed to the eclipse of British manufacturing by America and Germany. He quoted an article from *The Economist* of that time: 'London is often more concerned with the course of events in Mexico than with what happens in the Midlands, and is more upset by a strike on the Canadian Pacific than by one in the Cambrian collieries.' By today circumstances have changed, but attitudes are analogous.

The crude discussion of the consequences of this economic divide is nowhere better exemplified than in the debate on the Barnett formula, by which Scotland, Wales and Northern Ireland are funded. It is not only tabloid newspapers, but many politicians too, who portray this as a mere act of charity on the part of the south-east toward Scotland, Wales and Northern Ireland. There is no attempt to explain that such fiscal transfers are a feature of most civilised countries, where they are often attempted with a much greater degree of sophistication.

Iain McLean, professor of politics at Oxford University, and a specialist on these matters, has argued that Barnett 'punishes the territory which poses no credible threat to the union, viz. Wales'. As an alternative he has taken the Commonwealth Grants Board of Australia as a model for a proposed British Territorial Grants Board, that would operate at arm's length from Government, allocating money according to need, and able to operate on a four country basis or on a twelve territory basis, dividing England into its nine standard regions. He points out that there is inequity in England, too, where the distribution of money has tended to favour regions with a high proportion of marginal seats. Such schemes are very unlikely to commend themselves to central government or to the Treasury, and perhaps politics and controversy can never be entirely excluded from such calculations, but a review of the Barnett formula might at least allow the debate to achieve a higher plane, and offer the prospect of a just and rational settlement.

There is a debate beyond Barnett. To offer poorer parts of Britain very limited mitigation of the geographic impact of market dynamics, on the one hand, but no credible economic levers for self-recovery on the other, seems a recipe for long term disillusionment, outside England, with the union, and within England, with government generally.

Fourth, one could point to an unthinking English separatism, a disconnecting of the radar that spreads beyond the English border. This can be seen in the gratuitous disengagement of some ministries from consultation in areas where it is plainly desirable. For instance, Defra's publication of a draft Marine Bill for English waters, that, with no explanation, simply left the issue of Welsh and Scottish waters to be sorted out later by the devolved administrations. Even in the still unlikely circumstance of a complete break-up of the union, this is a field where concerted action might be thought to be desirable. Defra's chosen path might be construed as politeness to the devolved administrations rather than laziness, but the prospect of marine legislation around our collective shores being undertaken unilaterally by England does, at the very least, leave out of account the consequences for a benighted Bristol Channel flounder swimming from Weston to Cardiff.

Given the convolutions of the 2006 Government of Wales Act, designed to give the Assembly Government legislative responsibility by permit in order to retain the form if not the reality of a unitary juris-diction, it seems ironic that functions can be transferred to the Assembly or its Ministers by the unilateral actions of Whitehall depart-ments without formal consultation with the Assembly itself, as opposed to the Assembly Government.

Lastly, there is the neglect of the joint ministerial committees that in 1999 were seen as a mechanism through which heads of the British government and the devolved administrations, as well as other minis-ters and officials, might maintain regular contact. A House of Lords inquiry in 2003 commented on the way in which this mechanism had been neglected in favour of informal contacts that are possible only where all these governments are of the same political colour, a further example of the predilection for sofa government.

When the Lords reported in 2003, a health joint ministerial committee had met only once and its education counterpart not at all. Yet despite their lordships' strictures, the joint ministerial committee did not meet in plenary session from 2002 to 2007, and then only perfunctorily. A less lazy approach might, in future, give this at least the sort of attention and formality devoted, quite rightly, to North-South Ministerial conferences in Ireland. Who knows, reality television might find a meeting between Gordon Brown, Alex Salmond, Rhodri Morgan and Ian Paisley quite gripping.

Britain, as exemplified in the political power base of the south-east, has a strange capacity for denial whenever politics touches on identity. It is as evident in its grumpy membership of the European Union as in its responses to devolution. But there is also another force at work. What is happening in Scotland, Wales and Northern Ireland may be only dimly perceived in London because it falls between two very different fields of vision. The old guard finds it difficult to conceive of anything other than a state that is politically and emotionally unitary in its conception, while a new cosmopolitan culture, both immigrant and increasingly indigenous, and underpinned by London's status as a world capital in finance and culture, often sees the Scottish, Welsh and Irish politics of identity as old-fashioned or even regressive.

In the light of these failures of perception attempts to boost a sense of Britishness artificially through citizenship ceremonies or Union Jacks on the front lawn will always seem artificial in Scotland and Wales, and even counterproductive. They may even have a declining relevance for all but a minority in Northern Ireland. If stereotypes are put aside it is not impossible to envisage that Ian Paisley, the quintessential unionist who now presides over a Parliament that was the UK's first departure from the unitary state, Rhodri Morgan, the devolutionist who presides over a Welsh legislature in the name of the party of Aneurin Bevan, and his deputy, Ieuan Wyn Jones, leader of a nationalist party that puts an increasing stress on the inter-dependence of government at different levels, may be on strangely convergent courses.

This will be the backdrop to the evolving internal dynamics of England. Regionalism in England may struggle, but the increasing appeal of localism there will not be a mere priming of the parish pump. England's core cities outside the south-east, already in effective combination, may be more concerned with the country's imbalances than with answering the West Lothian question – for some, the one strangely indigestible anomaly in a constitution built on an accretion of ambiguities. The West Lothian anomaly is the premium paid by England for its dominance in an asymmetric union, and a funding system where, essentially, Welsh and Scottish block grants are determined by English spending decisions.

Different governments in Westminster may have more or less enthusiasm for what has already been put in place, but they will work with the grain of those changes. Those, both Welsh and English, who may resist the eventual refinement of Wales's current ingenious but impenetrably complex settlement, on the grounds of defending the union, will find themselves addressing an outdated question. They would be better employed pressing for a more active and nuanced union rather than hankering after a unitary past.

In a different context, Tony Blair talked of the kaleidoscope having been shaken and the pieces being in flux. The same could be said of Britain's constitution and the internal relationships within these islands. At the end of 2007, despit the stubborn weaknesses of our economy, when I see the increased energy of my own patch, when I see the open-ended possibilities for initiative and change, for more engaged government, and for a politics one can touch, the balance is positive and there is room for hope.

Index

A-levels 147
A Real Fire 77-8
Aberfan disaster 32-3, 142
Aberystywyth University 321
Abraham, William (Mabon) 83
Abse, Dannie 20
Abse, Leo 67
Academi 188, 189, 227, 248
Academy Health Wales 146
ACCAC 224
Adams, Jonathan 222-3
Alabama 82
All Our Lives 106
Allan, Andy 87
Alsop, Wil 105, 292
Alston, David 184, 226
Amsterdam concerts 166
And Did Corruptly Receive 81
Andrews, Leighton 220-1, 228
Angel of the North 292
Anglia Television 295
animations 122-3
Annett, Nigel 328
Arcade 76, 141–2
architectural programmes 104-5
architecture 271, 291-3
Argentina 74-5
Arizona 78
arm's length principle 212, 214-16, 218,
221, 224, 243, 248
Armstrong, Richard 172
arson attacks 77-8
Artes Mundi Art Prize 186, 262
artists 186
arts *see also* Arts Council of Wales: access
235-6, 237, 238, 256-7; amateur/profes-
sional 282-3; attendance figures 263-4;
civil liberties 249-53; democracy 247-9;
education and 269-70; funding 171-6,
181, 247, 273; independence of 252-3:
international strategies 167; politicians,
public and professionals 266-9
Arts Connection 199
Arts Council of England: chair 214;
clients 197; Covent Garden grant 154,
156; McIntosh review 234-5; stabilisation

scheme 172-3, 195
Arts Council of Great Britain 90-1, 156,
172
Arts Council of Northern Ireland 214
Arts Council of Wales: access 235-6, 237,
238; advocacy 242-3; arm's length principle 212, 214-16, 218, 221, 224, 243, 248;
arts director post 184; Assembly
Goevernment and 201-3, 210-12, 217-20;
clients 226; Collectorplan 213; creation of
181-2; Culture Board and 225-32; directors 226; foreign travel 167; funding by
173-4, 227-8, 260-1; funding for 156, 196-
9, 232-3; as intelligence centre 195;
literature and 188-9; performance of 228-
9; 'poisoned chalice' 180-1; recruitment to
233; research and development 240; resignation thoughts 229, 233-4; restructuring
182-5, 198-9; review 238-43; six companies proposals 227-8, 232-3, 238;
stabilisation scheme 173-4; strategic and
planning functions 225-6, 228, 231-3, 238,
240, 242; strategic capacity 194-6; submission 212-17; support for 219-23, 236-7,
248; survey on attitudes to arts 261-4;
sustainability scheme 195–6; workshop
meeting 230-2; writers' awards 180
arts councils 180-1, 214
arts development officers 272
'Arts outside Cardiff' 198
arts programmes 100-1, 104-5, 178-9
Artsmark 270
Arup Associates 105
Ascherson, Neal 58
ASPBs (Assembly Sponsored Public
Bodies) *see* quangos
Atlantic College 147
Audiences Wales 199
Audit Commission Wales 271-2
Azzopardi, Trezza 188

Babachina, Eliza 122
baccalaureate 146-8
Baker, Stanley 64
Baker, Tim 193
Bakewell, Joan 36

Bala National Eisteddfod 162
ballet 190
Balsom, Denis 106, 144, 209
Balsom, Sue 135
Bangor University 321, 331-2
Bank of Wales 54
Barcelona olympics 89, 289
Barn 21, 145
Barnett formula 338
Barrett, Lorraine 220
Barry 18
Barry Welsh school 20
Bartlett, David 25
Bassey, Shirley 222
Baverstock, Donald 23
BBC: Audience Council 124, 309; BBC Wales and 113-14; Broadcasting Councils 126-7, 131; central control 128-9; chairmen 98; Children's Department 124; 'climate change' 98-9; complaints against 250; consultants 99; controllers 126, 127; devolution coverage 131-6; digital services 311; directors general 97, 113; drama 115-19; Education 124; foreign concert tours 165-6; frequencies for Wales 294; funding 305-6; Funding the Future 93-4, 100; history programmes 106-7, 120; innovation 178-9; internal market 116, 118; licence fee 95, 109, 311; the nations 94-5, 96-7, 113-16; network output 119-20, 121; network schedules 69; news and current affairs 103; operas written for 162; organisational structure 113; programme costs 305; public value 267; radio talks 19; regional news 103-4; Royal Charter (1952) 124: Royal Charter (2006) 114, 124; S4C 73, 102-3; S4C and 109-11, 313; sports contracts 109; strategies review 105–6; Wales as separate region 296; websites 111; wedding presents 96
BBC 2 112, 121
BBC *Cardiff Singer of the World* 115, 167-9
BBC National Orchestra of Wales 166, 174, 252, 283; United Nations concert 165
BBC Northern Ireland 94

BBC Radio 3 121, 163
BBC Radio Cymru: budgets 101; digital services 112, 310; strike 107-8; transmission hours 103
BBC Radio Wales: budgets 101; digital services 112, 310; drama 122; Sony awards 103; transmission hours 103; on VHF 103
BBC Radio Scotland 101
BBC Scotland 94, 114, 115
BBC Trust 113, 124, 308
BBC Wales 92-112; animations 122-4; arts programmes 104-5; BBC and 113-14; bilingual appointments 101; Controller Wales 113; Broadcasting Council for Wales 70, 102, 124-8, 135; current affairs programmes 75; drama 115-19, 121-2; English language programmes 100; factual programmes 120-1; foreign correspondents 104; freed from BBC West 53; Funding the Future 93-4, 100; heads of programmes 101-2, 106; history programmes 106-7, 121; HTV and 100; ITV jobs comparison 95; music programmes 121; network output 114-17, 124; news and current affairs 104; programme strategies review 105-6; redundancies 95-6; regional broadcasters and 73; religious programmes 120, 123-4; resources 116-17; rugby coverage 109-10; S4C 100; S4C and 73, 102, 109-10, 122-4; Welsh language programmes 72
BBC Welsh Symphony Orchestra 163-4, 166
Beecham Report 241
Beleshenko, Alex 186, 265
Belfast protests 250
Belfast Telegraph 301
Bell, Stuart 88
Belonging 122
Bevan, Aneurin 38, 118-19, 325
Beveridge, William 325
Beynon, Ann 202
Beyond Boundaries 241
Bezhti 249, 250
Bhatti, Gurpreet Kaur 249
Binney, Marcus 154
Birmingham protests 249, 250

Birmingham pub bombings 37-8

Birt, John: analysis of 97-9; BCW and 127; cadres 92; as deputy director 103; digital services 111; *Holding the BBC Together* 134; at LWT 305; programmes and resources 126; style of 95

The Black Velvet Gown 90

Blair, Tony 134, 147, 151, 207, 340

Bland, Sir Christopher 98, 135, 202, 203

Blood and Belonging 120-1

Bofill, Ricardo 292

Bogdanov, Michael 136, 191

Book of the Year 185, 189

Border Television 295

Bormann, Martin 42

Bottomley, Virginia 150, 156

Boulding, Hilary 121

Boyce, Michael 152

Boydell, Peter, QC 46

Boyden, Peter 173, 192, 194

Boyle, James 214

Bragg, Melvyn 91

Bread and Roses 146, 160

Breitenstein, Rolf 57-8

Brinnin, John Malcolm 78, 79

British Bone Marrow Donor Appeal 31

British Territorial Grants Board 338

British Wales 144

Brittany 74

broadcasting: future of 308-15; regulation of 307-8

Broadcasting Act 1990 110

Broadcasting Act 1996 110

Broadcasting and the Nation 71

Brooks, Jack 33, 61, 152-3

BT 202, 203

Buchanan, Colin 33, 44

Burns, Lord 328

Burton, Philip 19, 21

Burton, Richard 19, 64, 222

business development 139-40, 330

Business in the Community 329

Bute family 279, 294

Butetown 280

Butler, Rosemary 213, 220, 237

Butler-Sloss inquiry 88

Byford, Mark 103, 114, 131

Byrchmore, Ruth 259

Caleb, Ruth 116

Callaghan, Jim 33

The Canterbury Tales 123

capital punishment 37-8

CARAD 199

Cardiff: as capital 275-7, 281, 283-4; centenary 256; cost analysis 280-1; councillors' arrest 45; and country 283-5; criticisms of 277-8; European Capital of Culture 193, 283; future of 285-6, 288-9; history of 278-9; planning 289-91; redevelopment 45-7, 279-80, 289-90; Welsh language and 278-9; *Western Mail* presentation to 39

Cardiff 2000 289

Cardiff Arms Park 284

Cardiff Bay Development Cor-poration 150, 151-3, 158-9, 276, 289

Cardiff Bay Opera House: architectural competition 150, 151-3, 156-7; funding for 155-6; vs. Millennium Stadium 153-5; name change 158; rejection of 149-50, 157-8, 159-60

Cardiff Bay Opera House Trust 150-1, 158

Cardiff Business Club 329

Cardiff Business School 141

Cardiff High School for Boys 275

Cardiff University 281–2, 321, 331

Cardiff Workers' Cooperative Garden Village 278

Care Council for Wales 224

Carleton Greene, Hugh 23

Carlton Television 302

Carr-Ellison, Sir Ralph 86

Casey, Luke 88

CBAT 199

Celf o Gwmpas 199

Celtic Film and Television Festival 112

Central Television 306

The Centralist Enemy (Osmond) 143

Centre for the Performing Arts 160

Centre for the Visual Arts 152-3

Jones, Hywel Ceri 60-1

chamber orchestras 186, 219-20

Chamberlain, Brenda 20

Channel Television 302-3

Channel 4 80, 310

Chaplin, Michael 89, 101, 102, 106, 117-18
Chaplin, Sid 89, 118
Chapter Arts Centre 227
Charles, Prince of Wales 38-9, 150, 154, 203
Charter 88 145
Checkland, Michael 92, 97-8, 115-16, 305
choirs 186
Christmas Films 122-3
Christopher, John 298
Church, Jonathan 249
cities, competitiveness of 281-2
citizen-centred government 266, 291-2, 334
Civic Trust 291
civil disobedience 38-9, 52
civil liberties 249-53
Civvies 116
Clarke, Gillian 188
Clarke, Jane 199, 226
Cleveland child abuse 88-9
Close the Coalhouse Door 89
Clwyd, Ann 143, 298
Clwyd Theatr Cymru 191, 193, 194, 219-20, 227
coal exports 277
Cold War 52
Collins, Allen 78
The Colour of Saying (A. Talfan Davies) 19
Commercial Bank of Wales 54
commercial radio 310
Commission on the constitution 55
Communities First 261, 262
community arts 258-9, 260-3
Community Dance Wales 189
Competition Commission 301
concerts 115, 163-6
Connolly, Brian 206
Conservative Party: conferences 34-5, 151; Council for Wales 54-5; devolution 61-2; education 147; future of 208; internal fault lines 335; support for 38
Cookson, Catherine 90
corruption scandals 45, 81
Council for Wales 54-5
Countryside Council for Wales 224
Covent Garden 154, 156

Cox, Sir Alan 149
Crawford Committee 70
Creative Conflict (Osmond) 143
Creative Futures 214, 232
creative industries 270
Creative Partnerships 270
Creative Wales Awards 185, 236-7
Crickhowell, Lord: ACW and 156; Cardiff Bay Opera House 157, 158, 160; as secretary of state 137-8, 151
Welsh Business Institute 139
Crouch, Sybil 182, 184, 191, 211
Crowther, Lord 55-6
Crowther-Hunt, Norman 56
Crying in the Dark 88
C3W 306-7
Cuba 74
cultural charter 243
cultural value 266-7
'culture' 265-7
Culture Board 225-32
culture ministers 221, 243, 265-274, 308
current affairs programmes 72-7
Curriculum Authority 224
Cyfarthfa Castle 51
Cymru Fydd 162
Cymru'n Creu 225
Cymru'r Byd 111
Cywaith Cymru 199

Daily Express 298
Daily Mirror 298
Daily Post 297, 302
dance 189-90, 256-7
Daniel, Emyr 73-4, 76
Daniel, Sir Goronwy 55, 71-2
Darlledu a'r Genedl 71
Dauncey, Jane 124
David, John 147
David Morgan department store 46, 47
Davidson, Jane 148, 331
Davies, Aled Glynne 107-8
Davies, Alun Talfan 16, 50, 61, 64, 70-1
Davies, Andrew (minister) 202, 203, 210
Davies, Andrew (scriptwriter) 116
Davies, Aneirin Talfan 14-20, 21-2, 26, 43, 70-1
Davies, Dai (ACW) 203-4, 229

Davies, Dai (trade unionist) 34
Davies, David, Lord Davies of Llandinam 170
Davies, Elfyn Talfan 15
Davies, Elinor Talfan 20, 24-5
Davies, Elizabeth Talfan 25, 62
Davies, Geraint Talfan: childhood 17-18, 20-2; courtship 25; criticised in Commons 67; early career 27-39; educational peregrination 39-43; opera introduction 161; university 25-6
Davies, Glyn 61
Davies, Goronwy Talfan 15-16
Davies, Grahame 188
Davies, Gwilym Prys 57
Davies, Herbert 25
Davies, Huw 64-5, 66, 302
Davies, Hywel 17, 21
Davies, John 80, 151, 279
Davies, John (photographer) 105
Davies, Kitchener 20
Davies, Mari Talfan 13-17, 20, 22, 24, 27, 43
Davies, Owen Talfan 17, 22-5
Davies, Phil 102
Davies, Rhys 80
Davies, Rita 23, 25
Davies, Ron 133
Davies, Roy 120
Davies, Stevie 188
Davies, Simon Talfan 24, 25
Davies, Reverend William Talfan 14
Dawns i Bawb 189
de Valera, Eamon 318
Dearing, Sir Ron 147
decentralisation 337
Decline of the Public (Marquand) 253
Deep Navigation 287-8
Defra 338-9
democracy: architecture and 291; central control 253; civil liberties 249–53; government conflict 247-9; newspapers and 296-8, 300-2; public bridges and 296-7; qualitative 254; template for 314
Demos 266
Denton, Charles 116
Department for Education and Skills 270
Department of Culture, Media and Sport

215, 265-6, 268, 270
Department of National Heritage 265
design 270-1
Design Commission for Wales 146, 213, 293
devolution: approaches to 29; arts 167; British press silence on 336; budgets for 36; debates about 34, 38, 41, 55-8; financial disadvantages 155-6; news coverage funding 135; No campaign 68; polls 57, 61; referenda 128-31, 145; referendum orders debate 67; state of the union 336-40; television coverage 67-8, 131-6; Yes campaign 56
Diana, Princess of Wales 128-9
Diannerch Erchwyn (A. Talfan Davies) 24
Dickinson, Robert 86
Digest of Welsh Statistics 35
digital services 111-12, 133, 309-11
disadvantaged young people 256-7
District Nurse 115
Diversions 178, 189, 227
The Divided Kingdom 144-5
Doran, Peter 191
Dr Who 124
The Dragon Has Two Tongues 137
drama 89-90, 115-19, 182
Dromgoole, Patrick 66
Drummond, John 163
Dumbleton, Bob 33
Dunwoody, Tamsin 209, 237
Duret, Vivien 24
Durham 40
Dyddiau'r Ceiliog Rhedyn (A. Talfan Davies) 16-17
Dyke, Greg 90, 103
Dylan Thomas in America (Brinnin) 79

Economic and Social Research Institute 318-20
Economic Research Advisory Panel 323
economics: advising Government 139; early strategies for 35-6; highly-paid jobs 270; research 321-4; unbalanced development 336-8
The Economist 55
Edmunds, Alan 236
education 146-8, 269-70, 281-2

Edward VIII 50
Edwards, Cenwyn 73, 76
Edwards, Dave 124
Edwards, Hywel 257
Edwards, Nicholas: see Crickhowell, Lord
Edwards, Wil 30
EEC 60-1
Eirug, Aled 76
Elfyn, Menna 188
Elis-Thomas, Dafydd 213, 237, 238
ELWa 201-3, 206
Ely 280
England, Wales and 334-5, 339-40
English language: English/Welsh programmes compared 100; English/Welsh speakers 69-70
Environment Agency 224
Epstein, Matthew 172
Equity contracts 65
Erfyl, Gwyn 66
Essex, Sue 213
European Capital of Culture 193, 283
European referendum 60, 61
European Union 335
Evans, Cerith Wyn 187
Evans, Delyth 209
Evans, Gwynfor 36, 57, 70, 71
Evans, Harold 40
Evans, Jonathan 208
Evans, Nick 103
Evans, Phil 206
Evans, Rhys 53
Evans, Sir Geraint 66, 162
Everitt, Anthony 182, 183 4
Eversheds 138
Everyman 120
Ewenny Priory 265

factual programmes 120
Falkland Islands 74-5
Fawkes, Richard 171
Ferris, Paul 79
fiction 188
The Fifteen Streets 90
Filipina Dreamgirls 116
Financial Times 298
Finch, Catrin 186
Finch, Peter 188, 278

Finnemore, Peter 187
Fisher, John 168
Fishlock, Trevor 58, 143, 298
FitzGerald, Garret 61, 315
Fitzgerald, Penelope 93
Food for Ravens 118-19
Foot, Michael 34, 38
Ford, Colin 158
Forgan, Liz 105
Fox, Paul 69, 115
Francis, J.O. 277
Francis, Karl 116, 118
Franks Commission 25-6
freedom of expression 215-6, 251-2
Freedom of Information Act 2004 167
French, Paddy 81
Freud, Anthony 168, 172, 201, 259-60
Y Fro Gymraeg 144
Frost, David 23
The Fruitful Earth 121
The Future of Welsh Conservatism (Evans) 208

Galeri 186
Galleries and Exhibition Spaces in Wales 196
Gardiner, Duncan 37
Gardner, Julie 124
Garfield, Leon 122, 123
Gec, Stefan 287
General Election 1966 35
General Election 2007 297-8
George, Phil 120-1
Geraint, John 121
Germany 74
Giddings, John 38
Gittins, Rob 78
Glamorgan University 321, 331
Glas Cymru 328
Glen, Hamish 250
Glynn, Victor 90
Goldie, Grace Wyndham 23
Goldsmith, Harvey 89
Goldstone, Ellis 33
Gooding, Alf 63
Goodway, Russell 150, 151-2, 159-60
Gormley, Anthony 292
government centralisation 301, 326-7, 337

Government of Wales Act 1998 208
Government of Wales Act 2006 145, 247, 327, 329, 339
Gower, Raymond 61
Grace, Chris 69, 122
Gramsci, Antonio 82
Granada 294-5, 302
Granjon, Paul 187
The Gregynog Papers 208-9
Griffiths, Dewi 109
Griffiths, James 53
Griffiths, Niall 188
Griffiths, Trevor 118
Griffiths, Tweli 73, 74
Gruffydd, W.J. 277-8
Guardian 250, 298, 302, 306, 313

Hadid, Zaha 149, 150, 154, 156-7
Hafren Television 63
Halligan, Brendan 316
Hands, Guy 328
Hands, Terry 193, 220
Hannay, Patrick 293, 329
Harding, Peter 229
Hargreaves, Ian 273, 297
Harlech Consortium 64
Harlech, Lord 63-4
Harri, Guto 104
Hart, Edwina 135, 261
Hasegawa, Itsuko 157
Hatch, David 119
Hawker, Graham 202, 203
Hay Festival 189
health issues 146
Health Professionals Wales 206, 224
Healy, Tim 89
Heddiw 15
Hen Atgofion (Gruffydd) 277
Henson, Jim 89
Heren, Louis 40-1
Heritage 266
Heritage Lottery Fund 158-9
Heseltine, Michael 150
Hewson, Alan 291
higher education 331-2
Higher Education Funding Council 224
Higher Education Wales 329
Highway 87

Hindell, Alison 124
Hiscott, Amber 186
Hoddinott, Alun 222
Hodge, Sir Julian 54, 141
Holden, John 266-7, 268
Holding the BBC Together (Birt) 134
Holland, Jools 87
Holland, Tony 115
Hooper, Alan 290
Hooson, Emlyn 35, 63
Hopkins, Anthony 118, 121
The House 172
Housing Act 1974 48
housing associations 48-9
housing issues 33
Howells, Geraint 35
Howells, Kim 262
HTV: arts programmes 162; BBC Wales and 100; documentaries 77-84; English language programmes 100; fourth channel 70; franchises 306-7; Head of News and Current Affairs 67; historical documentaries 80-4; licence renewal 63-4; network output 115; network schedules 69; news and current affairs 72-7; opera 162; rugby coverage 109; S4C and 73, 100, 306; S4C current affairs 102-3; underdog spirit 64-5; Welsh language programmes 65-6, 69-70, 72
HTV West 64, 115
Hughes, Aneurin Rhys 60-1
Hughes, Cledwyn 53, 54-5, 71
Hughes, Gareth 48
Humphreys, Emyr 188
Humphries, John 28-31, 37-8
Hunt, Tristram 337
Hussey, Duke 92, 98
Huws, Bethan 187
Huws, Meri 213, 225
Hyder 141

IBA Welsh Advisory Committee 70
illiteracy 262-3
In Blackberry Time 118
incitement to religious hatred 251-2
Independent Television Authority 303
Independent Television Commission 273, 300

Industrial and Maritime Museum 158-9
industrial revolution 276-7
inequality 325
Inkin, Sir Geoffrey 150, 152, 159, 160
Inner Space 89
innovation 270
Institute of Welsh Affairs: *Bread and Roses* 146, 160; Cardiff Bay Opera House 157-8, 159; creation of 139-44; *The Gregynog Papers* 208-9; influence of 146-8; Irish Institute of European Affairs 315-16; policy options 270; universities 322; *Wales 2010: Creating our Future* 147; Welsh baccalaureate 146-8
International Baccalaureate Organisation 147
Ireland: economic policy 318-20; history of 317-21; National Economic and Social Council 319; National Economic and Social Development Office 319-20; National Economic and Social Forum 319; newspapers 299; visit to 61; Wales and 316-17
Irish Development Authority 318
Irish Independent 299
Irish Institute of European Affairs 315
Irish Management Institute 320
Irish Times 299, 302
Is Wales Viable? (Kohr) 36
Isaac, Norah 20
Isaac, Russell 74-5
Isaacs, Jeremy 80, 87
Israel 74
Isserlis, Steven 165
ITN, news programmes 72-3
ITV: advertising 304-5; fourth channel 70; franchises 306; Independent Television Authority 303; Independent Television Commission 273, 300; mergers 302-3, 307; network schedules 89: news programmes 133; opera 162; programme costs 305; regionalism 303-5, 306; separate frequencies for Wales 294-5; share prices 305

Jackson, David 121, 129
James, Harry 187
James, Keith 138-9, 140
James, Pedr 122
James, Shani Rhys 186
Japan 164-5
Jay, Peter 40
Jenkins, Colin 147
Jenkins, Dafydd 15
Jenkins, David 206
Jenkins, Karl 136
Jenkins, Marged 17
Jenkins, Roy 53-4, 70
Jenkins, Rt. Rev. David 89
Jerry Springer: the Opera 250-1
Jervis, Margaret 257, 258
Jerwood Prize 186
John, Angela 81
John, Sean Tuan 189
Johnson Buildings 169
joint ministerial committees 339
Jones, Alderman Ferguson 46
Jones, Alun Ffred 73
Jones, Barry 33
Jones, Carwyn 209
Jones, Chris 328
Jones, Dame Gwyneth 222
Jones, David 222
Jones, Dr. Gareth 147, 148
Jones, Dr. Gwyn 125, 126, 127
Jones, Elinor 73
Jones, Emrys 34
Jones, Gareth (IWA) 159
Jones, Gareth (WNO) 186
Jones, Glyn 20
Jones, Huw 110-11
Jones, Jonathan 223
Jones, J.R. 71
Jones, Keith 111
Jones, Lyn 124
Jones, Naomi 124
Jones, Peter Elias 66
Jones, Roger 109, 110, 135, 202, 203
The Journal 39-40
journalism: future of 314-15; leader columns 37-8; letters pages 41-3; sub-editors 40
Jowell, Tessa 268

Kane, Vincent 75-6, 113
Kay, John 337

Kay, Norman 162
Kelly, Petra 74
Kennedy, Bruce 76
Kerr, Elizabeth 234
Kilbrandon Report 55
Kilfoil, Bethan 104
Kinnock, Neil 34, 68, 137
Knell, John 260
knowledge economy 266, 270, 281-2, 322-4
Kohr, Leopold 36
Koralek, Paul 154
Kroch, Henry 140-1

Labour Party: conferences 33-4, 151; devolution 29, 60-2; future of 209; internal fault lines 335; Liberal Democrats and 148
Ladd, Eddie 189-90
Lamb, Charles 122
Lamb, Martin 124
Lammy, David 234, 268
Lampeter 331-2
Latvian Radio Choir 265
Law, Peter 207, 237, 238
Law, Trish 207
leader columns 37-8
Lebanon 74
Lee, Jennie 171
Lee, Joseph 316, 320
Leipzig 164
Lemass, Sean 318
letters pages 41-3
Levin, Bernard 41
Lewis, Gwyneth 136, 178, 188, 222
Lewis, Huw 237
Lewis, Robyn 55
Lewis, Roger 239
Lewis, Saunders 14, 53, 162, 178, 180-1
Liberal Democrats: devolution 61; internal fault lines 335; Labour and 148; quangos 207, 208
Liberal Party 35, 38
Lightman, Ivor 145
Linbury Theatre 186
literature 15, 185, 187-9, 252
Live Theatre 89
Liverpool Daily Post 294

Llandaff 284
Llandovery College 23
Llangrannog 285
Lliw Valley Eisteddfod 71-2
Lloyd George, David 54, 325
Llwyd, Dewi 104
Llyfrau'r Dryw (Wren Books) 16
local government: arts and 268, 271-2, 273; Assembly Government and 281, 329; ASPBs and 208; corruption scandals 45, 81; culture and 271-3; grants 190; planning 290; reorganisations 54-5, 182
local radio 310
London, growth of 336-7
London newspapers 39, 41
Lord, Peter 186
The Lottery of Lottery Funding 158
Loughor 14
Loughrey, Pat 94
Loveluck, Paul 205-6, 239
Lowe, Jeremy 49
Luard, Roger 306
Lynch, Patrick 318

Mabon 83
McConnell, Jack 268
McCormick, John 114
McCrory, Helen 118
Macdonald, Vicky 239
McIntosh, Baroness (Genista) 234
Mackay, David 289
MacKenzie, Kelvin 309
McKerras, Sir Charles 172
McLane, Val 89
McLean, Iain 338
McMaster, Sir Brian 172, 268
Macmillan, Harold 52
Macmillan, Joyce 193-4
Mactaggart, Fiona 251
Major, John 145, 150-1
Making the Connections 198, 219
Mandelson, Peter 134
Mansfield, Henry 47
Manson, Helen 102
Marine Bill 338-9
Marquand, David 253
Marshall, Ray 90
Mather, Ian 75

Mathias, Glyn 104
Matthews, John 157-8
Maud, Ralph 19
Mazelis, Jo 188
Mears, Wyn 102
media policy 312-13
medical schools 332
Medley, Fran 195
Meredith, John 130
Merthyr 48-51, 259, 288
Metcalf, John 265
Michael, Alun 27, 157, 158, 159-60
Michelmore, Cliff 23
Middleboe, Penelope 124
Middlehurst, Tom 181
Militant Tendency 137
Millennium Commission 149, 155-6, 157, 158-9
Millennium Stadium 153-5, 284
Milne, Alasdair 23, 25, 97
miners' strike 83, 116, 137
mining, commemoration of 287-8
The Minister (Thomas) 19-20
Ministry of Defence 30-1
Mobile 82
Monitor 23
Morgan, Elystan 54
Morgan, Geraint 61
Morgan, Gwyn 60-1
Morgan, John 64, 67-8, 162
Morgan, Kenneth 80
Morgan, Professor Kevin 145, 207, 212, 218
Morgan, Rhodri: ACW and 218 19, 221-2, 226, 228-9; arm's length principle 224; clear red water 266, 334; father of 15; Public Service Reform 204-6; total recall 33
Morgan, T.J. 15
Morphine and Dolly Mixtures 116
Morris, Colin 94
Morris, Geraint 118
Morris, Jan 277
Morris, Jim 125
Morris, John 56-7
Moscow 123
A Most Peculiar People (Stephens) 277
motorway art 292

motorways 45
Ms Rhymney Valley 116
Mungham, Geoff 209
Murdoch, Rupert 306
Murphy, Gerald 81
Murphy, Suzanne 260
music 21
music programmes 89, 121
Music Theatre Wales 186
musicians 185-6

Nally, Donald 186
nation-building 296
National Assembly of Wales 213
national companies 227-8, 232-3, 238, 240, 247, 248
national curriculum 270
National Eisteddfod 30-1, 71-2, 162, 282
National Library of Wales 224, 330-1
National Lottery: arts councils and 156; grant-in-aid 197, 204, 215, 221-2; inconsistencies 158; reduction in 181, 182, 190, 195; Welsh Assembly and 218-19, 221-2, 232
National Museum Wales 224, 262, 283, 330-1
National Poet 188, 189
nationalism 55
Naughtie, James 129
Nazi criminals 42
Negroponte, John 74
Neil, Ron 94, 97, 99, 103, 127
Nevin, Professor Edward 35
new towns 44-5
Newcastle upon Tyne 39, 85 6, 88, 91, 163
Newport 281
Newport University 331-2
News at Ten 133
News of the World 45
news programmes: before devolution 72-7; after devolution 132-6; regional/central combination 132-3; research into 273
newspapers: democracy and 296-8, 300-2; influence of 27; national 297-8
Newydd Housing Association 48-9
NHS 224
Nicholas, Sir David 72-3, 306

Nicholson, Paul 86
Nicoletti, Manfredo 157
A Nightingale Sang 89-90
North East England 39, 85-6
North East Wales Institute of Higher Education 331
north/south 55
North Wales 284, 294
Northern Arts 90-1
Northern Ireland Assembly 135
Northern Life 88
Northern Sinfonia 163

O Flaen dy Lygaid 102
obituaries 42
Objective One 146, 330
Ofcom 295, 307, 308-9, 310, 312
Old Arcade 33, 50
The Old Devils 116
Oldfield-Davies, Alun 95
OpenDemocracy.net 314
opera see also Welsh National Opera: appreciation of 161-2; chamber opera 186; innovation 178-9: 'national' companies 177-8
Opie, Roger 36
orchestras 186, 252 *see also* chamber orchestras; National Orchestra of Wales
Orlova, Natalya 123
Ormond, John 40, 141-6
Osborne, Alan 259
Osmond, Henry 142
Osmond, John 57, 61, 76-7, 137, 209
Otaka, Tadaaki 163, 164-5
O'Toole, Peter 25, 255
outreach programmes 257-8
Owen, Elis 67, 76
Owen, Idloes 170
Owen-Jones, Jon 209
Oxford Mail 26
Oxford University 25-6

Paddington rail crash 130
Page, Jennifer 156, 158
Paisley, Ian 340
Paris Match 32
Parkinson, Ewart 45
Parliament for Wales Campaign 145

Parry, John 97, 125
Parry-Williams, T.H. 178
Patagonia 74-5
Patti, Adelina 177
Paul, Les 61
Peacock, Professor Alan 56, 305-6
Peacock report 87
Pembrokeshire County Council 272
Pentrebach 48-9
performing arts 220
Perlmutter, Dr. Howard 286
Pettifer, Julian 24
Philadelphia 286
Plaid Cymru: conferences 35-7; devolution 61; first MP 53; internal fault lines 335; quangos 208
Planet 137
planning 44-7, 290-1, 293
Plater, Alan 89, 117-18
Plowden, Lady 63
Pobl y Cwm 102
poetry 188
Points of View 23
political parties, future of 208-9
Pompeii 287
Pontcanna 64
Poole, Roy 78
Portman Productions 90
potato prices 28-9
potato principle 58
Powell, Enoch 57
Powell, Jonathan 116
Powell, Tristram 118
Power to Change 105
Prague 164
Pratley, David 196, 212
Prebble, Stuart 132-3
Price, Angharad 188
Prichard, Mathew 150, 153
Princess of Wales Building 169
print shop 40
Pritchard, Gwyn 101-2, 120
Pritchard-Jones, Eirlys 147
private sector, role of 138, 248, 300, 330
Producer Choice 116-17, 128
The Psychology of Distance (Williams) 208-9
public art movement 292-3

public domain 253
public expenditure 337
public sector, domination of 248, 279, 330, 337
Public Service Publisher 312, 314
Pugh, Alun: access 235-6, 237; ACW and 230; ACW and SCW 218-19, 223; as AM 211-12; as culture minister 182; *Jerry Springer: the Opera* 250-1; six companies proposals 233; theatre 194
Pugh Lloyd, Sir Hugh 30-1
Pugh, Sheenagh 188
Pullman, Philip 260
Punter, John 290
Purnell, James 268

quangos: changes 224; future of 208-10; justification for 207-8; reform issues 236; subordination 210; Welsh Assembly and 201-6
Quite Early One Morning (Thomas) 19

racial tensions 252
Radio Authority 206
radio budgets 101
radio, history of 294
radio odes 19-20
radio talks 19
radio transmission 309-10
Radiocommunications Agency 295
Raikes, Elizabeth 202, 206
Randerson, Jenny 182, 211
Ravenseft 45, 47
Rawlings, Keith 102
Reay, David 87-8
Rebecca 81
Rebecca's Daughters 116
Redesigning Democracy (Mungham) 209
Redwood, John 118, 150, 151, 281
Rees, Lucy 78
Rees, Marc 189
Rees, Merlyn 70
Rees-Mogg, William 40, 42
Reese, W.H. 15
Reeves, Robin 144, 298
referenda 60, 61, 128-31, 145
referendum disaster 68-9
referendum orders debate 68

regeneration 258
regionalism 281, 303-5, 306
Reid, Stephen 102
Reitell, Liz 78-80
Reith, Lord 294
religious controversies 249-52
religious programmes 89, 120, 123-4
Reminiscences of Childhood (Thomas) 19
Report Wales 69
research 320-4
Research Assessment Exercises 322
Reynolds, Henry 37
Rhondda Cynon Taf 261
Rhys, Matthew 204
Rhys, Milton 75
Richard Commission 56, 208
Richards, Ed 308
Richards, Menna 76, 124
Ridley, Viscount 86
Rizzi, Carlo 169, 172, 201
Roberts, Janet 236
Roberts, Michael 67
Robinson, Gerry 173
Roderick, Vaughan 104
Rogers, Ken 298
Rogers, Richard 186, 284, 293
Rome 161
Rosa, Carl 171
The Rose Affair (Kay) 162
Rosser, David 29
Rowe-Beddoe, David 149, 165, 222
Rowlands, Lord (Ted) 33, 50
Rowley, John 38
The Roxy 89
Royal Commission on Ancient and Historical Monuments of Wales 224
Royal Commission on the Consti-tution 55
Royal Opera House 172
Royal Society of Architects in Wales 293
Royal Television Society 88, 103
RTE 109
Ruane, Professor Frances 319
Rubicon Dance 189, 256
rugby coverage 108-9
Rugby World Cup 153
Russell Group 331
Russian visitors 57

S4C: animations 122-4; attitude to BBC 110-11; BBC and 109-11, 313; BBC hours 73, 102-3, 109-10; BBC Wales and 100, 122-4; Channel 4 and 310; current affairs programmes 102-3; documentaries 102; formation of 68-9, 71-2; future of 313; HTV and 73, 100, 306; legislation 110; news programmes 132-3; Nolan rules 238; non-news output 100; rugby coverage 109-10

S4C Authority 308

Safle 199

St. Fagans Museum 105

Schiff, Heinrich 163

Schumacher, E.F. 36

Scotecon 321

Scotland: national theatre 193-4; news programmes 132, 134-5; newspapers 299; universities 321; Wales and 56

Scotland and Wales Bill 61-2

The Scotsman 136

Scottish Arts Council 190, 197, 212

Scottish Council for Development and Industry 139

Scottish Cultural Commission 214, 268

Scottish Media group (SMG) 302

Scottish Parliament 135

Scottish Television 115

Sculptural Objects and Fine Arts Exhibition 186

Seawright, Paul 187

Secombe, Harry 87

Selected Exits 117-18

Sendall, Bernard 303-4

Senedd 186, 284, 293

sense of place 117

Seven Deadly Sins 178

Sgript Cymru 191, 194, 199

Shakespeare, William 122, 255-6

Shaw, George Bernard 192

Sheers, Owen 188

Sherman Cymru 199

Sherman Theatre 191, 194, 199, 227, 272

Short, Renée 171

Shortridge, Sir Jon 205, 214

Sikh protests 249, 250

Sinfonia Cymru 186

Six O'Clock News 135

Sky 313

The Slate 104

Slivka, Dave 79

Slivka, Rose 79

Sloman, Anne 129

Smith, Bill 171

Smith, Chris 265-6

Smith, Dai: ACW and 218-19; BBC and 81; Food for Ravens 118; history programmes 120; influence of 103, 105-6; scholarship 80

Smith, Julia 115

Smith, Julian 168

Smith, Sir Brian 281-2

Soar chapel 257

social equity 262-3

Sokhiev, Tugan 201

Sony awards 103

South Glamorgan County Council 33

South Wales Echo 27, 167

South Wales Evening Post 40

spectrum trading 312, 313-14

Spence, Basil 104

spirituality 325-6

sports contracts 109

Sports Council of Wales 218, 225

St David's Forum 144

St David's Hall 163

St Hilary transmitter 294

Stanley Jones, Geraint 93

Station Road 122

steel industry 137, 143

Steel, Janet 250

Stephens, Elan Closs 182, 238-9, 240

Stephens, Meic 189, 277

Stevenson, Michael 134

Sticky Wickets 116

Street, Rita 23

Streetlife 118

STV 302, 306

Summers, John 163

Sun 298

Sunday Times 40, 315

Sunderland, Eric 127-8

Sure Start 262

Swansea 16-17, 45, 289

Swansea University 321, 331

Tales from Shakespeare (Lamb) 122
Taro Naw 103
Taylor, Elizabeth 64
Teale, Owen 90
television licences 95
television transmitters 294, 309
Temple of Peace 170
Tender Loving Care 116
Terfel, Bryn 185
TG4 109
That Was The Week That Was 23
Thatcher, Margaret 138, 162, 265, 306, 326-7
The National Question Again (Osmond) 144
Theatr Clwyd 272
Theatr Genedlaethol Cymru 191, 227
theatre: access 255-6, 259-60; ACW and 199, 252; development of 190-4; national companies 227; Welsh Assembly and 252
This Blessed Plot (Young) 60
Thomas, Brian (B.K.) 153
Thomas, Colin 81, 83, 144
Thomas, David 39, 63
Thomas, Dylan 16, 19, 78-80
Thomas, George 53-5, 56
Thomas, Gwyn 117-18, 123, 277
Thomas, Hugh 141
Thomas, Iwan 92
Thomas, James 273, 301
Thomas, Ned 137, 299
Thomas, Peter 54
Thomas, Professor Wynn 239
Thomas, Rhodri Glyn 194
Thomas, Roger 138
Thomas, R.S. 19-20
Thomas, Ward 86
Thomas, Wynford Vaughan 64, 66, 80-3
Thompson, Mark 120, 124, 129
Thompson, Sada 78
Thomson, Lord 39
Thomson Regional Newspapers 27-8
Tiger Bay 122
Till, Ruth 256-7, 258
The Times 40-3, 298
tinplate works 34
Tonight 23-4
Top of the Pops 89

Torch Theatre 191, 194
Touchstone 293
Traherne, Lord Cennydd and Lady Rowena 68
Trawsfynydd nuclear power station 104-5
Tredegar House 213
Tresize, Rachel 188
Trewin, Ion 41
The Triangle 48-50
Trident Television 86, 91
Trinity Mirror 301
Trip Trap 116
The Tube 86-7
Tusa, John 247
Twine, Anne 182, 183-4
TWW 64
Tŷ Newydd 189
Tycroes 17
Tyndall, Peter: ASPBs 201, 217; as ACW chief executive 182, 199, 225-6; culture department 211; English language theatre 191; national theatre 194
Tyne and Wear County Council 85
Tyne Tees Television 85-91, 95, 162-3, 295, 304

UKIP 68
Ulster Television 306
unemployment 35
United Kingdom, devolution and 336, 339-40
universities 139, 281-2, 320-4, 331-2
University of Wales 331
Upton, Steve 218
urban development 276-7
Urdd Eisteddfod 149, 282, 285
USA 58-60, 74, 315
Ushida-Findlay 105
UTV 302

Vale of Glamorgan Festival 265
valley communities, future of 292-3
Valleys Kids 257-8
Vaughan, Aled 66, 162
Venice Biennale 186-7, 220
Vick, Graham 179
video on demand 314
Visions of Snowdonia 121

visual arts 186-7, 196, 220, 262
Voices of a Nation 136
Voluntary Arts Wales 261

Wales: geography of attitudes 55, 144; gross value 330; intellectual resources 320-4; musical tradition 176-7; myths about 81-2, 332-3; as non-sentient nation 187; plurality 106, 301, 310-11, 337; polycentrism 282; special needs 333-4
Wales and Monmouthshire Area Council of the Conservative Party 34-5
Wales Arts International 167
Wales Centre for Health 224
Wales Council for Voluntary Action 329-30
Wales Millennium Centre: benefits of 284-5; case for 160; dance 190; funding for 276; opening ceremony 222-3; planning 149
Wales on Sunday 31, 301
Wales project 137
Wales, the National Question Again (Osmond) 137
Wales, The Way Ahead 35
Wales This Week 75-6
Wales Today 104, 155
Wales Tourist Board 201, 203, 206, 270-1
Wales! Wales? 81
Wales West and North (WWN) 294-5
Walker, Peter 150
Wallace, Richard 181-2
Walsh, Dr. John 26
Walters, Sir Donald 140-1
Waters, Sarah 188
Waterstone, David 140
Watkin, Alan 239
Watkins, Alan 18
Watkins, Tasker 46-7
Watkins, Vernon 20
Webb, Sir Adrian 135
Week in Week Out 75
Weill, Kurt 178
Wells, Stanley 123
Welsh Affairs Correspondent 29
Welsh Arts Council 171
Welsh Arts Review 268
Welsh Assembly: abolition of 68; ACW and

182, 183-4, 201-3, 217-20; building 186, 284, 293; business liaison 320; Campaign for 144-5; Cardiff and 285-6; celebrations 135-6; centralisation 183, 184; culture department 210-12, 226-8, 247, 267-8; defeat of 237-8, 247-8; election turnout 326; issues and options 145; legislative powers 329, 339; *Making the Connections* 198, 219; news coverage funding 135; overview 327-31; policy options 223, 270; political parties 148, 207-8; Public Service Reform 204-6; public services 332; quangos 201-6, 213-14
Welsh baccalaureate 146-8
Welsh Book of the Year 187-9
Welsh Books Council 185, 188
Welsh Business Institute 139
Welsh Council 139
Welsh Courts Act 1942 15
Welsh Development Agency 126, 140, 201-3, 210
Welsh Economic Council 35
Welsh Economic Institute 139-40
Welsh Housing Quality Standards 293
Welsh Industrial and Economic Committee 139
Welsh language: broadcasting 296, 310-11; in Cardiff 284; English /Welsh speakers 69-71, 106; 'ghettoisation' of 70-1; newspapers 299; post-war emergence 20; spread of 69-70; television channels 65-77; television programmes 65-6, 68-9, 72, 100 *see also* S4C
Welsh Language Board 203, 213, 225
Welsh language schools 20-1
Welsh Language Society 38-9, 52-3
Welsh Local Government Asso-ciation 272, 329
Welsh National Opera: Cardiff Singer 168-9; chorus 186; collaborations 178; education department 175; funding for 171-6; history of 169-72, 176-7; innova-tion 178-9; *Katerina* project 259-60; Music Director problem 201; 'national' companies 177-8; opera house 159; on tour 282-3; track record 227
WNO Max 175, 259
Welsh National Party 14

Welsh Office 29, 53
Welsh Rugby Union 155
Welsh Rural Observatory 321
Welsh Union of Writers 142
Welsh Wales 144, 284
Welsh Water 327-8
Wenvoe transmitter 294
West Germany, visit to 58
West Lothian question 340
Western Mail: ACW and 236; Assembly
election 298; centenary 39; *Daily Post* and
302; devolution polls 57, 61; graduate
intake 27-8, 29-30; leader columns 37-8;
legendary characters 28-9; letters pages
42-3; as national newspaper 294; opera
house 155; political reporting 29;
profitability 300; and quangos 210; right-
wing pedigree 38; sales 297
Wheatley, Ossie 127
Wheldon, Huw 23
When was Wales? (Williams) 83, 137
Whitaker, T.K. 318
White, Eirene 35
White, Michael 154
Whitelaw, Willie 70, 72, 110
Wigglesworth, Mark 166
Wigley, Dafydd 35-6
Wilding Report 90-1
Wilkins, William 186
Williams, Anna 168
Williams, Bedwyr 187
Williams, David 76, 104
Williams, Glanmor 80
Williams, Reverend Gwilym O 23, 71
Williams, Gwyn Alf 50, 80, 81-3, 137, 288
Williams, Huw Tregelles 163
Williams, Hywel 150, 151
Williams, Iolo 121

Williams, John 188, 278
Williams, Llŷr 185-6
Williams, Merfyn 167-8
Williams, Phil 35-6, 208-9
Williams, Professor Jac L. 71
Williams, Rhodri 202-3
Williams, Sir William Emrys 171
Wilson, Harold 55, 56
Winchester, Simon 75
Wines, James 105
Wireless Group 309
Wix, Mandy 157
Wonfor, Andrea 86, 87
Wood, David 41
Woolley, Geoffrey 41-2
Wordley, Ronald W. 63, 65-6, 71
World in Action 69
World War II 16-17, 132
Wren Books 16
Wrexham 281
Wright, Frank Lloyd 44
Wright, George 61
Wyatt, Will 118

Y Byd 299
Y Byd ar Bedwar 72, 73
Y Dydd 69
Yentob, Alan 105
Ymryson y Beirdd 108
Yom Kippur War 47
Yorkshire Television 91, 295
Young, Hugo 60
young offenders 257-8
Yr Wythnos 69
Ysgol Lonlas 20

ABOUT THE AUTHOR

Geraint Talfan Davies is chairman of Welsh National Opera and of the Institute of Welsh Affairs. His career has spanned newspapers in Cardiff, Newcastle and London, ITV, first with HTV Wales and later as Director of Programmes with Tyne Tees Television, and ten years as Controller of BBC Wales before retiring in 2000. He subsequently represented Wales on the Radio Authority. Prior to his appointment as chairman of the Arts Council of Wales in 2003 he had been much involved with the arts as chairman of the public art agency, CBAT, and as a board member of the Artes Mundi Visual Arts Prize and the Wales Millennium Centre. He is a trustee of the Media Standards Trust and a non-executive director of Welsh Water.